Héctor P. García

HÉCTOR P. GARCÍA
Everyday Rhetoric and Mexican American Civil Rights

Michelle Hall Kells
With a Foreword by Rolando Hinojosa-Smith

Southern Illinois University Press
Carbondale

Publication of this book was underwritten by a grant from Southern Illinois University
Carbondale through its Reflective Responsive University Grants Program.

Library of Congress Cataloging-in-Publication Data
Kells, Michelle Hall.
Hector P. Garcia : everyday rhetoric and Mexican American civil rights /
   Michelle Hall Kells.
      p. cm.
      1. Garcia, Hector P., d. 1996—Language. 2. Rhetoric—Political aspects—United States—
History—20th century. 3. Mexican Americans—Civil rights—History—20th century.
4. Racism—Political aspects—United States—History—20th century. 5. Mexican
Americans—Politics and government—20th century. 6. Political participation—United
States—History—20th century. 7. Garcia, Hector P., d. 1996. 8. Mexican Americans—
Biography. 9. Civil rights workers—United States—Biography. 10. Political activists—
United States—Biography. I. Title.
E184.M5K45 2006
973.'0468720092—dc22
[B]   2006025042
ISBN-13: 978-0-8093-2728-7 (cloth : alk. paper)
ISBN-10: 0-8093-2728-7 (cloth : alk. paper)
ISBN-13: 978-0-8093-2729-4 (paper : alk. paper)
ISBN-10: 0-8093-2729-5 (paper : alk. paper)

Printed on recycled paper. ♻

The paper used in this publication meets the minimum requirements of American National
Standard for Information Sciences—Permanence of Paper for Printed Library Materials,
ANSI Z39.48-1992. ⊗

To my son,
Jacob,
Siempre hay fe

Contents

Illustrations

Foreword
Rolando Hinojosa-Smith

*D*r. Héctor P. García's parents, don José A. García and doña Faustinita Pérez de García, lived across the street from us in the "pueblo mexicano," the Mexican American part of town. The downtown district of the Texas Anglo part of town was called "El centro" for reasons I could not discover. But the division between the two societies was evident enough: South Ward Elementary was populated mostly by Texas Anglos kids and North Ward Elementary was one hundred percent Mexican American. Mercedes, town of six thousand at the time, had two elementary schools, one junior high, and the high school. The walls of the second story of the high school were lined with the graduation photographs of seniors past and present, and I would often stop and look at pictures of my family's friends, my two bothers and two sisters, and of course, the Garcías. My parents, Manuel G. Hinojosa and Carrie Effie Smith, were longtime friends of the Garcías; we lived across the street from one another. When I was five, my father became one of the three policemen in Mercedes, and this brought in a monthly income, although all of us worked for our own spending money.

My father was born on the Campacuás Ranch, three miles north of Mercedes, and my mother was born in Rockport, Texas; she came to the Valley at the age of six weeks. My father's father, grandfather, and great grandfather were also born on the ranch. The name Hinojosa appears in the 1750 census ordered by the Spanish Crown. My brothers and sisters graduated from Mercedes High, as I did; I probably occupied the same classroom chairs as my siblings and the Garcías. Of the five of us, four went into teaching as a profession. As I recall, the following were among Mercedes Texas Mexicans' paternal last names: Baum, Billings, Bowman, Brooks, Carr, Carroll, Closner, Foley, Gavlin, Handy, Heath, Howell, January, McGee, McVey, Moody, Parker, Pue, Rowland, Starcke, Thomas, and Werbiski. Other Valley towns reflected the same mixture: Atkinson, Chamberlain, Hatcher, Hon, Hull, Kingsvury, Putegnat, Ramsey, Randolph, Rutledge, Solitaire, and Turner. It was also the same in the cities across the Rio Grande: Braun, Brockman, Kelley, Schu, and so on.

Latin American, of course, was the polite name for us, the Americans of Mexican descent or, as they called us to our face, sometimes, and among themselves, all the time, I should imagine, *Messicans*. However, what counts is not what others say, but what one says of oneself, how one refers to oneself:

in Spanish, *mexicano,* in English, Texas Mexican. But, in those days, schools used the term Latin American. Leon R. Graham, our high school principal and later our superintendent, wrote his master's thesis at Southern Methodist University, and it helped to explain why our school remained on par, regarding the number of schoolrooms and the number of teachers, with the other elementary schools in the Valley. The reason, as stated in the thesis, was that the school board took cognizance, as it appears in the minutes of their meetings, of the Latin American politicians in Hidalgo County. Texas was a one-party state at the time; Texas Mexicans voted, and sometimes the poll taxes would be bought for some of them. But Latin Americans, to use that old term, were involved politically in the Valley, as they were in Laredo. My father was much involved, as were other Texas Mexicans in Hidalgo and Cameron counties. That the Mercedes school board (with not one Texas Mexican elected member) recognized the importance and influence of the Latin American politicians accounted for the equality in facilities in the two elementary schools.

Our teachers said we were Americans, but what we heard and saw said otherwise. It didn't much matter. Some of us complained among ourselves, but others didn't. Instead, we couldn't wait to compete with our age mates for grades and athletic glory once we would come together in the one junior high in the Mercedes Independent School District. These were the conditions in the 1930s, when the future Dr. Héctor P. García was finishing his high school studies. I was about four years old when Héctor García graduated from high school; the class of '32, if I remember correctly. I graduated at seventeen in 1946, so there was a substantial age difference: his friends were our cousin Gilberto de la Cruz Hinojosa and my oldest brother, Roy Lee. Our mothers visited daily and on walks would call on other friends as well. As the youngest, I would be babysat by my mother. I remember Héctor as witty and given to assigning nicknames to his friends.

He was called Neto; Emilia was referred to as Mila, and his older brother, José Antonio, as Pepe Toño. Dr. Cleotilde García was called Cota, although in Corpus Christi she is referred to as Cleo. Cuautémoc, who died during his undergraduate years at the University of Texas, was called Chino because of his curly hair. He was followed by Cuitláhuac, called Bonnie, and the recently dead Xicoténcatl was called Xico, the X serving as an aspirated H. The youngest, Dalia, was called Llalla, or Yaya. Héctor was regarded by his sisters and brothers as outgoing, popular, energetic, and athletic. Some forget to mention handsome and tall. He carried himself proudly but not aloof, and among us, he was Neto.

The 1930s should evoke images of the Great Depression among those who lived in those times. For those who didn't, there remained the memories of the older generation, who talked of it even during the time of World War II. What I remember most were the prices; for a penny, one could buy 5 Hershey kisses; Bright and Early Coffee cost nineteen cents and Admiration Coffee twenty-one. A twelve-pound bag of flour ran to thirty-nine cents; movies were a nickel for children, as was a bag of popcorn, and so on. I also remember young and old out of work. A steady job meant food on the table, and for some, the ability to continue schooling. The Depression was also a time of dislocation among families. It was no different in our neighborhood. Dislocation means movement: the Okies and others of the South who settled in parts of California; children being parceled out to friends or relatives; people who moved to be near make work programs of the Roosevelt administration, and so on. In our neighborhood, some families moved away never to be seen again. Along with the de la Torres, the de la Cruzes, the other Garcías, their cousins germane, as well as the Garzas, and many others, we stayed put and saw it through. The migrant farm laborers, as is usual in that hard life, would leave Mercedes and the Valley for work in what we referred to as "el norte," up North. A land of mystery to most of us, el norte meant work, that was it, and this too became part of the dislocation, since some people went to the Pacific Northwest and never returned, and, if they did return, it wasn't to stay.

In the midst of the poverty, Dr. García's oldest brother, José Antonio, earned his medical degree in Galveston. The future Dr. Héctor P. García worked to earn his keep, as had his brother, during his undergraduate days at the University of Texas; there was only one university at the time, in Austin. Some years later, their sister, Cleotilde A. García, also earned her baccalaureate degree at the University, and after marriage and childbirth, she turned to teaching school at North Ward Elementary, to earn and save money, thus enabling her to enroll at Galveston's medical school. She too earned her medical degree in Galveston; Héctor helped pay her way. After the end of World War II, a younger son, Cuitlahuac, followed in the same footsteps, and in the late 1940s and early '50s, the youngest son, Xicotencatl, graduated from the University of Texas and also won his medical degree. The third son, Cuahuctémoc, did not; he died young, during his undergraduate days in Austin. Producing six doctors is a remarkable feat for any family, but particularly in those hard days. Their father, don José, had been a teacher in northern Mexico before he brought his family to Mercedes, as his brothers, Antonio, Abel, and Odón, brought theirs. There all became successful businessmen.

I was presented with one of don José's books, a reading primer in Spanish, which I treasured, being a sickly child with ample time on my hands. I learned the term *onomaetopia* at an early age thanks to that book. The other neighborhood families also valued education, but none equaled, let alone surpassed, the Garcías' achievements. It would be most difficult for any family to have produced as many physicians as that family, under any circumstances, much less those as reduced as theirs were.

My choice of UT was based on a visit during a furlough, when I heard the stories of Mercedes friends who were studying there at the time. I knew nothing about requirements, its stature as a school or its worth; my older friends had gone there, and that was enough for me. I knew I wanted to teach, and I majored in Spanish. My brother René graduated from UT, and I stayed with him and his friends during my visit there from the Army. Somehow, in our innocence, and during the Depression, I knew it was expected of us to go a university, as did many of our other friends and neighbors. Like Héctor, I come from a family of readers; my parents read individually and also to each other. My brothers and sisters were also avid readers, and it was logical that I also follow the same pattern. As for Spanish, it was spoken at home along with English. Like many of my young friends, I attended schools that were called "las escuelitas"— these were private schools operated by men and women from Mexico living in exile during one phase or another of the Mexican Revolution of 1910, which lasted, off and on, for some twenty-five years. As for literature, we could read whatever we wished, and Mercedes, as small as it was, had a fine public library, as did the high school. We had two English teachers: Mrs. Merle Blankenship and Miss Amy Cornish. The latter taught juniors and seniors and sponsored Creative Bits, a creative writing program for juniors and seniors. Five of my pieces were accepted and remain in the Mercedes High School library.

Our families were close; my parents had baptized Dalia, the Garcías' youngest daughter, who also attended the University of Texas. The Garcías were, without our knowing it, what are now called "role models" and "achievers." We saw them as friends. The Garcías became doctors. I wanted to be a writer as a youngster, and I discovered I liked to teach during my military service. I made a sound choice by choosing those two careers. *Mi querido Rafa* is an epistolary novel about the Valley; one cousin writing to another. It's a political novel that shows how politics was run by both Texas Anglos and Texas Mexicans in the Valley. It was a world Hector García knew well.

After Dr. Héctor García's military service and his return to Texas, he opened his medical practice in Corpus Christi, where his oldest brother had been practicing prior to and during the war. There remained the usual residual racism, and some not so residual, and this led our Dr. García to take stock: Mexican Americans had served, had fought, and many had died during the war, and yet some restaurants were closed to the returning veterans; there being a shortage at the time, housing was also not readily available for the veterans who were eligible. Other signs of separatism also prevailed. The poll tax was a southern thing, and Texas was a southern state. The tax was also a money raiser. As for disfranchisement, the tax also excluded poor whites who couldn't come up with the $1.75 it cost. There was little to no legislative representation for Texas Mexicans, save briefly, in 1915, when Judge José T. Canales served in the legislature and almost did away with the Texas Rangers, missing it by one vote. Medical services were scarce, but Mercedes, small as it was, did have a hospital. When World War II came along, job opportunities increased, but many of the eligible men and women either enlisted or were drafted into the various services.

The germ for the founding of the American GI Forum by Dr. García came from all these conditions, and, as will be seen in Dr. Michelle Hall Kells's work, the organization formed as a result of racism; no other word fits. The Félix Longoria incident, where a veteran was refused burial, accelerated national growth of the GI Forum. The choice of the term *forum* was a proper one, since forums allow for voices. In this case, the forum provided many Spanish-speaking Texans, another euphemism, who had from little to no voice and thus little to no political representation, a place at last to be heard. The Longoria incident also brought then Senator Lyndon B. Johnson into the picture. This, too, is covered faithfully by Dr. Kells.

I've given a brief sketch of the family, and that is as it should be: the readers will judge for themselves the significance of one man's drive for equality and fairness for all citizens, and the disappointments faced in this undertaking, and not always overcome. Dr. García's acceptance of temporary defeats and setbacks was ever tempered by his readiness to fight for justice even where it was not always possible to be won. This is an important book for all Americans, not just for Texans, and I'm happy to have been selected to write the foregoing words as a prologue.

Acknowledgements

he journey began at Texas A&M University–Corpus Christi with Leonardo Carrillo, Patrick Carroll, Robb Jackson, Rich Haswell, and Javier Villarreal. My enduring appreciation to each. Donna Halford, David Sabrio, the late Joe Graham, and Miguel Leatham (Texas A&M University–Kingsville) further inspired and encouraged me. Mike Anzaldúa (Del Mar College) instilled a passion for teaching and community-based research. I was a research assistant at Texas A&M University–Corpus Christi during the summer of 1993 when I first learned about Dr. Héctor P. García. As a teacher of rhetoric and literacy studies to South Texas Mexican American college students, I was moved by the local significance and national import of García's story and disturbed that many of the same racial stereotypes and social configurations García had confronted some fifty years previously remained entrenched in the United States, as they do today. During the Dr. Héctor P. García Plaza Dedication at Texas A&M University–Corpus Christi on June 28, 1996, I decided to research Dr. García's civic discourse. Regretfully, I never had the opportunity to meet Dr. García. He died one month later, on July 26, 1996.

I started this research on Dr. García in 1998 at Texas A&M University in College Station. My work was supported by grants from the South Central Modern Language Association, the Race and Ethnic Studies Institute, the Center for Teaching Excellence, the Department of English, and the College of Liberal Arts (all of Texas A&M University). During the three-year period of archive research and field work, I circulated my writing widely among the Texas scholarly community. Invaluable to this work has been the guidance along the way of many Mexican American studies scholars, among them Marco Portales, Rogelio Sáenz, Carlos Blanton, and Armando Alonzo, of Texas A&M University; Ignacio M. García, of Brigham Young University; Thomas Kreneck and Anthony Quiroz, of Texas A&M University–Corpus Christi; B. J. Gallegos, of Sul Ross State University; Cynthia Orozco, of Eastern New Mexico University; David Montejano, of the University of California, Berkeley; Rolando Hinojosa-Smith, Neil Foley, and José Limón, of the University of Texas, Austin; and Rodolfo Rosales, of the University of Texas, San Antonio. The groundbreaking work of Tey Diana Rebolledo, María Dolores González, Enrique Lamadrid, and Tobías Durán, all of the University of New Mexico, has helped me to bring this research home.

Research discussed in this book has been presented at conferences of the Rhetoric Society of America, the Texas State Historical Association, and the

Program in Presidential Rhetoric at the George Bush School of Government and Public Service. Portions of chapter 4 were originally published in an essay, "Héctor P. García, Lyndon B. Johnson, and the Polemics of the *Bracero* Immigrant Labor Program: Questions of Race, Caste, and Citizenship," in *Who Belongs in America? Presidents, Rhetoric, and Immigration*, edited by Vanessa Beasley (College Station: Texas A&M University Press, 2006).

This research draws upon the insights of many intellectual communities, especially rhetoric. For their thoughtful guidance and criticism, I wish to thank M. Jimmie Killingsworth, C. Jan Swearingen, James Aune, and Leroy Dorsey, of Texas A&M University; Victor Villanueva, of Washington State University; Juan Guerra, of the University of Washington; Ralph Cintron, of the University of Chicago; and Vanessa Beasley, of the University of Georgia. Archivists Grace Charles, of the Bell Library, Texas A&M University–Corpus Christi; Margo Gutiérrez, of the Benson Latin American Collection; and Claudia Anderson and Linda Seelke, of the Lyndon B. Johnson Presidential Library, were critical to this research from beginning to end. My appreciation to my friends and colleagues Diana Cárdenas and Susan Wolff Murphy, of Texas A&M University–Corpus Christi; and Molly Johnson, of the University of Houston–Downtown, who have shared the joy of the journey. A special thanks to Jeff Felts of KEDT-TV in Corpus Christi, for helping to recover the García story.

To my mentors along the way, Larry Oliver of Texas A&M University and Scott Sanders of the University of New Mexico), thank you for sharing my Thanksgiving. The enthusiastic support of my colleagues at the University of New Mexico has helped me to find the inspiration to bring this book to completion: Carolyn Woodward, Charles Paine, Jesse Alemán, David Jones, Elizabeth Archuleta, Héctor Torres, Susan Romano, and Gary Harrison—*muchismas gracias por todo*. My students restore my passion and commitment to teaching, especially Bernadine Hernández, Isaac Cardona, Scott Rogers, Carson Bennett, Leah Sneider, Beverly Army Gillen, Dana Salvador, and John Bess. For the generous gifts of their stories, my deepest gratitude to Wanda Fusillo García, the late Dr. Xico García, Liz Carpenter, Virgilio Roel, the late Ed Idar Jr., Carolyn Swearingen, Agnes Horn, and Belia Chabot. My guide and guardian angel throughout the journey, Vicente Ximenes, continues to inspire me. For his editorial guidance and unwavering interest, I thank Karl Kageff at Southern Illinois University Press. Thanks also to my project editor, Kathleen Kageff. I am especially indebted to Ignacio M. García and Juan C. Guerra, my then-anonymous reviewers in rhetoric and history, for their thoughtful readings and suggestions in the early stages of this book. The intersections between the study of rhetoric in English and communications and the study of history offer new avenues of research for cross-cultural and cross-disciplinary studies of this kind. Finally, my son, Jacob, my daughter-in-law, Erin, and my daughters, Risha and Hallee, remain my most devoted supporters. And there are no words to express my appreciation to my husband, Ross, my most engaged reader.

Héctor P. García

Introduction: "The Rhetorics of the Everyday" and Civic Belonging

*T*he students for whom I wrote this book have long since left the classrooms of Texas A&M University–Kingsville. A small percentage have graduated. Most slipped away after their first year to return to their South Texas communities to take jobs and raise families, but none of them have faded from memory. All have a stake in this story. Serving as their teacher for four years did more to shape my understanding of citizenship and civic presence than any other single life experience. They voiced their lives in the arduous process of learning to write—Mario's essay on *barrio* life in South Texas, which he proudly sent to Henry Cisneros (then Secretary of Housing and Urban Development); Javier's campaign flyer for the Kingsville school board written in Tex Mex dialect; Terese's reader response journal describing her experiences of the stigma of speaking Spanish; Sergio's story of his teenage cousin secretly giving birth in his garage; Rosa's commentary on the omission of Chicano history from the high school curriculum. They told their stories and moved on with their lives. None of my students had ever heard the story of Dr. Héctor P. García, although it was for them that he left his legacy. All of them believed the civil rights movement was a thing of the past. I want to complicate the story of twentieth-century civil rights reform with the everyday life and words of a South Texas doctor.

The exercise and acknowledgment of voice within one's community is integral to becoming what Philippe-Joseph Salazar calls *homo faber* or "one included in the fabrication" of government and society. Through rhetorics of civic participation, we construct and reconstruct the national vision. Our twenty-first-century struggle to recover from invasion and war—the shadow of loss and death that has hung over the United States since September 11, 2001—intertwines with national memory. Current national discourse echoes themes resonant of the early post–World War II era. Questions about the limits of civil liberty, citizenship, immigration, and homeland security preoccupy the national imagination and are issues reflective of those that moved García to action in 1948. Recursive trends are played out in a post–9/11 America marked by the militarization of the U.S. Mexico border and patrols of vigilante Minutemen, the Patriot Act, color-coded terrorism alerts, racial profiling, erosion of affirmative action, censorship, and the political shift to the right. These developments evoke an American moment fifty years ago of *bracero* guest worker programs, the GI generation, the Eisenhower administration, the McCarthy hearings, "Operation Wetback," backyard bomb shelters, air raid drills, and the national struggle over racial segregation and civil rights. These threads of history weave through our national discourse where we are today, in the twenty-first century.

Dr. García gave voice to the fifty-year cacophony of American post-war revival through the rhetoric of civil rights reform. He built his rhetorical career by calling for the full inclusion of Mexican Americans in the civic life of the nation. Unlike separatist Chicano and African American activists who followed, García did not strive to spark an anti-American revolution. For him, flag-waving patriotism provided occasion for both reaffirmation of and resistance to American political practice. Education represented a conduit toward agency. García's everyday rhetoric of citizenship helped to reshape the post-war national imagination, public policy, and the civic presence of the Mexican American electorate.

García's rhetoric represented an adaptation of available civil rights language as well as a bold departure from the assimilationist discourses of earlier Mexican American reformers. In the aftermath of World War II, García's campaign against institutionalized discrimination appropriated and recast post-war reform rhetoric. From a platform he called the American GI Forum, García aligned the struggles of a "forgotten people" with America's collective assertion for universal justice and human rights. Drawing on New Deal liberalism and a rhetoric of public service, García reiterated a national call for justice and freedom. His campaign was an extension of the rally cry played out on the battlefields of Europe, brought home to the borderlands of the American southwest. War was his primary metaphor—the mythos of military service and meritocracy, and the collective values of honor, duty, and sacrifice. García performed his self-ascribed role of civil rights advocate through the offices of physician, veteran, community activist, and founder of the American GI Forum in the remote outposts of South Texas. For García, the everyday rhetoric of citizenship extended beyond oratory and formal public address to include a broad array of discourse practices that effectively engaged and empowered politically underserved constituencies. García's iterations of belonging, his speeches, letters, telegrams, memos, flyers, posters, radio announcements, pamphlets, resolutions, newsletters, and reports, served to rewrite the history of civil rights reform in the United States.

For García, dissent and resistance were American activities. The repressive forces of Cold War politics did not suppress his outrage. García stepped onto the scene as a naturalized citizen, a multifaceted social actor bearing the conviction that he was playing a vital part in the everyday work of American democracy. The ironies and contradictions in the terms of U.S. inclusion did not elude him. They incited him. For García, the everyday discourse exercised in the role of citizenship was the celebration of agency. "A true measure of the democratic evolution of our nation is always summed up by the activity of minority groups in political and civic action," García poignantly asserted in 1952 at the dawn of the Cold War.[1]

As twenty-first-century America resegregates itself along class and racial lines in schools and neighborhoods across the nation, García's succinct measure of democracy and national health is no less applicable today than it was fifty years ago. The wellbeing of the nation is inextricably linked to the full socioeconomic participation and political representation of America's minority populations. In terms of García's own constituency, Americans of Spanish-speaking origin now comprise the new majority in the U.S. Southwest and the largest, fastest growing minority throughout the country. They also represent one of the largest poverty groups in the nation. As García's story illustrates, the enduring underrepresentation of Latino groups in all circles of national life—academe, medicine, law, government, media, industry—reflects enduring historical patterns of discrimination.

This book focuses on García as a self-styled rhetor and the leader of an emerging post–World War II Mexican American civil rights movement. It examines García's evolution from social marginalization to national influence. García's rhetoric represents the fusion of will and imagination. He used simple, unadorned language to move people, mobilizing audiences into engaged and empowered citizens. García's civil rights rhetoric both traces the role of racism in the national narrative of progress and examines the structural nature of institutionalized discrimination. García's legacy offers a valuable study in the performance of public rhetoric, the formation of civic identity, and the possibilities of democratic participation in the shifting contexts of post-war America.

The Everyday Rhetorics of Civic Presence

The rhetorics of civic culture, or what Ralph Cintron calls "the rhetorics of the everyday," emerge out of the dynamic coexistence of cultures and communities "as systems of contention in which a contentious position does not exist without its structured opposite and the two together have much to do with generating the specificities of everyday life."[2] As an acting and speaking agent in the drama of American civil rights reform, García operated as an engaged citizen in the spaces between Anglo and Mexican American sociopolitical structures. García never held elected office. He wanted to remain, in many respects, an ordinary citizen. What distinguished García from his contemporaries was his knack for recognizing and honoring the common man and woman in the work of nation-making.[3]

This book resists the invisibility of marginalization and privileges the acts of self- representation of one man who consistently turned the tables on the powerful. Rather than a prescription, this book offers a description of the discursive practices of a behind-the-scenes activist who made immeasurable impact on local and national policymaking. García's everyday acts of public rhetoric are especially productive to the conversation about American democracy in the current historical moment. Through the everyday discourses of public service, García inscribed his own personal journey of desire and belonging into a rhetorical work with broad implications. Masked in the tropes of patriotism and male military *ethos*, he traced the dissonance and contradictions of our national myths. In García's experience of the United States, the metaphors, attitudes, and social practices central to civic inclusion circulated around the issues of race, class, and citizenship. García recast these Americanist tropes for a single purpose: "first-class citizenship" for Mexican Americans. In this single-mindedness, García both achieved and unraveled the mythos of American citizenship.[4]

To map García's journey across spheres of marginalization and inclusion calls for close consideration of both the form and content of the "rhetorics of the everyday." Discursive analysis of García's own texts suggests that the everyday rhetoric of citizenship is a tapestry of genres, codes, styles, and media that promotes deliberation, coalition-building, and community-based activism across disparate groups. García's everyday rhetoric of citizenship named and described the lived experience of a community, calling attention to the corporeal condition and social position of the Mexican American community.

Embedded in the discourses of the everyday, García's legacy reveals that civic identity is not a static condition. The construction of civic *ethos* is a dynamic process, a discursive exercise, a reiteration of national myth-making. García's South Texas was a forum for twentieth-century American civil rights reform, a training ground for citizenship. The *paideia* of García's movement focused on cultivating Mexican immigrants into citizens.[5] The *phronesis* instilled an ethic of learning to govern by doing.[6] *Koinonia* emphasized the cultivation of fellowship within a common *ethos* of American identity.[7] *Kairos* recognized right timing and mindful engagement with federal reform opportunities beginning with Harry S. Truman's administration and culminating with Lyndon B. Johnson's Great Society.[8]

As García demonstrated, everyday civic rhetoric is subjectively constructed and individuated at the same time it is collectively circulated. The embodiment of citizenship achieves voice through the symbolic performance of authorship and production of polyvocal discourse. I have attempted to represent García's texts as in a form as close as possible to their original orthographic form in order to illustrate García's distinctive style and rhetorical resonance.[9] I use primary sources such as speeches, letters, memos, radio addresses, interviews, oral histories, and other forms of instrumental discourse to construct a textual history of García's civil rights rhetoric. To attend to the gaps in archival records, I use interviews, dialogue, and participant observation to construct a textual history of García's civil rights rhetoric.[10]

The intellectual operating space of this study of García's civil rights rhetoric exists at the intersection between rhetorical studies and cultural studies. Thomas Rosteck contends that both projects share a common focus on the processes of influence, with this distinction: rhetorical studies is concerned with how the struggle for power happens through legitimate social institutions such as local and national elected officials; cultural studies, in contrast, operates on the assumption that political empowerment occurs outside sanctioned social institutions.[11] This research is an application of what Rosteck calls "cultural rhetorical studies" combining analytical praxis and theoretical inquiry to examine the transition from political and social marginalization to civic inclusion.[12]

Walter Beale's model of the aims of discourse, which locates instrumental discourse on the borders between rhetorical discourse and scientific discourse, offers an especially productive approach to García's text.[13] According to Beale, instrumental rhetoric emerges out of operational, ethical/ pragmatic, and formalistic dimensions. The primary aim of instrumental discourse is governance and social control. Documents such as contracts, letters, memos, constitutions, policies, and reports represent the textual products of instrumental discourse.[14] Whereas rhetorical studies tend to focus on oratory and essayist literacies as evidence that indexes the role of the rhetor, Beale's model of instrumental rhetoric recognizes the discourses of the everyday as a valid measure of rhetorical action.[15]

Increasing interest in the rhetorics of the everyday has helped to create the necessary theoretical and historical context within which García's community-based discursive practices can be recognized and analyzed. He so embodied the rhetorics of civic presence that it is now impossible to overlook him. The discursive features of his texts index not only García's role as rhetor, leader, and negotiator, but also the shifting rhetorical situations and audiences he sought to accommodate. As a Mexican-origin immigrant who achieved access to the sanctioned structures of the U.S. political system, García provides an important case study in the exercise of civic presence and rhetorical power in the democratic state. He interleaved empirical discourse (establishing and organizing "facts") with rhetorical discourse (shaping social action) into forms of instrumental discourse that helped to expose social inequity and engage the Mexican American electorate in the processes of policymaking and governance.[16] García was a walking exigence.

Lloyd Bitzer argues that exigence, both potential and actual, emerges out of a rhetorical situation, the complex and dynamic configuration of persons, events, and material conditions. Exigencies become the places around which arguments are formed. In Bitzer's model, discourse introduced into the situation can limit or bring about significant modification of events.[17] Exigence drives rhetorical action and calls discourse into being. In contrast, Richard Vatz argues that discourse is the tinder that sparks exigence. Vatz affords greater agency to rhetors and the discourses they generate. Reading García from Vatz's position would reveal an actor who stirs a situational response. While Bitzer would interpret García as a man of his times, Vatz would read him as a man who shaped the character of his times.

García's legacy suggests that the rhetorical situation both is shaped by discourse and shapes discourse. Exigence is more than a discernable social pattern, obstacle, obstruction, limiting condition, and rhetorical constraint. It is subjectively constructed by individuals and by groups. Exigence is holographic. It functions multidimensionally, resolving obstruction into a transformation or change, a rupture, an opportunity, an occasion for action, a galvanizing moment. Rather than an either-or binary, exigence can be both entropic and generative. Exigence manifests as a reductive event as well as an opportunity for growth, death, and regeneration.

Exercising his role in the rhetorical situation of post–World War II America, García forged as well as reacted to the exigencies moving the United States toward major civil rights reform. He made progress never achieved before, inroads with unpredicted reversals and uncertain ends. The texts García generated, the strategies he used, the alliances he formed coalesce, on one hand, into one of America's archetypal "bootstraps" narratives.[18] He dined with the presidents. On the other hand, study of the compromises he made, the challenges he faced, the sacrifices he endured can also be read as one of the great American tragedies. Moving from marginalization to national distinction, García's legacy of resistance demonstrates the precarious process of achieving enfranchisement—the risks, the rewards, the gains, and the losses.

Mobilization and Rhetorical Resonance

García's civic rhetoric reveals that mobilization is less about eloquence and more about resonance. García did not pen any memorable essays or speeches. He did not theorize about the condition of modern democracy nor generate a searing critique in the form of a polemic. Instead, he offered an enabling fiction of civic inclusion that promised Mexican Americans access to "first-class citizenship" by exposing the disabling fictions of institutionalized discrimination. García's representation of the Mexican American experience both challenged the myth of American exceptionalism and unmasked the nation's enduring patterns of racial oppression and exclusion. In a post-war period where dissent and difference were suspect, García complicated complacency, ideological homogeneity, and political passivity. He reinvented patriotism, resisting the post-war "view of America as an anointed nation," a people righteously above the atrocities it had fought overseas.[19] García exposed America to itself.

In 1949, in a series of letters to Texas governor Allan Shivers, García articulated the Mexican American struggle against discrimination. Reacting to recurring cases of discrimination and police brutality against Mexican Americans in South Texas, García wrote on November 22 to Shivers:

> Your people throughout the state are getting tired of such discriminatory actions as the one in Edna, Wharton, Refugio, Ganado, most of East Texas is typical. It is imperative in order to maintain friendly relations that your office come out with an official statement condemning such discriminatory and segregatory actions.
>
> We are not appealing this as Mexican but as Americans who destroyed such beliefs in the last war when we fought the Germans, etc. Am sorry in stating that your office seems not to care to solve the problem but hopes that sometime somewhere the whole thing may be forgotten which it will not. If you can convince me that such actions throughout the state are not Nazi in ideology then I will stop writing.

> Meanwhile we the forgotten citizens who are kept second and third class Americans by Texas customs hope that you see fit to issue such a statement thereby giving us a chance to become at least first class Americans though we remain third class Texans.[20]

In this letter, García has framed his protest through the lens of second person plural invoking the second person possessive, "your people," to establish Shivers's obligatory role to García and the Mexican American electorate as members of Shivers's constituency. Through this strategy, García forges an *ethos* of presence and authority. His use of the metaphors of place as illustrated in the catalogue of proper nouns, Edna, Wharton, Refugio, and Ganado, locates and specifies the growing wave of discontent. He creates a map of mobilization. By shifting subject positions to first person plural in the next segment, "we are not appealing this as Mexicans but Americans," García asserts identification with the national body politic. García's assertion of military participation invokes the unifying emblem of the war. Then in a typical García rhetorical twist he suggests that the lingering threat of "Nazi ideology," though defeated overseas, lurks unchecked on Texas soil, the enduring enemy of democracy. He challenges Shivers to debate the evidence with the promise of his own silence only when violence against Mexican Americans ceases. Through these strategies, García gives voice to a collective presence, "we the forgotten citizens who are kept second and third class Americans."

Following up on these challenges, García's letter of December 4, 1949 to Shivers, asserted:

> [I]n view of the fact that President Truman is so much interested in Civil Rights, naturally I believe that Texas should get interested in our own Civil Rights Program. . . . For three years I have been trying to approach the problem of discrimination and segregation against our people in the State of Texas by petitions, appeals, conferences, and I believe that it has been a complete failure. . . . Unless we get action from our state, we feel that we must go to the federal government to secure equal rights, equal opportunities, and equal protection under our Constitution and laws.[21]

Here, Constitutional rhetoric provides his primary defense. García demonstrates deference to the Constitutional U.S. government and at the same time asserts bold resistance to the state of Texas. As a former military officer, García clearly understood the protocols of hierarchy. His bold demand for action threatens to step over the local Texas chain of command and to appeal to the president as the ultimate authority. This is an act of rhetorical mutiny resonant of the opening lines of the Declaration of Independence, "when in the course of human events, it becomes necessary for one people to dissolve the political bonds." García dares to call Shivers' authority into question. He challenges the sovereignty of the Texas government, the historical memory of the Southern confederacy, and the cherished Texas Republic to invoke federalist intervention and Constitutional protection. García's letter metaphorically threatens to call in the National Guard to establish social justice in Texas. García crafted his message for an intended audience of white legislators situated in a political context where these charges would be received as nothing less than audacious and incendiary fighting words.

Acting as an arbitrator of civil rights, García exploited the privileged discourses of governance using "petitions, appeals, conferences" to participate in the work of civic reform. He taught his followers how to do the same. He exploited Constitutional rhetoric to make room in the national vision for a growing and vital Mexican American presence. García called upon New Deal liberalism to hold the state and federal government accountable to the common citizen. He appealed to a government with the will and structural capability to compensate and protect the working poor and disenfranchised classes. García demanded more from America and its leaders.

Inclusion was not a final achievement; it was a process. García joined the conversation on civil rights at the earliest stages of Truman's project, echoing the common theme of American reform rhetoric and calling for America to realize its most basic terms of citizenship.[22] For García, the process was neither direct nor decisive and was often marked by reversals, ruptures, and inconsistencies as well as by successes. Inclusion was a shifting target that he was constantly trying to pin down through discourse. Even after establishing a national reputation and the recognition of two presidents, García argued that "the American system is a farce" and that "discrimination against Mexican Americans has its roots imbedded in the 'manifest destiny' theory of American expansion."[23] He lamented that "Americans have forgiven the Germans for two world wars, the Japanese for Pearl Harbor—but not the Mexican Americans [for their historical ties to Mexico]."[24] The expansionist impulse of the nineteenth century had not enlarged the American imagination enough to permit the full inclusion of Mexican Americans. With the fervor of the newly converted, García took on the rights and responsibilities of citizenship.

García, Post-War America, and the Ideology of Citizenship

After serving overseas as an officer in the U.S. Army, García relinquished his Mexican citizenship to become a naturalized U.S. citizen. At the same time, he decried America's contradictory terms of inclusion and slanted view of egalitarianism based on race. García understood deeply that Americanism was an ideological commitment.[25] Becoming an American is not a matter of birth. It is a state of mind. García never rejected what he perceived as core American values. For García, exercising citizenship involved a commitment to civic engagement, political compromise, practical imagination, and the vigilant protection of civil liberties. He grappled with the inherent challenges of lobbying for civil rights reform within the ideological parameters of the American civic ethic.

García saw it as his duty, and the duty of every citizen, to join the national dispute about public policy and principles of citizenship. Silence and complacency in the face of injustice, not protest and activism, represented a disavowal of American ideals. The performance of civic identity represented rhetorical practice. For García, civic rhetoric involved exploiting all available means of persuasion toward productive action. Cultivating adherence and the meeting of minds were more critical to moving audiences to action than the eloquence of ceremonial discourse.[26] Impetus for rhetorical action began in the subjective and evolved into arguments founded on universalizable premises about justice and human rights.

García's national impact reveals that effective rhetorical action strikes a chord of discontent yet embeds itself with hope. As one deeply engaged at multiple levels with his community, García addressed the whole audience, not just singular facets of groups or individuals.[27] As veteran, physician, coalition-builder, and peacemaker, García demonstrated that effective rhetoric begins by negotiating power differentials and resolves by healing division. His earliest outreach efforts began in the early 1940s in the barrios of Galveston and Houston, where he taught public health and translated medical information from English into Spanish for the community while attending medical school at the University of Texas–Galveston.[28] García forged liaisons across disparate groups toward the achievement of common aims. García demonstrated that effective civic rhetoric emerges out of a confidence in the audience and its potential for action. Ever the pragmatist, he understood that encouraging an audience toward making "a choice rather than" toward "an irrevocable position" is the best a leader can expect.[29] He did not apologize for the ambiguities and contradictions in his own arguments and the positions of others. Action was everything.

García's brand of civil rights rhetoric distinguishes him from other early post-war civil rights activists such as Martin Luther King Jr., Bayard Rustin, and César Chávez. He was not the eloquent orator that King was. He was not a provocative essayist like Rustin. García did not become the national emblem of *la dignidad* and a collective *mexicano* identity that Chávez became. García, nevertheless, evolved into an embodiment of working-class aspiration and middle-class achievement. Mobility was the recurring thread running through García's civic discourse. The possibilities of America inspired him. His life was a model of American pragmatism and social mobility. He unabashedly demanded "first-class citizenship" for Mexican Americans in every sense of that term: access to higher education, economic upward mobility, political representation, professional status, and full participation in the post-war American Dream.

García did not critique the capitalist underpinnings of the American Dream; he simply wanted to enlarge it to encompass all Americans. His leftist politics leaned only as far as FDR. At the same time, he shared common enemies with America's political right. For García, communism, socialism, and fascism were the enduring threats to the American way of life. Unlike W. E. B. Du Bois, whose civil rights project gradually shifted toward Marxist ideology and capitalist critique, García's civil rights rhetoric remained deeply informed by New American pragmatism and New Deal idealism. He did not intellectualize his experience; he lived it. Citizenship was about the opportunity to fashion one's self and one's community.

García's primary constituency was returning veterans—the members of the American GI Forum — the urban working class, and rural farm workers. His audience responded to his pragmatic approach to democracy. The skillful use of influence through the instrumental discourse of governance and inquiry extended his agency across the nation. He compelled his people to recognize America's abundance rather than resolve themselves to its scarcity. For García, the great crime of America's system of inclusion was the denial of access based on race. He remained deeply conflicted by the contradictions in U.S. pigmentocracy and the complexities involved in social position ascribed by race.

Civic Belonging and American Civil Rights Reform

How García resolved the paradox, the irony, and the contradictions in the narrative construction of becoming an American is especially relevant to the current national conversation. García's legacy speaks to a post–9/11 era grappling with war and terrorism, definitions of patriotism, xenophobia, national security, ideological intolerance, immigration reform, militarism, and the contradictions of American exceptionalism. García's story can be read, by some accounts, as a tale of the unsung hero, as illustrated by Patrick Carroll's *The Wake of Félix Longoria: Bereavement, Racism, and the Rise of Mexican American Activism* and Jeff Felts's documentary, *Justice for My*

People. His story can also be framed as the recovery of an American anti-hero, as examined by Ignacio M. García's political biography, *Hector P. García: In Relentless Pursuit of Justice.* As a metanarrative, the rhetorical construction of García's legacy is unavoidably metaphorical—the ironic representation of a relatively unknown historic figure, the synedochic reduction of the parts of the man for the whole, and his metonymic association with a people.

As founder of the veterans' organization American GI Forum, García emerged as a mobilizing force in post-war Mexican American activism. Notified in January 1949 by Beatrice Longoria, the widow of Private First Class Félix Longoria, that her husband, posthumously awarded the Purple Heart for valor in combat, had been denied burial rites in their hometown of Three Rivers, Texas, García initiated and sustained a discourse of resistance to the ethnic apartheid that historically defined socioeconomic and political configurations in the region. Rolando Hinojosa-Smith, Chicano author, South Texas native, and neighbor to the García family in Mercedes, Texas, reflects:

> What the incident also pointed to was that despite Longoria's military service and death, it mattered little to the Anglo Texans from Three Rivers. Much had been expected by way of improvement in race relations [and] civil rights by Texas Mexicans and the Three Rivers experience reminded Texas Mexicans that military service meant from little to nothing to those people and, perhaps, to many other Texas Anglos in the state.[30]

The war created a "new kind of citizen" within the Mexican American community, which entailed a sense of national belonging and honor that García as a major in the Army not only shared but inspired.[31] The Félix Longoria incident of 1949, pre-dating the historic Rosa Parks case by six years, provided the single galvanizing event necessary to spark national coalition-building among Mexican Americans. García's rhetorical construction of the Longoria incident offered a unifying emblem for Mexican American mobilization. Moreover, the Longoria case provided a template for civil rights reform at the national level. The end result of García's reform effort was a Mexican American civil rights movement forged out of patriotic ideals and military participation. It focused on inclusion and mobility. The movement's emblems of inclusion appropriated Americanist principles and eschewed all residual symbols of Mexican nationalism.

Mexican-origin peoples in post-war America achieved a level of recognition never previously realized in U.S. history. As Rodolfo Rosales observes, inclusion was an ideal of Mexican American middle class before the war, but "the restrictive anti-Mexican environment dictated concessions as the practical goals of their participation."[32] Mexican American activism before the Longoria case remained localized and diffuse. Social conditions after the war combined with rhetorical action moved Mexican American activism beyond concession-making and into policymaking. The exposure and confrontation of racism was critical to that shift in Mexican American civic activism. After the Longoria incident, the realities of institutionalized discrimination and racist social configurations in America were no longer exclusively black and white issues. The slow progression of American civil rights reform leading to the passage of the historic 1965 Civil Rights Act was teleologically linked to the relationships and issues articulated by Mexican American activists and the events surrounding the Longoria affair.

Equally significant, the pragmatism and rhetorical strategies of García's post-war movement sparked the counterdiscourse of the *chicanismo*, a critical exigence for the emergence of the Chicano movement of the 1960s.[33] The new generation of Mexican American intellectuals would be the ones to eventually write the histories of the Mexican presence in America, framing the historical struggle for civil liberties largely from a Chicano nationalist perspective. The subsequent Meso-American mythos, embodied in the utopian notion of Aztlán, involved deconstructing a liberal democratic ideology and as such, disassociating from the values and political agenda of the first-generation Mexican American civil rights figures such as García. Chicano counterdiscourse reaped the harvest of resistance from post-war reform rhetoric and the activism of figures like García.

García's fifty-year legacy has been a call for inclusion, not revolution. He did not seek to overturn America's model of governance, but to participate within it equally and fully. He rejected anything that smacked of a separatist agenda. America, not Aztlán, was the object of desire. America was not a utopian dream. It was a paradox—the reality of García's own experience as an immigrant: the freedom to move—economically, socially, geographically, intellectually; the freedom to become a citizen—useful, resourceful in whatever ways he felt moved. The call to serve and to protect his family, community, and nation was an invitation to fulfill his ultimate purpose. García's vision was grounded in the experience of his own journey from Mexican refugee to American citizen. The process of becoming American was the source of his greatest satisfaction and deepest disappointment.

Recovery of Mexican American Civil Rights Rhetorics

In 1993, the American GI Forum, the largest and most politically influential Mexican American civic organization of the post-war era, was celebrating its forty-fifth anniversary while its founder, Dr. García— still practicing medicine at the age of seventy-nine— was guiding the establishment of the Dr. Héctor P. García Papers at Texas A&M University–Corpus Christi Bell Library. He declined offers from major universities around the country to house the records of his civil rights legacy, even turning down Yale University's proposal to establish an endowed chair in his honor. He left his extensive archive of over 390 linear feet of materials to the local community he had served for five decades.[34]When I began writing about García in 1998, an accretion of interest in his legacy and the post-war Mexican American generation was beginning to form.[35] Journalist Maggie Rivas-Rodriguez launched the *U.S. Latinos and Latinas and World War II* oral history project at the University of Texas in 1999 and organized the first conference on Latino/as in World War II in May 2000.[36] My dissertation, *Legacy of Resistance: Héctor P. García, the Félix Longoria Incident, and Construction of a Mexican American Civil Rights Rhetoric,* the first on García, was defended in March 2002.[37] Arte Público Press commissioned the first political biography about Dr. García, *Hector P. García: In Relentless Pursuit of Justice,* written by Chicano historian Ignacio M. García (no relation), released in December 2002.[38] A locally sponsored film, *Justice for My People: The Dr. Héctor P. García Story,* by Corpus Christi documentarian and producer Jeff Felts, was likewise in progress and released in November 2002.[39] Finally, an examination of the impact of the Longoria incident on the Texas political scene, *Félix Longoria's Wake: Bereavement, Racism, and the Rise of Mexican American Activism,* written by Latin American historian Patrick Carroll, was released in March 2003.[40] Thus, the problem of the obscurity of post-war generation reformers like García has been addressed most productively in the fields of political science, history, and journalism, not in rhetorical studies.

Historian Julie Lereinenger Pycior calls García "one of the giants of the twentieth century."[41] Ignacio M. García, in turn, calls Dr. Héctor P. García "the most famous unknown reformer in our community" and asserts that "there needs to be a García Age in Latino history of the United States."[42] García, whose numerous honors included being awarded the Presidential Medal of Freedom in 1984, represents one of the most prominent national-level Mexican American leaders in modern history.[43] Yale University's Chicano Research Center proposed but never filled the Héctor P. García Endowed Chair. The recent surge in attention focused on García suggests that his legacy has something to say to twenty-first-century American audiences. García's pragmatism, pluralism, activism, and liberalism reemerge as a counterdiscourse to the promulgation of American exceptionalism, elitism, passive patriotism, and neoconservatism in a post–9/11 era. His struggle over immigration offers a cautionary tale for twenty-first-century America border politics. García's bold embrace of liberal democratic principles offers discursive counterweight to the progressive erosion and retreat of liberalism in twenty-first-century U.S. politics.

The Tropes of History-Making

History as a rhetorical construction is as Hayden White argues "a poetic act" built upon the strategies of metonymy, metaphor, synecdoche, and irony. Constructing a historical field involves the articulation of the interpretive schema, the tropes that constitute explanation.[44] A tropological examination of García reveals a complex drama of shifting power relationships. The metonymic identification between García and the American GI Forum functioned as a strategic alliance that redirected power and allowed García to act as an agent for the Mexican American community (and, in some cases, the community to act as an agent of García). The Longoria incident, García's initiation rite into the art of moral protest, represents the dynamic interplay of irony and tragedy, a touchstone moment that both mobilized and symbolized Mexican Americans' position in relation to America's contradictory terms of civic inclusion. The rhetorical construction of the Longoria incident represents a pivotal moment in the emergence of Mexican American civic identity and the circulation of a Mexican American civic *ethos* into the national consciousness.

Civil rights activism is the exercise of transgressing subject positions. The act of claiming and exercising civil rights is an act of resistance—civil rights rhetoric as such is inherently contentious. *In American Exceptionalism: A Double Edged Sword*, Seymoure Lipset argues that "the greatness of free politics lies in the institutionalization of conflict, of the continued struggle for freer and more humanely decent societies."[45] For García, desire and dissent defined the American spirit. In a 1958 letter to the editor of the American GI Forum newsletter, Henry B. Gonzalez depicts García's leadership style in almost messianic terms. About the young García, Gonzalez notes, "He has taken upon himself the task of starting, organizing and guiding an organization that fills a gaping hole or vacuum in our milieu: a veteran's organization that shall channelize the aspirations, hopes, and ambitions of hundreds of thousands of our GIs."[46]

The will to imagine is an invitation to invent community. Civic rhetoric is not about only division and overcoming, but also unity and cooperation.[47] García's record suggests a gifted leadership style that induced cooperation, forged identification, and achieved consensus across social lines. García's reputation as a man of action evolved into a cache of prestige, a kind of embodied capital in his very person that extended to the organization that he led for nearly fifty years.[48] His authority was exponential. People emulated him and adopted his positions. From the construction of García's civic *ethos*, a generation of Mexican American civil rights reformers reimagined and repositioned themselves inside the American democratic saga.

García's model of civic inclusion and social reform seeded the careers of many Mexican American leaders, including the prominent White House appointee Vicente Ximenes, who was tapped for Commissioner of the Inter-Agency of Mexican American Affairs in 1967. García established a bastion of Mexican American political activism and forged enduring coalitions confident in nonviolent gradualism and accommodationist strategies over revolutionary tactics as measures toward social change. García resisted birth-ascribed status, struggling with questions of citizenship, as exemplified by his twenty-year struggle with the *bracero* migrant worker agreements. His own conflicted notions of race both resisted and complicated questions about the hereditary privilege of whiteness. He sought inclusion in diverse public spheres—medical, military, educational, political—writing and talking his way into prominence. He vacillated between hubris and humility—a heroic and tragic figure reflective of his mythological namesake, Hector.

Over the final decades of his life, the images of García became those of a frail, ill, and unimposing man with a soft voice standing at a podium in his American GI Forum uniform—someone upon whom to bestow honors. In old age, García embodied frailty and vulnerability—not the strength and virility America demands of its heroes.[49] He was not larger than life but lived his humanity openly and publicly—refusing to relinquish his medical practice or civic duties and politely fade into the background. When the Texas State Senate passed a resolution in 1989 praising García for his "lasting contributions to the cause of civil rights for Hispanics," the seventy-six year old physician accepted the honor with the sober comment "Our task is not finished."[50]

At the end of his life, García was hailed by the press as a great American leader and healer. The headlines announcing his death called him "the Martin Luther King Jr. of Mexican-American History."[51] García's enduring achievements were acknowledged by the Texas Council of Negro Organizations in 1955 with the "Democracy Forward" award, and by the Corpus Christi chapter of the NAACP in 1969 with the Humanitarian Award. In his liberal democratic view of social empowerment, education remained first and foremost. In recognition of García's dedication to educational equity, Guadalupe San Miguel Jr. dedicates *"Let Them Take Heed": Mexican*

Americans and the Campaign for Educational Equality in Texas, 1910–1981
to García with these words: "To Dr. Hector P. García and all those Mexican
American individuals who have struggled passionately for a more just and
equal society in this country."[52]

Neither direct nor decisive, García's mobilization of the Mexican
American people was a circuitous process marked by reversals, ruptures,
inconsistencies, and unprecedented successes. Shaped by the rhetorical
context of post-war America, the places around which García formed his
arguments of civic inclusion index not only the promises but the contradictions of the American democratic vision. Problematically, myth and lore
surrounding García's civil rights achievements and the Longoria incident
persist. Even the "Félix Longoria" entry in Meier and Gutiérrez's historical
compendium, *Encyclopedia of the Mexican American Civil Rights Movement*, reflects common misconceptions rather than archival evidence.
The citation on the Longoria incident indicates that "Dr. Héctor García
intervened locally in the affair, without success." The reference overlooks
García's liaison role and sustained coordination efforts and instead credits
Lyndon B. Johnson with the successful outcome. Juan Gómez-Quiñones's
Chicano Politics: Reality and Promise, 1940–1990 omits García's role in
the Longoria case and ignores his fifty-year platform of reformist rhetoric
yet credits the American GI Forum with providing a political foundation
for Chicano activism.[53] García's unswerving patriotism at the peak of the
Chicano movement and through the Vietnam War, emblematically represented in the American GI Forum uniform worn by García and the aging
first-generation reformers, alienated anti-war Chicano activists and intelligentsia of the 1960s and 1970s.[54]

Chicano activists of the 1960s and 1970s openly challenged the patriotic,
assimilationist stance of the American GI Forum. According to Rodolfo
Acuña, student organizers of the Mexican American Youth Organization
in 1964, felt that they had no place in the more established, middle-class
Mexican American organizations such as the American GI Forum and
the League of United Latin American Citizens (LULAC). Moreover,
they felt that García talked down to them. They resisted and distrusted
García's liberal political agenda and moderate leadership. In *Chicanismo:
The Forging of a Militant Ethos among Mexican Americans*, Ignacio M.
García elaborates:

> Why, unlike Mexican Americans during the integrationist years of the 1940s
> and 1950s, did Chicanos seek a different course? No longer satisfied with
> pluralism and liberal agendas, Chicanos and Chicanas rejected mainstream
> American society and clung to the idea of Aztlán—a social, political,

economic, and cultural utopia, free of liberal politicians, welfare programs, police brutality, discrimination, poverty, and identity crisis.[55]

García had no interest in advancing visions of a "cultural utopia" and regarded Chicano politics as politically naïve, economically unrealistic, and ideologically impractical—a retreat from the possibilities of America. Even more importantly, he recognized that Mexican Americans, on the whole, were more politically centrist and culturally conservative. As a youth movement, *chicanismo* had scant appeal to first generation Mexican Americans interested in acquiring economic mobility and political enfranchisement in the U.S. society. García knew that only a fraction of the post-war Mexican American generation would ever identify with Chicano ideology.

To consider the rhetorical action of Mexican American civil rights activists in relationship to modern civil rights history is to complicate the conversation on race and citizenship in the United States and to confront the grand narrative of civil rights reform. Representing García's legacy requires a recovery of the tropes of history-making. With the reversal and erosion of affirmative action legislation in all facets of American life over the past two decades, the misperception of already-achieved equity, a once-done-always-done notion of social justice, has become insidiously embedded in the grand narrative of civil rights reform. García's legacy complicates that narrative. His own journey from marginalization to enfranchisement and into obscurity suggests that civic inclusion cannot be secured as a final end; it must be practiced as a process. What the recovery of García's rhetorical career illustrates is that the process of civil rights reform grows out of the pragmatics of politics as well as the galvanizing moments of public protest. Current sources on Mexican American civil rights focus largely on the Chicano movement of the mid-1960s and the leading figure of the United Farm Workers movement, César Chávez. Winthrop Yinger's *Cesar Chavez: The Rhetoric of Nonviolence* and John C. Hammerback and Richard J. Jensen's *The Rhetorical Career of César Chávez* examine the rhetorical action of Chávez in his confrontation with exploitive farm labor policies and practices.[56] These volumes record, document, and analyze Chávez's life as rhetor without reference to the early post-war Mexican American reformers. Jensen and Hammerback's *The Words of César Chávez* offers close reading of Chávez's rhetorical practice by anthologizing and examining Chávez's most significant and representative texts.[57] Yet none situates Chávez within the rhetorical trajectory of early post-war reformers nor acknowledges the historical context giving rise to the 1960s Mexican American civil rights reform movement.

Hammerback, Jensen, and José Ángel Gutiérrez's *A War of Words: Chicano Protest in the 1960s and 1970s* begins to enlarge the scope of Mexican American civil rights reform rhetoric to include analysis of several national-level Chicano nationalists such as Reies Tijerina and Rodolfo "Corky" González and moderate reformists such as Henry B. González.[58] Héctor P. García, however, is not mentioned. Pre-dating César Chávez by nearly ten years, García cultivated the rhetorical field of Mexican American civil right reform before, during, and after the rise and fall of the Chicano movement. He remained in the rhetorical trenches of local and national politics longer than any other national-level civil rights activist.

Jorge C. Rangel and Carlos M. Alcala's article "Project Report: De Jure Segregation of Chicanos in Texas Schools," featured in the *Harvard Civil Rights–Civil Liberties Law Review* acknowledges García for "his relentless efforts, spanning twenty-five years to eradicate Chicano school segregation" and chronicles García's desegregation battle but does not examine the broad range of his rhetorical practices.[59] None of the aforementioned, including the more recent studies on García by Ignacio M. García and Patrick Carroll, examines through close reading the discursive strands of Mexican American civil rights rhetoric advanced by Héctor P. García and the early reformers of the post–World War II era.

Matt S. Meier and Margo Gutiérrez respond to the general absence of Mexican American civil rights history in *Encyclopedia of Mexican American Civil Rights Movement*. This resource guide emerges out of the recognition that Mexican American civil rights issues have been historically subsumed under language, citizenship, employment, immigration, and educational issues.[60] Meier and Gutiérrez define civil rights broadly, to include "those personal and property rights, political, economic, and human or natural, for the violation of which citizens may have recourse in the courts as a result of constitutional or statutory law." They argue that the Mexican American struggle for civil rights, although long-standing, has received little scholarly attention: "The Mexicano fight against discrimination and racism as manifested by Anglo political and societal institutions began in Texas at least a decade before the U.S.–Mexican War and the 1848 Treaty of Hidalgo. However, only in recent decades has the story of that striving begun to be included as a part of mainstream American history."[61]

Much of the public rhetoric and civil rights oratory related to Mexican American civil rights has not been archived. Additionally, literacy practice among Mexican Americans and Mexican immigrants in the border region has been limited—especially before World War II. This overall absence of an accessible body of Mexican American civil rights discourse demands finding new indexes of civic leadership and Mexican American participation in the national conversation on race and citizenship throughout U.S. –Mexico history.

The Paradox of Leadership

As a civil rights activist, García simply fails to fit comfortably into the traditional rhetorical narratives of U.S. civil rights reform. The irony and complexity of García's position in post–World War II America reverberate not only through political history but popular culture as well. His reputation, attracting the national notice of author Edna Ferber and providing background for her fictionalized account of García as the good doctor in her 1952 book *Giant* (and the film version following, in 1956), further problematizes García—a figure overshadowed on screen by Elizabeth Taylor, Rock Hudson, and James Dean, cinematic icons of white America.[62] Moreover, García's indomitable activism and unabashed Americanism profoundly complicate the left's conversation on Mexican American civic presence, leadership, ideology, and identity.[63]

Functioning on the borders of class, race, and culture, García remains a complex figure whose legacy resists compartmentalization. The dearth of scholarship on García and his role as a rhetor and civil rights activist can be largely attributed to the complexities of border politics: he cannot be categorized into either Anglo or Chicano narratives of Texas history. The underexamination of García's legacy represents a loss, a gap in the historical conversation that until recovered limits our vision and insight into possible responses to our current conditions as a nation. Interrogating discourses performed "at the intersections" between legitimate social institutions and non-sanctioned political formations demands looking beyond nation-maintaining offices of our elected officials to examine the impetus for social change.[64]

As examined by Garth Pauley in *The Modern Presidency and Civil Rights: Rhetoric on Race from Roosevelt to Nixon* and Eduardo Bonilla-Silva in *White Supremacy and Racism in the Post–Civil Rights Era*, rhetoric on questions of civil rights is formed in a centrifuge of social orders and discourses.[65] Furthermore, as explored by Russell Riley in *The Presidency and the Politics of Racial Inequality*, political institutions like the executive and legislative branches routinely serve as nation-maintaining institutions on questions of racial inequality. Elected officials are put in office to maintain national stability, the status quo, and the positions of those already in power. Change agents, therefore, must come from outside these institutions, are necessarily figures who irritate the status quo and push the discourse in new directions.

Several of García's followers attempted to establish García's place in the national narrative on civil rights reform. In 1958, Oscar Phillips, an American GI Forum founding member, described García in a submission to *Readers' Digest*:

> Shooting across the vast Texas horizon in 1948, he has ignited a movement for the renaissance of Mexican Americans that has overlapped into some 14 other states. Sometimes begging, sometimes cajoling, and at other times badgering potential leaders of Mexican descent into action, he has returned to these earliest Texans their dignity, prestige, and willingness to fight for their place in the hot Southwest sun.[66]

Outside of local lore, popular culture, and brief sketches within Texas historical studies, there is scant analysis of the rhetorical value of García's civic identity and discursive action—carefully coordinated performances which together challenged state and national civil rights policy and practice.

García consistently and persistently implemented the tools of instrumental rhetoric to make the injustices of racial discrimination, educational segregation, and labor segmentation palpable and present to the American gaze. García operated on the assumption that given evidence, "the truth," white America would see the injustices and social change would follow. García's entire civil rights project was built on the generation of empirical evidence and discourse to demonstrate the institutionalized denial of civic rights and privileges to Mexican-origin people in the United States.

García's reliance on inquiry and evidence-gathering, his liberal view of democracy, and his confidence in education and science to confront injustice in the world closely parallel W. E. B. Du Bois's earliest approaches to social reform. The epistemic nature of García's rhetoric aligns García with the "New American Pragmatism" of Du Bois and, at the same time, distinguishes it from other forms of civil rights discourses such as that of Martin Luther King Jr., which drew more heavily on pulpit eloquence.[67] The pragmatic civil rights rhetoric of García and the American GI Forum spurred the subsequent Chicano nationalist rhetoric of the 1960s, a counterdiscourse that resisted the Americanist principles García so ardently endorsed. García's rhetoric, in contrast, was largely secular and civic in nature, informed by the dominant discourses of the post–World War II era. It was performative, active, and empirical.

García's mode of governance reflected his approach to knowledge-making. García maintained faith in free conversation, the foundation of his vision for the American GI Forum. He considered democracy not only a way of governing but a way of knowing. Constantly immersed in the human condition, awash in the social, the bodily, the spiritual, and the political dimensions of daily life, García recognized that knowledge and justice are constructed through experience. His rhetoric proceeded not only from participant observation but complete immersion in the community he served. He privileged *phronesis*, practical wisdom—the stuff of life transmitted through language. García believed that at its heart, the American democratic experiment was an open process of deliberation. He fostered environments conducive to discussion and debate. García observed:

> I see it working—this war on poverty on the local level . . . where the lowest educated person or the poorest on the economic level can get up and talk to the mayor, or talk to the rich, or talk to the political leaders in a way that they would never talk before, say ten years before. And this is democracy at its best. It's working.[68]

Over the course of some forty years, unlike many civil rights activists whose brief lives did not allow a long-term view, García witnessed local and national-level changes. He mentored generations of new leaders such as Texas state Senator Carlos Truan, using the American GI Forum as a template of civic engagement. Throughout the journey, García celebrated and called for the authorization and mobilization of citizens at the grassroots level. He marveled:

> Practically illiterate people who get up and demand that the city repair the streets, that the city pick up the abandoned automobiles, and fix their streets and the city does it! Before they wouldn't do anything like that, they expected people like us to do it. Now we don't have to do it; in fact, they do it themselves. And I say this is not an experiment anymore, it's become a reality.[69]

García, however, understood that justice is a process, never a finished product. Justice, like rhetoric, is symbolic action.[70]

García's self-ascribed role as rhetor further reflects the "prophetic pragmatism" outlined by Cornel West in *The American Evasion of Philosophy: A Genealogy of Pragmatism*. West locates his notion of "prophetic pragmatism" within a Judeo-Christian world view and a deep confidence in human agency—individually and collectively. West's prophetic pragmatism recognizes the "irreducible predicament of unique individuals" and appropriately applies to García as a man of his time as well as a man ahead of his time. West argues that "the praxis of prophetic pragmatism is tragic action with revolutionary intent, usually reformist consequences, and always visionary outcome."[71] In the practice of prophetic pragmatism, García advanced a vision of inclusion, confronting individual and collective experiences of injustice "with little expectation of ridding the world of *all* evil."

Although he was a highly effective and very active orator, García believed that prepared speeches were somehow contrived and insincere. Contemporaries described García as an emotional and often passionate speaker. Critics depicted him as "a radical" who inflamed the poor, was capable of "stirring up his hearers," and spoke from "an emotional standpoint."[72] García understood that an effective speaker must empathize with the audience, and that to exploit *pathos* an orator must demonstrate *pathos*. He often boasted that he never "wrote" a speech and whatever he said came straight from the heart. The few film clips and audio recordings featuring García's public address indicate that García was neither an eloquent nor skilled orator. As a result, there is not a large repository of speech transcripts from which to analyze García's means of persuasion.

Moreover, García did not create a body of essays reflecting his experience or theorizing about civil rights leadership. He was, nevertheless, a gifted rhetorician and communicator. In the 1970s, he had plans to write a history of Mexican American civil rights but never found time for the project.[73] He recognized the political and historical value of the written text, however, and saved even the seemingly most insignificant fragments of writing. Yet García never considered himself a writer. He scribbled notes to himself and to others on prescription slips, typed letters to public officials between treating patients, dashed off telegrams from his medical office. García's approach to instrumental discourse reflects Beale's pragmatic model in which "[r]hetoric is performative in a teleological rather than a formal sense: it aims at participation in the actions of a community."[74]

This absence of a body of poetic and polemic literature accounts in part for García's omission from the historical construction of twentieth-century American civil rights. Unlike Du Bois or Martin Luther King Jr., whose eloquence in both speech and written text marked them as gifted intellectuals and exceptional orators, García left no literary legacy, social theory, or eloquent discursive fragments equal to Du Bois's notions of the "color line" and "double consciousness" or Martin Luther King Jr.'s "Letter from the Birmingham Jail" or "I Have a Dream."

García's literacy of social engagement relied on two linguistic codes and code alternation as a rhetorical strategy. He wrote in both English and Spanish and occasionally employed codeswitching within a single conversation or text as a solidarity marker, as illustrated in his January 1979 letter to the membership of LULAC. In this open letter, as in many texts that García wrote for a Spanish-English bilingual audience, García composed the body in English but closed with: "Para los 'LULACS' que dios los bendiga y les ayuda a nuestra organizacion hermana son los deseos de su hermano. Fundador de el American G I Forum, Dr. Hector P. Garcia."[75] [To the members of LULAC that God blesses and helps our sister organization. These are the hopes of your brother, founder of the American GI Forum.] The use of codeswitching in both his writing and speech signaled his identification with the Mexican American community he served. Codeswitching and Spanish function as symbols of intimacy and markers of belonging. García's strong identification with the Mexican American working poor, as well as his own communicative fluency within Anglo, English-speaking communities, enhanced his discursive agency.

Even for the most formal audiences, García's rhetoric did not indulge in elaborate figurative constructions or strive to translate lived experience into a polemic or poetic genre. He typed most of his correspondence and used full capitals for emphasis for both the salutation and body of the text. Both his oral and written English were frequently marked with nonstandard features, especially in terms of verb tense markers. Spanish was his first language and the only language spoken in his home while he was growing up. He learned English while attending the public schools in Mercedes, Texas. García's written prose in English, sometimes exhibiting unconventional features in syntax and spelling, as well as orthographic error, nevertheless affected his audiences. The fact that his writing was generally written in an accessible, informal, sometimes unconventional style, and approximated ordinary speech, is one of the keys to its success. "Our people don't like a man who stands too straight; it makes him seem too far above the people," García explained to Thomas Sutherland, former executive secretary of the Texas Good Neighbor Commission.[76] García's rhetoric in both speaking and writing exuded an authenticity and a highly evocative down-to-earth quality. He remained close to the subject of his discourse and near to the interests of his audience. In sum, García was a professional writing not a writing professional.

The following chapters focus on the *topoi* or places around which García found and formed his major arguments. These areas include García's discursive engagement with the Longoria incident, the *bracero* immigrant labor program, and his alliance with Lyndon B. Johnson. As responses to the conditions of the post-war rhetorical situation, these issues fueled García's primary arguments toward civil rights reform. While other exigencies such as the evolving role of women, the democratization of higher education, and the mission of the Catholic Church at the cusp of Vatican II precipitated, facilitated, limited, as well as super-charged García's civil rights movement, the Longoria affair, immigration, and partisan politics were the areas that demanded most of García's rhetorical energies. He was an activating agent in a dynamic forty-year chiasmus of social action. He seized the moment as well as helped to shape the moment. García's discursive impact was diffuse and immeasurable.

Chapter 2 examines the formation of García's civic identity and rhetorical career. As physician, social activist, and citizen, García used language, oral and written, to forge an *ethos* and a rhetoric of resistance. These roles among others constituted García's civic identity and framed his terms of national belonging. However, García was more than his constituent parts, more than his public roles. This chapter focuses on how García used discourse to construct his civic identity and how others discursively map García's leadership.

Chapter 3 centers on the Longoria incident as exigence, moving García into a stance of resistance and propelling him as an activist into the national arena. Responding to the post-war rhetorical situation and the antitotalitarian tenor of the era, García advanced a strand of discourse that became the initiating force behind the national drama of the Longoria affair. Through García's intervention and sustained leadership, the Longoria incident evolved into a galvanizing moment mobilizing and organizing disparate groups toward the formation of the post-war Mexican American civil rights movement. The occasion would provide García and his followers with critical training in moral protest. In the wake of the Longoria affair, the American GI Forum would become, under García's direction, the political conscience of an emerging Mexican American middle class.

Immigration issues were integral to García's civil rights effort. The growing presence of Mexican laborers, those protected under the 1942 *bracero* agreements and those working without documentation, represented an urgency that also moved García into a stance of resistance. Chapter 4 examines García's rhetorical engagement with the *bracero* program and the so-called "wetback problem" during the post-war era. The rhetorical practices exercised by García and the American GI Forum in reaction to the Mexican migrant labor situation generated some of their most problematic discourses. Calling for fair labor practices and greater economic mobility, García's rhetoric made visible discriminatory practices against Mexican-origin citizens in the United States.

From 1948 to 1968, García played an increasingly significant role in the post-war political landscape and in civil rights reform. Chapter 5 focuses on García's alliance with Lyndon B. Johnson and its importance to post-war civil rights reform. The meteoric rise of the American GI Forum and García's reputation as an advocate of Mexican American civil rights paralleled Johnson's ascendancy to national prominence. Through their collaborative and contentious engagement in partisan politics, García and Johnson helped to destabilize institutionalized discrimination in Texas and the nation. An examination of the García-Johnson relationship and the examples of their instrumental rhetoric illustrate how García and Johnson together contributed to a social mosaic of political discourses—some of which through complex sets of relationships and exigencies ultimately coalesced into public policy.

From the 1949 Longoria affair to President Lyndon B. Johnson's 1965 Voting Rights Act speech, García complicated America's terms of national belonging and recast the image of national communion. García's unique position as civil rights activist allowed him to operate at the nexus of a growing alliance between the U.S. government and an emerging post-war civil rights movement. For the first time in U.S. history, Mexican Americans in the post-war period took a seat at the national table and joined in full deliberation.

The American GI Forum and
the Rhetoric of Civic Presence

2

*I*n March 1948, Dr. Héctor P. García established a forum to represent the civic presence of disenfranchised Mexican Americans.
He called this coalition the American GI Forum. His organization began
as a veterans' rights group and evolved over the next twenty years into a
sociopolitical framework to launch local and national resistance to *de jure*
and *de facto* segregation. The American GI Forum became a training ground
of social activism for García and his followers. A witness to the devastation
of the Mexican Revolution and World War II, García rejected the tools of
war and looked to the art of rhetoric to do battle with the social injustices
of South Texas. Throughout his career as physician and social activist, he
sought to ensure the opportunity for "freedom of action" in his life and the
lives of others.[1] García's understanding of "freedom of action" included
the full range of intellectual, political, economic, religious, and social opportunities guaranteed to whites by the Constitution. He spent his entire
civil rights career grappling with the questions of race and citizenship that
historically impeded Mexican-origin people from attaining full access to
American mobility.

Fashioning his own journey from immigration to enfranchisement into a
narrative of the quintessential American dream, García constructed a civic
ethos to counter prevailing stereotypes of Mexican Americans. García's life
story was his rhetoric. This chapter textualizes the mythic construction of
García's civic identity, interweaving the rhetorics of biography, narrative,
and history. I examine the broad range of discursive representations used
to depict García and his civic presence over the span of his nearly fifty-year
career as well as examine the life experiences and relationships shaping
García's rhetorical legacy. As one of García's most savvy and enduring
rhetorical achievements, I set the landmark establishment of the American
GI Forum at the center of this discussion.

García publicly cultivated the role of the citizen as a change agent. Citizenship was not only a state of being, but a performative, purposeful action

toward the creation and re-creation of the American democratic vision. Through public and private discourse, García projected himself and was projected by his constituency as an archetypal leadership figure: a blend of the Trojan war hero Hector, the tragic Greek god Prometheus, and the self-sacrificing Judeo-Christian emblem of the martyr and saint. Perpetually broken by his quest, García faced a life task he could never complete. His life story and mythic civic identity evolved into local allegory, making concrete and particular the collective experience of his community. The American GI Forum gave the Mexican American electorate not only a forum for deliberation, but also a political presence in local and national policymaking, a safe haven for resistance, and an indisputably Americanist civic identity.

García and the leaders of the American GI Forum adroitly appropriated current discourse formations of the era, fusing New Deal liberalism and the Cold War anti-communist rhetorics to align themselves with the post-war structure of feeling.[2] They maintained a curious balance of staying in step with the nation they simultaneously resisted and celebrated. Through the governance of the American GI Forum García and his followers learned how to generate and circulate an array of instrumental rhetorics. The grassroots, everyday leadership of the American GI Forum achieved new levels of rhetorical authority through the effective manipulation of different genres, texts, linguistic codes, and messages in order to influence the attitudes and actions of diverse audiences. By his own example, García made instrumental rhetoric accessible and easily appropriated by uneducated Mexican American citizens. Unlike formal oratory and essayist literacy, which require varying levels of skill, training, and eloquence, García demonstrated to his constituency the power of the common voice.

A "Militant Moses"

García's performance of civic identity reveals the unique embodiment of an American *ethos*, his pragmatic approach to leadership, the historical moment in which García exercised influence, his use of the everyday rhetorics of citizenship, and his evolving engagement with the regional, national, and international context. By triangulating the discourses that García used to represent himself along side the discourses used by others to describe him—portraits etched from inside and outside his inner circles—a multifaceted rubric emerges of García in the practice of civic life. The myth was not the man; García the man eluded even those most intimate to him. The qualities he concealed and those he revealed shifted continuously.

García projected a heuristic for American civic life nuanced by the idiosyncrasies of his own individuality.[3] García fashioned a self-fulfilling prophecy for himself and his people. The social roles constituted by and for García ultimately constructed his civic identity and helped to reframe the terms of national belonging. García's persona, replicated through public rhetoric, media representation, and instrumental discourses of diverse forms transformed him into an emblem of both honor and controversy. He capitalized on the iconic value of his acquired reputation.

Seemingly tireless, García routinely worked late nights making hospital rounds and tending to the daily controversies of Forum business. In a letter to Concha Noyola, secretary of the American GI Forum Ladies Auxiliary, García reveals his strategic self-posturing in his confession: " were it not for the many friends who told me to ignore the attacks, I would have quit all of the work I have done for many years at great sacrifice of time, health, and money. . . . Please pardon my letter but I am typing it in my office myself at 11:30 tonight because that is the only time I have to do this work."[4] Short-tempered, demanding, and even authoritarian, this same man provided ice cream for the neighborhood children as they watched the "Ed Sullivan Show" on the black and white television in his office, the only television set in the community. Consistent with García's own self-representation as a self-sacrificing public servant, Pauline Kibbe, former executive secretary of the Texas Good Neighbor Commission, announced in a 1953 letter to the American Friends Service Committee that "the people of Mexican descent in Texas have at last found a leader" and described García as "fearless, tireless, selfless, and absolutely incorruptible. . . . available day or night, wherever problems arise."[5]

García's public persona countered pernicious stereotypes of Mexican-origin peoples and transformed collective shame into honor. He resisted the role of victim, and instead exercised the role of citizen.[6] He remained perpetually suspect of passive compliance in the face of injustice. García demanded the same kind of critical activism from his followers, knowing that oppression is perpetuated by silence and invisibility. García confronted the cycle of victimization and internal colonization by becoming vocal and visible. His embodiment of American virtue countered every prevailing Mexican stereotype; he was resourceful, faithful, hard-working, patriotic, assertive, prudent, intelligent, and articulate. He accentuated the virtues of ordinary citizenship to extraordinary dimensions. Sacrifice transformed García into public icon, a representative of American ideals.

As a member of a well-educated clan, respected on both sides of the border even in impoverishment, García straddled spheres of privilege and deprivation his whole life. The border was more than a geographical reality. It was a social, political, cultural, intellectual, and spiritual condition that challenged him to envision social configurations differently.[7] García resisted the narrow definitions of Mexican civic identity imposed by Anglo-dominant institutions, demanding equal access to education, housing, employment, legal representation, and political participation. Functioning on the borders of class, race, culture, and citizenship, García remained a complex figure his entire life. His legacy resists compartmentalization. García's keen ability to accommodate diverse audiences was as much a response to his own personal condition as it was a reaction to the world beyond the U.S.-Mexico border. Alongside his unwavering patriotism, García imagined himself a world citizen and took tremendous pride in representing America to the world. He explained in an interview with Thomas Kreneck, Texas A&M University–Corpus Christi Special Collections curator:

> From the very beginning, I told you that some of the people have asked me how I was able to do all these things, and my answer being constantly, (still looking for that thing), that I am and I was very adaptable to changes. Here I am a United States Army officer, that's all I am. . . . I was not a Mexican-American officer, I was an American officer, same thing when I was ambassador to the United Nations. . . . I was not a Mexican-American ambassador, I was an American ambassador. I'd become adaptable to changes like that, and I was very good at it.[8]

Adaptability remained a key word in García's conceptualization of citizenship, practice of leadership, and construction of resistance rhetoric. As one who understood how to straddle diverse cultures, García liked to represent himself as "the helpful go-between," a liaison between the disfranchised and the privileged elite.[9] He resisted the label of "power broker" and preferred to see himself as "a conduit for people to get solutions to their problems."[10] Maury Maverick Sr., the liberal ex-mayor of San Antonio, once described García as a "rough and tough" leader who could "talk to people in their own language."[11] Descriptions of García span the spectrum. He was labeled an agitator, a subversive, and a radical by the Texas Anglo establishment. A four-page newspaper exposé on García in the mid-1960's headlined "A Man of Controversy" reports:

> Admirers and critics alike have referred to him as a Mexican-American Martin Luther King, but their meanings are vastly different. To some, he is a radical who inflames the poor and the uneducated, although he drives a Cadillac and lives in a large brick house on Corpus Christi's south side. Others see him as a militant Moses, leading his people out of the wilderness. Men who know him have strong opinions about him. He is variously described as warm, kind, cold, selfless, glory-seeking, dictatorial,

emotional, calculating, a natural leader, a self-appointed boss and a believer in democracy.[12]

The inconsistencies, the paradoxes, the contradictions of García's character contributed to the complex construction of the *ethos* and mystique that never failed to attract the attention of his followers and his adversaries.

Gilbert Casares, former chairman of the Corpus Christi–based Héctor P. García chapter of the American GI Forum, worked closely with García for over forty-five years helping to establish American GI Forum chapters around the country, driving five and six days at a time to remote corners of the country with García in the doctor's light blue Cadillac. "He could get action just like that," Casares recounted. "He never turned any one down. He could pick up the phone and call the president. Dr. García was aggressive as hell."[13] Tom Kreneck confirms, "You didn't walk away from Dr. García. He walked away from you."[14]

García remained a man of contradiction his entire life. He represented a dissonant presence during the Eisenhower halcyon years, demanding that the federal government address South Texas social inequities. He helped to stir national political shifts when he mobilized Spanish-speaking voters in unprecedented numbers during the 1960 Viva Kennedy and 1964 Viva Johnson campaigns. In 1968, García was appointed to the U.S. Civil Rights Commission by President Lyndon B. Johnson for his progressive yet moderate leadership style, then was removed from his appointment by President Richard Nixon for being too extreme. "In the view of some I am a radical. I am a radical in that I am for equality," García confessed.[15]

He fought for the civil rights of South Texas Mexican Americans under the aegis of the American GI Forum at the same time he resisted civil rights labels. "Yes we do fight cases that need our help wherein the rights of our citizens have been violated but we are not and never have been a civil rights organization," García wrote to the secretary of the Crystal City American GI Forum in 1954. "Personally I hate the word."[16] He nonetheless appropriated the terminology, designated funds for "civil rights" cases in the American GI Forum operating budget, and began promulgating a Mexican American civil rights discourse as early as 1948.[17] By the 1970s, García no longer shunned the civil rights label and regarded himself as being at the forefront of modern American civil rights history.

No other Mexican American figure has received more appointments, accolades, or honors—including the Presidential Medal of Freedom presented by President Reagan in 1984. None before him has wielded more influence with high level public officials nor held sway over a national-level Mexican American constituency as long. An endowed chair was named in his honor at Yale University at the Chicano Research Center in 1985. A statue of the young Dr. García dressed in his American GI Forum uniform and holding a book marks the Texas A&M University–Corpus Christi campus, where his papers were donated in 1990.[18]

García interrogated and implicated the disparities of America's terms of national inclusion. He knew his words would be empty rhetoric if he and his followers did not exercise the role of citizen above reproach. After countless confrontations with institutionalized discrimination, decades of retaliatory action against him and the American GI Forum, and untold setbacks, García insisted, "The biggest impact I had was that I never pushed or favored any demonstrations to tear down the system. I always thought the system would work with us."[19] In practice, he shuttled between acts of resistance and civil *obedience*, acting out an unwavering confidence in democracy and American pragmatism.

García's primary rhetorical aim was to make the condition of the Mexican-origin peoples in America present and palpable. In the tradition of American pragmatism, he believed that "truth can be made, just as health, wealth, and strength can be made in the course of experience."[20] García's engagement with the Longoria incident, the anti-*bracero* campaign, and democratic partisan politics were all endeavors to make Mexican Americans present, active, and vocal. He used a broad range of civic discourses to grapple with the American paradox, or what social scientist and race relations scholar Gunnar Myrdal called in 1944 "the American Dilemma:" the conflict between the national creed and social practice.[21] García operated "under the spell of the great national suggestion," the belief that liberal, humanistic tenets of the "American Creed" guided the nation.[22] As a practical idealist, García functioned under the belief that if he exposed the disparities corrective action would follow.

The Practice of Civic Discourse

García keenly recognized the inconsistencies in the ideals and practice of American democracy. Because of his tenacious engagement with the American dilemma, García was perpetually writing and speaking his way into and out of conflict. He recognized that engaging dissonance is precisely the work of civic discourse, of taking on the role of citizen, of belonging to a human community—the reconciliation of difference through language. García believed his voice mattered. Even more, he believed his voice would be heard. And it was—by ten presidents from Truman to Clinton; countless public officials; international dignitaries from Latin America to the West Indies; audiences across the nation for over four decades.

García expected the United States to live up to its contract of equal protection under the law. In his October 30, 1947, letter to the editor of the *Corpus Christi Caller Times*, a young Dr. García appealed to his community. Serving as liaison for the Veterans Administration to receive the remains of war casualties returned to Corpus Christi for burial, García wrote:

> These soldiers, both Latins and Anglos laid down their lives in the same Altar of Sacrifice for the same country—our country. Schooling of language difficulties or inability to speak English did not make any difference when the call came. They fought and died in foreign and hostile shores believing in their country and what to them it represented. They firmly believed in the Ideals of Democracy: Liberty, Equality, and Freedom of Education. Today they are returned to the same land where they were discriminated against and where their brothers, sisters, and their own children are still segregated.[23]

The points upon which García hinged his veteran and civil rights rhetoric remained the same. He argued that war was the great equalizer in which Mexican Americans had paid at the "Altar of Sacrifice" with their lives for the civil liberties historically denied them. The Judeo-Christian metaphor of blood sacrifice prefigured the arguments García would construct to represent the Longoria case two years later. Invoking images of bloodshed spilled on "foreign and hostile shores" for the "ideals of democracy, liberty, equality, and freedom of education," García fused Revolutionary and Judeo-Christian symbolism with liberal and traditional republican political values.

Ironically, García's argument for individual rights and the protection of civil liberties appealed to America's historical memory, a historical memory in which Mexican Americans had no place. Casting himself as what Texas state Senator Carlos Truan once called "a prophet of honor," García framed the demand for equal protection through a rhetoric of "atonement."[24] Although the suppressed premises in García's enthymematic constructions shifted, the conclusion reflected this one pivotal Judeo-Christian tenet: sacrifice renders inclusion. Because Mexican Americans had paid the sacrifice they should be included in the national communion.

The peculiar, enthymematic quality of García's rhetoric reflects the kind of non sequitur logic characteristic of most his arguments. His arguments generally evolved informally, uninformed by the rules of formal deduction. Suppressed premises gape around the fabric of his arguments like dropped stitches. García evidenced little inclination to resolve the inconsistencies and gaps. Truth for García was a kaleidoscope of multicolored fragments.

Reality was teleological: the end was contained in the beginning. As illustrated in his 1947 letter to the editor, García's rhetoric does not establish a logical connection between the primary premises of his argument, "schooling of language difficulties" or "inability to speak English" with the sacrifice of Mexican American lives on the battlefield. He expected his audience to fill in the enthymematic gaps with collective knowledge.

García and his constituency knew that inequitable social configurations economically, educationally, and politically contributed to the overrepresentation of Mexican Americans on the frontlines of military service—exposed to the highest risk of harm and death. He did not need to spell out these realities to his constituency. These kinds of suasory moves enhanced García's rhetorical effectiveness. Rather than amplification, he relied on simplification, rarely belaboring the intricacies of an issue. He didn't burden or insult his audience with too much information. Instead, he appealed to *phronesis*, practical wisdom. The tenets of his own pragmatic style insisted on sufficient and relevant evidence, no more. García relied, therefore, on sparse pragmatic rhetoric, symbolic performance, collective knowledge, and metaphor to communicate what deductive reason alone could not.

Through his own public and personal performance, García helped to shape the drama of American civil rights history. In South Texas, where "Jim Crow" practices still permitted restaurants to post signs "No dogs or Mexicans allowed," García struggled to make visible the displaced and exploited Mexican American population. He saw an unjust social situation that called for a response. Considered neither white nor "colored," Mexican Americans were historically excluded from the national discussion on civil rights. The condition of Mexican Americans in the Southwest escaped the general notice of scholars, legislators, and the American public. There were no statutes of law forbidding Mexican-origin people equal access to public facilities and the privileged social strata. Social convention, however, subordinated Mexican-origin peoples to what García called "third-class citizenship." Positioned in this ambiguous space between white and black America, there were no mechanisms for the redress of discrimination. In a May 5, 1948, letter to the U.S. Civil Rights Commission reporting on the substandard living conditions in Texas migrant labor camps, García pleaded:

> We, the American Citizens of Latin American origin in Texas feel that conditions like this warrant the direct action from the Federal Government because the Texas Officials will not do anything about it, no matter how long we wait. When the health and welfare of the Citizens is threatened as it is here, by negligence of Officials, we would like to know what we can do

to secure the help of your Civil Rights Commission and our good President, Mr. Harry. S. Truman.[25]

García's rhetorical strategies for this audience contrast dramatically with his pleas for action directed to Texas state officials. His appeal for assistance from the federal government conveys a strong sense of U.S. identification as illustrated in his opening statement: "We, the American Citizens of Latin American origin in Texas." His tone of supplication suggests the voice of one crying out from the wilderness on the behalf of a tribe of the dispossessed, the diaspora of unclaimed American citizens forgotten by the state of Texas. Although he directly addresses his message to the officials of the U.S. Civil Rights Commission, García demonstrates an almost boyish and naïve deference toward his implied secondary audience, "our good President, Mr. Harry S. Truman."

García called for the federal government to recognize the plight of Mexican Americans. He looked to Truman's emerging civil rights agenda and federal government welfare programs to compensate for the failures of the state of Texas. García attempted to forge the identification of public officials with Mexican Americans by cajoling, berating, celebrating, and even rewarding them for their interest. García and the American GI Forum eventually awarded Harry Truman honorary membership in the Forum in recognition of Truman's leadership in civil rights reform and the elimination of the poll tax.[26] Through metonymic association with the American GI Forum, García fashioned his own system of political leverage.

By calling attention to Mexican Americans' position in America's social system, García worked to change the national conversation about civil rights reform. In his April 14, 1951, letter directed to Harry Truman, García asserted a growing Mexican American presence and identification with U.S. interests. Through an appeal to the male military *ethos*, García reminded Truman of the dedication and the plight of Mexican Americans:

> Yes we who have served and know discipline feel that all officers under the chief have to be disciplined when they act out of harmony and out of line with your policies. We Americans of Mexican origin still feel that your name will go down in the history of our country as one of the greatest presidents. We are still very thankful to you for your interest and help in our minority problems and hope that you keep working at them. . . . I hope President Truman that what we say and what we believe may help you in your hard moments. We know what it is to make decisions more so when we are always in a minority group, and we know the suffering of criticism and vile slandering.[27]

García addresses Truman as his commander-in-chief, reaffirming his commitment as an officer of the U.S. Army to the president and the nation on behalf of Mexican Americans everywhere. His brief message of encouragement demonstrates praise, gratitude, compassion, and identification. The assumption undergirding García's message rests on an unfounded confidence in President Truman as an advocate for Mexican Americans in Texas and an unstated belief that Truman valued, respected, and welcomed García's words of encouragement. García so keenly personalizes his relationship to the presidency that reading his words now without the benefit of history might dismiss this kind of rhetorical action as an exercise in folly and wishful thinking. Like a child mailing letters to the North Pole, García sent off his wish lists to the presidents of the United States with an unwavering confidence that his words were worthwhile and welcome. Ironically, over the course of the next two decades García's deep identification with the office of the president became a kind of self-fulfilling prophesy as presidents turned to him for guidance and support.

"They Were a Conquered People, and We Were Unconquerable"

Shaped by generations of displacement and the struggle for social mobility, García embraced his role of leadership—a response to his understanding of civic duty. In an interview for the forty-fifth anniversary tribute to the American GI Forum by the *Corpus Christi Caller Times*, García reflected: "You know, sometimes, I think that as long as I was in this country, I would help people who needed me the most. It just so happened here the Mexican-American people needed me the most."[28] As the child of Mexican immigrants fleeing the Revolution and the descendent of Sephardic Jews escaping the Spanish and Mexican Inquisition, García keenly understood the conflicted ethnic and racial status of Mexican-origin peoples in America.[29] He once recalled, "I've been asked why is it that I'm so interested in those people. It is because those people are my people. I like they suffered in poverty and knew hunger."[30]

The personal history of Héctor Pérez García and his family intricately connects him to the social trends of the twentieth-century U.S.-Mexico borderland. García, a Mexican immigrant, was born on January 17, 1914, in Llera, Tamaulipas, the second son of José and Faustina García. He emigrated with his family to Mercedes, Texas, at the age of three in 1917. One of García's earliest memories was of Mexican revolutionary soldiers storming the streets of Llera, Mexico. He recalled: "I can remember those days because there was a lot of shooting around, that was the beginning, or during the Mexican Revolution of Madero, Pancho Villa, and Carranza. So

naturally, a kid is impressed very much when they shoot all around you."[31]
His parents abandoned their home in Mexico to rebuild their lives with
their children in Mercedes, Texas, where Hector's father would join his
brothers in business and manage a dry-goods store.

Upon his arrival in the United States, Héctor was fascinated by the
uniformed U.S. soldiers protecting the border at Camp Mercedes. "I remember seeing the soldiers, beautiful uniforms and then, the army doctor,"
he recounted.[32] These earliest images would shape García for a lifetime.
García's parents remained Mexican citizens their entire lives. His father,
José, was invited to return to Mexico after the Revolution to help write
the Mexican Constitution but declined because he wanted his children
to have the opportunities offered by the United States. José respected the
American vision, but in many ways his heart remained Mexican. Héctor,
however, became a naturalized U.S. citizen, but not until after serving in
World War II.

A recurring narrative of displacement and repatriation inflected the
lifelong journey of Héctor García and his siblings. His sister, Dr. Clotilde
García, recounted with vivid detail the intellectual and social climate of
the modest home in the desolate borderlands of Texas that produced six
physicians.[33] Poverty would not permit the nine children shoes for school
and demanded that each family member work. One sister died in early childhood from burns sustained after falling into a lime pit because no medical
care or funds for travel to a hospital were available. Héctor's brother, Xico
P. García, recalled gathering the discarded fruit and vegetables from the
local packing sheds to help feed the family. Héctor hitchhiked to college
because the family could not afford the bus fare.

García's father, José G. García, was a descendent of Sephardic Jews
and the early colonists of Mexico who settled in the northern territories
to avoid persecution during the Spanish Inquisition.[34] The myth of racial
purity and white supremacy had coalesced in South Texas for centuries,
nourished by ideological influences from north and south of the border.
The blood purity myth, codified in fifteenth century Spain as *los estatutos
de limpieza de sangre*, had been imported to the Americas by the earliest
colonizers and took root in the New World well before the first English
settlers set foot in North America.[35] Blood cleanliness or purity codes had
provided the ideological impetus for the expulsion of Jews and Moors from
Spain in 1492 and fueled the two-hundred year reign of terror imposed by
church inquisitions throughout Spain and Mexico. Conflicted discourses
on racial identity circulated on both sides of the Greater Mexico border.
The enduring elitism of Spanish "purebloods" and pigmentocracy within

Mexican society inflected South Texas social structures when José García crossed the U.S. border with his family.[36]

José had studied to become a lawyer before the Mexican Revolution erupted. He fought in the Revolution, eventually becoming an elementary school teacher and writing an elementary school primer, *Lea y Escriba*. Hector's mother, Faustina Pérez de García, was likewise well educated and a descendent of the earliest Spanish colonists who came with land grants to Llera, Tamaulipas. She taught school in Mexico before marrying José in 1910. Together José and Faustina García tutored their children in music, art, history, mathematics, and world literature. García's mother regularly read aloud from *La Prensa*, a newspaper established in San Antonio, detailing the developments of the Mexican Revolution and other events on both sides of the border. The family sustained close cultural ties to Mexico. Defying Christian tradition, José named three of his sons after Aztec rulers: Cuautemoc, Cuitlahuac, Xicotentactl. Héctor was named in honor of the mythical warrior and hero of the *Iliad*. Although Faustina practiced Catholicism, José remained distrustful of the Church and kept his children on guard against the clergy because "they would control your mind."[37]

Héctor was the most prominent of the García children to forge a legacy of community service, leadership, and educational advocacy in South Texas. Six García children attained professional degrees and practiced medicine. From his meager savings and income as a merchant, José supported each of his children through college—insisting that even his daughters attain higher education. He sold his life insurance policy to pay for Héctor's college tuition. Clotilde (also known as "Dr. Cleo") recounted: "My father just told all of us we had to be physicians, because that's a profession that nobody can take anything away from you, and you can keep on being educated, and people will respect you. You don't have to be hired by anybody, or dismissed by anybody. It was, he said, it was the only true profession."[38]

The García family was unique not only to the Mexican American community in Mercedes, but to the Anglo community as well. Most of the residents, Anglo as well as Mexican, were laborers and farmers with limited education. According to Dr. Cleo, the most educated members of the desolate borderland were immigrants from Mexico, intellectuals and professionals displaced by the Revolution. There was an acknowledged social and intellectual distance that separated the Garcías from other Mexican Americans in Texas. However, they transformed this distance into a deeply felt obligation to serve their community. As Dr. Cleo observed, "They were conquered people, and we were unconquerable."[39] The sense of entitlement that came with being one of the original colonizing families in the Rio

Grande Valley certainly shaped the García family's notion of belonging. Clotilde summed up their sentiments as Spanish land-grant descendants: "They sent us here to settle the land and, dammit, we are still here. We did not come as ignorant people, picking cotton, as we have been stereotyped. We brought religion, art, and literature with us and built forts, missions, and cities where we went."[40] The García family felt a defined sense of place and entitlement within the history and landscape of Greater Mexico.

Héctor graduated from the University of Texas, Austin in 1936, forming relationships along the way with respected Mexican American intellectuals including Carlos Castañeda, archivist and historian, and eventually forming alliances with his civic and political mentor George I. Sánchez, professor of education and strong supporter of New Deal liberalism.[41] Castañeda had known García's father in Mexico before the Revolution. Like Garcia's father, Castañeda had fled Mexico, yet retained a strong identification with the culture of the motherland. Although Héctor was not politically active during college, focusing exclusively on his studies, he was nevertheless intellectually and socially impacted by the work of his mentors.

Castañeda actively recruited and trained emerging leaders from the Mexican American community, believing that leaders are made, not born. In his opinion, higher education was the key to Mexican American enfranchisement. Historian Richard A. García explains, "Sounding like the black intellectual W.E. B. Du Bois, [Castañeda] urged LULAC [League of United Latin American Citizens] to establish endowed scholarships at different colleges and universities" to advance Mexican American leaders throughout the state and nation.[42] In contrast, George I. Sánchez advanced a doctrine of social advancement combining "a philosophical-psychological orientation (Americanism), a psychological-emotional flexibility (tolerance), and an understanding of others (pluralism)."[43] In his role as a leader of LULAC, Sánchez challenged members of the Mexican American middle class and LULAC to be on guard against "narrow and undemocratic thinking."[44] Both Castañeda and Sánchez imagined a "new consciousness for *los mexicanos de adentro*" (Mexicans from "within" U.S. borders—geographically, spiritually, emotionally).

García eventually responded to Castañeda's call for leadership as he advanced Sánchez's "Americanist" principles and vision of the place of Mexican Americans in the liberal democracy. After graduating from the University of Texas in 1936, García attended medical school at the University of Texas at Galveston. Héctor was the second in the family to earn his medical degree and would help to support the four other siblings who followed him through medical school. García initiated his first service project during medical school from 1936 to 1940. While studying medicine, García established a health education program for the residents of a Mexican labor colony in Galveston, translating material from English into Spanish and teaching about hygiene, sanitation, immunization, diabetes, tuberculosis, and cancer. García's project was recognized with an Honor of Merit award from *the Federación Regional de Organizaciones Mexicanas de la Confederación Estatal de Galveston* in 1940.[45] He would eventually extend this project to Corpus Christi in the early 1950s when he launched an aggressive campaign to confront the high rate of tuberculosis within *las colonias*, collecting the signatures and raising the votes to pass a $700,000 bond to fund a hospital.[46]

García received a commission in the army after summer training with the Civilian Military Training Camp at Camp Bullis in Texas. He completed his internship and residency at St. Joseph's Hospital in Omaha, Nebraska, in 1942. After completing his medical training, he served in Europe, first in an infantry division, then in the medical corps. As a major in the Army Medical Corps who drove an ambulance in the European theater of operation, García understood the corporeal and symbolic exchange demanded of Mexican Americans for citizenship and enfranchisement. He was awarded the Bronze Star for service achievement while running operations across enemy lines.[47] His two-year stint in the army allowed him to travel to the places about which he had read: Ireland, England, Scotland, Morocco, Algeria, Tunisia, France, and Germany. In his April 9, 1943, letter to his father, García chronicles his attempt to learn Italian, Arabic, and French. Although Spanish was the language spoken at home, García wrote to his father in English:

> I hope that you got a box of books and other things I sent about two month ago. . . . Right now I am trying to pick up a little Arabic here and also learning a little Italian. The Italian is easy but oh Lord the Arabic is hard. For instance to say good morning the say something like "sbalaj her" and to say good evening "celiam alley kum." And also to say how are you they say something like "keraack" and all right is "klabes." The whole language is guttural. However Italian is easy and I have read an Italian French dictionary and will try to learn it easy. For instance how are you they say "commo se va" and good day "bon jorno." It is a combination of Spanish and French and I can listen to the radio here and get or understand everything of the Italian propaganda and talks. So I won't have any trouble.[48]

García was fascinated by language and the study of language. He minored in English as an undergraduate student. An unabashed and prolific letter writer, García's style nonetheless violated many of the conventions of edited American English. Seemingly oblivious to error, García never allowed the limits of his communicative abilities to squelch his self-concept or self-expression. His wife, Wanda, recounted that García would get flustered reading the Italian newspapers because the words he read were not the variety of Italian he recognized and used. He insisted the newspaper editors had made the grammatical mistakes which impaired his comprehension. Wanda noted that, in truth, he spoke a variety of Italian mixed with Spanish. Nevertheless, García believed he had reached a level of native fluency in Italian. Wanda never challenged his misperception.

García met his wife, Wanda Fusillo, in Naples during World War II while she was finishing her Ph.D. in liberal arts. She shared García's passion for language, studying French, German, and Latin, and teaching herself English after her arrival in the United States. Her parents were teachers like García's, imparting a love of learning and culture.[49] Wanda came from a long line of accomplished scholars—her parents held Ph.D.'s as did her grandmother. "Héctor was always very proud that I had a Ph.D.," Wanda reflected, an accomplishment that distinguished her from most American women in the 1940s.[50] Married in 1945 in Naples at the Church of Santa Maria de Pedigrotta, with a special dispensation from the cardinal to marry an Italian citizen and an audience with the Pope at St. Peter's, García understood how to get what he wanted. He courted Wanda with a determination and resolve that both surprised and fascinated her. García knew how to circulate successfully in multiple spheres, to function effectively within diverse cultures and different sets of expectations. "My wife, even now, she still wonders how the dickens I was able to get [the special dispensation to marry her]," he once reflected.[51]

García's sense of his place in the global community and his passion for exploring different cultures was cultivated early in his life; he read history and literature at the library after school whenever he wasn't playing sports. Although he spent his entire youth in Texas (except for occasional visits to family in Mexico), García could imagine a world beyond Texas's borders. He read voraciously his entire life. "I always studied literature and poetry and Italian history and a little music," he recalled.[52] Throughout his youth, García was fascinated by Greek and Roman mythology, the history of the Catholic Church, and the writers and painters of the Renaissance.

García considered himself a global citizen, identifying with European thought and culture and promulgating an Enlightenment view of the world. He never abandoned his sense of Mexican identity, but that did not preclude embracing the tenets of American citizenship as well as a European predilection for art, music, literature, and philosophy. He cultivated a cosmopolitan identity through his love for language and culture. García claimed that he learned to speak English with an Irish brogue while stationed in Ireland and had eagerly picked up Arabic while in North Africa, French while in France, and even a bit of German. "Being that I had historical background, I was ready, I felt like I was visiting places I'd known about." After marrying Wanda, García affectionately maintained that he was "half Italian." He insisted, "Well, if my wife's my better half and she's Italian, [that] makes me half Italian."[53]

Wanda was stunned to learn that inside his own country her husband was considered a second-class citizen because of his Mexican origin. "In Italy and in many European countries that I have visited the word America is always associated with liberty, equality, and freedom of opportunity," she once observed.[54] This contradiction in America's bold democratic vision that consumed her husband without respite would puzzle her most of her life. "I consider myself an American now," Wanda later reflected after over fifty years in the United States, "but I still don't understand" how these inequities could still persist.[55]

As a well-educated European woman, Wanda expressed her own enduring discomfort and dismay at the social conditions in South Texas, the lukewarm reception she received from the extended García family upon her arrival in the U.S. with their first child in arms, and Héctor's indomitable determination to change the world he had left behind when he went off to war. Coming to South Texas meant something very different to Wanda. It was not the mythical land of opportunity that García had portrayed to her. When she finally joined García in America after the war, Wanda was escorted to the hospital by the American Red Cross where she found her husband suffering from nephritis and depression. García was moved to political action by a radio broadcast he heard while recovering. Disheartened by the news report describing the segregation of Mexican children in Texas schools, García vowed to spend the rest of his life working for his people if he recovered his health.

From the moment of his recovery until his death, García was on a mission that left little time or energy for the family they ultimately built together. "We had no family life," Wanda lamented. García remained physically weakened by illness and a heavy workload his entire life, aging quickly and growing irritable, depressed, and chronically fatigued by midlife. He suffered two heart attacks before he was fifty. "I lost my husband" and their four children "lost a father" to the American GI Forum, she poignantly confided. Wanda had little intimacy with the Garcia extended family and little involvement with the American GI Forum. As a beautiful, educated European war bride, Wanda extended a certain amount of cultural capital to Héctor's civic identity and social status, but at great cost to her and their own nuclear family. In the highly racially segmented social world of South Texas, Wanda found it difficult to find complete acceptance. As an immigrant white woman married to a Mexican American, she existed on the complex social borders of race, caste, class, and citizenship. Héctor's father, José, objected to the marriage because he thought that the responsibilities of family life would interfere with Héctor's career and duties to his siblings. Wanda saw the García family and the American GI Forum as competing for Héctor's scant time, energy, and money. For Wanda, García's great American success story was a private tragedy—a long journey of loss and loneliness.

Upon his discharge, Héctor joined his brother Dr. J. A. García in Corpus Christi and established his medical practice in 1946, serving primarily veterans and the poor. García joined LULAC, the leading Mexican American civic organization of the period, soon after arriving in Corpus Christi. J. A. García had been an active member and leader of LULAC through the 1930s and 1940s. Héctor, following J. A.'s example, served as the president of LULAC Council No. 1 and led a LULAC committee investigating segregated Mathis school facilities and labor camps in 1948. He assisted with fundraising efforts for the Delgado segregation case against the Bastrop Independent School District, a groundbreaking decision that outlawed discrimination against children of Mexican origin in the public schools of Texas.[56] García eventually resigned as president of LULAC in 1948 after establishing the American GI Forum. Even though Garcia's poor health would not permit him to serve in a leadership capacity for both organizations, he consistently maintained strong ties to LULAC.[57]

García confronted the inadequate medical services for Mexican American veterans in South Texas, arguing with the Veterans Administration for additional hospital space for ill-served veterans. In these early moments of activism, he distinguished himself as a medical practitioner who was intellectually critical and socially engaged. A rigorous "organic intellectual" who reveled in the life of the mind and yet had the uncommon capacity to translate ideas to collective practice, García recognized early the need for a political forum for social action.[58]

García's advocacy of women prevailed throughout his career, especially toward his sister, Clotilde, also known "Cota" or "Dr. Cleo." His relationship with Dr. Cleo was most likely the longest, and most enduring personal relationship of his life. García adored his mother. He never completely

recovered from her loss when she died suddenly while his was completing his internship in Nebraska. She had been a model of compassion and
social engagement throughout his life; it was her devotion to the poor and
the oppressed to which García attributed his own commitment to service.
In many respects, he was able to keep alive this spiritual kinship with his
mother through his enduring devotion to his siblings, in general, and to
Cleo, in particular.

Dr. Cleo became García's helpmate in medicine, an ardent American GI
Forum supporter, frontline social activist, respected educator, published
author on Spanish colonialism, and personal confidante. Dr. Cleo, who
became a public figure in her own right, was inducted into the Texas Wom-
en's Hall of Fame after thirty years of medical service by Governor Mark
White in 1984. Among her many activities, Dr. Cleo served as a member
of the Texas Constitution Revision Committee, regent of Del Mar College
in Corpus Christi, board of directors of the Nueces County Antipoverty
program, and member of the Texas Historical Foundation.

In the tradition of her older brothers, Cleo had applied and been accepted
to the University of Texas medical school in 1942. However, she declined
admission after deciding to get married and become a teacher instead.
When the marriage failed, Héctor intervened on her behalf to help her gain
readmission to medical school. In February 1948, during a painful period
of recovery and growth in his own professional and personal life, García
wrote to his mentor at the University of Texas at Galveston, Dr. George
Herrman. He appealed for guidance:

> I am writing you about my sister Clotilde who will apply to medical
> school before March. I am asking for your kind advise as to how to go about
> it. You have been so kind and have given me much good advice before that
> I am certain you will not mind my asking for more again. . . .
>
> She has decided that she would like to go to Galveston. I am certainly glad
> of that because she will make a good student and a good doctor. Naturally,
> I am willing to help her financially for any amount of money she needs so
> that she will not have to work while in school.[59]

Dr. Cleo earned her Masters degree in education from the University of
Texas in 1950 and completed her MD degree from the University of Texas
School of Medicine in 1954 with García's continuous support. During this
same period, García provided substantial financial support to his father
and two brothers, Xico and Cuitláhuac, as well.

In the decade following his discharge from the military, García built a vibrant new civic organization, a young family of his own, and a growing medical practice while providing free health services to the poor and extensive financial support to Cleo and the rest of his extended family. García's conviction and commitment to the educational, political, and social advancement of women was as strong as his advocacy of Mexican American civil rights. He was revolutionary in his insistence that women take visible leadership roles in the American GI Forum. In a 1949 memo to the leaders of the American GI Forum planning for the first state convention, García directed the members: "It is imperative that you sign up your wives and girlfriends, sisters, widows, mothers, etc. in the Ladies Auxiliary so that we can bring them in as delegates also."[60] Officers of the Ladies Auxiliary were featured in the American GI Forum State Convention program and described as "hard-working." Their list of activities included circulating petitions for a TB hospital, collecting and donating college scholarships, and conducting poll tax campaigns to help voters pay their fees.

Progressive in many respects, and highly conservative in others, the American GI Forum was as much a paradox as its founder. García's insistence that women should have an equal vote in American GI Forum elections distinguished the organization from other male-only civic and veterans organizations of the era. Women were at the frontline of American GI Forum civic action. Without question, the rapid mobilization of the Mexican American community and effective transmission of time-sensitive information throughout the American GI Forum were the results of an empowered and engaged membership that included women. The formal and informal communication network of the American GI Forum relied on women. García knew from the experience of his own mother and her compassionate service to the people of South Texas that women were not only the heartline of the family, but the heartline of community. García reported in a 1952 address focusing on civic participation:

> In our experience we have found that women are better workers once they are organized and usually end up by being the best participants in civic work. It is usually our women's groups who raise the funds for Red Cross work, crippled children's drive, charity drive or scholarship money. They are harder to get together in the beginning, but once started they usually carry on easier and smoother.[61]

García knew that women could achieve a level of coordination at the grassroots level that men alone could not. García activated that capacity for mobilization with unprecedented results.

García founded the American GI Forum in Corpus Christi, Texas, in 1948. In a February 3, 1948, letter inviting his older brother Dr. J. A. García to help in the formation of what would become the American GI Forum, Héctor defined the South Texas rhetorical situation:

> It is regretful [to] admit that a large percentage of our quarter of a million of children of school age are being denied this right [of equal educational facilities] even at this age of tolerance and enlightenment. As citizens and residents of this country we must combat and destroy certain ideologies or native totalitarianisms which are not conducive to the general welfare of our country and for them we can wholeheartedly enter into the struggle against foreignism which threaten our country at this time.[62]

This new advocacy group for veterans eventually became the largest and most influential Mexican American civic organization in the country, a coalition substantial enough to play a significant role in Texas and U.S. politics for over thirty years. U.S. Representative Solomon Ortiz (D—Corpus Christi) lauds the American GI Forum's remarkable development: "The American G.I. Forum was originally intended to guide World War I and World War II veterans through the maze of bureaucracy to obtain their education and medical benefits. And it grew into the highly acclaimed Hispanic civil rights organization that it is today."[63]

García argued that he had no "blueprint" or plan for the American GI Forum when he called the first meeting in 1948. He did not set out to establish a civil rights organization. Rather he responded to the needs of his patients—largely veterans and the poor of the community. Reflective of what Cornel West has termed "prophetic pragmatism," García conceptualized his project into something palpable, possible, and positive.[64] Demographic and socioeconomic shifts in the wake of World War II represent significant dimensions of the rhetorical situation in which García emerged as a leader. The formation of the American GI Forum paralleled the establishment of a Mexican American middle class. This new middle class grew as World War II Mexican American men and women veterans returned to South Texas to embrace and realize to an increasing degree the "American Dream." The socioeconomic possibilities of the post-war era became increasingly visible if not accessible to returning GIs. In *Among the Valiant: Mexican Americans in World War II and Korea*, Raul Morin recalls:

> [W]e left the other side of the tracks and began to move to town. We moved to better neighborhoods and, thanks to the GI bill, we continued our education. We were able to buy new homes. We began to go into business for

ourselves, obtain better positions of employment and some even managed to get chosen, appointed or elected to public office."[65]

Educated veterans like García and his American GI Forum contemporaries, Ed Idar Jr. and Virgilio Roel, who earned law degrees, were able to break into the professional class. They acquired new levels of economic prosperity. Some sectors of this new middle class continued to ascend the social ladder and never looked back, abandoning the use of Spanish in the home, enrolling their children in private schools, and carving a niche as *la gente decente* within the South Texas community. Others like García and many first generation Mexican Americans realized that the majority of their people were still locked in place by poverty and institutionalized discrimination.

To say that segments of the Mexican American community prospered is not to claim that the post-war socioeconomic pie was ever evenly distributed among Mexican-origin groups. In spite of García's argument that war was the great equalizer, the socioeconomic consequences of the war aggravated disparities between groups as much as it alleviated them. Mexican Americans as a cohort paid dearly in the war. Disproportionately represented, Hispanics were the largest minority group in the military in terms of their percentage of the U.S. population. This overwhelming presence of Mexican Americans in military service served to realign the collective sense of their rights and privileges as U.S. citizens. Their set of expectations changed. Morin describes the flood of Mexican Americans that had enlisted in the armed services:

> The draft boards in Los Angeles, Nogales, Albuquerque, San Antonio, El Paso, Corpus Christi, and the Lower Rio Grande Valley of Texas were never caught short-handed when they had large quotas to fill. These boards were loaded with Spanish names on their files; and very few were ever exempted, reclassified, or found too essential to be drafted. Local rural youths were being drafted so fast in comparison to others, that land owners of large farms and ranches, faced with manpower shortage, voiced stern protests with the local draft boards.[66]

Moreover, as a cohort, Mexican Americans in World War II received more military honors than any other single ethnic group.[67] Their substantial and devoted service to the war effort would have far-reaching implications. Morin articulates the shift in consciousness among Mexican American veterans: "For too long we had been like outsiders. It had never made very much difference to us and we hardly noticed it until we got back from overseas. How could we have played such a prominent part as Americans over there and now have to go back to living as outsiders as before?"[68]

When García issued his call to unite South Texas veterans, he struck a chord of growing discontent. Foreshadowing the Longoria controversy, an editorial in the July 1945 *LULAC News* describes the post-war setting that returning GIs faced and openly questions how Mexican American "soldier-citizens" would be received.

> They are coming home with a feeling of equality tinged with fraternity which they have learned in the training camps, in the far-flung outposts, and on the battlefields throughout the world. They have learned equality through the uniformity of uniforms, pay, food, and housing; through the distribution of ranks, awards, and citations based on merit; and the similarity of hardships, pain, and horror. They have learned fraternity . . . through the hard won knowledge that dissension, bigotry, and prejudice hold no place among people whose mutual safety depends upon unity. . . .
>
> Will the appreciation of the rest of the American people for the contributions of the Latin Americans be so little that they will revert to that superior feeling of origin—that Nazi-inspired feeling that plunged a world into [war]?[69]

The minimization of Mexican American sacrifice in the war effort, the persistence of white supremacism, and the general insensitivity within Anglo society toward Mexican-origin peoples were critical pressure points within the Mexican American community even before the Longoria incident erupted into an international controversy. The meritocracy of the military had opened new opportunities for Mexican Americans, opportunities that were quickly foreclosed once they returned to Texas' social configurations.

García's vision for the American GI Forum, however, was not only shaped by the social trends of the post-war era but deeply influenced by the reformist rhetoric advanced by his mentors, George I. Sánchez and Carlos E. Castañeda. Moreover, García's strand of liberal democratic discourse aligned him with an active, vibrant community of Texas intellectuals and professionals such as the prominent South Texas attorneys J. T. Canales and Alonso Perales, vocal activists of the World War I era.[70] García's model of civic engagement connected him to democratic political thought not only rooted in South Texas but extending throughout the country for more than two decades.

García's message was not new. It was, however, bold. García understood how to capture the civic pulse that had prompted the formation of LULAC in 1929 in Corpus Christi. His agenda for Mexican Americans paralleled a similar movement calling for racial justice among Texas African Americans, a struggle that led to the establishment of the El Paso chapter of the National

Association for the Advancement of Colored People (NAACP) in 1915. The NAACP coalition in Texas, in fact, had become the organization's largest sector but foundered under the persistent attacks of white supremacists, until a resurgence in membership occurred in the post-war era. Growing resistance to institutionalized discrimination was gaining a foothold in Texas when García assumed a leadership role.

In many respects, the history of the American GI Forum is also the history of LULAC. The establishment of LULAC in 1929 signaled a shift within the Mexican-origin populace away from mutual aid societies and toward civil rights campaigns.[71] For the next two decades, LULAC did battle in the courts on behalf of "Spanish-speaking Americans."[72] The growth of LULAC between 1929 and 1949 "signified an emerging Mexican American identity and shift away from a Mexican identity," an agenda that decidedly excluded Mexican immigrants from membership.[73] Early LULAC members identified themselves as "México Tejanos," an act of nominalization meant to distinguish them from newly arrived Mexican immigrants. LULAC, like the American GI Forum, poised itself to defend the interests of citizens of Mexican-origin in the racially stratified system of the United States that afforded Mexican immigrants and Mexican migrant workers no role in its civic organization. García picked up where LULAC left off.

With these common threads between LULAC and the American GI Forum it is difficult to separate their intellectual and political activities, especially during the late 1940s and 1950s.[74] García's formation of the American GI Forum does not represent a distinct second stage of political activism but an extension and amplification of LULAC leadership and ideology. Overlapping ideas, leaders, and strategies are simply too strongly evidenced to distinguish these two Mexican American mobilization efforts as separate stages. García retained strong ties to LULAC throughout his career, as reflected in his January 1979 congratulatory letter to LULAC on its fiftieth anniversary.[75] His emphasis on cultural pluralism, Americanist principles, patriotism, and "first class citizenship," central American GI Forum tenets, strongly reflects LULAC ideology codified by its constitution.

García himself was shaped under the tutelage of LULAC leader George I. Sánchez, coordinating many of his efforts with his University of Texas mentor, as indicated in the 1949 American GI Forum resolution "opposing the expenditure of federal funds in the support of schools that practice segregation of children of Mexican descent."[76] García asked Sánchez to draft one of the first resolutions of the American GI Forum to resist school segregation, citing the *Delgado v. Bastrop Independent School District* case that LULAC had won in 1948. García's movement, therefore, was an expansion and transformation of the LULAC model into something different. Ideological overlap with LULAC ultimately helped to advance García's new organization but also may have contributed to García's conflicted record on the Mexican immigrant labor issues or what he termed the "wetback problem" (the impact of the *bracero* immigrant labor program on García's civil rights efforts is more fully examined in chapter 4).

Both organizations exploited the xenophobic tenor of the era. "LULAC'ers" and Forumeers joined the constant alert against subversives and spies.[77] LULAC leaders, like García, reacted strongly to being identified as a political organization and confronted all claims to that effect.[78] LULAC and the American GI Forum did their political work under the guise of civic service. LULAC promoted voting, education, cultural pluralism, literacy, and community service and aggressively confronted school segregation and discrimination in public facilities—all projects that the American GI Forum advanced.

García did depart from the LULAC agenda on matters of constituency. LULAC appealed largely to middle-class Mexican Americans, professionals, intellectuals, and entrepreneurs. García structured the American GI Forum, in contrast, to respond to a larger constituency. The American GI Forum appealed to not only to middle-class Mexican Americans, but also more broadly to veterans of the urban and rural working class. Throughout his career, García consistently represented himself as an advocate of the poor.

García's leadership experiences with LULAC informed his vision for the American GI Forum. On March 26, 1948, García called the first meeting of the American GI Forum at Lamar School in Corpus Christi, Texas. Circulars in Spanish and English called the community to gather. Local veterans' loss of pension and medical benefits and the lack of Mexican American representation on draft boards stirred García to action. He had notified the Veterans Administration, the American Legion, the Veterans of Foreign Wars, and the American Red Cross of the problems in January 1948, but to no avail. He quickly turned to coalition-building strategies to intervene on behalf of his many patients who suffered with little or no recourse for acquiring necessary medical service. Over seven hundred veterans and their family members were in attendance at that first meeting. Anglo as well as Mexican American veterans were welcomed equally. The group moved to become a permanent organization, proposing the names "GI Co-Op," "GI Joes," and "American GI Forum."[79]

In his April 5, 1974, interview, García recounted the process of choosing a name for his new veteran's rights organization: "We are American citizens of Mexican origin, so let's point that out to the people that we are really

Americans. GI merely means that we are ex-soldiers or ex-GI's. The word 'Forum' was like the Roman open forum derived from the fact that we were hoping this would be an open meeting and open discussion for everybody taking part."[80] Put to a vote, the name of the American GI Forum became official and García was elected president in 1948.

García's vision for the American GI Forum was at its core an act of social criticism situating politics in the everyday lives and experiences of ordinary people. García grappled with the day-to-day manifestations of racism—the subtle and the glaring. He challenged the members of the American GI Forum to confront dehumanizing social configurations in many forms: segregation practices in private and public sectors, unchallenged cases of brutality and murder by law enforcement agents, and the lack of legislative and judicial representation.

Through collective action at the polls, in the schools, in the courts, in their neighborhoods, at social events, in their churches, and among their families, he believed the American G. I. Forum members could establish a presence and voice resistance. His proactive movement didn't wait for justice to come but operated on the assumption that change was possible and the American system of self-governance was not only redeemable but achievable. In a letter to the American Friends Service Committee, Pauline Kibbe, former executive secretary of the Good Neighbor Commission and author of *Latin Americans in Texas*, describes the American GI Forum under García's leadership:

> The Forum's program is broad and militant. It investigates and actively prosecutes every valid case of overt discrimination, such as refusal of service, any where in the state. It is eternally vigilant in seeing that the Federal Court decision of 1948 [*Delgado v. Bastrop Independent School District*], outlawing discrimination in the public schools, is enforced. It sponsors education of all kinds, the most important of which is political education, beginning on the precinct level. This campaign of political education and participation has been so successful that—to mention only a few examples—Corpus Christi now has two Latin American members of the school board; Del Rio, for the first time in its often bitter history, has a Latin American member of the City Council; and, and also for the first time in history, the Maverick rump Democratic State Convention in San Antonio last year elected five Latin American delegates to the National Convention, four of whom were members of the American GI Forum. . . . About Dr. Garcia himself I can never say enough. . . . He has one of the keenest minds it has ever been my good fortune to encounter. He is fearless, tireless, selfless, and absolutely incorruptible. . . .

> In my opinion, it would be not only useless but foolhardy for any one to even consider attempting a program in Texas involving Latin Americans without first coordinating his efforts with Dr. Garcia and the work of the American GI Forum.[81]

García's authority grew as admirers and followers persuaded new groups to follow.

García traveled to communities throughout South Texas promoting his new civic organization. He formed chapters wherever he was able to stir interest. García's model of *paedia,* civic formation, education, and mentorship remained focused on recruiting leaders from the local community. Vicente Ximenes, an early organizer who García frequently credited as the "co-founder of the American GI Forum," recalls that it was not uncommon for him and García to drive all day to meet with less than a dozen new members to teach them how to grow their own chapter of the American GI Forum. "It was a slow and difficult process, but it worked," Ximenes remembered.[82]

A poster with a photograph and caption of a young, handsome, well-dressed, and very sincere-looking "Héctor García, M.D." calls veterans to a "gran junta" sponsored by the American GI Forum in December 1948 in Taft, Texas. "Of course he captured their attention. He looked like a movie star," observes archivist Grace Charles.[83] The 1948 announcement declares: "¡Atencion Veteranos! Se invita a todos veteranos de Taft, Portland, Gregory, Ingleside, Rockport y Aransas Pass y pueblos vecinos a oír al Dr. Hector Garcia, Major F. Dixon, Arturo Cantu y Luis Bryan, Joe Zapata Jr., de Sinton, Texas, explicar la razón porque debemos unirnos como Veteranos se hablara de asuntos de importancia."[84] [Attention veterans! All veterans of Taft, Portland, Gregory, Ingleside, Rockport, and Aransas Pass and neighboring cities are invited to hear Dr. Héctor García, Major F. Dixon, Arturo Cantu, and Luis Bryan, Joe Zapata Jr., of Sinton, Texas explain the reason we should unite as veterans who talk together about important issues.] The text invokes the attention of veterans from towns throughout South Texas to discuss such issues as segregated schools, student enrollment, VA pensions, bonuses, hospital facilities, and the draft.

In "A Short History of the American GI Forum," García explained the impetus and growth of the organization:

> The American GI Forum became an organization of necessity . . . to protest the reduction of beds available to Veterans at the Corpus Christi Naval Base. The group was a group of both Americans of Mexican origin and Anglo origin. . . . By the end of 1948 the American GI Forum had groups

in approximately 40 communities in Texas. . . . The American GI Forum became a State Organization in Sept. 24, 1949 when they had their First State Convention in C.C. Texas. . . . During the year 1949 and thru the year 1951 the American G. I. Forum of Texas spread to a total size of 150 groups.[85]

The growth of García's group captured the attention of the media and Texas politicians as well. Within one year of its foundation, García had become a recognized spokesman for the Mexican American community in South Texas. In June 1949, state senator Rogers Kelley appealed to García for his help in promoting a constitutional amendment to abolish the state poll tax.[86] In 1949, García attracted the attention of popular novelist Edna Ferber, who gave him copies of her books and maintained contact with García for a number of years.[87] As the daughter of Hungarian Jewish immigrants, Ferber found in García a kindred spirit and sought to immortalize him in her work. She traveled to South Texas to meet García personally and study the living conditions of Mexican immigrant laborers. Her best selling novel *Giant* (examined in chapter 4) contains scenes based on events and conditions revealed to her by García.

García keenly understood that the measure of rhetorical influence is the ability to direct the attention of an audience and to recirculate power. Coalition-building helped to make Mexican Americans' politically weak position stronger. In order to direct the course of the conversation, García brought to focus many issues facing Mexican peoples in the United States including the intolerable labor conditions. In a letter dated October 4, 1949, to W. F. Kelly of the U.S. Immigration and Naturalization Service, García asserted:

> If counties like Hidalgo, Cameron, Nueces, and others would pay our Citizens a reasonable and humane wage then there would not be this suffering migratory movement and would allow our citizens to take roots and become more stable and better American citizens than they are now; as a result of removing their children approximately 100,000 from school in order to work to feed themselves and their children.[88]

He documented the mass migration of Mexican American citizens from their South Texas communities, families leaving their homes and pulling children from their schools. He also exposed the high incidence of child labor in Texas fields.[89]

The American GI Forum under García's direction promoted the social advancement of "Spanish-Speaking" people, vowed to uphold the American Constitution, pledged to protect the United States, confronted institutionalized discrimination, promoted cultural pluralism, and awarded scholarships to deserving students. The military aegis of the American GI Forum enhanced its *ethos* in the victorious aftermath of World War II.[90] García was careful, however, not to restrict participation exclusively to Mexican Americans. To further enlarge membership, García disassociated his organization from a strictly "Latin American" identification. Names of Anglo veterans were included on the roster of the first chapter of the American GI Forum.[91] Ramos explains:

> The absence of direct ethnic identification with the Mexican-American community was intentional and largely the result of García's thinking. The intent was to emphasize that members, though distinct in ethnic and cultural orientation, were just as American as Anglos.[92]

His insistence on ethnically integrating the American GI Forum was not the only progressive feature of García's organization. His insistence on "orderly" discussion and non-violent protest practices produced a civic organization both reflective of the post–World War II American society and also remarkably distinct.

As Ramos suggests, "This institutional commitment to non-violence—a concept earlier developed by Mohandas Gandhi in India and later popularized in the United States by Dr. Martin Luther King, Jr.—was still somewhat ahead of its time in 1948 America."[93] Unlike other veterans' organizations of the period, García preached non-violence to a constituency of military men and their families and gave women members an equal vote in organizational elections. In 1949, the American GI Forum adopted the "Prayer of St. Francis" as its official benediction, reinforcing the organization's commitment to non-violent social action.[94] García's organization was as paradoxical as its leader. Beneath the aegis of a veterans' organization, García cultivated a coalition of freedom fighters committed to non-violence.

The rituals and protocols of the American GI Forum resembled LULAC as well as other veterans' organizations of the period. Members wore uniforms, took minutes of their meetings, kept records, gave reports, marched in parades under the American flag, and represented themselves to the community as patriotic, law-abiding citizens. Unlike LULAC leaders such as Alonso Perales, Albert Peña Jr., J. T. Canales, and Gus García, all prominent South Texas attorneys, García executed the office of president under the title of physician, typing letters in his medical office between patient visits. He extended his *ethos* as physician over his role as social activist, appropriating even the language of medical science for political purposes. In a letter to Texas Governor Allan Shivers concerning an incident of discrimination in Seguin, Texas, García writes, "we ask you earnestly to devote some of your valuable time to this cancer in the democracy we all love."[95]

"Education Is Our Freedom"

García and the American GI Forum did not rely on acts of civil disobedience to resist discrimination and injustice but instead practiced highly visible forms of civil obedience and proactive social engagement. García's goals were to mentor leaders, make his people visible, and position capable Mexican Americans throughout the community who would conduct themselves above reproach. This primary tactic, the construction of visible civic presence, was manifested in an array of community practices: conducting scholarship fund-drives, organizing poll tax fund-raisers, and promoting back-to-school campaigns. Although not averse to conflict, García cautiously avoided dishonor. He wanted above all else for the American GI Forum to embody the values of patriotism, community service, education, and moral leadership.

García founded the American GI Forum as a constitutionally based organization under an elected leadership.[96] Although he employed a military model of hierarchical leadership, García also engaged members in democratic practices. Ramos notes that the American GI Forum was the first Mexican American organization to do serious business with national-level officials. García trained his followers for broad-based civic engagement. He enlarged his audience to include not only the Mexican American constituency of South Texas, largely poor and working-class veterans and their families, but also powerful public officials at the local, as well as the national level. In a letter guiding the formation of a new American GI Forum chapter in Freer, Texas, García reminded organizers, "Acuerdese que esta organizacion no es para hacer ganacias, sino para ayudar a los pobres, nesecitados y los que no saben desfenderse."[97] [Remember that this organization is not for profit or gain but for helping the poor, the needy, and those that don't know how to defend themselves.] García's organizational model helped to shape a collective sense of empowerment and build Mexican American civic *ethos*. These strategies along with his unrivaled ability to forge alliances across social boundaries were key to his political effectiveness. García coalesced disparate groups of people toward common goals at a moment in history when racism fractured local communities and divided nations across the globe.

Within ten years, García's talent for grassroots organizing and mobilizing enlarged the American GI Forum to over 20,000 members with groups in twenty-one states.[98] "Without organization nothing can be accomplished," García wrote in a memo to all chapters of the American GI Forum.[99] García's mobilizing ability was a quality both valued and critiqued. Six years after the first meeting of the American GI Forum, Ed Idar Jr., American GI Forum Texas state chairman, advised García in a May 19, 1954, letter:

> I think you ought to give some thought to where you want the Forum to go, Hector. You apparently concentrate on only organizing and more organizing without giving adequate thought to the basic program we are following and to whether or not we are implementing it.[100]

Clearly, García's vision was not as legalistic as Idar, an attorney, would have wanted it to be. García's approach was more deliberative, focused largely on consciousness-raising and coalition-building. There was no attainable "basic program." There was not just one legal issue under scrutiny. García wanted to build a collective, responsive, and flexible civic presence capable of putting pressure on the Anglo power structure whenever and wherever needed. García wanted "first-class citizenship" for his people in a system that invidiously replicated white supremacist values. A pragmatist who sought the most reasonable and expedient solution, García reached for the greatest good for the greatest number of people.

With aims so diffuse and needs so disparate it was impossible to coalesce action into one defined achievable goal. Inclusion proved a constantly shifting and elusive aim in a system of ascribed privilege. García subscribed to the liberal belief that American institutions, given the proper information and guidance from the people, could become effective executors of social change. Applying an empirical model, he used instrumental discourse to keep the government informed.

Guadalupe San Miguel Jr. argues in "Mexican American Organizations and the Changing Politics of School Desegregation" that the legalistic focus of 1960s and 1970s desegregation activists following in García's wake helped to confront old patterns of discrimination but failed to eliminate the structural causes of educational inequality. He concludes, "Emphasis on legal and administrative challenges to segregation served to deflect serious analysis of the complexity and of the serious sources of inequalities in the society."[101] García's organization would never become the kind of single-issue group some followers may have wished it would be. The American GI Forum's effectiveness was its localized nature and its ability to adapt according to the needs and demands of the community.

For García, education would be the means by which Mexican Americans achieved the promises of democracy. The American GI Forum not only elected officers, drafted a constitution, crafted an emblem, and recruited members; they advanced a credo. The American GI Forum motto asserts enthymematically, "Education is our freedom and freedom should be everybody's business." Emblazoned on newsletters, letterhead, and banners, and inscribed on the base of the statue bearing García's image at the plaza in front of the library of Texas A&M University–Corpus Christi, this statement is a two-fold indictment. The premise implicit in this patriotic declaration celebrates Enlightenment ideals as well as intimates that Mexican Americans, because they are not educated, are not free. The American GI Forum motto functions a bidirectional charge: first, to Mexican Americans to fight as fiercely for education as they fought for America's freedom, and second, to Anglo Americans to make the education of Mexican Americans "everybody's business."

President John F. Kennedy characterizes the unifying theme of García's struggle in his August 1, 1961, letter to García, thanking him for his leadership role:

> Our Nation was born of the first great revolution which man undertook to secure his political and economic liberty under a democratic form of government. . . .
>
> The American GI Forum has, throughout history, espoused those principles which call for a better life for all men everywhere. Your dedication to the true spirit of the American Revolution is patent evidence to the world that the United States is disposed to realize its destiny, and support those nations and peoples who likewise seek a life free from those conditions which stifle man's spirit.[102]

Representing the Civic Self

The practice of medicine, like the practice of rhetoric, emerged from a common impulse: to serve and to heal. Like Franklin D. Roosevelt, García's impetus for leadership was forged out of an acute awareness of mortality and human suffering. As one of García's most enduring models, the leadership of President Roosevelt represented an empathic rhetorical response to America's economic and spiritual bankruptcy. García's invitation to Eleanor Roosevelt to speak at the 1953 American GI Forum in Fort Worth, Texas, affirmed his enduring identification: "Mrs. Roosevelt I like the rest of the American people of Mexican origin in the Southwestern United States are great admirers of the Roosevelts. We were and are great admirers of your husband Mr. Franklin D. Roosevelt. We are great admirers of your great humanitarian work and we are proud of your efforts to establish permanent peace."[103]

There is much about García's civic honor, stoic service, and selfless resolve that, like Roosevelt, suggests a leader who was, beneath the public veneer, a "wounded healer."[104] Although often in disguise, García's and Roosevelt's styles of leadership styles were informed by their own long and painful struggles with illness. Garry Wills's examination of the motivating pulse behind Roosevelt's presidency prefigures the impetus that would drive a young García a decade later: "As a president, Roosevelt came to minister to a sick nation. . . . He knew the soul needed healing first. . . . He understood the importance of psychology—that people have to have courage to keep seeking a cure, no matter what the cure is."[105] Similarly, García responded to the call for leadership with an understanding of the psychology of the oppressed. In his letter celebrating LULAC's fiftieth anniversary, García reflected on the social history of Mexican-origin peoples in America. He recounted: "50 years ago the suffering, abuse, and exploitation of the Mexican American people in Texas seemed to be a hopeless and lost cause. We were a class of people that were swept across the state by the winds of prejudice and hatred. Unwanted and homeless for over 100 years we seemed to have been forsaken and without friends."[106] The American GI Forum became the collective entity from which García mobilized his campaign against institutionalized discrimination. The arts of healing, physical and rhetorical, were his tools.

It is likely that García's educated and socially and politically conscious family listened to Roosevelt's fireside chats on the radio and saw Roosevelt in the performance of the presidency on newsreels in the local Mercedes, Texas, theatre that García's family owned and operated. García, like Roosevelt, often exploited the medium of radio to inform, move, and build consensus within the South Texas Mexican American community. García's own style of public leadership reflected Roosevelt's pragmatic and sometimes inconsistent style. Often to the consternation of his followers and derision of his enemies, García was willing to cooperate with unlikely individuals and entities, if collaboration translated into practical action toward justice. Like Roosevelt, García "would make deals with the devil in order to keep his hold on those who might respond to his call."[107] Both were inconsistent and ambiguous—expecting their followers to fill in the gaps. In many respects, García's contradictory stance on Mexican immigration and conflicted position on segregation reflects Roosevelt's own mixed record on race.

Garth Pauley characterizes Roosevelt's "rhetorical program on race as neither dynamic or sustained."[108] Nonetheless, Roosevelt's *ethos* as the compassionate leader and his reliance on symbol, or what Wills calls the "semaphore of hope," prefigure the role of García as a healing leader in his own fractured time and place.[109] García's sense of assuredness, like FDR's, even more than his eloquence, lifted others and moved them forward into action. Like FDR, the strength of García's rhetoric rested in the magnitude of his *ethos* as a healer.

García exercised an unwavering identification with the larger fraternity that had framed the American Constitution—a community of visionaries that transcended the time and place in which he lived. "Texas is not worth fighting for. We are fighting for our country!" he once declared before the Texas Advisory Committee to the U.S. Commission on Civil Rights.[110] "We Mexican Americans would rather trust the federal officials, presidents, vice presidents, senators, congressmen than Texas officials," he explained.[111] Texas was a segregated Southern state, historically governed by Anglo political bosses. García maintained confidence in the "national manhood" of the federal government, although no less white than Texas, because it held out the promise of inclusion.[112]

Like African American civil rights activists of the era, García recognized that Mexican Americans would have to appeal to the federal government in order to secure the protection of their civil rights. Texas, like other southern states, was deeply invested in institutionalized discrimination economically, socially, and politically. Segregation affected every dimension of public life. García tirelessly resisted the Anglo political machine of Texas, pushing for changes at all levels of government. The civil rights acts of 1964 and 1965 did not end segregation patterns in Texas. Nearly a decade after President Lyndon B. Johnson's historic Voting Rights Act, García continued his campaign for equal rights in the state. In a rare instance of staged civil disobedience, García was arrested in August of 1972 with seventeen young Mexican American students when he staged a sit-in at the Corpus Christi Independent School District office to protest discriminatory educational practices.

García maintained a daily Spanish radio program introduced by a bugle call. Sponsored by the American GI Forum in Corpus Christi, García used the medium of radio for decades to make club announcements, promote poll tax drives, launch back-to-school campaigns, address veteran affairs, and stir political awareness. He used the radio to educate the people, crossing the boundaries of class and culture and even national borders into Mexico to broadcast information on health and politics. "He was bold because he was telling people to get an education, to vote, to stand up for themselves," notes archivist Grace Charles.[113] For these acts of mobilization, he was considered a subversive and a rabble rouser by the Anglo majority.

"García is considered an able speaker, capable of stirring up his hearers and his more emotional speeches come in for criticism," one article reported in 1966. "He uses the ignorance of the masses. . . . He speaks from an emotional standpoint, appeals to nationalistic ties of the Mexican American to his homeland. And they rally around him."[114] García's activism ruptured the South Texas status quo and reverberated throughout the nation. "His rhetoric was not violent and therefore not threatening. It may have been strident but there was coherence in his arguments, and this aside from money, is what usually gets the attention of politicians," observes author Rolando Hinojosa-Smith.[115]

However, with shifting political and ideological currents through the 1960s and 1970s, an unresolved schism divided García and emerging Chicano activists. Militant activists tagged him an accommodationist and assimilationist and they dismissed him as overly conservative. Some Chicano activists accused him of sleeping with the enemy, the Anglo elites. Juan Guerra recalls, "As a Chicano who came of age in the 1960s and was influenced by the highly charged anti-American rhetoric of the time, I found García's response to the challenges of the day dangerously reactionary. In our eyes, García was *un vendido*, a sell out."[116] This audacious, self-authorized, highly visible, and irrepressibly vocal advocate of Mexican American civil rights who dared to publicly proclaim that "We are sick and tired of being abused by the power structure!" was reduced by the close of the 1980s to an aging and irrelevant icon of elitism among Chicano intelligentsia.

Textualizing an American Experience

García struggled to circulate his story and at the same time protect his legacy. He enlisted the help of the media early in his civil rights project, orchestrating press releases of American GI Forum events and exposing incidences of discrimination. *Border Trends*, a newsletter reporting "Anglo-Latin relations in the South West" published by the Unitarian Church in McAllen, Texas, carried the announcement of the formation of the American GI Forum in its September 1948 issue: "Corpus Christi recently saw the birth of a new veterans' organization called the American G I Forum, which has rapidly spread over South Texas and is extending itself into the central and western regions of the state. It is estimated that there are now 1,000 members in the Corpus Christi area alone and about 3,000 throughout the state."[117] The press frequently provided García and the American GI Forum rhetorical leverage against the local power structure.

García vectored the persuasive power of the media whenever and wherever possible to confront voting rights violations, police brutality, migrant labor abuse, inequitable school facilities, and discrimination in housing, employment, and medical care. In 1951, *Quick* magazine featured a photograph and notice about the work of the American GI Forum in an article entitled, "Civil Rights: Strength or Weakness?" Consistent with the prevailing discourse of the period, the *Quick* magazine article echoes García's recurring argument that civil rights violations in the United States provided fodder for Cold War propaganda in Asia and Russia. The article reported:

> For every instance of U.S. failure to fulfill its promise of civil rights is seized upon by our critics, weakens our efforts to offset Red propaganda in much of the world. . . . As with Negroes, discrimination against Mexicans in the Southwest, West, and Midwest runs to housing, eating places, hotels, schools. State and civic agencies say they are making headway in eliminating these inequalities. The G.I. Forum of Texas, made up of U. S. war veterans of Latin-American descent, has successfully attacked efforts to keep Mexicans out of many public eating and recreation spots. . . .
>
> Thus, by court order, by civic group attack and by state directive, the U.S. is seeking to fulfill its promises of equal opportunities. Insofar as America succeeds, it strengthens itself against the pointing fingers of Red propaganda.[118]

García complicated the narrative of progress of civil rights reform by demonstrating the intractability of racism in Texas. Moreover, his rhetorical embedding of Mexican American civil rights issues into the prevailing anti-Communist discourse of the era proved especially productive in gaining the attention and approval of the dominant Anglo culture. These rhetorical strategies helped to confront charges lobbed against his organization by Anglo conservatives who sought to label his activities as subversive or un-American.

An even more significant article, entitled "Texas' Forgotten People," was released in 1951 by *Look* magazine and featured an eight-page exposé of García's work.[119] Heavily infused with *pathos*, this full photographic representation depicts García in his role as a physician treating ill and impoverished migrant workers. The impact of the 1951 *Look* magazine article was far-reaching, propelling readers from around the country to send letters of response. A physician and fellow serviceman from García's military unit wrote from his office in New York:

As I glanced over this week's issue of "Look" magazine & commenced reading about the situation of those Texans of Mexican extraction, I thought about Garcia. You can imagine my surprise to turn the pages & look at Garcia in the photo. . . . In all the years we spent overseas together, I never got a hint that there was any discrimination such as is mentioned in Look—either from you or the others in our outfit."[120]

Readers sent cash gifts to the editors of *Look* for the families featured in the article. The editors forwarded the gifts to García for the intended families. A Corpus Christi resident received a three dollar gift from a reader in Syracuse, New York. Manuel Reyes thanked the donor on behalf of his wife and nine children: "I am very grateful to you and for the very nice magazine LOOK. I can assure you the money will mean very much to me and my children. I have received many things for them including clothes and food."[121]

García's reputation also graced the pages of the media mainstay of postwar Americana, the *Saturday Evening Post*. Thomas Sutherland's 1952 article "Texas Tackles the Race Problem" offers this portrait of García:

Dr. Hector Garcia, a Corpus Christi physician, spellbinds the Mexican American war veterans and is putting on an evangelical drive to get them hospitals, better housing facilities, dignity and all that goes with it. Many veterans who felt let down after the war are being trained by him for leadership. . . .

His American GI Forum is teaching political action in the tortilla flats of Texas, and they also know García's name, though, not so reverently out in the Scotch-and-soda sections.[122]

The mystique of García's persuasive powers rests at the heart of Sutherland's portrait. Moreover, Sutherland recognizes the Longoria incident as a galvanizing event for Mexican American civil rights and links "the current caste system founded on color" to an "American agriculture based on black slavery."[123] Connecting civil rights violations to issues of national security, Sutherland argues:

Proud Texas has been unfair to her Latin citizens, often ostracizing them, once refusing a man even the human decency of a proper funeral. . . .

News about insults to our Spanish-speaking neighbors is eagerly dispersed by enemies of the United States. . . .

We Texans are still a conservative, tough-minded rural folk, not far removed in time from a frontier history of bloody conflict with Indians, Mexicans, and Yankees. Thus more inclined to action than to thought, we are loyal in our affections, but stubborn in our attitudes even when they are wrong—as they usually are toward other peoples, since we are experienced only in the combative approach.[124]

The symbolic mix of García as a passionate civil rights activist and noble physician wrapped in a patriotic military veneer proved time and again a potent emblem for media circulation through the post-war era.

García similarly recognized the value of the academy and professional scholarship to help legitimize his aims and efforts. His 1958 "A Brief History of the American GI Forum of the U.S." traces the ten-year evolution of his organization, claiming 20,000 members in twenty-one states. Although never published, this account would become the nucleus for Carl Allsup's historical examination, *The American G.I. Forum: Origins and Evolution*.[125] Both the *Stanford Law Review* and *Harvard Civil Rights–Civil Liberties Law Review* featured articles referencing the work of the American GI Forum and García.[126] However, García was not always pleased with the academy's treatment of his legacy. He welcomed circulation of his ideas and achievements but wanted to retain authority over his own story.

In 1977, García lambasted political scientist Richard H. Kraemer and coauthors Ernest Crain and Earl Maxwell for errors in *Understanding Texas Politics*.[127] There were two issues García wanted to keep clear. First, the American GI Forum was a veterans' organization and not a political group (not even a civil rights group). Second, neither García nor the American GI Forum ever adopted the Chicano ideology or label, firmly resisting identification with this militant strand of civil rights rhetoric. It was very important to García that the record reflect the fact that his civil rights efforts predated the Chicano movement by some twenty years. He strongly resented the tendency in the 1970s for historians to locate the beginning of the Mexican American civil rights movement with the emergence of Chicano nationalist activism of the 1960s.[128] García disapproved of many of the strategies and aims of the Chicano movement, and his civil rights project consistently promoted a vision of civic inclusion, not the separatism advanced by Chicano nationalists.

Kraemer's chapter includes a brief overview of the Chicano political party *La Raza Unida*, a group that coalesced in the 1960s in the wake of the Viva Kennedy campaign. García and Albert Peña Jr. were key players in the formation of the Viva Kennedy clubs and instrumental leaders in the creation of the national-level coalition PASO (Political Association of Spanish Speaking Organizations) in 1961. PASO held together for less than two years, during which time García lamented the difficult struggle to organize diverse Latino groups. García did not approve of the strategies PASO sought to employ and resigned in a dramatic walk-out that became a defining moment in García's mind separating his generation of post–World War II reformers and Chicano activists.[129] García questioned the ties of PASO to the Teamsters union and resisted the growing militancy of the Chicano leaders. Although García was instrumental in organizing PASO (as discussed in chapter 5), he wanted no part of their politics. PASO eventually crumbled, but *La Raza Unida*, bolstered by some of the remaining PASO leadership, would evolve into the Chicano *La Raza Unida* political party. *La Raza Unida*, responsible for overturning the Anglo "good ol' boy" network in South Texas's Crystal City election, developed into a militant separatist Chicano organization from which García remained aloof.

Kraemer's account of the formation of *La Raza Unida* treads on tenuous territory. He opens with a brief and inaccurate gloss of the American GI Forum after discounting the role of LULAC as "not very effective." Kraemer makes the glaring mistake of describing the American GI Forum as a Chicano organization. The American GI Forum predated the Chicano youth movement by some fifteen years. Even more significantly, García never aligned forces with Chicano nationalists. It is understandable why Kraemer's account was so problematic for García. Kraemer does not outline any of the precedent-setting activities of the American GI Forum or the post–war reformers. He claims that the American GI Forum "was a more militant organization with wider appeal among Chicanos," inaccurately assuming that American GI Forum members had adopted the label and ideology of Chicano nationalists. Kraemer fails to recognize the distinctions in civic identities and politics among the Mexican American populace since World War II. In Kraemer's textbook, Mexican American civil rights activism begins and ends with *La Raza Unida*, an organization which ultimately broke apart before the close of the decade. García's letter challenged Professor Kraemer:

> As founder of the American G.I. Forum and as an officer of this veterans organization I wish to strongly protest your errors intentional or otherwise in your book "Understanding Texas Politics," . . .
>
> Page 76 under heading of "political parties" you have included with "La Raza Unida Party" the "LULAC is middle class oriented, moderate, and not very effective."
>
> "After World War II, Dr. Hector Garcia founded the American G.I. Forum, a more militant organization with a wider appeal among Chicanos. The trigger for the establishment of the Forum was furnished by a Three Rivers Funeral Home that refused to bury the body of Felix Longoria, a military veteran . . ."

My objection is the fact that we are not a political party and neither is the "LULACS." Secondly, Felix Longoria was not a military veteran but was an active duty infantry soldier who was killed on a voluntary military action in W. W. II in Luzon, Philippines. . . .

I am rather surprised that persons of your scholarly ability and political experience should have made so many errors. . . .

We, Mexican Americans, both as American G.I. Forum and LULAC members are used to unjust, unfair, and racist criticism by racial and prejudiced bigots. But when this is done by people of your stature it is time to raise the question. Why?[130]

Kraemer's lengthy response argues that admittedly LULAC and the American GI Forum do not represent political parties but "the activities you engage in do have political impact." He admits that Félix Longoria was inaccurately depicted as a veteran rather than a soldier, but asserts that no other errors exist in his account. Kraemer closes with this note: "I am considering turning your letter over to my attorney to ascertain whether or not we have grounds for legal action against you for defamation of character."[131] García was unmoved by Kraemer's threat.

The reply by Kraemer's coauthors, Ernest Crain and Earl Maxwell, however, takes a more conciliatory tone and squarely places the error on Kraemer for the writing of the offending chapter on the American GI Forum. Crain and Maxwell also indicate that the relationship formed with Kraemer had been "dissolved for a variety of reasons" and that *Understanding Texas Politics* would not be published in a second edition.[132] This would not be the last time García sparked such diametrically opposed reactions in audiences, or the last time he challenged academics about their uneven attention to the history and experience of Mexican Americans.

Discursive Agency and García's Legacy of Civil Rights Reform

García's record of shuttling between working-class Mexican American and elite Anglo discourse communities has no precedent. He forged a political discourse that effectively negotiated geographical, social, and cultural borders toward the construction of a Mexican American civic *ethos*. While García's extensive archive of political discourse aligns him with many of the major events and leaders of the twentieth-century United States, it is difficult to assess the exact impact of his texts. His words were incendiary, sparking action and reaction. His arguments drew steady fire. García saw himself as an unrecognized harbinger of American civil rights reform. He once asserted:

You've heard it said that the Mexican-Americans are following in the black people's civil rights trail. I have only admiration and respect for the black civil rights movement. But for it to be said that we followed in the tracks, no, I think it was the other way around. We established points in law, precedents they followed through.[133]

Problematically, however, García himself never authored the bills that would become law nor argued the cases in court. He did not approach civil rights reform as a lawmaker, but as a physician. He was writing prescriptions, not legislation, for social justice.

García engaged in the political process first through his role as healer, realizing early in his career that treating the symptoms of social inequity would never eradicate the social ills themselves. His father and his family in Mercedes, Texas, were never politically active. Throughout his youth, García avoided engaging in political activity. Even at the peak of his activism in the 1960s, García had no designs on holding public office. Political ambition did not motivate him—justice did. James De Anda, national chairman of the American GI Forum, defends the Forum and García against claims of acting out of self-interest and anti-Anglo sentiments in his August 15, 1963, letter to the editor of the *Corpus Christi Caller Times*: "This has been the consistent position of the Forum and its founder, Dr. Hector P. Garcia. That the situation can be remedied by the united efforts of all citizens is obvious. Experience and common sense show this."[134] De Anza chronicled García's record of advocacy on behalf of Mexican American laborers, veterans, patients, public leaders, and candidates for public office as well as García's history of supporting Anglo as well as Mexican American leaders. Fusing García's public identity with the organization, De Anza asserts: "The American G.I. Forum and Dr. García have advocated in the strongest terms, unity of all Americans." García and his organization formed a mnemonic structure, a metonymic device; the man and his organization were interchangeable tropes.

Had García held an elected post like New Mexico Senator Dennis Chávez, Texas Senator Henry B. González, or San Antonio's Mayor Henry Cisneros, García may have enjoyed a more secure place in history. But he always saw himself as healer first, social activist second. García's combination of social roles evolved into a unique model of civil rights activism. As a result, García's political discourse, generated and circulated from his position as a self-authorized advocate, complicates the interpretation of his agency. Although he remained suspect of the moral conscience of the Texas Anglo majority, García stood resolute in his faith in the principles of the Constitution and his place among the nation's "imagined fraternity."[135]

García's rhetorical power was not invested in cultivating the image of the eloquent orator but rather in performing the role of the grassroots practitioner who gets things done. He spoke a variety of Mexican Spanish occasionally inflected with lexical items characteristic of border Spanish or "Tex Mex" for rhetorical effect.[136] However, he took pride in his "perfect" Spanish. "All of us knew Spanish, written Spanish, reading in Spanish, we knew the alphabet in Spanish, we knew the numbers in Spanish, 'cause Father taught this to us," García recalled.[137] García's linguistic repertoire enhanced his *ethos* not only among South Texas Mexican Americans but among dignitaries in Latin America. When introduced to the ambassador of Spain while serving as a Special Ambassador to Venezuela in 1964, García was mistaken for a doctor of letters rather than of medicine. "In fact," García recalled, "I could never convince the ambassador from Spain that I was not educated in Spain or Mexico."[138]

García was a border figure in many dimensions. He resisted the historical stigmatization of Spanish-accented English and asserted his voice on radio and at public events. His passion and dedication overpowered his reserve. His fidelity to his beliefs, his community, and his colleagues was unwavering. García respected authority but wasn't afraid to go against the grain. He adopted the brand "liberal maverick," and at the same time, unabashedly appropriated the discourse of conservative McCarthy-era politicos, as reflected in his statement to the 1960 Democratic National Committee Nationalities Division.[139] In this statement, García invokes both liberal democratic ideals and Cold War xenophobic alarm in his call for appointments of Mexican Americans to diplomatic posts in Latin America and Asia:

> On the surface this omission [of Mexican American appointments] appears harmless but it reaches serious proportions when we are trying to combat communism and do not realize that we are unable even to sell democracy because we are not making use of our greatest salesman of democracy. That is the Americans of Latin American origin who would be the greatest salesmen of democracy to their brothers in those countries.
>
> Therefore it is of great importance and of great significance that the president in 1960 make immediate plans to use this vast number of loyal citizens who can not only serve their country but perhaps save it from the grasps of communism by selling democracy to our friends.[140]

García appropriated disparate discourses toward a single objective—the heightened political presence of Mexican Americans in every facet of U.S. civic life.

The desire to belong, to be useful, to be of service to his people was at the heart of García's political action. His colleague and fellow serviceman, Dr. Daniel McAteer, Jr. reflects, "You are a good M.D. Hector. I realized that when I saw how you gave ungrudged attention to medical indigents of the civilian population overseas."[141] García practiced medicine for forty-seven years, serving homeless patients in the indigent health center at Memorial Medical Center past the age of eighty.[142] "I'm not doing anything for anybody. I'm doing it for myself in a way and reminding this country and this land that this is America," García claimed.[143] His entire public life was an exercise of praxis, action that had potency with the intention of making a difference in the world. Former mayor of Corpus Christi Luther Jones described García as "a fighter—there's no question about that."[144] He reportedly spent as much as $10,000 per year of his own money to help fund the American GI Forum. "Here is a man who could have earned a lot more money just practicing medicine," reflects Eddie Cavazos, former state representative for Corpus Christi.[145] Instead, García devoted the majority of his time to civil rights and to healing the poor.

Not only did he feel called by the political situation in which he found himself, García called others to respond—even those who resisted the demands of time, energy, and resources. He was a compelling presence. Collaborative action by countless supporters allowed García to perform his multiple roles. He did as much as any one person could do because he operated out of a collective identity. His younger brother, Dr. Xico P. García, who was still practicing medicine at the age of seventy-one in Corpus Christi, often covered Héctor's practice for him—allowing Héctor to continue to participate in civil rights efforts. In a 1981 letter of appreciation to his younger brother, Héctor disclosed: "Mi Querido Hermano; Mi familia y yo estamos eternamente agradecidos a ti y a tu familia por tanto que han hecho por mi durante mis largas y dolorosas enfermedades. . . . Le pido a Dios buena salud y que sigamos adelante juntos con animo y carino y con forteleza por nuestras familias, para nuestras responsibilidades a nuestras profesiones y nuestro deber a la humanidad."[146] [My dear brother, my family and I are eternally grateful to you and your family for all that you have done for me during my long and difficult illnesses. I ask God for good health and that we move forward together with strength and affection for our families, for our responsibilities to our profession, and our duties to humanity.] The demands García placed on himself not only impacted his life but the lives of everyone around him.

Throughout his civil rights career, García relied heavily on others because so many relied heavily on him. He refused to allow his own failing health to impede him. He felt called to moral action to counter the unjust conditions eroding America's vision of equality. In this 1969 interview for the National Archives and Records Service, García describes the struggle of forging a Mexican American national identity:

> Psychologically we Mexican Americans want to belong. In other words, I say this: we always want to end our days in somebody's arms. Is it our mother's arms, is it our wife's arms, is it our priest's or minister's arms, is it our children's arms, we want to be loved and to [be] taken in by someone. We Mexican Americans up to the time of 1960 were dejected people because we were rejected by everyone. In Mexico we were never accepted by the Mexicans, and here we were not accepted by the Texans. So since 1960 is the first instance that we feel that we are Americans.[147]

García saw the election of John F. Kennedy and Lyndon B. Johnson to the White House as a watershed year for Mexican Americans, a political shift García and the American GI Forum worked diligently to achieve through mobilization of the Mexican American electorate. Driven to bring his people under the umbrella of the "imagined fraternity" promised by the Kennedy and Johnson administrations, García embraced a civil rights project that yielded uneven results. García contended:

> For instance, up until about 1960 we Mexican-Americans had never made the federal people realize first that we were a minority of any numbers, Secondly, they never realized we had specific problems. It was the Civil Rights Act of 1960 that we were able to start moving into the field of civil rights. Previously we moved in other fields But I think these civil rights acts were the ones that gave us the feeling—that we also had civil rights and the voting rights. The repeal of the poll tax on federal elections which involved the presidential and federal nominees helped. This was a most important thing, because the federal law made the State of Texas repeal the prerequisite of voting, which was the poll tax. And this happened only about '65 or '66, not too long ago.[148]

García's faith in the American democratic experiment and willingness to negotiate with the Anglo majority of Texas politics over decades of service are among the many features that distinguish his remarkable career as a civil rights activist.

García was the one people called. The community recognized a powerful presence in him—even as a frail bedridden man. According to those who worked closest with him, people came to García for help even near the end of his life, and he refused to say no. People sought his endorsement for political appointments, for letters of recommendation for jobs and college, for the symbolic gestures that would place them beneath the umbrella of his expansive *ethos*. In turn, he called his followers to be a bold civic presence, to make the sacrifice of time, energy, and resources for a larger vision of equality. "Great leadership is not a zero-sum game," concludes Garry Wills. Both leaders and followers "get by giving."[149]

García projected a model of commitment few could emulate. His single-minded determination to make a difference in the lives of Mexican Americans demanded a lifetime of action. García embodied Thoreau's charge to "to cast your whole vote, not a strip of paper merely, but your whole influence."[150] The act of casting his vote with his "whole influence" rendered García a complex, contradictory, and controversial figure, giving his days and his nights, his wealth and his reputation, his foibles and his strengths to service. A living sacrifice. He was "a great humanitarian," recalls Belia Chabot, a nurse who served beside García for over twenty years, walking with him as he made his midnight rounds through the Corpus Christi Memorial Medical Center.[151]

Perhaps this is why his legacy has remained, until very recently, untouched in historical and rhetorical studies. "Not many people vote with their whole lives," explains Garry Wills. "But those who do have a disproportionate impact on society."[152] There is something incomprehensible, something mythical, something paradoxical about a leader who can exercise such power and at the same time exude tremendous vulnerability. García's fragility and magnanimity, his insistence on being heard and his humility overwhelmed even the most powerful people.

García demanded that the record reflect not only his presence but the civic presence of his people. He refused to be erased and furiously resisted misrepresentation. García worked sixteen to eighteen hours per day for over forty years with one eye focused on the future and the other on the past. "I only hope he has enough health to see some of the fruits of his labor," his wife, Wanda Fusillo García once poignantly reflected.[153] In June 1996, only one month before García's death, U.S. Representative Solomon Ortiz saluted García's contributions to American civil rights to the 104th Congress. The *Congressional Record* of June 26, 1996 reads:

> Dr. García is a different breed of patriot and citizen. Long before the issue of civil rights was on the national radar screen, he recognized the need for equal rights for the citizens of South Texas and the United States. . . .
>
> Today, Dr. García's message is political gospel to which we all adhere. While others fought the system, often unsuccessfully, he worked within the system to open it up for everyone to participate. . . .

While the nation began to understand civil rights in the 1960s they never quite recognized the fact that Dr. García founded the cause so successfully in 1948. He fought for basic, fundamental civil, human, and individual rights. He has been a successful warrior for his cause—democracy, decency, justice, and fairness.[154]

García battled injustice and illness for five decades in both his private and public life. From the moment of his return to the United States after the war, García suffered from a series of incapacitating illnesses. In many respects, he never enjoyed the fruits of his labor. The collective sacrifices that he and his family made were directed to often unattainable aims. "It was very hard for me growing up and hard for other members of our family," remembered Cecilia, García's eldest daughter.[155] Loss, grief, and frail health marked his final years. "He was his work," Wanda reflects.[156] In the decade since his death, García's legacy hovers somewhere between obscurity and myth.

The Félix Longoria Incident: Drama, Irony, and "The American Dilemma"

3

> Beautiful that war and all its deeds of carnage must in time be
> Utterly lost,
> That the hands of the sisters Death and Night incessantly softly
> wash again and again, this soil'd world.
>
> Walt Whitman, "Drum-Taps"

*I*n January 1949, Hector García incited a maelstrom of national disputation and indignation around an ordinary reality that would become the extraordinary case of Private Félix Longoria. War was the backdrop. The hero was only a memory, a name. With a few simple words, García gave voice to the tragedies of war and racism in America.[1] As the leader of an emerging veterans' rights organization, García's rhetorically measured response to an everyday act of discrimination permanently seared the American conscience. The rhetorical force of the Longoria incident began months before with the formation and coalition-building activities of the American GI Forum. When the moment presented itself, García was ready.

García's symbiotic identification with the American GI Forum provided the mechanism for moral protest. García's empathic representation of Private Longoria and protection of Longoria's widow, Beatrice, set the drama. This chapter examines García's leadership strategies, and his adroit representation of the Longoria affair exercised both at the forefront of action and behind-the-scenes. It situates the Longoria affair inside the historical moment of 1949, a critical juncture in national race relations, to highlight García's mobilizing role. The Longoria incident as exigence moved García into a stance of resistance and propelled him as an activist into the national arena.

Straddling the "Color Line"

By making Mexican-origin people visible, García sought to complicate the black-white binary of race in America. He struggled to demonstrate the variant forms of bigotry. García argued again and again that Mexican Americans were not only an exploited people; they were a "forgotten people." In the pigmentocracy of the U.S. social system, racism and discrimination impacted all peoples of color. Convincing whites of that reality was García's primary challenge. He used the methods of American pragmatism to do so, fore-grounding concrete and specific cases of discrimination to index a general trend. Consistent with the model of knowledge-making delineated by William James, "The pragmatist clings to facts and concreteness, observes truth at its work in particular cases and generalizes."[2] For García, white Americans did not accept the truth of racism because they did not see it. His job was to make white America see the truth of racism by vividly representing real and particular cases of discrimination against Mexican Americans.

According to Greenfield and Kate's examination of contradictory court rulings on the racial status of Mexican-origin people, individuals of Mexican descent have been, in general, considered "nonwhite" throughout U.S. history and have endured "substantial discrimination" as a result of that perception.[3] The first U.S. naturalization laws in 1790 did not include members of "the so-called Latin races" under its umbrella term "white persons."[4] Mexicans, as such, were labeled "half-breeds" because of their mixed Spanish and indigenous lineage.[5] Existing in the undefined space between white and black in the racially polarized system of America's seg-regated society, García worked to assert a new level of Mexican American civic presence.

García both enacted and challenged the ideals of what Gunnar Myrdal called the "American Creed." In his comprehensive examination of national character and the entrenchment of racism in America, Myrdal reported, "These ideals of the essential dignity of the individual human being, of the fundamental equality of all men, and of certain inalienable rights to freedom, justice, and a fair opportunity represent to the American people the essential meaning of the nation's early struggle for independence."[6] Through the Longoria case, García exploited the American *ethos* and national disposition toward moralism, rationalism, pragmatism, and optimism.

In the backdrop of García's civil rights project, political and social shifts at local and national levels signaled heightening awareness of U.S. racial inequities. The Truman administration's civil rights agenda was forging new ground when García called the first meeting of the American GI Forum. Although inconsistent and considered suspect by social activists like W. E. B. Du Bois, Truman extended the conversation on racism in America in new ways. Truman's 1947 State of the Union address, condemning racism and bigotry and challenging the limits of the current legislation to protect the civil rights of citizens, signaled a new level of consciousness within the majority population.[7] The sociopolitical context in the post–World War II era proved a fertile period for social activism and critique.

Like Mexican Americans, African American reformers mobilized throughout the 1940s in vocal and visible ways. The first "March on Washington," although not executed, had been planned as early as 1941 by A. Philip Randolph, founder of the Brotherhood of Sleeping Car Porters. World War II conscientious objectors Bill Sutherland and George Houser established the Congress on Racial Equality in 1942.[8] At the close of the war, fifteen thousand protestors marched to the Lincoln Memorial in 1946 reacting to a lynching in Monroe, Georgia, and calling for anti-lynching legislation.[9] The first "freedom rides" and "sit ins" by black civil rights activists occurred between 1942 and 1947 and were events that met with mixed reactions from the American public. The formation of the American GI Forum and the drama of the Longoria incident not only reflected the rhetorical situation of the post–World War II era, but also García's keen sense of *kairos*.

The American GI Forum was not the only organization to enjoy increased membership at the close of the war. LULAC enjoyed a surge in membership as did the NAACP at the end of World War II.[10] Additionally, the Texas Good Neighbor Commission, established in Texas in 1943 as a liaison organization to forge goodwill with Mexico, took an expanded role in mediating relations between Anglos and Mexican Americans. The Good Neighbor Commission, a clearinghouse established to address issues related to Mexican nationals working in the state, foundered before the close of the decade. Without legislative or political clout, the Good Neighbor Commission remained a relatively impotent organization during its brief tenure amid "the climate of hate in Texas."[11]

In concert with intellectual and political predecessors such as Alonso Perales and LULAC, García, however, resisted identification with African Americans and Mexican immigrant groups. García, like LULAC leaders, cited the "Caucasian Race Resolution" to assert Mexican American entitlement to equal access and treatment under the law. The "Caucasian Race Resolution," introduced into the Texas state legislature in 1943, a precursor to the formation of the Good Neighbor Commission, declared that Mexican-origin peoples belonged on the "white" side of the color line.[12] Subscription to this legislative act of racial naming limited the rhetorical parameters of García's civil rights project.

Discourses of resistance were circulating in Texas and throughout the United States. In 1948, Héctor reflected in a letter to his brother, Dr. J.

A. García, "The minorities of our country, among which, unfortunately we find ourselves making a decided stand at this time for their rights and privileges guaranteed everyone under our Constitution and laws."[13] The Garcías had broken through the economic and educational constraints they faced growing up on the borders of U.S. enfranchisement and civic inclusion. Reconciling America's racial division would become Héctor's more enduring and problematic endeavor. This private struggle aligned with a period of mounting tensions over enduring inequities within global, national, and local spheres—conditions calling for response.

After the euphoria of victory in World War II had died, Americans grappled with the ominous task of national as well as global reconstruction. After the Depression of the 1930s and World War II in the 1940s, America struggled to find the "will to recover."[14] Facing loss and devastation demanded leadership at every level from the local to the international. It was a period in search of the means to bridge social divisions and heal communities. In a detailed post-war examination of the global consequences of colonialism and totalitarianism, race theorist, historical sociologist, and "father" of modern civil rights, W. E. B. Du Bois daringly called attention to the invidious forms of white supremacism. He argued that minorities and depressed classes at all points of the world were forming "one increasing cry for freedom, democracy, and social progress."[15]

Du Bois's investigation of historically colonized and enslaved peoples revealed that the "color line" in the twentieth-century confined not only Blacks but all people of color across the globe.[16] In "The Color Line Belts the World," Du Bois charged, "the white races have had the hegemony of civilization—so far so that 'white' and 'civilized' have become synonymous in everyday speech."[17] Du Bois maintained that the subjugation of peoples of color was not only manifested in practices of segregation but was most insidiously and effectively reproduced through language, the oral and written tenets of society and culture, and Anglo-Euro-centric ideologies and myths that sustained the sense of a unified identity within colonizing nations.

The race debate played out in U.S. courts and universities. "Some of the most pernicious racial theorizing emanated from the nation's prestigious universities, including Harvard and Columbia," notes Lawrence Oliver.[18] "Academic racism," as such, rested at the center of the American educational system, implicitly and explicitly promulgated through the "rhetoric of American consensus."[19] Sociologist Franklin H. Giddings's 1900 *Democracy and Empire* and 1903 "American People" advanced the notion of American exceptionalism on purported Anglo-Teutonic "race traits," myths reproduced at every level throughout the U.S. educational system.[20] Colonial conditions and political configurations throughout the world justified the domination of peoples of color with the "scientific" claim that as a result of genetic and cultural evolution peoples of color were "naturally inferior" and "incapable of self government." This racialized narrative of human progress, placing members of the Caucasian race at the apex of human development, in effect helped to sustain racial hierarchies in the United States and throughout the world.

At the first Universal Race Congress in 1911, Du Bois, counting Mexican-origin people among the subjugated populations across the globe, contended:

> Under the aegis of this philosophy strong arguments have justified human slavery and peonage, conquest, enforced ignorance, the dishonoring of women and the exploitation of children. It was divine to enslave negroes; Mexican peonage is the only remedy for laziness.[21]

Du Bois's arguments closely reflected social configurations in 1949 South Texas where for over a century, Anglo colonizers in Texas operated under the belief that Mexicans represented a "mongrel" race. In *Anglos and Mexicans in the Making of Texas, 1836–1986*, David Montejano explains that although there was "no constitutionally sanctioned 'separate but equal' provision for Mexicans as there was for blacks . . . the separation was as complete—and as 'de jure'—as any in the Jim Crow South."[22] Armando Alonzo further elaborates in *Tejano Legacy: Rancheros and Settlers in South Texas, 1734–1900*: "In a way reminiscent of their treatment of Blacks, they [Anglo settlers] condemned dark-skinned Tejanos to the bottom of society . . . setting up social and physical boundaries that later developed into patterns of segregation."[23] Co-opting land with the contention that "this region of the United States would have never have prospered and developed in the hands of the Mexican government and Mexicans," Anglos asserted dominance through political, economic, ideological, and educational means.[24]

Consistent with the prevailing ideology of racial genetics and the myth of racial "purity," Anglos believed that because Mexicans belonged to a "mixed" race their "low" intellectual and cultural development made them well suited for manual labor and servitude.[25] Montejano summarizes, "in political and sociological terms, blacks and Mexicans were basically seen as different aspects of the same race problem."[26] As early as 1840 with the western expansion under the Polk administration and Secretary of State James Buchanan, a "scientific" ideology was promulgated throughout the Southwest that assigned racial supremacy not to all whites, but only to those from northern European origins, termed "Anglo-Saxons" or "Anglo-Normans."[27] These Anglo-American colonizers believed that the earliest Spanish *conquistadores*, although white, represented inferior European stock because they "had bred" with the indigenous peoples and brought forth "wretched hybrids."[28] The historical ambivalence toward *mestizo* ("mixed race") peoples was reproduced not only by Anglos but by elite Spanish and Mexican-origin groups claiming "pure" Spanish lineage.[29]

Consistent with Du Bois's observations of colonized peoples throughout the world, social and ideological systems of white supremacy were not only integral to the maintenance of Anglo domination in South Texas but Spanish domination throughout Latin America and Mexico as well.[30] As a citizen of two worlds, Mexico and the United States, García inherited the complex racial attitudes and belief systems integral to both cultures.

The systematic perpetuation of racial stereotypes about Mexican-origin peoples in Texas served as a means of forming and sustaining a separate civic identity, a way of differentiating the emerging Republic of Texas from Mexico.[31] Texas civic myth-making suggests a discursive process not unlike the formation of the Southern slave culture.[32] The circulation of racial stereotypes about Mexican peoples in American civic and popular culture throughout the twentieth-century, as a result, reflects many of the stereotypes used to maintain African Americans in subordinate social conditions: the faithful servant, the stoic peon, the shiftless outlaw, the tragic whore, the long-suffering mother. From its earliest period as a colony, a graduated system of inclusion based on color forged the enduring pigmentocracy of Texas, a system of hereditary privilege under which García himself both prospered and struggled.[33]

In *Color and Democracy: Colonies and Peace*, Du Bois argues that vast populations of exploited peoples around the world were calling for liberation and inclusion in democratic progress. This theme of universal resistance was not new. Du Bois's 1906 article "The Color Line Belts the World" claims, "The awakening of the yellow races is certain. That the awakening of the brown and black races will follow in no time, no unprejudiced student of history can doubt."[34] With the global defeat of Nazism, imperialism, and fascism on foreign shores, Du Bois's anticipation of the universal uprising of subjugated peoples in their own lands was close at hand.[35] The challenge facing twentieth-century social activists everywhere was the reversal of "oligarchical control of civilization by the white race."[36]

At the cusp of the Truman administration's civil rights program, race scholars such as Gunnar Myrdal and W. E. B. Du Bois argued that the maintenance of Jim Crow practices and America's racial hierarchy—especially glaring with the defeat of Hitler and his master race project—was a destructive contradiction at home and abroad. At the close of World War II, Myrdal observed: "The subordinate position of Negroes is perhaps the most glaring conflict in the American conscience and the greatest unsolved task for American democracy."[37] Likewise, Du Bois argued in 1945, "The attitude of the United States in this development puzzles the observing world of liberalism."[38] García advanced a similar argument in his 1949 letter to Governor Allan Shivers, when he pointed out, "It is a great shame that our sister republic and a true good neighbor, Mexico, feels that Texas is a backward state. They also feel that discrimination is practiced widely."[39]

The contradiction between America's celebrated egalitarian ideals and the entrenched practices of institutionalized discrimination were for Du Bois and Myrdal the root of the trouble in America. Du Bois succinctly argued, "The problem is the spirit of caste that is arising in a land which was founded on the bedrock of eternal opposition to class privileges."[40] The Félix Longoria incident on a local, national, and even international level profoundly drove home the point that racism in America was not only a black and white issue. This deeply private occasion evolved into a highly public and heavily coded event. The final burial of this Mexican American soldier from South Texas at Arlington National Cemetery, the site of the nation's honored dead, symbolized both a moment of national division and reconciliation. The national ceremony to restore the dignity of Private Félix Longoria represented a landmark national occasion, a drama resonant of the *epitaphios*, funereal ceremonies, performed beside the grave sites of Gettysburg.

The Burial of Private Félix Longoria

The Longoria incident represents the metaphorical and rhetorical acts of recovering and honoring the dead. After receiving news from the Department of the Army that her husband's remains would be shipped back to the United States from the Philippines, Beatrice Longoria took a three-hour bus ride on January 8, 1949, from Corpus Christi to their hometown of Three Rivers, Texas, to make funeral arrangements.[41] A letter dated December 1, 1948, from William E. Smith, county clerk of Live Oak County, informed the Office of the Quartermaster of the American Graves Registration that Beatrice Longoria "desires to have the body sent" to the Rice Funeral Home in Three Rivers.[42] A prior agreement with Rice Funeral Home was reportedly made by Beatrice after Félix was killed on June 16, 1945, in the Philippines. According to a published statement by the director of the funeral home, Thomas Kennedy, Beatrice had arranged with him to accept the remains of her husband two months before her trip to Three Rivers in January of 1949.[43] However, final arrangements did not go as Beatrice had hoped. Thomas Kennedy refused to allow her husband's body in the chapel, suggesting she hold the funeral rites in the vacant house she once occupied.

Informed by Kennedy, the director of the only funeral home in town, that he would not allow her husband's body in the chapel because "the whites wouldn't like it," she returned to Corpus Christi.[44] Upon the advice of her sister, Sara Moreno, who knew first-hand about García's civil rights work, Beatrice telephoned García the next day.[45] "I returned to Corpus Christi to consult with my family," Beatrice later testified. "One of my sisters got in contact with the American GI Forum . . . and I authorized Dr. Garcia to try to get the use of the chapel for my husband's services."[46] Testimonies by García and Beatrice Longoria both indicate that Beatrice's hope was that García would persuade Thomas Kennedy to change his policy so that she could conduct the funeral in Three Rivers as she had initially intended.

García's timely and decisive response transformed what might have been dismissed as a common daily experience of institutionalized discrimination into a national event. The drama that followed poignantly illustrates that texts not only happen to situations but situations happen to texts. While there are no indexes for assessing the direct and long term impact of the event on the course of civil rights reform, it is possible to connect this moment teleologically to Lyndon B. Johnson's historic 1965 Voting Rights Act speech (examined in chapter 5). Furthermore, archive evidence points to the initial link from which the chain reaction began. Beatrice Longoria's indignation provided the spark. Her resistance born of anger and grief both authorized and moved García to action. It was García who wrapped public language around Beatrice's private words and experience. The rest is history or lore or a combination of both.

The media called the moment "a cause."[47] Si Dunn's 1975 retrospective for the *Dallas Morning News* recognizes Félix Longoria as "a symbol of victims of racial discrimination."[48] In 1986, almost forty years after the event, the sesquicentennial collector's issue of *Texas Monthly* lauded the controversy as a defining moment in Texas history, and the article itself is a symbolic act of acknowledgment within Texas elite culture. The *Texas Monthly* describes:

> The three-month-long Longoria affair helped the nascent Mexican American movement channel its discontent into disciplined activism. It demonstrated with such appalling clarity the depths of white prejudice that even politicians could not afford to look the other way.[49]

The obstacle imposed by the funeral director in Three Rivers presented an exigence for action, an exigence García both recognized and embraced. García's engagement set off a course of events like a string of firecrackers. The results stunned not only the nation but García and his followers as well. The rhetorical power of a Mexican American leader and his people was vividly evidenced for the first time in modern history.

The Longoria incident was shocking not only because it was such a clear and glaring example of racism; it was so humanly intimate. How does such an intimate moment become transformed into a public display of resistance capable of moving people so geographically and socially removed from the event?

First, it is necessary to recognize that significant groundwork needed to be done before a situation like the Longoria case could capture attention and move international audiences. García's growing visibility as a leader and his behind-the-scenes experience in community affairs had to be previously established. His reputation as an accessible and responsive advocate of civil rights had to be secure. This kind of local knowledge needed to be in place in order to inform Sara and Beatrice's choice about where to go in a moment of crisis.

Secondly, we must realize this was a private issue, the kind of issue a woman brings to a doctor or a priest. García was an experienced mediator. Failure to recognize Beatrice's vulnerability and her willingness to disclose her plight to García is to overlook the kind of trust and rapport García engendered in people. With confidence in his *ethos* as a physician and the founder of the American GI Forum, Beatrice was secure enough to authorize García to take action in her name.

Thirdly, it is important to understand that Beatrice risked considerable exposure. She had to trust García to protect her. Publicly announcing her anguish and rage toward her hometown was a risky practice. Not only could she face humiliation and reprisals for taking such action, her in-laws were also at risk. In 1949, social and cultural conventions restricted a Mexican American woman from calling public attention to herself. Beatrice's public indignation was a violation of cultural and gender roles, a breach in convention for which the leaders of Three Rivers would retaliate. The mayor and other officials in her hometown would, in turn, attempt to discredit Beatrice by claiming that it was because of bad blood between Beatrice and her in-laws for some unsubstantiated infidelity that Thomas Kennedy refused Beatrice access. However, her father-in-law, Guadalupe Longoria Sr., and the entire Longoria family would officially refute this accusation.[50]

Acknowledging the intimacy of the issue and García's rapport with the community is significant to this examination in order to counter accusations that García's actions were politically calculated. To the contrary, evidence suggests that García's response was cautious. He knew how contentious the matter might become but did not attempt to manipulate the case as some disgruntled Anglos asserted. García did not act, as one South Texas observer suggested, like "some hot-headed Latin American [who] jumped to his feet and hollered 'PREJUDICE.'"[51] García took a pragmatic approach with dramatic results.

García's effective use of instrumental rhetoric in each of the roles he performed on behalf of Beatrice Longoria and the Longoria family served not only to initiate, but also sustain resistance to this incident of discrimination. Throughout the entire affair, however, García wanted to respect Beatrice's wishes, which remained consistently the same—to honor the memory of her husband. First, García verified and circulated the facts of the case. He enlisted a witness, his secretary Gladys Blucher, to record his conversations and actions. He wrote letters and telegrams and made phone calls from his medical office. By wrapping his aegis as a physician and the founder of the American GI Forum around the issue in his correspondence with state and national officials, he both certified the validity of Beatrice's claim and staked his credibility on it. Next, by negotiating with Anglo officials like Lyndon B. Johnson, García played the critical role of arbitrator, bridging not only political and rhetorical positions, but cultural and linguistic perspectives as well. He exercised this liaison role, protecting the Longorias from the wrath of public opinion and the manipulative actions of Anglo officials, throughout the entire affair. Finally, García acted as mobilizer, moving the Mexican American community to protest and to rally financial and social support for the Longorias. In the end, García would stand witness to the events that occurred, withstanding scrutiny and attack from a state legislative investigation designed to discredit him.

Immediately following Beatrice Longoria's plea for assistance, García made a phone call to Thomas Kennedy of the Rice Funeral Home to verify the report, asking his secretary to listen in on the line to serve as a witness to their conversation.[52] When the funeral home manager refused to relent on his position, García contacted George Groh, a reporter for the *Corpus Christi Caller Times* to confirm the story.[53] García also sent telegrams to seventeen state and federal officials dated January 10, 1949, and notified the press. García's message to Senator Lyndon B. Johnson, President Harry S. Truman, Texas Governor Beauford Jester, Texas Attorney General Price Daniel, and state representatives John Lyle and Lloyd Bentsen and others relayed the situation and called for action:

> The American GI Forum an independent veterans organization requests your departments immediate investigation and correction of the un-American action of the Rice Funeral Home Three Rivers Texas in denying the use of its facilities for reinterment of Felix Longoria soldier killed in Luzon, Philippine Islands and now being returned for reburial in Three Rivers, based solely on his Mexican ancestry. . . .
>
> In our estimation, this action is in direct contradiction of those same principles for which this American soldier made the supreme sacrifice in giving his life for his country and for the same people who now deny him the last funeral rites deserving of any American hero regardless of his origin. . . .
>
> This is a typical example of discriminatory practices which occur intermittently in this state despite our efforts to prevent them. We believe action from your office will do much toward elimination of similar shameful occurrences in the future.[54]

García exploited his metonymic relationship with the American GI Forum through the construction of two personas: third person singular as the entity of American GI Forum and first person plural "we." This multifaceted persona enhances García's *ethos*, making him larger than a sole individual acting on his own accord. García did not meet with the members of the American GI Forum before writing the telegram but assumed a stance of authority to speak for the American GI Forum nonetheless. Although some might argue he overstepped the democratic process of his organization, García knew that quick action was necessary and was willing to risk raising criticism and the ire of his followers. Moreover, the mnemonic structure of García's civic identity and the American GI Forum fused them as common entities, interchangeable social figures.

García interjected the word "American" four times into his brief message, reinforcing not only his sense of allegiance but status of citizenship that he and Private Longoria shared in common with the readers. He does not mention the name of Beatrice Longoria, a strategic omission that both protected Beatrice and assuaged possible claims that he was acting on behalf of an emotional, overreactive woman. The text reveals García cautiously stepping clear of gender and racial stereotypes. Nothing about his word choice suggests "a hot-headed" author. His tone exudes confidence in the recipient's willingness and capacity to act in a rational manner. Finally, García's assertion that this case represented not an isolated incident but a pattern of discrimination reaffirms the reality Texans knew existed but didn't openly discuss. García's words had more immediate impact and extended further than even he expected.

García had been sending off telegrams of admonition to public officials complaining about incidents of discrimination for several years under the auspices of LULAC and, more recently, the American GI Forum. None stirred the kind of response that this one did. The content of this message struck a deep chord. García's statement recounts in detail the sequence of events from his perspective. In this testimony, recorded for the state legislative committee that followed the incident, García makes it clear that Beatrice authorized his actions from the onset. He references Beatrice's requests for intervention twice; first, to talk with the funeral director by phone and second, to make more satisfactory funeral arrangements with the director. García reported:

> I made a long distance call to Three Rivers and asked to talk to the owner of the "Rice Funeral Home." The person that answered the phone said "I am Mr. Kennedy." I stated that I wanted to talk to the owner and he stated: "he would take care of any business."
>
> I informed Mr. Kennedy that I was Dr. Hector Garcia from Corpus Christi and that I was talking by authority of Mrs. Beatrice Longoria and I proceeded:
>
> Mr. Kennedy, Mrs. Longoria has authorized me to ask you to please let her use your funeral home to bring the remains of her husband Felix Longoria.
>
> Mr. Kennedy replied: "It can't be done, and besides we reached an agreement with Mrs. Longoria whereby she would use her home instead and she seemed satisfied."
>
> Mr. Kennedy, Mrs. Longoria was not satisfied and she has authorized me to ask you to please let her use your funeral home.
>
> "That cannot be done," said Mr. Kennedy.
>
> I answered by saying: "But, why, Mr. Kennedy?"
>
> Mr. Kennedy answered "Well, you see, the last time the Latin Americans used the home they had fights and got drunk and raised lots of noise and it didn't look so good. You understand how some of them are."
>
> I said, "Yes, I understand."
>
> Then Mr. Kennedy proceeded: "And what's more the 'whites' here in town would not like it so much and I want to run my business in such a way as so not to hurt them. There are some differences and I am sure that the 'whites' here wouldn't like them to use my funeral home. We have not let them use it and we don't intend to let them start now."
>
> I said "But Mr. Kennedy this man is a veteran, I mean, Soldier who was killed in action and he is worthy of all our efforts and our greatest honors. Doesn't that make a difference? Can we use your funeral home?"

He answered, "No, No, it can't be done and it doesn't make any difference. I don't dislike the Mexican people but I have to run my business so I can't do that. You understand the whites here won't like it."

I answered: "Yes, I understand Mr. Kennedy, Thank you."[55]

García's statement was corroborated by *Corpus Christi Caller Times* reporter George Groh, García's secretary Gladys Blucher, Beatrice Longoria, and even Thomas Kennedy himself. Investigations conducted by John B. Connally, Lyndon B. Johnson, Frank Oltorf of the state legislature, Thomas Sutherland of the Texas Good Neighbor Commission, and Paul J. Reveley from the State Department confirmed the content of the conversation between García and Thomas Kennedy.[56] A report filed by Shag Floore, an information specialist for the American Graves Registration, likewise corroborated García's statement.[57] García's testimony did more than substantiate Beatrice's claims against the Rice Funeral Home and reaffirm his role as mediator in the affair. His account helped to construct the core of the Longoria affair as text. Testimonies derived from García's account would generate and circulate additional layers of discourse, validating the gravity of the matter.

Within twenty-four hours of his conversations with Beatrice Longoria, García took action in his role as mobilizer. He called for the collective response of the Mexican American community. On January 11, García organized a protest vigil at Lamar School in Corpus Christi. The American GI Forum provided the political platform of resistance. The poster announces:

> GRAN JUNTA DE PROTESTA. . . . Cuando una casa Funeraría se Niega a Honrar a los RESTOS de un Ciudadano Americano solamente porque es de origen mejicano entonces es TIEMPO que no unicamente el American GI Forum sino todo el pueblo se levante a protestar esta injusticia.[58] [When a funeral home fails to honor the remains of an American citizen solely because he is of Mexican-origin then it is time that not only the American GI Forum but all the community raises up to protest this injustice.]

Hundreds attended, including Beatrice Longoria and three of Longoria's brothers. Building a coalition of resistance, García circulated widely the telegram he had received from Senator Lyndon B. Johnson:

> I deeply regret to learn that the prejudice of some individuals extends even beyond the grave. I have no authority over civilian funeral homes, nor does the federal government.
>
> However, I have today made arrangements to have Felix Longoria reburied with full military honors in Arlington National Cemetery . . . where the honored dead of our nation's wars rest.[59]

García exercised considerable political leverage over the incident by leaking Lyndon Johnson's telegram to the press. Circulation of Johnson's message to the general public opened the flood gates of debate as "critical and even abusive wires" flowed in from the citizens of Three Rivers to the office of Senator Johnson.[60] Johnson was both confused and distressed over the Three Rivers hate-mail. In a letter to Shag Floore of the American Graves Registration Division, Johnson laments: "Not a single individual [of Three Rivers] has taken the pains to give me any facts concerning the matter, but contented themselves with trying to place at my door the blame for an incident, about which I knew nothing and over which I had no control."[61]

The Forum's protest vigil elicited responses from other national, state, and local leaders.[62] García received a telegram dated January 12 from Major General Harry H. Vaughn, military aid to President Harry S. Truman, declaring, "Discrimination and intolerance unfortunately not illegal, public opinion only weapon for use against" racist actions like those reflected in the Three Rivers case.[63] Apologies poured in from Governor Beauford Jester, Representative John Lyle, Attorney General Price Daniel, R. E. Smith, chairman of the Texas Good Neighbor Commission, Three Rivers mayor J. K. Montgomery, and Thomas Kennedy of the Rice Funeral Home.

Thomas Kennedy's January 12 letter of apology to Beatrice describes the incident as a "misunderstanding" and claims that "at no time did I refuse to bury your husband . . . but I tried to discourage you" because of alleged trouble between Beatrice and her in-laws because of previous family conflicts.[64] However, Kennedy was a newcomer to Three Rivers and had limited previous personal experiences with Beatrice and the Longorias before their meeting. Kennedy's assertion simply reiterates the unsubstantiated claim fabricated by Three Rivers leaders to counter the negative press that poured in from around the country when the incident hit the newspapers. The accusation held no sway over general public opinion, however. Eventually the mayor of Three Rivers relented and issued Beatrice an apology, offering to hold the funeral in his own home after media reports cast the town as bigoted and uncivil.[65]

News of the Three Rivers incident circulated across the nation within days. The *New York Times* headlines announced on January 13, 1949, "GI of Mexican Origin, Denied Rites in Texas, to Be Buried in Arlington." Paul Reveley, Chief of the Division of Mexican Affairs in the State Department, informed Senator Lyndon B. Johnson, "Unfortunately, newspaper articles regarding the case received adverse publicity in the Mexican press and were not conducive to the strengthening of relations between the United States and Mexico."[66] The chain reaction following in the wake of the Longoria affair stirred collective identification in ways that civil rights incidents against Mexican Americans of previous decades throughout the twentieth-century failed to engender.

The discursive and semiotic dimensions of the Longoria incident reenacted the painful funereal scene of Gettysburg and the rhetoric of America's most tragic period in history, words and images of a country divided against itself. The collective reaffirmation of America's egalitarian vision in the wake of World War II foregrounded the basic principles for which the nation fought to protect. Reacting to the news of the Longoria event, the *Detroit Free Press* admonishes:

> He was an American citizen who put on the uniform of his Country in order that this Nation might continue to be free; that men might always enjoy the guarantee of human liberty and dignity contained in the Bill of Rights; that the immortal words of Jefferson in the Declaration of Independence—'life, liberty, and the pursuit of happiness'—might be more than empty words.[67]

The site of Arlington National Cemetery, like the cemetery at Gettysburg, became for twentieth-century America the "supreme locus of liminality . . . the borderland between life and death, time and eternity, past and future," a center of national division and reconciliation.[68] The final burial of Private Félix Longoria at Arlington National Cemetery harkened America back to a moment in which Garry Wills describes as "the crucible of the occasion," a symbolic event that "distilled the meaning of the war, of the nation's purpose, of the remaining task" of a broken nation.[69]

The article on the front page of the January 13 issue of the *New York Times* recounted to the world, in the words of Dr. Héctor P. García, the reasons that the manager of the Rice Funeral Home in Three Rivers, Texas, denied services to the Félix Longoria family. "White people object to the use of the funeral home by people of Mexican origin," explained García. García's pivotal statement excerpted from his January 11 telegram to the lawmakers of the land would reverberate throughout the country in countless iterations to become a national rallying cry for racial justice. García's charge, recirculated in countless venues across the nation, asserts:

> this action is in direct contradiction of those same principles for which this American soldier made the supreme sacrifice in giving his life for his country and for the same people who now deny him the last funeral rites deserving any American hero regardless of his origin.[70]

Reports of the Longoria incident appeared in newspapers across the

United States and Mexico. The *Detroit Free Press* declared on January 14, "A Hero's Return: Bigotry in Texas" and published a political cartoon of a rifle-bearing figure in a Ku Klux Klan hood sitting in front of a flag-draped coffin inscribed with the words "Pvt. Felix Longoria Luzon War Hero of Mexican Descent." The figure of death gazing down on the coffin with black hollow eyes menacingly bars the entrance to the "Three Rivers Funeral Home" beneath the caption, "D'ya Think We Want the Flag of Texas Sullied?."[71]

Letters from around the country followed. In a January 17, 1949, letter of protest, a resident from Flint, Michigan, reacts to Senator Lyndon B. Johnson in disbelief, "To me it does not seem possible that such action could have occurred in the United States." A resident of Los Angeles, California, responds, "It is most disgraceful to have such reactionary attitude toward class and color distingtion [*sic*]."[72] A member of the Young Men's Christian Association at Texas A&M College in College Station, Texas, writes, "Any American who gave his life for the cause of Democracy shed red blood regardless of the color of his skin."[73] Moved by the news of Johnson's intervention on behalf of the Longoria family, Nelson A. Rockefeller writes, "Dear Lyn . . . your action . . . is one of the most heartening things I've read in a long time."[74] A citizen from Washington, D.C., laments, "This is only an example of how a small minority of ignorant, prejudiced 'White' Texas-Americans can besmirch our idea of American Democracy, not only in the United States, but in foreign countries where we are trying to propound democracy against the outrageous suppresion [*sic*] of personal rights and liberties by fascism and communism."[75] The regional director of the National Labor Relations Board in Fort Worth, Texas, praises Johnson:

> I want to express to you my deep appreciation. . . . This healed greatly the wound to his [Longoria's] family and to our State. . . . This action is proof of your liberal statesmanship, and in reviewing the history of our people who have represented us in high offices I find that only the liberals are those who do have a lasting and honored place in our history.[76]

The January 30 issue of the *Dallas Morning News* followed the event closely with reports of the maelstrom of negative press and hate-mail pouring into the town of Three Rivers under the headline "Three Rivers Digs Out of Blizzard of Abuse." Bulletized descriptions depict the tensions that ruptured the naturalized system of institutionalized discrimination in South Texas. "The story exploded over America and Mexico. Indignation meetings followed. Abusive letters, some obscene, and telegrams poured into Three Rivers, a South Texas town of 2,000 people, a quarter of them of Mexican descent."[77]

At the center of the controversy, García emerged as the primary liaison between the Longoria family and public officials, confirming funeral arrangements, negotiating mounting tensions within the Three Rivers community, and meeting with the press. News of the Longoria case spread south of the border, requiring that Governor Beauford Jester meet with Mexican President Miguel Alemán in Matamoras to restore diplomatic relations and pledge to fight discrimination in Texas.[78] Shag Floore went directly to Three Rivers to investigate and indicates in his report to Lt. Col. Stanley H. Partridge, Chief of the American Graves Registration Division: "Various citizens of Three Rivers have an accumulation of communication—letters and wires—that I should say was from six to eight inches high."[79] With hate mail arriving from around the country, R. E. Smith of the Texas Good Neighbor Commission urged García to persuade Beatrice Longoria to reconsider having her husband buried in Texas to restore the peace instead of at Arlington as arranged by Lyndon Johnson. Smith wrote:

> We all agree that the happening at Three Rivers is to be regretted, and we must bear in mind that the reputation of Texas will be at stake in history's recording of this very delicate matter.
>
> If you will talk to the widow of Felix Longoria and ask her if she would be agreeable to a change of plans whereby this American soldier's body would be brought back to Texas for reburial at Three Rivers, or at least in Texas. . . . [T]he Governor will do everything possible to show her that he approves of this action [to] bring the Hero's body back to Texas where it should be, and would have been had it not been for whatever action that caused all of this trouble.[80]

Beatrice, however, felt that the Three River apologies and offers had come too late and wanted an Arlington burial for her husband.[81] Her letter to Thomas Kennedy, which was published in the January 20, 1949, issue of the *Three Rivers News*, reasserted her decision to bury Félix at Arlington with this closing note: "I want to let you know that I bear no grudge and still think greatly of all the people from Three Rivers."[82] García stood firm with her. He organized fund-raising efforts to underwrite the travel expenses for the Longoria family's trip to Washington, D.C., reporting over $1,522 had been raised by the American GI Forum, schools, and other civic organizations.[83]

As pressure mounted to keep Longoria's body in Texas, García remained at the center of the fray protecting the wishes of Beatrice and her family. On January 14, Shag Floore went to Corpus Christi to interview García after meeting with citizens of Three Rivers. Floore's report indicates that García wanted to restore harmony to the community and sought Floore's help in having Félix's body promptly returned to the family.[84] After his meeting with García, Floore called Governor Jester to ask his prompt intervention. Floore also makes note that the animosity directed at García from Representative Jeff Gray of Live Oak had "a political angle" because of García's ardent opposition to Gray's 1946 candidacy for the state legislature during which time García "went all over the county talking against Mr. Gray who was defeated." In 1948, Gray ran again "with Dr. Garcia working against him but Mr. Gray was elected this time."[85]

Representative Gray, in concert with the leaders of Three Rivers and Live Oak County, considered García a troublemaker and dismissed García's involvement in the Longoria matter as little more than a rhetorical ploy to gain political leverage over Gray. In a memo to the American GI Forum membership, García reported:

> Rep. [J. F.] Gray from Live Oak County is sore . . . because we exposed Mathis with its bad schools and its bad labor camps. Now this year we have exposed the Longoria incident at Three Rivers and also the practices of segregation in George West County, seat of Live Oak County.[86]

Under the aegis of LULAC, García had led an investigation of discrimination practices throughout Representative Gray's area of jurisdiction. Apparently, he and members of the state and local leadership had not forgotten García's name or civil rights agenda. They might not have reacted as quickly or as vehemently toward García if he had been an unknown agitator. Moreover, they might have been more prone to ignore García as a potential threat to their political positions had they not had previously dealings with him. But when news of the Longoria case broke, the rhetorical tug-of-war was on. They knew García was a tenacious advocate of Mexican American issues, and they reacted as if they had a tiger by the tail (or a tiger had them by the tail). These Anglo officials were not above discrediting García and making false statements about the Longoria family in the local newspapers.

On January 31, the Longoria family met with García to make the final decision about Félix's final resting place. John B. Connally, a legislative assistant, informed Lyndon Johnson that Mexican officials had registered their complaints about the matter with Paul Reveley of the State Department and wanted the "salutary effect" that an Arlington burial would provide. Connally conveyed his conversation with Reveley:

> Mr. Reveley pointed out that in the past few years, including last year, that the agreement in which the United States signed with Mexico concerning Mexican workers entering the United States during certain periods of the year . . . excluded Texas because of incidents which have arisen regarding

the treatment of Mexican labor in the State. Mr. Reveley told me that he thought the [Longoria] incident might have a disastrous affect [*sic*] on their negotiations unless they were able to present the solution in such a way as to counteract the incident itself . . .

He pointed out that of course the Mexican government officially could take no position in the matter since Felix Longoria was an American citizen, but that wasn't the point at all—not what they said officially but how they felt unofficially would more often than not affect our relations with them.[87]

The Mexican government and Reveley extended the suggestion that Johnson's office pressure García and the Longorias to agree to the Arlington ceremony. How much of this information reached García and the Longorias is not clear. If García wanted to sabotage *bracero* negotiations, a binational agreement he strongly opposed, he could have steered the Longorias away from the more conciliatory gesture of an Arlington funeral. García did not, however. He did not use the Longoria affair for political leverage against the *bracero* program. He honored the wishes of the family and he honored Johnson's generous offer to intervene on their behalf. The Longoria family accepted Johnson's offer for an Arlington burial in a January 31 letter confirming funeral arrangements and thanking Johnson. "According to instructions given us by Dr. Garcia, we the widow Mrs. Beatrice Longoria, the father and mother and brothers of Felix Longoria wish you to arrange for the funeral . . ."[88] They requested that a Catholic service precede graveside rites at Arlington. García made all travel arrangements for the family.

Private Félix Longoria was buried with full military honors on February 16, 1949, in a ceremony honoring nineteen other soldiers at Arlington National Cemetery. Beatrice and her daughter, Adelita, attended with members of the Longoria family by her side. Senator Johnson and Lady Bird Johnson were in attendance as was Dr. Héctor García, Representative John Lyle of Corpus Christi, Major General Harry Vaughn and First Secretary Justo Sierra of the Mexican Embassy. Officials from the Mexican Army and Navy "brought a huge wreath from the Ambassador."[89] The Chief of the Division of Mexican Affairs, Paul Reveley likewise attended. The *Dallas Morning News* depicts the scene:

Whether there had been "discrimination"—even after death—against Pvt. Felix Longoria was still a subject of dispute as the last sweet notes of "Taps" echoed over the rolling knolls and around the white marble tablets that mark the final resting places of America's war dead.[90]

No one lingered long after the ceremony, promptly returning that same day to their homes and offices. But the Longoria affair was not over.

Héctor P. García, Lyndon B. Johnson, and the Rhetorics of Disputation

The Longoria event, in many respects, prefigured the rhetorics of disputation that García and Johnson would eventually engage in not only in this early post-war historical moment, but beyond with the introduction of the 1965 civil rights legislation sixteen years later. This incendiary event continued to spread through the national media for several months in spite of Johnson's stated wishes that the matter would be immediately closed. Johnson's February 16, 1949, letter to García calls the event an "impressive ceremony" and thanks García for his helpfulness. Johnson closes his letter reasserting, "As I told you, I have not sought and do not seek any personal attention for my small role in this. I hope there will be no further reason for this to linger in the newspapers or instigate unnecessary contention."[91] In spite of Johnson's hope that the matter would quietly fade, the burial of Private Felix Longoria was promptly followed by a tense, lengthy, and hotly contested legislative investigation. Longoria's burial did not issue in a moment of closure but opened up an occasion for ongoing disputation. An article in the *Corpus Christi Caller Times* reports, "Citizens of Three Rivers will leave no stones unturned to counteract the 'bad publicity' to which their town has fallen victim."[92] An editorial in the *Santa Fe New Mexican* observes:

> Everywhere people are speaking out against such intolerance and are happy that arrangements have been made to give the Texas GI an honorable funeral in Arlington National Cemetery. The furor raised by the shoddy treatment for the bodies of our dark skinned soldiers indicates that maybe we are coming of age at last with a promise of becoming a nation of freedom and equality that we talk so much about but have never achieved.[93]

Thomas Sutherland of the Texas Good Neighbor Commission reported to the press that diplomatic negotiations with Mexico over the *bracero* immigrant labor program had "stopped because of the Longoria incident."[94]

Not all public reactions demonstrated solidarity with the Longorias nor applauded García and Johnson's acts of intervention. A resident of Three Rivers charges in a letter to Johnson, "I believe you did more harm for the state of Texas in five minutes of unguarded speech than you can undo in the few years and possibly a very few you are a U.S. Senator."[95] In an open letter to Johnson, the editors of the *Three Rivers News* lamented:

> Senator, you can very easily understand why the citizens of Three Rivers are so stunned. . . . If you could read some of the vile letters that we businessmen and officials are receiving blaming the citizens of Three Rivers, Live Oak County, and State of Texas, you could not but feel that you had some part in it.[96]

The divisions that ruptured the town of Three Rivers in 1949 over the Félix Longoria incident were emblematic of the unrest erupting within inequitable social orders throughout the nation and the world. In the wake of World War II and the international struggle against totalitarianism, the Longoria incident made visible the violations of basic social rights and civil liberties at the most local level. The Three Rivers controversy rocked the nation, coalescing conflicts on the home front over disparities between Americanist egalitarian principles and the practice of "ascriptive inequality."[97]

García and Johnson remained in the hot seat even after the Longorias resumed their lives. Sara Moreno Posas, sister of Beatrice Longoria, reflected decades later on García's role, "We were very, very grateful. We just did not expect any action like that. At the time, things just did not get done like that. There were no other people who would take action."[98] García would serve as a key witness in the contentious hearings that followed, while Johnson waited out the storm back in Austin. Convened by state Representative J. F. Gray of Live Oak County, this legislative panel sought to restore the reputation of his Three Rivers constituency and to dismantle the Texas Good Neighbor Commission to keep troublemakers like the executive secretary, Thomas Sutherland, and activists like Héctor García from exposing other cases of this kind. The day after the Longoria funeral, Gray presented the following resolution during the fifty-first legislative session on February 17, 1949:

> Whereas, International publicity has been given to the reburial of one of our returning soldiers, Felix Longoria, and
>
> Whereas, So many conflicting reports have been circulated and continue to circulate, some such reports alleging that discrimination had been shown in the handling of his funeral arrangements, and
>
> Whereas, to establish the accuracy of such acquisition or the incorrectness of such acquisition is now absolutely necessary for the continuation of good relations among the peoples of South Texas and to our international relations. . . .
>
> Now therefore be it resolved by the Members of the House of Representatives that the Speaker of the House, at his earliest convenience, be instructed and is hereby instructed to appoint a committee composed of five members from the House empowering such committee with authority to subpoena witnesses and administer oath and to take evidence and that the committee be instructed to do all things necessary to find and report back to this House the truth in this controversy not later than March 1, 1949, to the end that justice may be done.[99]

Justice would "be done," but only after a long, circuitous process. LULAC attorney Gus García represented the Longoria family in the investigation. Described as "brilliant, flamboyant, with eyes that bored into one's soul," Gus García was a proven "master of courtroom debate."[100] The five-member investigative committee, consisting of Cecil Storey, Frank Oltorf, Byron Tinsley, Thomas Cheatham, and James Marvin Windham, went to Three Rivers to interview witnesses. The tension outside the Rotary Club building as Héctor García, Sutherland, and the Longorias testified before the committee reflected what Sutherland later compared to a showdown in an old Western movie. Sutherland, who eventually became an English professor at the University of Texas at Arlington, described:

> It was a dangerous atmosphere. It was like high noon in a Western movie. That's how ugly the attitude of the hangers-around was. One man showed a Bowie knife. And other men said in loud voices so they could be overheard: "You know, really, this Longoria bunch, they're just a bunch of greasers. . . . [A] South Texas sheriff with a reputation as a killer of Mexicans also was present—just standing around with his gun on . . . and long and lean and looking just as mean as his .45.[101]

During the five days of hearings, the funeral director, Thomas Kennedy, admitted saying "whites would not like it" if Beatrice Longoria used the chapel for the funeral. Headlines in the *Corpus Christi Caller Times* on March 11, 1949, at the peak of the investigative hearings, announced "'Obscene' Mail on Longoria Case Sent Three Rivers Mayor: Dr. Garcia Repeats Forum Charge of Discrimination."[102] Reports of the hearings spread throughout the nation and Mexico.

Gus García's March 16, 1949, letter describes the committee's aim to blame Johnson and Héctor García for fabricating the incident for political leverage. He apprised Johnson:

> The Chairman wanted to establish the theory that you and Doctor Garcia had ramrodded the whole thing for the publicity purposes, but I believe the record is clear on that point. . . . It is my opinion that the committee will probably render a four to one report clearing Three Rivers of discrimination, but certainly the language will have to be very soft because the record is overwhelmingly conclusive that there was discrimination at the onset. Furthermore, Frank (Representative Frank Oltorf) intends to write a blistering dissent and I am going to help him prepare it.
>
> The committee is so confused by the unexpected turn of events that it has obtained a two-weeks extension from the legislature for the filing of the its report. Doctor Garcia made a splendid witness. He was calm, deliberate,

and well-informed. He dispelled any idea that might have existed that he is a "crackpot" or rabid rabble-rouser.[103]

Gus García's March 25, 1949, letter to Johnson further describes the mounting tension as the investigation came to a close. Gus García reported:

> [T]he loaded committee is now having a difficult time making up its mind . . . because of the tremendous pressure being exerted by powerful political figures including the Governor himself. . . . [T]his is the first time that all the conservative elements including some notorious Dixiecrats are on my side of the argument.
>
> This attitude of course is due to the International implications that they attach to this matter. They undoubtedly are recalling the repercussion that the incident had in Mexico and since the International labor agreement is hanging in the balance, they probably fear dire results if the report is too obviously a whitewash.[104]

When the final majority report was released on April 7, 1949, Gus García sent these words of encouragement to Johnson and John B. Connally: "I suggest that we adopt the motto of the tool grinders' union: 'illegitimi non carborondum . . . don't let the bastards grind you down.'"[105] The investigating committee had taken testimonies from nineteen witnesses and generated three volumes of material, "aggregating some 372 pages." The majority report signed by Storey, Cheatham, Windham, and Tinsley concluded:

> This committee therefore concludes that there was no discrimination on the part of the undertaker at Three Rivers, Texas, relative to the proposed burial of the body of Felix Longoria.[106]

One committee member remained unconvinced. The dissenting minority report filed by Frank Oltorf countered the majority report's conclusion with this closing statement:

> The statements of Mr. George Groh, a disinterested reporter, are indisputable and undeniable. I cannot look into the heart of Mr. Kennedy to ascertain his true intent but can only accept his oral words which appear to me discriminatory.[107]

It was not the outcome Johnson or García had hoped for, but it was a better outcome than the situation might have rendered. The following day, on April 8, Tinsley requested that his name be removed from the majority report with this explanation, "It was my feeling that there was haste in making a majority report into the Longoria incident."[108] State Senator Rogers Kelley publicly condemned the majority report, calling it a "tragic blot on the democracy of

Texas and the United States."[109] The report was not accepted by the House and the matter was given no further legislative attention.

Héctor García returned to his medical practice and the gritty work of organizing the nascent American GI Forum. Three weeks after the legislative reports were released, García wrote to an American GI Forum leader in Robstown, Texas: "We have to forge ahead and work. . . . We will keep on working and organizing. If you know any towns that wish to be organized send me somebody's name . . . and I will take care of it."[110] Gus García returned to his San Antonio law practice, chalking up another victory to LULAC's longstanding record fighting discrimination in the state. It was, however, an unprecedented moment for Héctor García and the American GI Forum. The Longoria incident represented their first civil rights case. It was international in scope and had won over the support of some of the most important figures in the United States and Mexico. Dignity restored, honor became "the capital of the dispossessed."[111] The victory, however, was short-lived and elusive. No new laws were made. No monetary reparations were realized. No books were written. Longoria as a folk hero never evolved into a collective "mythic symbol" of American civil rights reform or enduring emblem of social justice beyond South Texas.[112] The symbolic value of the Longoria case was, nevertheless, far reaching.

A Dramatistic Analysis of the Longoria Incident

Kenneth Burke's dramatism provides a useful framework for mapping rhetorical action in the Longoria case.[113] García as an agent acting on behalf of Longoria and his family through the agency of instrumental rhetorics set the stage for Mexican Americans' purposeful engagement with national politics. Symbolic value was constructed around the Longoria incident through the production and interpretation of disparate discourses. Moreover, rhetorical construction of the Longoria incident makes visible the ideological implications and the normative function of the history-making processes surrounding the event. Dramatism foregrounds "the constitutive role of discourse in human culture and knowledge."[114] The Longoria incident, as such, functions as a useful representative anecdote to illustrate the struggle for inclusion by a people juxtaposed geographically, politically, linguistically, and culturally and reenacting tropologically the sacrifices implicit in America's terms of citizenship.[115]

In "Dialectic of the Scapegoat," Burke's notion of sacrifice as a means of forging solidarity and collective identity aptly applies to the drama of the Longoria burial. The mythic construction of the scapegoat that undergirds the Judeo-Christian model of redemption, as well as epic narratives of war, becomes especially relevant to an understanding of the symbolic power of the Longoria affair. The remains of Longoria as "scapegoat" or "charism" served as an object of "atonement" or "vessel" that embodied the suffering of the group. Burke suggests: "For the scapegoat is 'charismatic,' a vicar. As such, it is profoundly consubstantial with those who, looking upon it as a chosen vessel, would ritualistically cleanse themselves by loading the burden of their own inequities upon it."[116]

The Longoria affair demonstrates how the process of death and identification has been integral to the history of Mexican American civic inclusion. Conflicts over national inclusion and membership between "'one's own' and the 'other'" function as critical facets of national behavior.[117] Conflicts over citizenship reflect not just what our "society holds most dear . . . but also who has the power ultimately to settle disputes."[118] What U.S. society has held most dear hinges like a swinging door on issues of race. The Longoria case suggests that civic identity, rather than being a static condition, is a performance, linguistically and rhetorically constituted. Even dead citizens can take on (symbolic) lives.

Through the discursive circulation of the Longoria incident via García, government officials in the United States and Mexico, the media, and Mexican American protesters, the civic identity of Longoria took on a narrative life. Longoria became a text, a strand of discourse from which other strands evolved. The post-war folk song, *"el corrido de discriminación a un mártir,"* evolved into what Manuel Peña describes as "prosaic rhetoric" about the "Mexican's oppression at the hands of insensitive Anglo American society.[119] Recast twenty years later in the post-Chicano era by Israel Bustamante's "A Soldier Named Felix Longoria," the mythical Longoria is cast as "a young Chicano who so proudly went along."[120] The politicization of Longoria's identity from "Mexican" to "Chicano" over time stands in puzzling juxtaposition against the consistent absence of García and the persistent presence of LBJ in both accounts.

Through the process of textual construction, Private Félix Longoria acquired more symbolic value in death than he would have had he returned to the United States alive. Thousands of decorated Mexican-origin soldiers returned from the war without so much as a ripple in the national narrative fabric. Their poignant lives of service remained unrecognized. Here then is the symbolic value of García's role. Adopting the collective persona of the American GI Forum, García acted as a speaking agent on behalf of Beatrice, directly, and Félix, indirectly. His discursive performance transformed the inert civic identity of Longoria, a dead soldier, into a viable and problematic presence. And America took notice.

Metaphorically, synedochically, and metonymically, the burial of Private Félix Longoria evoked an unprecedented response in the American public. Media coverage throughout the twentieth century of mob violence and lynchings never captured the attention of as many levels of American society as the Longoria incident did. The Longoria story stirred elite whites such as Nelson Rockefeller and Lyndon B. Johnson, military figures such as Major General Harry Vaughn, left wing labor activists, right wing military organizations, religious groups, local, national, and international leaders and citizens. Longoria galvanized not only Mexican Americans but Americans from other diverse positions as well to recover the democratic vision threatened by the war.

By giving public language to the personal experience of one Mexican American family, García helped to complicate the conversation on race in America and reshape the rhetorical situation of modern civil rights reform. Chapters 4 and 5 examine how the discussion initiated with the Longoria affair was recirculated over the following two decades. The textual history of the Longoria incident illustrates that the tropological value of the moment endured even while the initiating sources were effaced from the record. The archeology of the Longoria incident, therefore, is most productively recovered through its tropes.

As metaphor, the death of Private Longoria operated as an emblem around which disparate social groups found meaning, a potent symbol of heroism and sacrifice. Americans from every facet of the post-war situation could identify with the dead soldier as trope, an emblem of loss touching every family regardless of race, class, or culture. Returning Mexican soldiers had regularly been denied dignity and access to public services for years without the slightest concern or objection from the local or national community. Death, however, became the rhetorical device around which individuals and groups would forge identification. Death represented an absence calling for communion and solidarity.

Synedochically, the body of Félix Longoria became a trope representing the man, whole, heroic, noble. The remains of this Mexican American soldier evoked more response than any other entity related to the Mexican American civic identity. The dead soldier depicted in the media headlines and photographs became a profound and compelling imaginary construction: the image of the Longoria family gathered beside the flag-draped coffin; Félix Longoria's eight-year-old daughter, Adelita, staring hauntingly at the coffin; his wife, Beatrice, huddled and bowed against the drizzling rain and cold, accompanied by Major General Harry Vaughn, Senator Lyndon B. Johnson, Representative John Lyle, and Justo Sierra, First Secretary of the Mexican Embassy. The death of Félix Longoria was both a reduction and an amplification—the reduction of the man, the amplification of a people.

Metonymically, Longoria represented the honor and value of being Mexican in American society. As a metaphor of resistance, Longoria both embodied American values of duty, service, and sacrifice and counteracted America's exploitive, imperialist past. Longoria, like the celebrated folk heroes of the Mexican Revolution, represented a paradoxical emblem.[121] Private Félix Longoria as a Texas Mexican American became larger in death than life itself. As representative of a "forgotten" people, Longoria would become a symbol for all Mexican Americans. The *Dallas Morning News* describes the iconic performance: "The women wept quietly at the grave. . . . Little Adelita was curious, understanding little even as her mother laid a picture on the grave of the mustached boy who had been her father."[122]

The *Austin American* captures the *pathos* as well as the *ethos* of the event and recounts the patriotic ritualism of the scene signifying Longoria's elevated status as an American war hero: "His reburial was not far from the burial site of General of the Armies John J. Pershing. . . . When the firing squad had fired three rounds and taps were sounded General Vaughn, Johnson, and Lyle were among the first to step up and offer their condolences to the family."[123] Longoria as an absence was transformed into a collective presence representing the countless Mexican American soldiers who served honorably in the war effort.

The Longoria incident as a galvanizing event became a crucible of national identification making the plight of Mexican Americans and the inequities of hereditary privilege visible. Death became an index of life, an impetus for confronting the contradictions of being a Mexican in American society. It was an occasion to which García applied the kind of radical rhetoric and coalition-building strategies that civil rights activists in his wake would come to employ some ten to fifteen years later. García's discourse of resistance and the subsequent semiotic construction of the Longoria burial ritual forged America's identification with the condition of the Mexican American in a way that had never been seen. The American public as well as state and national elected officials joined in García's cry against the violence of racism and discrimination.[124]

García's telegram informing public officials of the incident called attention to the "sacrifice" that twenty-six year old Private Félix Longoria made on behalf of his country. In the tragic action surrounding his funeral, Longoria became the sacrificial lamb of his people, a forgotten tribe. His dishonor is transformed into the honor of his people on both sides of the border. At multiple dimensions, the Longoria incident both relieved and exacerbated the burden of America's inequitable social order.

In many respects, the Longoria case united Mexican Americans with the national community, a response resonant with America's reaction to the tragic drama performed on the battlefields of Gettysburg. The twentieth-century national symbolic sacrifice of the Mexican American soldier, refused burial upon his return to the U.S. border, profoundly aligned with America's great nineteenth-century civic tragedy. Soldiers, black and white, slaughtered on the boundaries between the North and the South, symbolized both the loss and the possibility of a mythic national order. The reinterment of Private Félix Longoria at Arlington National Cemetery enacted a democratic ideal boldly envisioned and painfully unrealized. In this gap, symbolic caesura between the achieved and the unachieved, García transformed the tragedy of the Longoria incident toward a dialectal movement.

Leland Griffin's model of analysis, "a dramatistic theory of the rhetoric of movements," helps to situate the Longoria incident as critical to the emergence of the Mexican American civil rights movement that followed in its wake.[125] Griffin argues that movements begin when "some pivotal individual or group" suffers alienation within a certain social situation and is motivated by the vision of a "mythic order" or social structure.[126] Operating on the assumptions that all movements are essentially political and moral—"strivings for salvation, perfection, the good"—Griffin maintains that movements are studies of progression, drama, and form.[127] Cycles of hierarchical assertion, guilt, sacrifice, atonement, and redemption which mark the course of human history also inform the cycles of group formation, growth, death, and regeneration.[128] Recognizing the mobilizing value of the Longoria case, Manuel Peña contends:

> The Longoria incident was thus important because, while it was by no means the first time that Mexicans had mobilized their resources to right what they considered a wrong committed against them, it did serve to highlight (to act as a "catalyst" for) the intensifying civil rights activities that marked the post-war phase of the Mexican in the United States.[129]

Auxesis and the Construction of the Longoria Incident as National Drama

García's handling of the 1949 Longoria incident demonstrated that he understood the rhetorical device of *enargia*, the use of vivid, palpable description. The application of *auxesis*, the rhetorical strategy of amplification designed "to make something more important" by situating it in a climactic series functioned as a key strategy in the construction of the national drama of Longoria incident.[130] García's use of *auxesis* in his representation of the Longoria affair reflects the same approach he used to stir social action around other instances of discrimination such as school segregation, migrant labor camps, poll taxes, and access to public services. Like Du Bois's sociological approach to exposing international conditions of subjugation, García relied on instrumental discourse and layers of evidence as a primary device. His pragmatic application of inquiry, evidence gathering, verification, and reporting to build a body of "fact" leaned heavily on empirical methods, as well as local knowledge and experience. Evidence provided amplification. García approached the Longoria affair in "a practical, atheoretical way . . . and by injecting an element of cultural moralism."[131]

As a practitioner of both rhetorical and medical arts, García's role in the Longoria case connects him not only to a circumscribed historical moment but also to a long legacy of healing. From Socrates to Burke, the notion of rhetoric as a healing art shapes the backbone of Western historical thought. Rites of reburial, the festival of the fallen soldier, and the performance of *epitaphios*, funeral oratory, represent the earliest forms of Athenian rhetorical practice.[132] Designed to laud the dead and lead survivors into the future, the art of rhetoric has functioned as the historical verbal balm to heal the wounds of loss and death. In Plato's *Phaedrus*, Socrates offers this analogue: "The method of the art of healing is much the same as that of rhetoric. . . . In both cases you must analyze a nature, in one that of the body and in the other that of the soul."[133] García's capacity to respond to the whole person, in life and death, distinguished him as a physician and rhetorician. Likewise, Kenneth Burke's assertion that rhetoric, like love, is "a communion of estranged entities" aptly captures the significance of the Longoria case to American civil rights history.[134] The rhetorical import of the event coalesced around the communion of disparate groups that ultimately joined at Arlington National Cemetery in January 1949 to honor the fallen soldier.

García's appropriation of the dominant discourse, his effective manipulation of the genres of instrumental rhetoric, and his stirring evocation of America's collective memory successfully implicated America's failure to live up to its democratic ideals. In an April 16, 1949, letter to Pauline Kibbe, García describes a dramatization of the Longoria affair broadcast over the radio. García reports: "Only last week in a radio program (Civil Rights?) Claude Rains dramatized the incident taking the part of Felix Longoria. The dramatization was carried out to empahzie [*sic*] the Constitution."[135] While the content of this transcript is not known, the dramatic reconstruction of the event suggests that the community both recognized and celebrated the symbolic value of the moment.[136] Unfortunately, the dramatization seems to have existed only as an oral performance. Without a text, there remains only the memory of the community and the body of instrumental discourse García generated and instigated to represent the intricacies of the Longoria affair.

Responding to the post-war rhetorical situation and the anti-totalitarian tenor of the era, García advanced a strand of discourse that became the initiating force behind the national drama of the Longoria affair. Through García's intervention and sustained leadership, the Longoria incident evolved into a galvanizing moment, mobilizing and organizing disparate groups toward the emergence of a post-war Mexican American civil rights movement. The occasion would provide García and his followers with critical training in moral protest. Although the Longoria incident endured in the collective memory of the community at the level of lore, as exemplified in the folk song, *"el corrido de discriminación a un mártir"* and the poem "A Soldier Named Felix Longoria," the event circulated without explanatory apparatus or a body of text to bear witness to García's role or to interpret the event in light of Mexican American civil rights activism. Until very recently, Lyndon B. Johnson, not García or the American GI Forum, has received primary recognition for the outcome of the Longoria case.

It is also important to consider that without the patriotic aegis and grassroots support of the American GI Forum, García's radical rhetoric implicating America and the disparities in the twentieth-century justice system would never have achieved such far-reaching impact. Echoing Raúl Yzaguirre, president of the National Council of La Raza, Henry A. J. Ramos argues that the American GI Forum was the only Hispanic organization in that era that could withstand the threats of anti-communist groups. Because of a membership comprised of veterans, families, and a highly active Ladies Auxiliary, the American GI Forum did not reflect the profile of what McCarthy-era watchdogs regarded as subversive "anti-American" organizations.[137] Under the banner of the American GI Forum, Mexican American civil rights activists were able to negotiate political and social terrain foreclosed to other minority advocacy groups.

In the following five decades of historical recasting, the Longoria case continues to acquire layers of significance for Texas Mexican Americans and the Texas Anglo establishment. García and the American GI Forum initiated the drama and infused the Longoria case with the allegorical impulse and historical resonance. In the wake of the Longoria affair, the American GI Forum would become, under García's direction, the "political conscience" of an emerging Mexican American middle class.[138]

The Longoria incident unequivocally illustrated the fact that racism extended beyond "the color line" of black-and-white as well as challenged citizens across the country to consider America's historical contradictory terms of inclusion. Without the Longoria incident as precedent and the formation of enduring coalitions forged by García between grassroots activists and elected officials from local and state levels up to the presidency, it is worth considering whether civil rights reforms of the 1960s would have advanced as they did.

Major Héctor P. García, U.S. Army, serving in Europe during World War II.
Dr. Héctor P. García Papers, Special Collections and Archives, Mary and Jeff Bell Library, Texas A&M
University–Corpus Christi.

Major Héctor P. García and Mrs. Wanda García on their honeymoon in Naples, Italy, 1945. Dr. Héctor P. García Papers, Special Collections and Archives, Mary and Jeff Bell Library, Texas A&M University–Corpus Christi.

Portrait of Major Héctor P. García from World War II.
Dr. Héctor P. García Papers, Special Collections and Archives, Mary and Jeff Bell Library,
Texas A&M University–Corpus Christi.

Burial site of Private Félix Longoria, February 16, 1949, at Arlington National Cemetery. *Front right:* Beatrice and Adelita Longoria. *Second row, right:* Major General Harry Vaughn.

Dr. Héctor P. García Papers, Special Collections and Archives, Mary and Jeff Bell Library, Texas A&M University–Corpus Christi.

Dr. Héctor P. García at an American GI Forum meeting in Corpus Christi, December 1956.

Dr. Héctor P. García Papers, Special Collections and Archives, Mary and Jeff Bell Library, Texas A&M University–Corpus Christi.

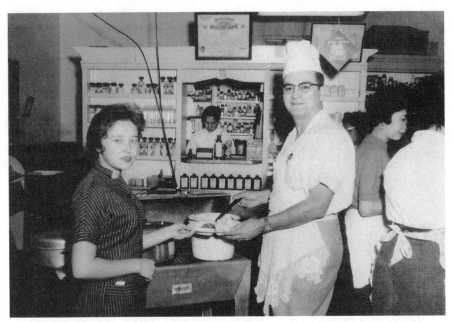

Dr. Héctor P. García serving dinner to members of the American GI Forum Ladies Auxiliary at his Morgan Avenue pharmacy, Corpus Christi, 1957. Dr. Héctor P. García Papers, Special Collections and Archives, Mary and Jeff Bell Library, Texas A&M University–Corpus Christi.

American GI Forum members rallying for the Viva Kennedy Campaign.
Dr. Héctor P. García Papers, Special Collections and Archives, Mary and Jeff Bell Library, Texas A&M University–Corpus Christi.

Dr. Héctor P. García, Lyndon B. Johnson, and Lady Bird Johnson on the campaign trail, 1960.
Dr. Héctor P. García Papers, Special Collections and Archives, Mary and Jeff Bell Library, Texas A&M University–Corpus Christi.

Dr. Héctor P. García and the American GI Forum televised tribute to the late President John
F. Kennedy, November 1965. Dr. Héctor P. García Papers, Special Collections and Archives, Mary and Jeff Bell
Library, Texas A&M University–Corpus Christi.

Dr. Héctor P. García and Vicente Ximenes at the Lincoln Memorial, Washington, D.C., 1961.

Dr. Héctor P. García Papers, Special Collections and Archives, Mary and Jeff Bell Library, Texas A&M University–Corpus Christi.

Dr. Héctor P. García and President Lyndon B. Johnson on the White House lawn, 1965.
Dr. Héctor P. García Papers, Special Collections and Archives, Mary and Jeff Bell Library, Texas A&M
University–Corpus Christi.

Dr. Héctor P. García *(seated)* and Vicente Ximenes at the Cabinet Committee Hearings on Mexican American Affairs, El Paso, 1967. Dr. Héctor P. García Papers, Special Collections and Archives, Mary and Jeff Bell Library, Texas A&M University–Corpus Christi.

Dr. Héctor P. García *(far right)* and Dr. Cleo García *(far left)* participating in La Marcha farm worker protest in Corpus Christi, 1966. Dr. Héctor P. García Papers, Special Collections and Archives, Mary and Jeff Bell Library, Texas A&M University–Corpus Christi.

Dr. Héctor P. García giving testimony in Corpus Christi during the school desegregation hearings, 1969. Dr. Héctor P. García Papers, Special Collections and Archives, Mary and Jeff Bell Library, Texas A&M University–Corpus Christi.

Dr. Héctor P. García and Dr. Cleo García participating in a local protest, Corpus Christi, 1978. Dr. Héctor P. García Papers, Special Collections and Archives, Mary and Jeff Bell Library, Texas A&M University–Corpus Christi.

Dr. Héctor P. García giving an address at the American GI Forum Convention, Corpus Christi. Dr. Héctor P. García Papers, Special Collections and Archives, Mary and Jeff Bell Library, Texas A&M University–Corpus Christi.

Immigration and the Rhetorics of Race, Caste, and Citizenship   4

*H*éctor P. García emerged onto the national scene after the Longoria incident as a political insider, reweaving the discourses of the military, medical, legislative, academic, and political communities to demand inclusion of Mexican-origin citizens in U.S. democratic participation.[1] García's strand of rhetoric represents a "counterstory" within the narrative of post-war civil rights activism that demonstrates the contradictory ideologies embedded within the "open texture" of U.S. civil rights policies and immigration law.[2]

Immigration issues appeared early in García's civil rights rhetoric. The growing presence of Mexican laborers, those protected under the 1942 *bracero* agreements and those working without documentation, represented an urgency moving García into a stance of resistance. This chapter examines García's rhetorical engagement with the *bracero* program and the so-called "wetback problem" during the post-war era. The rhetorical moves exercised by García and the American GI Forum in reaction to the Mexican labor situation generated some of their most problematic discourses. Calling for fair labor practices and greater economic mobility, García's rhetoric made visible discriminatory practices against Mexican-origin citizens in the U.S., particularly farm laborers. These tactics, however, frequently compromised the dignity and human rights of Mexican "guest workers" and undocumented laborers who were competing for the same economic opportunities as Mexican-origin U.S. citizens.

This chapter traces García's immigration discourse from 1949 through 1960. It begins with an overview of the South Texas socioeconomic and political situation, followed by examination of the impact of the *braceros* on Mexican American social development and civil rights. Two government policies, the *bracero* work program agreement of 1942 and the Texas Caucasian Race Resolution of 1943, shaped the discourses of inclusion generated by García and his generation of post-war reformers.

As a historically colonized people, Mexican-origin people claim a long and conflicted experience within U.S. and Texas socioeconomic and political configurations. Mexican-origin groups have lived for centuries on what is little more than an artificial barrier dividing a contiguous region some call Greater Mexico. The ubiquitous presence of documented and undocumented immigrants has profoundly influenced the Mexican American struggle for national inclusion. For these reasons and many others, questions concerning citizenship and national identity have been central to Mexican American civil rights issues for over a hundred and fifty years.

A critical moment in the historical process of Mexican migrant circulation begins with the institutionalization of the *bracero* immigrant labor program nearly sixty years ago. Paralleling the emergence of the "Mexican American Generation" of the mid-twentieth century, the massive influx of undocumented workers and Mexican laborers known as *braceros* permanently reconfigured the socioeconomic and political landscape of Texas and the United States. U.S. participation in World War II and the consequent loss and reappropriation of industrial and agricultural labor left a void that Mexican migrant workers surged to fill. As a tertiary and expendable labor force, the *braceros* moved with the ebb and flow of U.S. labor demands for over two decades.

The binational agreement known as the *bracero* labor program, conceived and drafted in Mexico City during the Inter-American Conference on Agriculture by the U.S. Secretary of Agriculture and Mexican government officials, was institutionalized and implemented on August 4, 1942.[3] The primary objective for the United States was to secure access to a ready supply of agricultural laborers. Mexico's primary interest was to enact "strict guarantees governing wages, transportation, housing, and protections for its workers against discrimination and exploitation."[4] This binational agreement held for over twenty years. Intricately linked initially to the U.S. investment in the war and then to the maintenance of the supercharged post-war economy, the *bracero* program catalyzed the largest exodus of Mexican emigrants, legally and illegally, into the United States since the Revolution of 1910.[5]

The introduction of the Caucasian Race Resolution by Governor Coke Stevenson and adopted by the Texas state legislature in 1943 further complicated and racially polarized the Texas sociopolitical climate. The Caucasian Race Resolution made the bold declaration that Latin America peoples belonged on the "white" side of the color line. Approved on May 6, 1943, the Caucasian Race Resolution represented a rhetorical act of international diplomacy in the wake of the *bracero* agreements. It was passed by the Texas forty-eighth legislature to placate the Mexican government following the adoption and implementation of the 1942 *bracero* program.[6] Increasing incidents of discrimination and hate crimes against Mexican-origin people in the United States prompted the Mexican government to threaten suspension of the guest worker program.[7] According to Chandler Davidson, whites in Texas during the mid-1940s were "deadly intent on maintaining their privileges through a system of brutal racial domination."[8]

The *bracero* agreements explicitly delineated: "Mexicans entering the United States as a result of this understanding shall not suffer discriminatory acts of any kind in accordance with the Executive Order No. 8802 issued at the White House June 25, 1941."[9] This was the first federal document to suggest that Mexican-origin peoples were vulnerable to discrimination. Nonetheless, this codified constraint represented a binational economic agreement not a legislative act to reverse discrimination and historical patterns of segregation. The *bracero* pact provided labor protection for Mexican nationals but did not shield them from the discriminatory practices embedded in the Texas social system.

The Caucasian Race–Equal Privileges resolution attempted to address discriminatory social conventions but, in reality, was little more than a superficial discursive measure designed to shore up the *bracero* agreement's impotent guarantee of equal treatment of Mexican nationals working in U.S. industry and agriculture. Discrimination and exploitation against Mexicans in America persisted in spite of the guarantees of the *bracero* program. The Caucasian Resolution was but flimsy rhetorical reinforcement of the binational agreements. It was never intended to disrupt the racial hierarchy of the State or to equalize historical disparities, but rather to represent a stronger stance by Texas government on behalf of Mexican-origin people. The resolution asserted:

> Whereas, the citizens of the great State of Texas are interested in doing all that is humanly possible to aid and assist the national policy of hemispherical solidarity; therefore be it resolved by the House of Representatives of the State of Texas, the Senate concurring, that the Forty-eighth Legislature of the State of Texas go on record as declaring the following to be the public policy of this State:
>
> 1. All persons of the Caucasian Race within the jurisdiction of this State are entitled to the full and equal accommodations, advantages, facilities, and privileges of all public places of business or amusement, subject only to the conditions and limitations established by law, and rules and regulations applicable alike to all persons of the Caucasian Race.

2. Whoever denies to any person the full advantages, facilities, and privileges enumerated in the preceding paragraph or who aids or incites such denial or whoever makes any discrimination, distinction, or restriction except for good cause applicable alike to all persons of the Caucasian Races . . . shall be considered as violating the good neighbor policy of our State.[10]

The opacity of the language, in effect, masks and reaffirms the entrenched system of white hereditary privilege since Spanish and Anglo colonization of the Southwest. The agreement defends *de jure* and *de facto* segregation against peoples of color at the same time reaffirms the exclusionary privileges of whites.

As would be expected, the Caucasian Race Resolution did not overturn a hundred and fifty year legacy of exclusion. It did not quell incidents of discrimination against Mexican nationals in Texas as illustrated by George Martinez's examination of the litigation experience of Mexican Americans from 1930 to 1980.[11] This gesture of international diplomacy not only failed to promote racial justice north of the border but further problematized the national question of where Mexican-origin peoples should be assigned in the binary racial system of white and nonwhite classes. The Caucasian Race–Equal Privileges resolution HCR No. 105 restricted discrimination against "Caucasians" in public places, protecting access for whites and implicitly condoning discrimination against blacks.

Although the preamble of the resolution does not directly identify Mexican-origin peoples as "white," it suggests by geographic and metonymic association that "our neighbors to the South" are to be afforded equal privileges within the jurisdiction of the State of Texas.[12] The primary impetus and economic intent of this gesture is carefully masked behind World War II nationalist rhetoric portraying North American and Latin American countries "banded together in an effort to stamp out Nazism and preserve democracy."[13] The suppressed premise in the enthymematic structure of the Caucasian Race Resolution, however, offered a tiny legalistic loophole through which some early Mexican-origin reform groups sought inclusion. Through the rhetorical assertion of whiteness, post-war Mexican American reformers launched a campaign to clarify the racial categorization and naturalization of Mexican-origin peoples. For the post-war reformers, whiteness was an elusive object, a moving target.[14] Because Mexican Americans were historically and traditionally regarded as nonwhite in Texas, even after the assertion of their whiteness, post-war Mexican Americans remained an excluded class.

As a historically marginalized group, Mexican-origin peoples existed in a social position between the white and black color line. Fernando Peñalosa's examination of discrimination patterns in the United States notes that "dark-skinned Mexicans suffered about the same type of discrimination as Negroes, but the medium complected Mexicans were able to use second-class public facilities."[15] Peñalosa also observes that "even light-brown skinned Mexicans were excluded from high class facilities, while 'white' Mexicans might be freely admitted, especially if they spoke fluent English."[16]

The Caucasian Race Resolution did not usher in first-class citizenship for Mexican Americans but rather reinforced the racialized narrative of social progress. It further polarized Mexican-origin peoples across national lines, fueled anti-immigrant sentiments among Mexican Americans, and sustained racial hierarchies in the state and nation. The Caucasian Race Resolution also provided a framework from which to set the rhetorical parameters of early post-war Mexican American civil rights activism. It offered legal leverage upon which Mexican American civic organizations such as LULAC and the American GI Forum initially forged resistance to the ethnic apartheid that historically defined social relationships throughout the region.

In "Becoming Hispanic: Mexican Americans and the Faustian Pact with Whiteness," Neil Foley argues: "The history of Mexican Americans in the Southwest is . . . more than the history of their 'becoming' Mexican American or Hispanic; for many, especially those of the middle class, it is also the history of their becoming white."[17] Harkening back to Constitutional-era white privilege, post-war Mexican Americans subscribed to a belief system that reasserted their European ancestral lineage and represented themselves as "inherently civilized, capable of republican government, and deserving of citizenship"[18] Additionally, Cheryl Harris observes that identification with whiteness or "passing" is not unique to any one group or historical moment. "The persistence of passing is related to the historical and continuing pattern of white racial domination and economic exploitation that has given passing a certain economic logic," Harris contends.[19]

García paddled with and against the currents of post-war racist ideology in the United States, and in some instances, was caught in the undertow of racist, anti-immigrant discourses. As Foley observes, "Mexican Americans reasoned that if the law said they were White, then Anglos broke the law by discriminating against them as non-whites."[20] They fused what Foley calls "Latin American racialism with Anglo racism," at the same time carefully negotiating themselves around the black civil rights movement of the early post-war period.[21] Within this historical and ideological climate, García and the American GI Forum grappled with, and in some instances, exploited prevailing stereotypes of Mexican-origin immigrants.

In terms of immigration policy, the American GI Forum followed in the footsteps of its sister organization, LULAC, whose foremost goal was "To develop within the members of our race the best, purest and most perfect type of a true citizen of the United States of America."[22] This notion of the "best" and "purest" members of the "race" became an ideological snag ultimately complicating the role of the American GI Forum as an advocacy group for the rights of Mexicans living and working in America. The nationalist rhetorics circulated by LULAC, and even by the American GI Forum, in many respects, echoed the elitist discourses of early Spanish colonialism and the edict of "blood purity" or *limpieza de sangre*.

Governor Coke Stevenson signed the Caucasian Race Resolution forbidding discrimination against "Caucasians" in public places, implying, as George Green suggests, "that it was all right with the state if discrimination against black Texans continued unabated."[23] Neil Foley argues in *The White Scourge: Mexicans, Blacks, and Poor Whites in the Texas Cotton Culture* that the Caucasian Race Resolution "was intended to convince Mexico that discrimination against Caucasians would not be tolerated in Texas, the assumption being that Mexicans were, of course, members of the Caucasian race."[24] García and the American GI Forum framed their civil rights agenda at these political and social crossroads, falling into some of the same ethical fissures into which their LULAC predecessors had foundered.

Aligning the American GI Forum with the anti-immigrant stance of post-war xenophobia served to protect and, inadvertently, promote the nativist, racist discourses and stereotypes García so ardently resisted in the Longoria case. Blanton observes, "The patriotic citizenship mantra of the Longoria case is nothing without its flip-side, the use of that very same idea of citizenship to loosen their ties to more problematic, less controllable members of the population [the *braceros* and the "wetbacks"]."[25] The rhetorics of race became further problematized in the face of growing Mexican immigration. As Haney López notes, World War II spurred national "reconsideration of the racism integral to U.S. naturalization law."[26] The United States was the only nation in the world other than Nazi Germany with restrictive racial naturalization laws. Ironically, both the Longoria case (which aligned Mexican-origin peoples with U.S. identity) and the anti-*bracero* effort (which distanced Mexican-origin peoples from U.S. identity) demonstrate the elusiveness and instability of "whiteness" and our national terms of inclusion. Both function as constructs under cover.

The performance of civic belonging in post-war American society involved reaffirmation of the racial hierarchy and whiteness as the most basic tenets of inclusion, a contingency of U.S. citizenship since the first naturalization law was drafted in 1790. Although inconsistently defined and applied, "the white person prerequisite" remained integral to U.S. naturalization law until 1952.[27] The vestiges of racial exclusion of U.S. naturalization law were not removed completely until the signing of the immigration bill of 1965, removing national origins restrictions. Racially restricted naturalization laws explicitly shaped the ethnic and racial composition of U.S. citizenry. As Haney López recounts, "legislatures and courts have served not only to fix the boundaries of race in the forms we recognize today, but also to define the content of racial identities and to specify their relative privilege or disadvantage in U.S. society."[28]

In this ideological configuration, citizenship is reduced to innate, predetermined physical features rather than the process and product of socialization. García and the American GI Forum both resisted and reconciled themselves to this historical social order. The flood of Mexican immigrants, the legally admitted *bracero* and the illegally present *"mojado,"* became the distinguishing case, the class unsuitable for inclusion or citizenship. In other words, the American GI Forum's mantra of resistance to immigrant waves asserted: "We are fit to be Americans, and they are not." They drew the line on Mexican immigration according to class and caste. This was a traditional Americanist rhetorical move.

In *Civic Ideals: Conflicting Visions of Citizenship in U.S. History*, Rogers Smith labels the ideology of innate superiority the "inegalitarian ascriptive Americanist tradition," a system of thought that emphasizes the value of "involuntarily acquired traits that differentiate people" as suitable for citizenship. Those who subscribe to an ascriptive ideology tend to support "exclusionary and hierarchical citizenship policies" and segregated social configurations.[29] The prevailing goal of this country's exclusionary system of citizenship is to protect the "purity" of American civilization. In his examination of U.S. naturalization law, Gold delineates the legacy of white citizenship and the duty of Congress "to insure the perpetuation and the preservation, in its purity, of the American type of civilization."[30] The increasing presence of Mexican laborers as an indeterminate caste racially and nationally complicated the social assimilation of Mexican American citizens into the cultural and economic fabric of American life.

The Braceros *and Questions of Inclusion*

The impact of the *bracero* agreement was far-reaching, permanently altering the ethnolinguistic, socioeconomic and demographic conditions of the United States. Research guided by García and sponsored by the American GI Forum on the *bracero* program and "wetback problem" over the course of two decades generated interest from a wide range of groups: political entities such as the Texas State Federation of Labor; academic sectors such as the *University of Texas Inter-American Education Occasional Papers* and the *Stanford Law Review*; and popular media, such as *Look* magazine, which in 1951 featured the exposé "Texas' Forgotten People," and Edna Ferber's 1952 novel, *Giant*, and the subsequent 1956 film.[31] Because it plumbed directly into American fears and Cold War consciousness, the American GI Forum's "wetback" propaganda generated more sustained interest and engendered more public discourse than any other social issue the American GI Forum brought to the foreground.

The term *bracero*, derived from the Spanish word *brazos*, meaning "arms," signifies a legally contracted Mexican agricultural or railroad worker. More than 4.5 million Mexican nationals were legally contracted for work on U.S. farms over a twenty-two-year period until the program's termination on December 31, 1964.[32] Additionally, a class of undocumented Mexican laborers commonly known as *mojados* or "wetbacks" figured in this picture, the exact numbers of whom remain unknown. Their magnitude, however, was at least equal to that of legally contracted laborers, if not greater. According to the U.S. Immigration and Naturalization Service, for the period between 1951 and 1964 more than 3.6 million undocumented workers were recorded.[33] Obviously, expiration of the binational labor agreement did not stem the demand or flow of Mexican labor across the border. Sixty years later, U.S.-Mexico immigrant and migrant circulation remains the world's largest, involving over three million people each year.[34]

At the close of World War II, as an emerging middle class of Mexican-origin U.S. citizens grew, the desire to differentiate between classes also increased. The emergence of a South Texas Mexican American middle class ushered in "a collective Mexican American mentality" and the formation of various mechanisms of class distinction.[35] The sustained infusion of Mexican nationals into Mexican American communities complicated the Mexican American process of assimilation—if assimilation was the goal, and for many it was. Large sectors of the Mexican American post-war generation began speaking English in their homes and stopped teaching their children Spanish. Fluency in English became a goal. The middle class left the *barrios*, joined civic organizations, went to night school, ran for political office, and sent their children to colleges, especially to institutions focused on the needs of the Mexican American community, such as St. Mary's University in San Antonio and Texas A&I University in Kingsville. The persistent presence of the *bracero* and the undocumented worker, however, remained constant and disturbing reminders to citizens of Mexican-origin that in the pigmentocracy of the U.S. social system they were a caste, a race set apart irrespective of socioeconomic level, military participation, or cultural achievement.

David Gutiérrez asserts that Mexican Americans have long been divided over immigration issues. The social, economic, and emotional fissures extending between communities and families over the immigration debate remain deep and enduring. Generations of binational/bicultural families have struggled with the contradictions and challenges of belonging to competing national interests. Gutiérrez concludes that Mexican American attitudes fall between "two essentially polar positions:" immigrants viewed compassionately as "los recien llegados" (the newly arrived) and immigrants viewed as a threat.[36] The larger economic and historical forces at work categorically repositioned post-war Mexican American laborers. As Alexander Monto explains:

> Once established the growing labor circulation developed into a network tying particular labor source areas in Mexico to specific sites in the United States. Now nearly a century old, this circulation has been institutionalized in the social and economic structure of the sending and receiving areas and it persists despite the predominance of wage labor in Mexico.[37]

Positioned on the borders of great international economic shifts, Mexican Americans who found themselves standing in line for the same jobs as the *braceros* perceived the continuous flow of Mexican immigrants as the driving force behind their own displacement rather than the consequence of much larger economic and political global changes.

For working-class World War II veterans competing with Mexican laborers for low wages, the *bracero* and the "wetback" became a target of blame, the root cause of the community's social and economic hardships. Growers' increasing reliance on low-wage Mexican laborers destabilized already unjust conditions of employment for Mexican American workers. With a ready supply of "cheap" foreign labor, local farm workers lacked collective bargaining leverage. It was a "take it or leave it" wage system, and Mexican Americans and poor whites were often the ones forced to leave.[38]

Lyndon B. Johnson's senatorial labor files contain correspondence detailing the increasing dependence of Texas growers on Mexican laborers over the two decades of the *bracero* program. Telegrams and letters tell the story of large and small farming operations as well as processing plants and financial institutions dependent on the readily available agricultural labor offered by documented and undocumented workers in order to remain solvent. As one telegram to Johnson described:

Sufficient local citizen labor not available, as certified by Tex. Unemp. Comm. Millions of dollars of crops now growing stand to be lost and much unemployment in plant, processing, and handling labor will result unless sufficient *bracero*s for harvesting are made available.[39]

Another farmer pleaded to Senator Johnson succinctly, "Need help immediately. Get more braceros to save crops. Situation serious."[40] With the presence of foreign labor competition and without union organizing opportunities, Mexican American agricultural workers were routinely displaced from their Texas communities and forced to move out of state to find work. The Mexican American agricultural labor class of the early post-war era remained a dispensable segment of the American work force—politically disfranchised and educationally underserved.

As a leading voice in the South Texas sociopolitical scene and activist for the Mexican American poor, García emerged as one of the strongest opponents of the *bracero* agreement and post-war Mexican immigration. His own immigrant background did not mitigate his opposition to the growing influx of immigrants from south of the border. García was especially disturbed by the migration trends he saw among naturalized citizens like himself. He witnessed the mass migration of Mexican American citizens from their South Texas communities. His early research of migrant labor camps in 1948 called for action from state and national officials. During the first Annual convention of the American GI Forum in September 1949, García introduced and passed a resolution condemning migrant labor policies and practices. The resolution exhorted that "the American GI Forum of Texas go on record as opposing the practice (of importing foreign farm labor into the State of Texas, etc.) and demand that such practices shall immediately and forthwith cease."[41] The resolution was circulated widely to President Harry S. Truman, Lyndon B. Johnson, Secretary of Labor Maurice Tobin, Governor Allan Shivers, and others. According to Ralph Guzmán, García's anti-immigration tactics were sometimes controversial, stirring the public with exposure of shocking conditions.[42]

As a young physician, García named the conditions that plagued his community, investigating living conditions of migrant labor camps, examining "Mexican" schools, and conducting educational radio broadcasts to combat dysentery and high infant mortality rates.[43] Acting as the chairman of the LULAC investigative committee, García reported his findings to Truman's Civil Rights Commission, sending detailed descriptions and photographs: "As to the Labor Camp situation, the Committee believes that the condition existing there is of an EMERGENCY nature and should be attended immediately."[44]

Examination of García's public and private discourse in the form of letters and reports reveals strategic rhetorical shifts around racial identity. In his 1949 letter to Maurice Tobin, Secretary of Labor, objecting to the *bracero* program, García eschews all ethnolinguistic markers and describes his newly established American GI Forum as "a group of veterans organized to bettering ourselves and our family as American citizens."[45] In a 1951 letter to a legislator calling for improved medical facilities, García labels his group "American Veterans of Mexican Origin" and appeals to a common bond of national fraternity. García explained: "We have suffered enough and have been exploited enough in our state by our own brother Texans and we are looking up to MEN like you in Washington to help us all around."[46] Describing economic hardships in South Texas in a 1949 letter to Philip Murray, president of the CIO, García assumed the role of spokesman for the region. He asserted: "We are presenting our position and viewpoints in this matter and are voicing the opinion of approximately 1,200,000 Americans of Mexican origin residing in Texas."[47]

Geographically, ethnically, and nationally locating himself, García exercised identification with those he represented to enhance his authority as a local insider. During one interview with an Anglo reporter García depicted the struggle for inclusion by distancing himself and his generation from negative historical stereotypes. García claimed: "We were Americans, not 'spics' or 'greasers,' because when you fight for your country in a World War, against an alien philosophy, fascism, you are an American and proud to be an American."[48]

In this declaration of self-identification, García resists the pejorative labels "greasers" and "spics" as devices of dissimulation and effaces racial labels for the American GI Forum constituency altogether. García frequently represented himself and his people as simply "Americans."

A 1953 letter to Ed Idar, executive secretary of the American GI Forum, illustrates García's claim to white privilege in his appeal for confronting segregation practices in a veteran's hospital where Mexican Americans were placed in "Negro" wards. García instructed:

> Dear Ed, Do you remember a letter you sent me sometime in May about the clinics in Colorado City that were having the same rooms for Mexican people and the Negroes? I have been thinking this thing over, and beiebe that the best approach on the matter will be to write the clinics a letter from Auxtin and suggest to them that our legal advisor write them a letter first asking that this is wrong and this will lead to trouble in black-listing of those counties. . . . [T]hey are violating the law because the Mexican people are white and they are not doing it right. I believe we might be able to stop them. . . . The situation is critical. Your friend, Hector P. Garcia, M.D.[49]

García's assertion that "they are violating the law because the Mexican people are white" leans not on federal statute but relies on the Texas Caucasian Race Resolution for legalistic leverage. No law existed, either state or federal, that unequivocally recognized Mexican people as white. García exploited the only legalistic rhetoric available. However, while he used the claims of the Caucasian Race Resolution to resist institutionalized discrimination against Mexican Americans, he did so without acknowledging the resolution's implicit intent as rhetorical reinforcement of the *bracero* program he so ardently opposed or racist ideologies. Acts of naming and self-identification by García varied according to context and audience.

As illustrated in his 1959 address to the National Advisory Committee on Farm Labor, García's public discourse shifts ethnic and racial labels to accommodate audiences. He identifies his constituency as "American veterans of Mexican origin" in the opening of his address, then categorically parses Mexican Americans within the Texas population as "white persons of Spanish surname," distinct from Anglo and "Negro" populations.

In a 1961 letter to George I. Sánchez, long-time mentor and Mexican *compadre*, and fellow American GI Forum and LULAC insider, García shifts subject positions and codeswitches into Spanish, identifying himself with *los mejicanos* (spelled with "j" instead of the anglicized "x"), writing:

> We here in Corpus Christi elected two Mejicanos for the first time in the history of the region, to the city council. But like I say, kiddingly, que aunque me aborescan los hombres, estoy contento que quieren las mujeres bonitas [although the men abhor me, I'm happy that the beautiful women love me]. This is not as bad as it sounds, but nevertheless it is a good method of escaping the pressure and criticism that we get from all sides.[50]

The act of codeswitching operates as a solidarity marker, building identification between speaker and audience. García used a similar strategy, evoking Mexican solidarity, in a 1961 letter to friend and confidante Manuel Avila, to whom he reports that the Corpus Christi school board hired "only three *Raza* . . . to teach only Spanish and band." García lamented, "I tell you Manuel we are tired and sick of this foolishness. We are still victims of segregation and discrimination."[51] In the very same letter, García demonstrates racial solidarity as *la raza* and, at the same time, disassociates himself from Mexico. Tired of "being suspected that we may be loyal to Mexico instead of U.S.A.," García asserted, "We fought for the good old U.S.A. not Mexico. We are 'Americans' not 'Mexican citizens.'"[52] Within this single discursive unit, García illustrates the conflicted status of Mexican-origin peoples based on racial identification and national origin.

Ethnolinguistic labeling patterns, like race, are unstable categories. Mobilization terms shift meaning over time. García and his generation of reformers understood that first-class citizenship demanded, at some level, engaging in protean acts of identification with the dominant group. Straddling identities was, however, a precarious process that sometimes resulted in complete alienation from *la raza*, the *mexicano* community. A 1956 letter to Vicente Ximenes from one Mexican American organizer reports on the difficulty of consensus building and labels dissenting Mexican American professionals "jellyfish Chicano politicians" and "Chicano Uncle Toms."[53] Those who identified too closely with white America were regarded as sellouts and traitors to *la raza*.

García and the post-war reformers exercised varying degrees of identification with white America. Interpretation of their rhetorical choices must be inflected with an understanding of the material culture and legal precedents from which they constructed their arguments for first-class inclusion. They practiced a kind of strategic whiteness, perhaps not unlike the strategies practiced by the crypto Jews during the Mexican Inquisition operating under cover. Ethnolinguistic labeling patterns index the perspectival and attitudinal stances of speakers concerning themselves and their audiences, acts of shuttling between identities for different audiences.[54] Montenegro delineates the varied terms adopted and applied to peoples of Mexican-origin through history. Some of these terms include: *la gente mexicana, hispano-americano, hispano, mexicano*, Latin-American, Spanish-speaking, white persons of Spanish surname, Spanish American, Chicano, and Mexican American.[55] If a Mexican American "is light, he may become acceptable to the dominant society by mastering English and ignoring his culture," Montenegro argues. "If he is dark, he may intermarry so that his children or grandchildren will lose the stereotypic appearance (short, stocky, and dark) and the stigma attached to it."[56] García and the leaders of the American GI Forum clearly understood these racialized terms of inclusion. Like García, a number of the American GI Forum leaders acquired a college education, joined the professional class, married European war brides, and identified with the prestige symbols of white America. As an educated professional, married to a fair-skinned, blue-eyed European war-bride, and living in one of the most exclusive Anglo neighborhoods in Corpus Christi, García knew how to manipulate these implicit racial codes for gaining social status.

The ideology of race embedded in the discourse of U.S. citizenship laws, the national narrative of social mobility, and the material conditions of white privilege set the "limits of legal imagination" for García's civil rights campaign.[57] García straddled two social systems of race: white and *mexicano.* His own misunderstandings about racial purity myths and conflicted notions about *mestizaje,* along with his complex position as an immigrant and naturalized citizen, complicated his perception of the place of Mexican Americans in the national racial hierarchy.

The privileges of whiteness favored García in both elements of morphology and ancestry. His physical features more closely resembled his fair-skinned, green eyed father than his *indio* and *mestizo* ancestors. He unwaveringly identified himself as white not *mestizo* and the dominant European traits he inherited from his Spanish father permitted him to "pass."[58] Like many elite and middle-class Mexican immigrants, he ardently resisted representing himself and Mexican Americans as a people of color. His dark-skinned sister Clotilde, however, who carried the indigenous features of their *mestiza* mother, incurred persistent rejection and shame throughout her childhood within the family and outside of it.[59] Racial identity, as such, was a problematic issue for García both personally and publicly—perhaps his most enduring wound.

In the complex process of constructing and performing an American identity, García engaged in the "ultimate identification" or what Foley calls the "Faustian Pact with Whiteness."[60] Foley notes that in the early stages of the Mexican American civil rights movement, Mexican Americans had to decide what side of the color line they were on and demanded recognition as whites. It would represent an oversimplification of the post-war social context, and a wholesale dismissal of the legal constructs that defined membership in racial categories, to claim that García and the American GI Forum were simply imitating Anglo prejudice by failing to openly align themselves with black activists. García and his followers constructed a civil rights movement along side the intellectual and social crosscurrents of the period.

García's rhetoric of resistance and model of organization accommodated conditions and audiences located in this highly contentious historical moment. Negotiating volatility in multiple domains, political, educational as well as professional, he eschewed all practices that might incite violence. During the race riots of the 1960s, García steered clear of radical African American and Chicano nationalists. However, García would demonstrate increasing solidarity with nonviolent black civil rights activists through the 1950s and into the 1960s as evidenced by his receipt of the "Democracy Forward" Award by the Texas Council Negro Association in 1955 and the Humanitarian Award by the NAACP in 1969.[61] In January 1952, only three years after the Longoria incident, the America GI Forum Newsletter reported on the refusal by a mortuary in Phoenix, Arizona, to provide funeral services for "a Negro soldier killed in Korea."[62] In 1953, García accepted an invitation from the NAACP to serve as a keynote speaker for the 17th Annual Convention of the Texas Conference of Branches.[63] In 1960, demonstrating strong solidarity with the African American civil rights movement, the American GI Forum passed a resolution commending the "sit in demonstrations" at lunch counters and public accommodations staged by black civil rights activists.[64]

Conflicting accounts of García and the American GI Forum's record on African American civil rights advocacy, nevertheless, endure. Carlos Blanton challenges the allegation in Patrick Carroll's *Felix Longoria's Wake: Bereavement, Racism, and the Rise of Mexican American Activism* "that Mexican Americans, like other white immigrants in the United States, were seduced into anti-black racism."[65] Citing Carroll's claim that "these well-to-do and successful Tejano leaders seemed to be aping and perhaps even strengthening the climate of racism that prevailed in the Nueces Strip up until the immediate post–World War II years," Blanton contends, "This serious charge, however, is unsupported by evidence and internally contradicted."[66] Archival evidence indicates that García and the American GI Forum provided sustained, behind-the-scenes support of African American civil rights. Although there were no public acts of solidarity and staged events of civil disobedience on behalf of black activists, as in the lunch counter protests or freedom rides, García and American GI Forum demonstrated support consistent with their own political activism style through the instrumental rhetorics of American GI Forum governance and ceremonial discourse.

García's evolution toward universal civil rights, however, was incremental not immediate. He did not initially decry all segregation as a social practice but resisted segregation, in particular, against Mexican Americans. By the 1960s, though, García was publicly demanding equal rights for Mexican Americans and African Americans. García's statement of protest to Governor Price Daniel in 1961, which was circulated to President John F. Kennedy, represents a bold reaction to the refusal of a Houston hotel to provide accommodations for Undersecretary of Labor George L. P. Weaver because he was African American. García asserted, "I hope that some action is taken," toward acts of discrimination "against our colored citizens [and] Americans of Mexican origin."[67] Initially García did not align forces with African American activists, emphatically identifying Mexican Americans as "white" or "Spanish-speaking Americans." García, like his LULAC predecessors, appropriated the rhetorical strategy of labeling Mexican-origin citizens as a "linguistically constructed" minority rather than politically aligning with African Americans as a people of color and a racially discriminated population.[68]

In many respects, García's ideological inconsistencies and discursive contradictions reflect the era in which he lived and worked. In *The Retreat of Scientific Racism: Changing Concepts of Race in Britain and the United States between the World Wars,* Elazar Barkan observes:

> Racism is a universal, but its representation as an oppressive and dogmatic ideology captured center stage only during the years between the World Wars. Prior to that time, social differentiation based upon real or assumed racial distinctions was thought to be part of the natural order.[69]

Barkan argues that the scientific rebuke of racist ideology evolved over three periods from 1933 through the 1950s, a time frame paralleling the emergence of García's entrée into civil rights activism through LULAC and eventual leadership over the American GI Forum.

The first period of U.S. scientific resistance to racist ideology began with the reconsideration of the notion of race and concern over Jewish refugees in 1933–34 but failed to coalesce into a direct action. This first period coincides with García's undergraduate studies at the University of Texas, Austin, where he first encountered the work of Mexican American scholar Carlos Castañeda. Barkan maintains that the second period of scientific racist consciousness reached a stalemate from 1934 to 1938, a period paralleling García's medical school training and first experiences in social activism in *las colonias* of Galvaston. Because of this scholarly gap, it is unlikely that García was formally exposed to these emerging scientific anti-racist discourses during his medical school period.

Finally, in the third period, from 1938 to the 1950s, the atrocities of the holocaust and Nazi racial policies exposed racism in international politics and spurred the gradual decline of scientific racism in intellectual circles. However, as Barkan notes, the majority of U.S. scientists resisted jumping into the political fray of "the intellectual battle to discredit racism."[70] Although Nazi racist ideology had been universally challenged in 1945 when García returned from overseas duty, U.S. racial segmentation and white privilege remained largely unaddressed and intact. These contradictory terms set the conflicted backdrop of García's civil rights activism. For García and the post-war generation, the unexamined dissonant chord of inclusion vibrates around the question of whiteness.

"Wetbacks," Whiteness, and Tropes of Inclusion

The earliest phase of García's civil rights activism was focused on keeping Mexican American workers in the state and keeping Mexican American children in school. García led a LULAC investigative committee in 1948 to examine the conditions of labor camps in the South Texas town of Mathis. García and his committee toured camps comprised of little more than small shacks lacking flooring, plumbing, ventilation, appliances, and even beds. Families lived together in single rooms without even the most basic necessities. García's investigation on April 22, 1948, records overflowing sewage disposal and pit privies filled to capacity, an absence of water, garbage cans, windows, and cleaning equipment. He documented shacks infested with rats and insects and crowded with children infected with dysentery, diarrhea, and other illnesses. "People lived and slept on the bare ground," García wrote. "A better combination for fly breeding and rat breeding could not be found anywhere in the world." By comparison, the livestock existed in better conditions.[71] García linked the high infant mortality rates in the region to poor living conditions, boldly charging the city of Mathis with criminal neglect. He argued:

> It [labor camp] proves conclusively that neither the camp owner nor the city authorities nor state authorities are concerned about giving human beings facilities to meet even the lowest standard of living. Both the camp owner and the city officials are interested only in exploiting these poor people to the point that they risk their health and their lives, as shown by the high infant mortality rate of San Patricio County.[72]

García sent a full report with photographs of Mathis labor camps and the equally appalling conditions of the area's segregated "Mexican" schools to Governor Beauford Jester, the Good Neighbor Commission, the Texas State Department of Health, the U.S. Civil Rights Commission, and the Mathis School Board of Education.[73] Lacking confidence in the moral conscience of the state, García asserted: "We are taking up the matter with the Civil Rights Commission because we feel the State of Texas is not doing everything they can to protect the health and welfare of its Citizens."[74] García placed considerable pressure on the Good Neighbor Commission to intervene on behalf of Mexican farm workers and their children.

In a May 5, 1948, letter to Thomas Sutherland, executive secretary of the Good Neighbor Commission, García argued:

> All the citizens of Latin American origin in Texas are indignant and aroused at such conditions. We don't want any compromise. If your Commission is to function as a truly Democratic Good Neighbor Commission, then after having seen the evidence sent there, they should go on record as desiring all of the communities involved to stop all segregation [in Texas schools] at once.[75]

García saw labor and education issues as two interlocking parts of the problem. To attack one issue demanded attention to the other. García's labor investigations continued under his leadership as the founder of the American GI Forum into the 1950s. In a letter to Senator Lyndon B. Johnson, García reported:

> It is no secret to know that Texas permits the hiring of children in agricultural pursuits. It is no secret that Texas has for the past 100 years and to a certain extent still segregating our children hoping to retard them and to discourage them from seeking higher education so that they would furnish cheap labor. ... It has been stated that the children like to pick cotton. It isn't so; if they pick cotton it is because they have to.[76]

García's investigations were not limited solely to South Texas but extended across the state. He demonstrated that the exploitation of Mexican farm workers was a statewide issue not just a border problem. Taking up García's cause, Thomas Sutherland cites García's research as evidence of the exploitation of child labor in Texas fields. In this 1949 letter to the Texas State Labor Commission, Sutherland reported:

> Dr. Hector Garcia of Corpus Christi has reported to this Commission that he saw and talked with large numbers of children who are working in the cotton fields of West Texas; he estimates that there are at least five thousand children of migratory families now employed in the cotton fields.[77]

State officials were obligated to investigate the charges, even though little change was made on the behalf of domestic or foreign farm workers.

García turned to colleagues and friends to help him confront farm labor problems. In 1949, García wrote to a South Texas friend and fellow leader of "este moviemiento" [this movement], informing him of recent *bracero* negotiations in the area and explaining his objections to the program. García explained,

> yo le dije que eso de legalizar los "mojados" en el valle seria una cosa buena si fuese por un sentido humanitario y segun reportes en los periodicos de valle Usted aseguraba esto. Ahora si eso fuera asi porque es que los agricultures no levantaron los 50,000 mojados legalizados. La razon es sencilla come siempre ha sido. No los levantaron ni los levantaran porque nunca intentaron ni intentaran pagarles un centavo mas de 25¢ por hora y por la misma razon deportaron mas de 50,000 pobres. Esto siempre sera una verguenza para todos nosotros porque debiamos de habernos preparado para esto ya que sabemos y sabiamos que estos grupos no buscan mas que una cosa en el valle "Cheap labor at any price."[78] [I tell you that legalizing the "wetbacks" in

the valley would be a good thing in a humanitarian sense if it was according to the newspaper reports as you assure me. Yes, if that is how it really is but agriculture did not raise the wages of 50,000 legalized wetbacks. The reason is simple as it always has been. They do not raise them nor will they raise them because they never intended and never will intend to pay them a penny more than twenty-five cents per hour and for the same reason they will deport more of these 50,000 poor people. It will always be a shame for all of us because we should have prepared ourselves for this. We already knew and should know that these groups look for nothing more in the valley than "cheap labor at any price."]

News of García's migrant camp research and his back-to-school campaigns extended throughout the region, enlarging his reputation as an activist. García also analyzed the economic dimensions of the labor situation. His field notes taken in the Rio Grande Valley calculate the farm worker wages in relation to farmer profits. He wrote:

Millions of dollars a year are being made in the Rio Grande Valley on cotton, but the pickers are not paid enough to live on. . . . The first picking around July 1st paid wetbacks $1.25 per hundred pounds. As proof that this is not a living wage for American citizens, there are only a few families in the Valley.

The Valley farmers have a racket. They have some of the best land in the country; they have the cheapest labor; their cotton comes in a month or two before the rest of the country so they get the best prices—they sell their cotton before the market is flooded and the prices drop.[79]

García concluded that valley farmers' unfair advantage over Mexican laborers demanded wide public and government intervention at the federal level. He argued that the state was more interested in maintaining the status quo than representing the interests of its Mexican-origin population.

García employed a variety of means to launch protests. He used radio announcements, back-to-school rallies, circulars, and letters to newspaper editors to promote community action on behalf of farm workers and their children. In many instances, the community responded to García's urging. In this 1948 letter, a teacher in the Petronila School in South Texas implored García for assistance:

We are now in our fourth week of the first school month, and thus far we have enrolled only a very small percentage of our Spanish-speaking scholastics. . . . We feel that since you have been able to accomplish so much for the educational betterment of these children, perhaps you would now be able to carry on an educational campaign among the Spanish-speaking parents of this community.[80]

Mexican Americans and even some Anglo community leaders began to take notice. In these ways, García's emerging civil rights project evolved as a reaction to the health, labor, and educational issues of Texas Mexican Americans.

Relying on *logos* and the rhetoric of statistics as well as his *ethos* as a doctor and former resident of Hidalgo County, García defined the educational situation for Mexican American children. García understood that institutionalized discrimination is systemic, impacting every dimension of society. From his own life experience, he knew that economic viability is directly linked to educational opportunity. In his early texts, García did not overtly name racism and bigotry as a factor in the educational exclusion of Mexican American children. Rather, he implicated school authorities, community leaders and the press for the overall educational neglect of the region's children. In his January 7, 1949, letter to the editor of the *Edinburg Valley Review*, García wrote:

> The number of children in Hidalgo County who do not go to school is exceedingly great. Edinburg itself is the worst city with 2,807 children not attending or not enrolled in school as brought out by the figures which were taken from the "Thirty-Fourth Biennial Report" published by State Department of Education [in] 1945–46. . . . The rest of the Valley towns such as McAllen, Mission, Weslaco, Pharr, San Juan, Donna, etc. are not any better. It is certainly "food for thought" and a challenge to school authorities, *the Edinburg Valley Review*, and the community leaders to bring this figure down. I have many fine friends in Edinburg that I know would be surprised at these figures since I attended Jr. College [in Edinburg] for two years.[81]

García did not attack his South Texas colleagues and neighbors in this letter, but challenged the community to consider local educational access issues.

If García couldn't bring his audience to the evidence, García would bring the evidence to them. His approach suggests an underlying belief that racism and injustice could be countered by reason and rhetoric. García's rhetorical action exhibits a measure of faith in his audience. He approached his audience as responsive citizens who by learning the "truth" would take the right action. In his letter to the editors of *Life* magazine, García exhorted:

> As to the Labor Camps, it is hard to believe that such a condition could exist in a civilized and so called modern State. We are at the breaking

point of patience and we would like to appeal to your liberal magazines, "Time" and "Life" to come to our help. . . . We are sending you the report we submitted and the pictures for your use. You certainly are welcome to use everything we have sent you. We invite you and your photographers to visit Mathis, Texas and check on the schools and labor camps to verify our contentions. Again let me thank you in any way you can help us because we need help badly.[82]

García appealed to media seemingly sympathetic to the liberal democratic vision in the post-war period.

With a national consciousness increasingly celebrative of American civil liberties and global human rights, García hoped that instruments such as *Life* and *Time*, voices of liberal white America, would help to bring his people under the broadening national umbrella of good will. The human-interest stories regularly featured in these types of publications seemed to suggest that they could serve as appropriate launching pads for his campaign. He believed that the story of his people would appeal to their audiences. García asserted in his letter to the editorial department of *Life*, "we are White and Citizens of the United States," implying that Mexican Americans were just like their readers. García's appeal to the "imagined fraternity" of liberal white America failed, however. Neither magazine published García's reports.

García's identification with whiteness, a rhetorical move he used on a number of occasions, was a persistent and precarious strategy for many reasons. Texas Anglos, even under the mandate of the Caucasian Race Resolution, adamantly resisted Mexican Americans' claim of whiteness. This assertion held no suasory value whatsoever. Since the Constitutional era, the "imagined fraternity" of white America was a closed class. More importantly, García's failure to decry all segregation practices violated his own deep commitment to human rights and set him at cross-purposes with himself. In this early period of his civil rights vision, García's pragmatism seems to have led to him to believe that in the post-war moment it would be easier for Mexican Americans to gain inclusion as white Americans than it would be to demand full inclusion for all Americans. This rhetorical compromise complicated García's record both in terms of Mexican labor issues and Mexican American civil rights.

García worked to build coalitions with other South Texas leaders and implored them to join his campaign against unjust labor conditions. In his May 7, 1949, letter to a colleague investigating the migrant labor situation in Brownsville, Texas, he reported:

> I have made several trips to the valley trying to get interest of the Valley
> leaders in getting our people educated so that they may have better standards
> of living. . . . If too many "wetbacks" are hired in the valley; or if "prevailing
> wages of wetback scale" are established all of the Veterans and their families
> will suffer more and automatically lower their standard of living which is too
> low as it is. Bear in mind that as far as the Mexican people are concerned
> the Valley is still one of the worst places to live according to mortality and
> morbidity rates published by the State Dept. of Health.[83]

Not only did García urge the leaders of South Texas communities to launch
back-to-school drives and to help increase the attendance of Mexican
American children, he pleaded with them to fight school segregation across
South Texas. García challenged, "Valley leaders should show more interest
in all of these conditions in order to better the condition of the residents
of the Valley who have the highest mortality rates in the state; the lowest
standard of living; and a very high grade of illiteracy."[84]

García understood that action at the regional and state level would not
be sufficient to change conditions. He advised national leaders including
President Harry Truman of the local situation. In his October 5, 1949, letter, García depicted the Texas socioeconomic condition of South Texas
Mexican Americans:

> with the increased closing down of military and naval installations in Texas,
> our veterans and other American citizens of Mexican origin are taking a
> beating. . . . There is a yearly migratory movement from Texas to other
> states because of low wages . . . paid to our workers in the local areas. This
> migratory movement of American citizens involves about 250,000 men,
> women, and children.[85]

García's message, however, met with silence from the president. Confront-
ing the indifference of the nation's executive office to the plight of Mexican
Americans would be an enduring struggle for García. At the peak of the
American GI Forum's anti-wetback campaign, García challenged President
Dwight D. Eisenhower in an October 17, 1953, letter during a presidential
tour of South Texas. Focusing attention on the substandard Rio Grande
Valley communities, García encouraged the president to visit the migrant
neighborhoods which he labels a "Little Mexico." He wrote:

> Congratulations on visiting our State. . . . Would kindly and humbly request
> that during your stay in the Rio Grande Valley . . . that you would . . .
> familiarize yourself with the "Wetback Problem." This group of veterans.
> . . . are deeply interested in trying to stop the influx of "Wetbacks" who

displace our American workers of the State of Texas and who undermine the standard of living of these American workers because of the cheap wages that the "Wetbacks" work for. The situation is critical in that the "Wetback Invasion" is the cause of the migratory problem."[86]

Eisenhower offered no reply. John F. Kennedy would prove equally mute on the matter. Eliciting no direct response, García's September 30, 1961, telegram to President Kennedy declared, "It is a disgrace when Congress guarantees foreign worker wages and benefits that they cannot give our people. Mexican bracero program is a farce."[87]

García directed his appeals to the Mexican government, hoping to persuade officials to limit if not sever altogether the supply of *braceros* to Texas. If he could show an enduring pattern of abuse and negative repercussions of the *bracero* program, García believed that the program would be dismantled. In a 1949 letter, he urged the minister of international affairs to investigate the Texas situation. García's appeal to the U.S. embassy in Mexico asserted:

> Naturally, we, the "American GI Forum" who represents not only the poorest Veterans, economically speaking, in Texas, but also the 1,200,000 people of Mexican origin in Texas who in the majority are American citizens, wish to make our position clear.
>
> We are indeed sorry in having to state to you that the International agreement bringing imported labor into Texas has hurt us severely. With the increased lay-offs of our people by the thousands in the military and naval installations in Texas as a result of your economy drive, we are suffering a great reduction in our incomes, greater number of unemployment and a drastic lowering of our American standard of living. Needless to say, this importation of labor which does not have our approval, neither were our working Citizens represented in it, has caused the whole problem to suddenly become critical.
>
> We kindly beg you, Honorable Wheeler, that before any more agreements are made, that our position as that of working Americans also be taken into consideration. . . . Please conduct a thorough investigation by your Department in this matter before any more agreements are reached.[88]

García requested that a full investigation be launched before renewing the program. The *bracero* agreements were ultimately renewed with no appreciable improvement realized by Mexican laborers or Mexican American citizens.

Grappling with local, state, federal, and even international authorities on the *bracero* issue for more than fifteen years sharpened García's political skills and helped him connect the local situation to larger trends. Ironically, even as his sphere of political influence expanded and his grasp of the national picture increased over the course of his career, García's solutions to the immigrant labor issues narrowed and foundered. García's opposition to the *bracero* program was initially informed by his direct contact with the lives of exploited farm workers, Mexican citizens as well as American citizens. Above all else, he wanted to alleviate suffering. After years of sustained resistance, García made no significant impact on *bracero* legislation. Contrary to the claims of the American GI Forum, García's campaign did not stem the overall flow of Mexican immigrants, documented or undocumented, into the United States. Moreover, the program remained in effect in spite of all García's efforts to reverse it.

Over the decades, García's focus began to shift from legislative solutions to enforcement strategies. Because he could not control growers' demand for labor and he could not influence state and national legislation, he tried to exercise influence over the supply of Mexican laborers. García and the American GI Forum's response to this impasse was to wage a rhetorical battle against the "wetback." Although some American GI Forum leaders celebrated García's anti-wetback program as an important contribution to improving the social condition of Mexican Americans in South Texas, examination of the rhetorical practices exercised to eradicate Mexican laborers from the region reveals one of the darkest chapters of García's legacy. His rhetoric of resistance reflects a series of ethical ruptures. García and the American GI Forum's myopic course of action devolved into a campaign of blaming the victim. In these ways, García accepted and advanced oversimplified answers on the Mexican labor issue.

The Polemics of the Bracero *Immigrant Labor Program*

According to García and the American GI Forum, repeal of the *bracero* immigrant labor program was among the most urgent issues of the Texas sociopolitical scene demanding remedy if Mexican Americans were to attain full status as American citizens. Linking the problem of Mexican American labor displacement with "wartime statements of national principles" and a growing global awareness of human rights issues, García and the American GI Forum struggled to achieve recognition for Mexican Americans as "fully vested citizens" of the United States.[89]

Judith Shklar argues in *American Citizenship: The Quest for Inclusion* that dignity of work and personal achievement have been integral in the formation of an Anglo American civic *ethos*.[90] Economic dependence "renders any group or individual unfit for citizenship."[91] Good citizens fulfill the demands of the polity through work and obedience to the laws they frame.[92] Since the framing of the first naturalization law in 1790, the privileges of citizenship (the right to vote and the opportunity to earn) have been aligned with issues of race (whiteness and non-whiteness) and caste (hereditary privilege and birth-ascribed status).[93]

These conflicted terms of citizenship informed civic and social practice in Texas through the first half of the twentieth century as comprehensively as the first citizenship laws shaped slaveholding America in 1790. The privileges of "first class citizenship" remained unattainable for the vast majority of Mexican Americans through tightly imposed racial restraints. A segregated educational system prevented professional mobility. Unskilled jobs and low wages kept families at below subsistence levels of existence so they could not even afford to pay their poll taxes in order to vote. The two marks of public standing, the opportunity to earn and the right to vote, were denied to the Mexican American working-class majority who remained locked in a migratory and underpaid social class.

The growing presence of Mexican nationals, further complicating conditions of civic inclusion for post-war Mexican Americans, "set the stage for a broad and deep reevaluation among Mexican Americans of both the significance of ongoing immigration and the political and social salience of their own sense of ethnicity."[94] The polemics of the *bracero* issue, as such, touched on a full range of domestic and foreign policy issues, including Mexican American civil rights.[95] In the midst of the *bracero* debates, Gutiér-rez observes, "Mexican American activists often found themselves in an ambiguous moral and existential borderland in which questions of political and cultural identity were muddled in ways most Americans never had to consider."[96] Because of the proximity to the border, enduring historical and cultural ties to Mexico, and the continuous flow of newcomers, post-war Mexican American activists faced a rhetorical situation unlike many other immigrant population. Gutiérrez explains:

> Ironically, it would take the opening of the border to Mexican immigrant labor in 1942 to jar Mexican American activists on both sides of the issue to renewed awareness that previous periods of immigration had created a large subpopulation of Mexican Americans for whom Americanism and assimilation had little appeal.[97]

García, as a leading voice of the South Texas Mexican American community, joined forces with disparate groups across the state and nation to address the problems. However, the demands of working on the healing edge of medicine as well as the cutting edge of politics complicated García's participation.

García struggled to accommodate diverse ideological positions and competing interests, often negotiating with groups operating at cross purposes with one another. Over the course of fifteen years confronting the Mexican labor issue, García eventually joined forces with other fierce opponents of Mexican immigration. Coordinating efforts with such disparate political forces such as LULAC, the Catholic Church, the U.S. Immigration and Naturalization Service, and the AFL against the *bracero* program helped to advance García's influence but it also challenged his effectiveness. In terms of the *bracero* issue, political bifurcation resolved into short-sighted solutions.

Although García realized early in his civil rights project that immigration issues and civil rights issues were tightly bound together, he failed to see that U.S. and Mexico socioeconomic futures were also closely intertwined. He believed a fixed and impermeable border was possible and necessary. Taking a pathologist's point of view, García approached the *bracero* program and the "wetback invasion" as a social disease. He focused on the workers themselves as the problem, attacking the symptoms of inequitable social conditions rather than critiquing the complex socioeconomic configurations giving rise to the immigrant labor situation. His was a very surgical solution—simply remove the afflicted part of the condition and suture the border closed.

García might have focused on organizing a farm workers union, a strategy César Chávez would employ in the 1960s. The revolutionary tenor that inflected the rhetorical situation of the 1960s helped to make César Chávez's bold farm workers' revolt possible. However, calling for the collective unionization of Mexican American and Mexican national agricultural laborers in García's era would have been a risky if not fatal rhetorical move in the "red-baiting" Cold War climate of the 1950s. Furthermore, García was confident in Mexican Americans' newfound civic status as veterans. Mexican American veterans were claiming rights and privileges and practicing authority in the community in ways not previously exercised.

García's faith in the American democratic experiment and his abiding confidence in the role of federal government to act as leveling agent on behalf of his people would not allow him to critique the economic system supercharging the post-war era. His fealty, so strong and enduring, was refractive, ultimately turning back in on itself. García and the American GI Forum advanced their troubled political stance on Mexican immigration through an array of instrumental rhetorics: correspondence, resolutions, American GI Forum–sponsored research and pamphlets, and popular media.

The 1954 pamphlet *A Cotton Picker Finds Justice: The Saga of the Hernandez Case* evolved as a collective effort between leading South Texas political figures such as ex-mayor of San Antonio Maury Maverick, LULAC attorney Gus García, University of Texas scholar George I. Sánchez, and Héctor P. García to educate the public about precedent-setting Mexican American civil rights cases. Listed beside their successes fighting discrimination in jury selection and school segregation cases, the battle of the American GI Forum against the "wetback menace" is touted as one of their shining moments.[98]

To align his stance on the *bracero* issue with the dominant discourse of the post-war era, García infused his anti-immigrant rhetoric with a motley composite of "Americanist" principles and patriotic tropes. In his October 4, 1949, letter to Don Larin, chief of the Farm Placement Service for the U.S. Department of Labor, García admonished:

> We are beseeching our Government to thoroughly and impartially investigate this situation and give us representation in their hearings and arrangements and to think less of "cotton, grapefruit, and vegetables," and more of "men, mothers, and children."
>
> . . . The American G. I. Forum finds that its work is hampered and its program of Americanism is delayed by this unnecessary migratory movement of our own people.[99]

The alliterative use of "more," "men," "mothers," "American GI Forum," "Americanism," and "migratory movement" creates a pattern of associations designed to evoke *pathos* and nationalist solidarity. The metaphor of "mother" functions as the central patriotic image, resonating notions of the American home, hearth, and heart. García's request to "thoroughly and impartially investigate this situation" and "give us representation" reflects the application of *logos*, an appeal to reason, as well as conveys confidence in the authority of modern empirical methods and democratic practice. Together these discourse features combine to cast García's project as an example of American pragmatism at work. The underlying meta-narrative of progress, the subliminal suggestion of America's "progress toward an ever broader human liberty," runs through García's rhetoric and aligns his appeal with the larger nationalist discourse.

García's appropriation of the dominant discourse of the post-war era for his anti-immigrant campaign helped to advance the aims of the American GI Forum. Operating under the fear-inciting banner "wetback invasion," García and American GI Forum were able to gain notice, build their reputation as guardians of democracy, and promulgate their civil rights agenda with a sense of urgency. However, this same discursive strategy also severely compromised the integrity of García's newly evolving civil rights project.

Beginning with the generation and circulation of the American GI Forum's resolution of September 26, 1949, García took increasingly aggressive measures to combat the presence of foreign labor. The resolution, drafted by García and sent to state and national public officials, reads: "Therefore be it resolved that the American GI Forum of Texas go on record as opposing this practice [of importing foreign farm labor] and demand that such practice shall immediately and forthwith cease."[100] The first step in framing resistance demanded that García name the problem. The next step, establishing legal recourse, would prove more problematic.

García exploited the terms of the *bracero* agreement to build his case. García employed the terms of the *bracero* agreements as well as the liberal, pluralistic rhetoric inherent in the Good Neighbor policy both to demand Mexican Americans' recognition as first-class citizens of the United States and to call for the termination of the *bracero* program. In his *Social Science Quarterly* article "Texas, Good Neighbor," Otey M. Scruggs underscores the global symbolic intentions of the Texas Good Neighbor Commission and the *bracero* agreements toward quelling the negative representation of U.S. race relations. Scruggs observes:

> Since the Second World War, the United States has been criticized by the rest of the world as never before in history. In no area of their national life have the American people been more severely attacked than in the sensitive area of race relations. . . .
>
> The communist countries, for propaganda purposes, the Latin American states, with their large Indian and Negro populations, and a host of newly emergent, Afro-Asian nations have been quick to play up instances of racial prejudice and discrimination in the United States to the detriment of the American image around the globe.[101]

García appropriated these discourses to bolster Mexican Americans' social standing and to argue for the elimination of Mexican laborers in Texas.[102] The Texas Good Neighbor Commission, set in place after the signing of the *bracero* agreement to stabilize relations with Mexico, provided García the necessary, if tenuous, rhetorical leverage.

The *bracero* agreement, the first and only federal statute forbidding discrimination toward Mexican-origin peoples, implicitly acknowledged the presence and possibility of racism against Mexican-origin peoples in the United States. Additionally, the *bracero* agreement was the only statute to secure wages of agricultural workers, an inconsistency in U.S. labor policy that García emphasized. Without union organizing rights guaranteed under the 1935 National Labor Relations Act, U.S. agricultural laborers remained comparatively disadvantaged.[103]

U.S. agricultural workers were not entitled to the minimum wage, unemployment insurance, health insurance, collective bargaining or pensions. Ironically, Mexican laborers contracted under the *bracero* agreements had more protection than their U.S. counterparts: contract guarantees for transportation, living expenses, and a minimum wage.

García leaned heavily on the *bracero* provisions and the Good Neighbor Commission for two purposes. He used the office of the Texas Good Neighbor Commission and national Good Neighbor rhetoric to advance the interests of citizens of Mexican-origin and to decry acts of discrimination. In his April 8, 1949, letter to Thomas Sutherland, García wrote, "we know fully well that there is a 'Great Need' for your Commission and certainly for a larger Commission and one who will apply more pressure and penalties on responsible individuals and agencies."[104]

García also used the Good Neighbor Commission to expose violations of the *bracero* agreements within Texas with the clear aim of eradicating the *bracero* program altogether. García sought to demonstrate the injustices of the migrant labor system to U.S. as well as Mexican government officials. In his January 19, 1951, letter to the Mexican Consulate General, Miguel Calderon, García reported an incident of discrimination in Seguin, Texas, against an immigrant. García advised:

> The discrimination of which Mr. Patlan was the victim is practiced against persons of Mexican or Latin-American descent, regardless of their citizenship. For this reason we urge the desirability of your government placing Guadalupe County, in which Seguin is located, off limits for purposes of *bracero* labor during the year of 1951.[105]

García rallied for support on both sides of the border, appealing to a binational audience to censure Texas and to end discrimination and the *bracero* program.

Within the context of the xenophobic Cold War era, however, García's anti-immigrant strategy took on a rhetorical life of its own. The Mexican labor issue gradually began to dominate García's focus as a target of attack, and his civil rights initiatives became entangled in a web of nativist discourses and rhetorical scapegoating. Through a complex rhetorical twist, García and the American GI Forum cast the Mexican national as the threat, the hindrance to Mexican American political, economic, and social inclusion. As a trope, the "wetback" became the primary symbol of Mexican

American displacement. The Mexican laborer was a "container" for all the ills facing middle class America. The solution appeared simple: close the border and eradicate the "wetback" and the *bracero* from the scene.

As reflected in his February 10, 1962, letter to Jerry Holleman of the U.S. Department of Labor, García relied on empirical evidence to call attention to Mexican American labor displacement:

> I just wish the Department of Labor would send an investigating team into the Rio Grande Valley and run a survey as to how many of our people are unemployed and how many *bracero*s are employed and consequently would our people get those jobs?
>
> . . . It is a shocking shame that with as many friends as we have in the Department of Labor and in the Attorney General's office that nothing has been done about the commuter's [Mexican labor] problem.[106]

Not only were Mexican laborers blamed for lowering wages, displacing American workers, interfering with unionizing efforts, spreading disease, increasing welfare costs and crime rates and heightening the risk of communist invasion, but they were also held responsible for lowering educational achievements and economic mobility of Mexican Americans as a class.[107]

Advanced through the primary premises of military service and citizenship, and reinforced by the suppressed premises of race and caste, the polemics surrounding the *bracero* immigrant labor program became integral to the advancement of Mexican American civil rights. Metonymic and synedochic emblems, the figurative disembodied arms and backs of the *bracero* and "the wetback" form the core of García's political discourse formations. Characterized as illiterate, diseased, uneducated, shiftless, immoral, and un-American, Mexican nationals became synonymous with what 1950s America feared most: subversives, spies, communists, invaders. Through rhetorical acts of disassociation, García found a strategy by which to demonstrate Mexican American veterans' repositioned status as citizens and their identification with the ideals of republican citizenship: literate, hard-working, educated, and civic-minded.

García and the American GI Forum's fifteen-year campaign for the repeal of the *bracero* labor program and support for the massive repatriation and relocation of Mexican laborers was rhetorically driven, directly and indirectly, by a discourse of dissimulation.[108] By forging metonymic and synedochic contrasts, the rhetorics of the American GI Forum cast the Mexican laborer as a dark specter, a shadow, a disembodied "other" beside the full-bodied, patriotic Mexican American citizen.

The American GI Forum's 1953 pamphlet called *What Price Wetbacks?*

constructs the image of the "wetback" into an emblem of threat, a device by which to define their mission as a civic organization. The introduction announces:

> The American GI Forum of Texas is an independent veterans' organization open to all honorably discharged veterans from either of the two World Wars or the Korean War. Its entire program, however, is aimed at improving the status of the Spanish-speaking population of the Southwest. . . .
>
> It is interested in the wetback problem because it considers this the fundamental problem facing the Spanish-speaking population in the Southwest. For this reason, the organization from its inception has been an ardent advocate of a border barred to illegal aliens, of stronger immigration laws, and of more personnel and facilities for the U.S. Border Patrol.[109]

By representing Mexican laborers as a threat to the "American way of life," García and the American GI Forum found a rhetorical strategy by which they could distance themselves from the Mexican immigrant and refashion an American identity. The dialogue and dialectic circulated among García and the American GI Forum reflect, among other things, a discourse moving toward the formation and adoption of a mainstream middle-class American civic identity.

To stir public outrage over the flood of Mexican immigrants, García and the American GI Forum collected and circulated "evidence" through reports, memos, letters, and resolutions depicting Mexican laborers as a caste prone to perpetuating disease, immorality, sexual promiscuity, crime, and multiple other social ills. In *What Price Wetbacks?* the American GI Forum asserted:

> We, as Texas citizens of the United States, living in the midst of the disputed economy of the border area, seeing wetbacks daily, watching our neighbors depart on the annual migration as a result of the wetback invasion, decided to make a report to the American people on what we saw happening around us. Perhaps, with our on-the-spot interviews with wetbacks, we can help awaken the people of America to the danger of this wetback invasion. Perhaps with pictures showing wetbacks and the conditions under which they live, we can convince the skeptics that there are actually wetbacks, and that they actually are a threat to our health, our economy, our American way of life.[110]

This appropriated nativist discourse did not originate with García or his vision for the American GI Forum. Fibers of the discourse remain inextricably linked to Constitutional-era immigration discourses and are tightly woven into the structure of feeling of mid-twentieth-century America.[111]

As veterans and as members of an emerging middle class, García and the American GI Forum found a way to construct an identity consistent with the aims and attitudes of the dominant U.S. middle class and the historical vision of democracy.[112] Exploiting the xenophobic tenor of the McCarthy era and fears of an immigrant "invasion," the American GI Forum and García used the "wetback problem" as a galvanizing issue to assert their own inclusion in the national fraternity. "An open border is a constant invitation to subversives and spies. . . . The answer lies in strengthening the immigration laws—and then enforcing them. Only then can the American people relax, secure in the knowledge that the threat of the wetback invasion has been halted," argued the American GI Forum.[113]

This shift to the political right was, in part, a pragmatic ploy to deflect Communist hysteria away from the American GI Forum as a civic organization. The "ethnic militancy" of the American GI Forum as the foremost national Mexican American organization made it especially vulnerable in a historical moment suspicious of leftist political action.[114] By naming and claiming common enemies, the American GI Forum was able to secure a place in mainstream America. Over time, the *bracero* question transformed into a litmus test of American-ness.

The December 1953 issue of the *American GI Forum News Bulletin* links the Forum's attack on the "wetback problem" with nationalist concerns over anti-American activities and the communist threat. The American GI Forum declared: "the existence of the wetback lowers health standards and poses a major threat to the security of the country in the sense that the wide open border poses a definite avenue for the infiltration of Communist agents and spies."[115]

The alignment of immigration issues with national security concerns gave the American GI Forum a way to vocally circumscribe Mexican Americans within the limits of U.S. social, economic, cultural, and geographical borders. The anti-*bracero* campaign of García and American GI Forum went beyond rhetorical action, however, and involved direct participation in covert paramilitary efforts along the southern borders patrolling, reporting, and subduing undocumented immigrants.[116] García was personally involved in the program but strategically remained in the background while American GI Forum officer Ed Idar Jr. took an active leadership role.[117]

In July 1954, leaders of the American GI Forum actively assisted with the implementation of "Operation Wetback," a "mass roundup and repatriation" effort coordinated by the U.S. Immigration and Naturalization Service under the direction of Lieutenant General Joseph M. Swing of the U.S. Army.[118] García did not participate in the apprehension efforts but was directly informed and approved of the operation. According to Idar, García chose to keep a low profile role throughout the mission. He did not directly aid in the round-up efforts. Tragically, he did not condemn them either. It is not clear whether or not García and the American GI Forum knew that General Swing was a notorious "Mexican hater" and had accompanied General Pershing in 1916 during the Mexican Revolution on a "Punitive Expedition" against Pancho Villa.[119] As the newly appointed commissioner of the INS, General Swing aggressively militarized U.S.-Mexico border operations. The American GI Forum did coordinate efforts and correspond with General Swing for "Operation Wetback." Moreover, García and the American GI Forum approved of applying aggressive military solutions to the "wetback problem."

With the knowledge and support of García and the American GI Forum, Swing's Mobile Task Force arrived in McAllen, Texas, on July 3, 1954 to execute "Operation Wetback." Border patrol units established roadblocks, patrolled railway lines, and apprehended undocumented workers.[120] Members of the American GI Forum assisted in the round-ups. Immigration officials reported the apprehension of increasingly larger numbers, beginning with the roundup of 1,500 Mexican nationals on July 6. On July 15, over 4,800 migrants were apprehended and transported back to Mexico. By July 29, officials in the lower Rio Grande Valley had apprehended 41,951 laborers.[121] The INS deported 1,035,282 Mexicans in 1954 at the peak of "Operation Wetback."[122] Speaking for García and the American GI Forum, Ed Idar congratulated Swing on the results in an August 14, 1954, letter:

> On behalf of this organization, I would like to extend to you and to the officers and men of the U.S. Immigration and Naturalization Service and the U.S. Border Patrol our sincere appreciation and gratitude for the extraordinary efforts that have been made in the drives along the Mexican border to enforce our immigration laws. . . .
>
> We are cognizant of the fact that some newspapers in the Rio Grande Valley have been critical of these efforts, but I would like to state that the Service has had and will continue to have the whole hearted support of this organization and of the Spanish speaking population.[123]

Not all the Texas Spanish-speaking population applauded the program. Depicting the historical moment, Emma Pérez situates the xenophobic tenor of the era:

> I was born in 1954, the year civil rights was initiated once again through "Brown vs. the Board of Education" in Topeka, Kansas. In the 1950s, pretension superseded reality. McCarthy must have frightened some

Mexicans into patriotic idiocies. How many turned their back on *mojados*? The wetbacks of ancestry forgotten.[124]

The incidence of violence and inhumanity of "Operation Wetback" are further chronicled by Rodolfo Acuña:

During the raids, U.S.-born citizens became entangled in the web. It was a victory for the INS and a blow to the human rights of Mexicans. Every brown person was suspect. Homes were searched illegally and U.S. citizens were seized and detained illegally.[125]

The practice of buslifting and boatlifting undocumented workers to the interior of Mexico continued through the end of 1955.[126]

García's cooperation with INS and his proliferation of anti-immigrant rhetorics deeply problematized his role as a civil rights activist. Because the target of García's anti-immigrant campaign were the poor *mestizo* caste of Mexican society, his strategies were ultimately racist and elitist. He forged compromises with the dominant social group to redress the inequities facing Mexican American citizens, resulting in shortsighted solutions that gave little relief to the poverty of Mexican American farm workers and failed to improve border living conditions overall. García's alliances with the Anglo hegemony, a political scope within which Lyndon B. Johnson figured prominently, were often conflicted by competing motives and ambiguous aims.

García and the Struggle Toward Citizenship

The discourse between García and Lyndon B. Johnson over the *bracero* issue and the "wetback problem" reveals enduring tensions associated with the Mexican American struggle to forge a national identity and to gain inclusion in American civic life. The anti-*bracero* rhetorics used by García and the American GI Forum, framed frequently in the form of appeals to Lyndon Johnson, demonstrate historical divisions based on race, caste, and citizenship. As two emergent voices in the national political scene of post-war America, Héctor P. García and Lyndon B. Johnson mirror membership within "two interlocking public orders, one egalitarian, the other entirely unequal."[127]

García and Johnson's discourse on the issue of Mexican immigration reveals the formation of a deep comradeship forged around questions of citizenship, race, and caste. Their dialogue also exposes two conflicting orders of discourse—the enfranchised "fraternity of white males" to which Johnson as a wealthy, established Anglo claimed by virtue of hereditary privilege, and the "imagined fraternity" to which García and Mexican Americans veterans as a cohort aspired.

After the furor of the Longoria incident had died down, García undertook a letter-writing campaign to Senator Johnson to address the issue of the "wetback labor problem." García outlined his concerns in this October 6, 1949, letter to Johnson:

> As our Senator, we are asking you to please consider our position and attack this problem on the basis of human beings and not merely grapefruit, cotton, tomatoes, etc., as some of the interests in the Valley have done so in the past. The first obligation of our government is to its citizens and I believe it is not too hard to see now that the whole importation of labor and the legalizing of wetbacks has only one object "cheap labor."[128]

Johnson's October 13, 1949, reply marked the beginning of the protracted pattern of appeal and appeasement between García and Johnson over the Mexican migrant labor issue. Much of the correspondence between García and Johnson through the 1950s centers on Mexican labor issues, with García voicing his objections to *bracero* legislation and Johnson placating. This fifteen-year pattern is reflected in Johnson's reply:

> Dear Dr. García, I appreciate the frankness with which you wrote your letter of October 6th. It is quite obvious that you have given this problem long and careful study and your views are both interesting and intelligent.
>
> I think you realize that I am as anxious as anyone to see that minority groups in Texas and in the Nation are protected from exploitation wherever possible. Certainly if our relations with Mexico are to continue on the friendly basis of the past, some suitable solution to the wetback labor problem is going to have to be worked out. . . . [129]

However, contrary to Johnson's assertion that "some suitable solution" to the "wetback labor problem" would need to be worked out, Johnson never took an active role to reverse the *bracero* program or to confront the exploitive labor conditions of Mexican laborers. Johnson, a rancher, a *bracero* user, and political figure with strong agricultural support, had many reasons for resisting García's anti-immigrant labor agenda. However, Johnson also had much to gain by securing political alliances with García and the Mexican American electorate. The end result was a fifteen-year stalemate in which Johnson couldn't afford to either accommodate or to alienate García on the issue.

Consequently, the "wetback problem" drives much of the rhetorical action between García, the American GI Forum, and Johnson during this early post–World War II period. Moreover, the Mexican labor issue would cause the only major rupture in what would become a durable and affectionate twenty-five year alliance between García and Johnson. Negotiating dividing interests and disparate alliances, García and Johnson would never directly tackle the issue together head-on, rather they danced warily around it for fifteen years, repeating the same steps to the rhythm of different tunes.

García inundated Johnson's office with letters, memos, reports, circulars, pamphlets, and articles. As García's coalition expanded from a local organization into the national-level American GI Forum, his anti-immigrant coalition enlarged to include other highly vocal opponents to the *bracero* program. From García's first letters to Senator Johnson concerning the "wetback problem" in October of 1949 until the termination of the *bracero* labor program on December 31, 1964, Johnson remained a primary recipient of the American GI Forum's appeals calling for the elimination of the program.

Of the more than one hundred items of correspondence in Johnson's Senate files concerning the *bracero* issue, however, there is no evidence of Johnson's resistance to the *bracero* program specifically or U.S. dependence on Mexican labor in general. As an Anglo Texas rancher himself and a strong representative of Texas growers, Johnson cautiously straddled conflicting interests over the matter. When the *bracero* program came up for renewal in 1958 as Public Law 78, growers bombarded Johnson's senatorial office demanding that he support the law. "[S]ince I understand you are a [*bracero*] user yourself, I know that you even more than most, will be able to appreciate our position," wrote the president of a Texas county grower's associations.[130]

In spite of García's vociferous anti-*bracero* campaign aligning himself with religious, labor, civic, and federal organizations, Johnson unofficially sided with those opposing a minimum wage for farm workers and quietly supported the renewal of the *bracero agreements* through Public Law 78.[131] Records suggest that Johnson's primary allegiances rested with the Texas growers and their demands for reliable and "cheap" labor offered by the *bracero* agreements. With the passage of Public Law 78, the president of the Texas Cotton Ginners' Association thanked Johnson for his help on the behalf of growers offering "appreciation for the efforts that you have given in the recent *bracero* labor fight."[132] Signaling the happy close of an extended strand of correspondence with Johnson concerning farmers' dependence on the *bracero* program, one owner of a small farming operation thanked Johnson "for the interest you have shown in my and other small farmer's behalf."[133] Johnson's passive if not direct support of the *bracero* program would in effect help to sustain Mexican Americans and Mexican migrants within the U.S. labor caste system.

In 1952, realizing their tenuous position among competing agricultural interests, García and the American GI Forum exercised a rhetoric of censure to protest Johnson's indifference to their position on Mexican migrant labor issues. The earliest and most significant rupture in the García-Johnson alliance came on July 6, 1952, during the American GI Forum convention in San Antonio. The America GI Forum adopted a resolution against Senator Johnson for his failure to support an appropriation bill designed to bolster the U.S. Immigration and Naturalization Service and Texas border patrol and to subsidize the airlifting of "wetbacks" back to Mexico. The American GI Forum resolved that Johnson's inaction was "in utter disregard of the friendship and high regard in which he has been held by thousands of citizens of Mexican-descent."[134] Resolution No. 1 of the American GI Forum of Texas 1952 convention reads in part:

> Whereas, The American GI Forum, the League of United Latin American Citizens, and other organizations have communicated frequently with U.S. Senator Lyndon B. Johnson on the so-called Wetback Problem, placing extensive documentation at the hands of Senator Johnson and making their stand known on this question; And
>
> Whereas, State and National officers as well as local Forums and Councils of both organizations . . . communicated by telephone and telegraph with Senator Johnson seeking his support for an appropriation for the U.S. Immigration and Naturalization Service of $4,001,000 with which the Service would have continued the airlifting of wetbacks to the interior of Mexico, would have strengthened its Border Patrol, and would have operated detention camps for wetbacks pending their deportation. . . .
>
> Whereas, Senator Johnson owes in large measure his position in the U.S. Senate to the vote of thousands of citizens of Mexican descent in South Texas . . .
>
> Whereas, Senator Johnson's actions have been contradictory to the principles of liberalism expounded by the late Franklin D. Roosevelt who was primarily responsible for Senator Johnson's elevation to the position of Congressman, and for the opportunities accorded to Senator Johnson as a Congressman which enabled him to acquire the prominence necessary to launch his campaign for Senator. Now, therefore, be it
>
> Resolved, That this fourth Annual Convention of the American GI Forum of Texas condemn Senator Johnson's vote on the Senate floor of June 26, 1952, against the appropriation for the Immigration Service as being in line with efforts in South Texas to continue the peonage and exploitation of human beings at all costs.

> Be it further Resolved, That Senator Johnson's vote is in utter disregard
> of the friendship and high regard in which he has been held by thousands
> of citizens of Mexican descent.[135]

García and the American GI Forum wanted decisive intervention. They
wanted to send the "wetbacks" back to Mexico as quickly and expediently
as possible. The appropriation bill under discussion would have helped to
accomplish this aim (if even only temporarily). It also would have bank-
rupted many growers. In the end, Johnson did not support it.

The pattern of rupture and repair between García and Johnson in the
wake of the American GI Forum resolution reads like scenes from a tumul-
tuous courtship. Fearing the loss of support from the Mexican American
constituency, Johnson responded quickly to restore his relationship with
García and the American GI Forum. As in other controversial actions
concerning the Mexican labor issue, Ed Idar, Texas state chairman of the
American GI Forum, took the role as the "front man." Although the action
against Johnson was a team effort with García, Idar was the one to push
the hard line and to "take the heat." This was a rhetorical strategy he and
García exploited on a number of occasions to protect García.[136] In this case,
the "good cop, bad cop" scenario yielded results.

Johnson's lengthy emotional reply in a letter to Idar dated November 14,
1952, appeals to a shared national fraternity. His highly charged lexicon
includes the words: "sorry," "regret," "disappointment," "desires," and
"friendship." The American GI Forum's censure aroused sufficient alarm in
Johnson for him to arrange a meeting with García and Idar in Austin before
Johnson's departure to Washington, D.C., for the upcoming congressional
session. Johnson writes:

> I am sorry that the friendship that I have shown throughout the years for all
> the Latin-American people should be forgotten or cast aside because I did
> not accept a belated request from a bureaucrat to give him substantially more
> money than he needed, was entitled to, or even than the budget contained
> for him. . . . There is no group for which I have done more or to whom I feel
> more kindly that the Latin-Americans. I have tried to show my friendship
> for them in a number of practical ways and I shall not be deterred from
> continuing to do so by resolutions which, at least to me, seem unfair.[137]

These rituals of rupture and repair suggest Johnson's heightened recognition of the growing power of the Mexican American electorate. Johnson
increasingly realized the importance of the Mexican American constituency
to his career. After the 1952 resolution, Johnson restored relations with
García and accepted García's invitation to address the 1953 American GI

Forum convention in Fort Worth as a keynote speaker. Furthermore, the "good cop, bad cop" strategy allowed Johnson to renew ties with García with only minimal damage incurred to their relationship. Johnson's subsequent 1953 address to the American GI Forum, effervescent and highly personalized, signaled the formation of strengthened alliance with García and the Forum. The opening remarks of Johnson's speech set the tone of his relationship with García and the Mexican American community that would endure over the next two decades. Johnson asserts: "You know—when I am with you, I have the sure-and-certain feeling that I am among friends. This is a marvelous feeling to have on an occasion such as this."[138] As will be discussed in chapter 5, the theme of brotherhood contained in the 1953 address would reappear in future correspondence between García and Johnson and resurface in Johnson's presidential Voting Rights Act Speech of 1965. Revealing his appreciation for García, Johnson's August 11, 1953, thank-you letter to García confided:

> The occasion of my appearance with the American GI Forum group in Fort Worth last week was one of the genuine highlights of my experiences during the last year. . . . I think it is most commendable that you have dedicated your services to advancing the rights of American citizens and if at any time I can ever assist you or the Forum, please give me the opportunity.[139]

The American GI Forum resolution had captured Johnson's attention, warranted a quick and strong response, and solidified the García-Johnson relationship, but the censure did not change Johnson's stance on immigrant labor. The *bracero* program continued in full force and the flow of undocumented workers increased.

Over the following decade, García did not curtail his anti-*bracero* campaign nor cease lobbying Johnson over Mexican labor issues. However, García did moderate his discourse with Johnson as their friendship and political interdependence strengthened. By early 1960 when Johnson had his eyes on the White House, García was eager and ready to help him get there. As illustrated in García's April 15, 1960, letter, rather than censure Johnson for resistance to his anti-*bracero* stance, García assumed a more conciliatory tone and advisory role. He invoked empirical evidence as the basis of his argument, assuming Johnson had read his report.[140] García respectfully informed Johnson at the cusp of the 1960 presidential election:

> As you know I have made a special study of the *Bracero* Program and I believe that is a needless program because it displaces American workers of Mexican origin in our country. I believe that our government should give protection and opportunity and good pay to its workers before importing outside workers. . . .

> I believe that some government whether it be the Federal Government or
> the State Government should give our farm workers a minimum wage. . . .
> However I do not want to appear demanding or abusive. . . . I respectfully
> submit this for your consideration and ask you to do everything in your
> power to help us out with this problem.[141]

Johnson's carefully crafted reply of April 28, 1960, reflects an appeal to
pathos and a common fraternity. He echoed a shared concern for the plight
of farm workers and a perfunctory promise to look at the situation further,
but makes no commitment to García's position. Johnson reassured:

> I certainly share your concern for the position of the farm worker in our
> economy. He has never had a fair share of our nation's prosperity. . . . I will
> keep a close watch on developments in connection with these bills, and
> you can be sure that if any of them reach the Senate, I will have your letter
> in mind.[142]

By and large, Johnson's rhetoric toward the *bracero* issue, as evidenced in
this letter and the following sample, is consistent with replies of the previous
decade. He remained conciliatory, passive, and noncommittal. His notes to
his May 31, 1960, letter to García concerning *bracero* legislation read: "Dear
Hector, I was deeply moved by your letter of May 18. I know that your interest in *bracero* legislation is motivated only by a high sense of public duty
and a strong feeling of compassion."[143] Beneath a penciled cross-out mark
is the line "You know I share these feelings." In the margins are Johnson's
hand-written notes to his secretary James Wilson: "Jim doesn't this commit
us to Hector's position?" signed with the initials "LBJ." Johnson wanted
to cultivate García's allegiance, but at the same time, retain control of the
relationship and avoid commitment on the immigrant issue. Johnson's letter
of reply conveys a more familiar and personal tone, no longer addressing him
as "Dr. Garcia" but rather "Hector." Johnson's discourse suggests García's
strengthening but still tenuous inclusion in Johnson's fraternity.

From their disparate positions, nevertheless, both García and Johnson
contributed to the reproduction of the system of pigmentocracy integral to
the dominant social and political configurations of Texas and the United
States. Johnson's passive stance on the *bracero* issue and the "wetback
problem" indirectly, if not directly, helped to sustain exploitive work conditions for Mexican-national as well as Mexican American laborers. On the
opposite pole, García's active anti-*bracero*, anti-"wetback" campaign served
to reinforce stereotypes and social divisions in U.S. border society based
on race, caste, and citizenship. The American GI Forum under García's
leadership exacerbated the exploitation and powerlessness of the Mexican

migrant laborer, misrepresenting the phenomenon of Mexican immigration as the source rather than a symptom of much larger structural issues within the North American socioeconomic picture.

Moreover, Johnson's failure to identify with García and the American GI Forum concerning the "wetback problem" and his lack of support for a minimum wage for farm workers signaled overt acceptance of the liminal status of Mexican-origin populations in the U.S. political, social, and economic scene. Johnson's contradictory pattern of support for Mexican American concerns and his own vested interests in Mexican labor reflects similar findings concerning his conflicted record on black civil rights issues. Johnson's unsympathetic stance on the *bracero* issue represents not only an index of Mexican Americans' fragile position in the Texas political machinery but also measure of García's tenuous standing in Johnson's "imagined fraternity," precariously positioned for as long as the *bracero* agreements remained in effect.

Rhetorics of Making Racism Visible

If there is a prevailing theme uniting each facet of García's civil rights efforts it would be making racism visible. García used linguistic coding (English and Spanish), imagery, symbolism, metaphor, and the national collective memory to construct a Mexican American civic identity—the honorable citizen and exploited victim. This strategy, however, turned in on itself as García intensified his anti-immigrant labor campaign. García's anti-"wetback" discourse was a refractive rhetoric, bending around and revealing not only the racist tenor of the dominant population but also the distorted and racist representations of the Mexican immigrant by García and the American GI Forum. Many of these discursive representations of the Mexican immigrant were reproduced and transformed into other discourses and genres. One example of a racist discourse formation advanced by García and the American GI Forum can be found in the Lyle Saunders and Olen E. Leonard publication of 1951. García's support of the research and circulation of the controversial report by Saunders and Leonard, "The Wetback in the Lower Rio Grande Valley of Texas," signaled the American GI Forum's first concerted effort to resist the growing presence of Mexican laborers in Texas.[144] Although García and the American GI Forum did not author the pamphlet, García approved its publication and authorized members of the American GI Forum to support the research.[145] Even more important, the tone, style, purpose, and empirical approach used in the Saunders and Leonard publication provided the template for the production of the subsequent 1953 American GI Forum pamphlet, *What Price Wetbacks?*

Significantly, García endorsed the research conducted by Saunders as early as 1949 with an initial field report entitled "Wetbacks" sponsored by the Advisory Committee for the Study of Spanish-Speaking People of the University of Texas.[146] The American GI Forum used this and subsequent research by Saunders to advance their anti-immigrant campaign. Not all leaders of the Mexican American community celebrated the release of the 1951 report. The content of *The Wetback in the Lower Rio Grande Valley of Texas* caused significant division and conflict not only within the ranks of the American GI Forum, but among Mexican American leaders throughout South Texas. Although García maintained a low profile role in the production of the publication, he came forward in the public debate to quell the volatile reactions it sparked. García did not anticipate the "disunion" that followed.[147] It was a division García would, nonetheless, struggle to mend.

In collaboration with George I. Sánchez, sociologists Lyle Saunders of the University of New Mexico and Olen Leonard of Vanderbilt University conducted their research for *The Wetback in the Lower Rio Grande Valley of Texas* in 1950 along the U.S.- Mexico border. The foreword by Sánchez begins with this description:

> Every citizen of the state . . . shares . . . in the evil effects and devastating repercussions that derive from the presence in the state of a hundred thousand to half a million homeless wanderers—men, women, and children without legal status, without skills, and without opportunity for improving their condition. No citizen of the state . . . can escape the consequences . . . which appear in the form of poverty, disease, slums, ignorance, dependency, low wages, and social and personal disorganization.[148]

The report defends the use of the local pejorative term "wetback" as a label for the subjects of investigation. "Illegal Mexican aliens are referred to in the Valley, and elsewhere, in the Southwest, as 'wetbacks,' a term which undoubtedly derives from the fact that so many of them arrive by swimming the Rio Grande," explain Saunders and Leonard in a footnote to the preface.[149] The stated purpose of the report is to "determine the extent and to outline the major implications of the periodic migration of illegal aliens into the Valley." The chapters include "An Introduction to the Lower Rio Grande Valley," "Profile of the Wetback," "The Problem of the Wetback in the Valley," and "The Wetback in the Valley."

The section of the report that caused the strongest objections was a segment in chapter 4 labeled "Relations with Anglos," an examination of Anglo attitudes toward Mexican-origin peoples based on anonymous interviews. "Almost any Anglo that one talks to in the Valley can discourse at length on the characteristics of 'Meskins' and why they are and must remain an inferior race," report Saunders and Leonard.[150] The report claims to document patterns of racial myth adherence among Anglos by depicting "an account of three fairly typical interviews on the matter in the Valley." Problematically, the authors declined to reveal the identities of the informants and footnote their entries with this inexact explanation: "These are not verbatim accounts, but rather summarized reports of points of view expressed in interviews lasting from one to three hours."[151] Some readers charged that Saunders and Lyle had fabricated the interviews for rhetorical effect. Without accountable sources, the report unabashedly promulgates pages of racist commentary and stereotyping.

A Valley politician supposedly said that "the local Spanish-speaking people have a gypsy spirit which makes them want to travel. They just can't resist going north each year, and it is fortunate that there are wetbacks around to take their place."[152] This same Anglo interviewee explained that segregation in the Valley is for "hygienic, not racial reasons. . . . We just can't have all those dirty, possibly diseased people swimming with our wives and children."[153] A state employee with a master's degree describes Mexicans as "creatures of impulse. . . . Mentally, they are all children." This second interviewee pointed to "five hundred years of burden bearing and animal-like living" as the reason that Mexican-origin peoples suffer poverty and underemployment.[154] The third interviewee, a farmer, complained, "The local Mexicans are no good. They've been ruined by being partly Americanized. They've been spoiled by the unions with their talk of a forty hour week and security for everybody."[155]

The authors of the report use this "evidence" to conclude that the characteristics described by these Anglos have been unilaterally attributed to all peoples of Mexican-origin because of an inability on the part of Anglos to make distinctions based on class, caste, and citizenship. They suggest that the influx of Mexican nationals must be curtailed in order to reduce Anglo antipathy toward local Mexican American citizens. The report concluded:

> And since the wetback, for reasons explained in a previous section of this report, is hardly representative of the best of Mexican culture, the characteristics believed to be those of local Mexican people are not such as to inspire in the Anglos any great liking for the group.[156]

The incendiary nature of these claims sparked protests by members of the American GI Forum, letters to South Texas editors, and divisions among Mexican American community leaders.

Alonso Perales, an established San Antonio attorney, World War I era civil rights activist, and founding LULAC leader, registered his complaint both personally and publicly.[157] In his December 3, 1951, letter of protest, Perales demanded the identities of the informants and asserted, "The statements are unfair because they are untrue and cowardly because the names and addresses of the interviewees were not given."[158] A public debate between Perales and Sánchez was played out in South Texas newspapers. A group calling themselves the "Leaders of the Latin American Citizenry of the Rio Grande Valley" circulated a flyer in Spanish and English calling for an "importante junta" in Mission, Texas. The group held protest rallies and called for a resolution to publicly condemn the three undisclosed interviewees, the researchers, the University of Texas, Sánchez (who had procured the funding for the research), as well as organizations such as the American GI Forum that had supported and praised the findings.[159]

J. T. Canales, a well respected Brownsville attorney, directly admonished Héctor García for his approval of the report. In an April 29, 1952, letter to García, Canales chastised García for his role in the controversy. Canales charged:

> It was therefore an error of yours and Ed Idar's part to give approval to the whole pamphlet, without reservation. . . . I did my best, as your friend . . . to get you to correct this mistake, but neither agreed with me—hence this unfortunate result of the division in our ranks. Now, Doctor, we all make mistakes; and neither you nor Ed Idar are exempt from this human weakness.[160]

The fissures between the Mexican American leadership widened rapidly. Threats of lawsuits flew. García regretted the divisions between two of the most respected senior leaders of the South Texas Mexican American professional class. On December 13, 1951, García submitted a letter in both Spanish and English to the editor of the San Antonio-based newspaper, *La Prensa*. As the founder of the newly established American GI Forum, García raised his voice in the hopes of bridging the seemingly irreparable chasm. García advised:

> As representative of this organization and as intimate friend of Attorney Perales and Dr. Sanchez, I want to say that I am very sad that there are differences between two great leaders of our race. I am very sorry that these personal differences have been carried to publication.
>
> With all sincerity and with all respect, I would like to beg these two men of ours who are loved and respected by all our people that they drop these differences and that they no longer publish anything criticizing each other. I

do not intend to take sides nor to say who is good or bad, I want only to beg
that there be no public attacks between our two dear brothers. . . .

Personally, knowing the prejudice that exists against our poor people in
the state I personally believe that there are individuals capable of saying that
which was published and much more. But, at the same time, I want to make
clear that what they said were lies and exaggerations, because all of us know
that our people may be poor but are good and clean and hard working.[161]

In spite of García's claim that he did "not intend to take sides," he identified
most closely with Sánchez, his long-time mentor. If García had had any
misgivings about the report, he did not allow them to squelch the overall
project that the Saunders and Leonard report purported to accomplish.
García stood firmly behind Sánchez. In his December 20, 1951, letter to
García, Sánchez thanked García for his enduring support and wrote:

I appreciate your congratulations. Such kind words are particularly
appreciated in light of the defamatory remarks being made by others. I'm
quite hurt and grieved that Perales and *La Verdad* should attack me in such
an unwarranted manner. After all, I'm guilty of nothing—unless sticking
my neck out for them and my people generally constitutes guilt.[162]

García lamented in his December 31, 1951, reply to Sánchez, "Personally,
I am fed up myself and although I feel sorry for the lot I still don't see why
I should be spending my money and killing myself physically for them
[Canales and his supporters]."[163] Some of the fissures never healed.

García and the American GI Forum were making a strategic shift to the
right, and not all Mexican American activists followed. Attorney and activist Albert Peña Jr. of San Antonio steered away from García's viewpoint,
eventually joining forces with labor interests. García focused on repairing
divisions within the American GI Forum. A resolution was passed by the
board of directors of the American GI Forum of Texas in San Antonio on
January 20, 1952, calling for the elimination of the offensive, anonymous
interviews from the Saunders and Leonard report. García wanted to restore
peace within the Mexican American community and his organization. The
resolution stated:

The method used of publishing anonymous opinions under the guise of
interviews is both obnoxious, unscientific and unlawful. The value of an
opinion or interview lies not so much as what is said; but on who said it. . . .

These three purported anonymous interviews add nothing constructive
to the pamphlet, which otherwise can be of useful service to us in Texas.
For these reasons we respectfully request the authors and publishers of said

pamphlet that the objectionable matter be suppressed in any future printing or reprinting of said pamphlet . . . [164]

The matter rested for a while. Nevertheless, by 1953, McCarthyism and the rhetorical "red-baiting" of the era were in full force and the questionable methods employed in the controversial Saunders and Leonard report were applied once again in the American GI Forum pamphlet *What Price Wetbacks?* The fact that García and the American GI Forum published their own anti-immigrant propaganda only two years after the release of *The Wetback in the Lower Rio Grande Valley of Texas* suggests that García neither regretted the American GI Forum stance on the "wetback problem" nor its strategies. *What Price Wetbacks?* unabashedly advanced prevailing stereotypes of the Mexican farm worker. The report categorizes "wetbacks" according to class distinctions:

> The vast majority of wetbacks are plain agricultural workers, including women and children, mostly from the peasant class in Mexico. They are humble, amenable, easily dominated and controlled, and accept exploitation with the fatalism characteristic of their class. . . . He accepts good or bad treatment, starvation wages, diarrhea, and other sickness for his children from contaminated drinking water and unsanitary living conditions—all this he accepts stolidly and philosophically. He does not think in terms of native labor displacement, lowering of economic standards, and the socioeconomic effects of his presence in the U.S. Ideologies are beyond his comprehension. He understands only his way of life: to work, to suffer, and to pray to the *Virgen de Guadalupe* for a better life in the hereafter.[165]

The American GI Forum circulated over 3,000 copies of *What Price Wetbacks?* to public agencies and officials. In his May 19, 1954, letter to García, Idar reports on the impact of the American GI Forum's "wetback" study published in the *Stanford Law Review,*

> please note the number of times that the name of the American GI Forum is used—perhaps this will give you an idea of the importance of the report and the recognition the Forum is getting as a result of it. Frankly, you have not the slightest conception of the great amount of prestige that we are gathering.[166]

Appropriation of the dominant discourse and immigrant scapegoating represented in the 1953 American GI Forum publication did not stir the kind of resistance that the Saunders and Leonard pamphlet had sparked. McCarthyism held a grip on the nation. McCarthy's anti-communist crusade reached its peak in the spring and summer of 1953 with the McCarthy hearings.[167] To demonstrate identification with outsiders was to risk being labeled a communist. This context permitted García's group to advance their campaign of rhetorical scapegoating with little resistance. The tactics paid off with great dividends, advancing their visibility and their reputation as guardians of the national welfare. The American GI Forum anti-immigrant campaign went on unabated until the termination of the *bracero* agreement in 1964.

Although the American GI Forum anti-*bracero* campaign failed to make legislative change, it did capture the attention of proponents of the program. García and his followers complicated the debate and even helped to stir a counter-campaign. A number of discourses in defense of the program emerged to quell the barrage of bad press raised against the program, especially from the U.S. government and Texas growers. Pamphlets such as the 1958 *Progress in Housing for Migratory Farm Workers*, sponsored by the U.S. Department of Labor the same year the *bracero* agreements came up for renewal, represent the working conditions of Mexican laborers in glowing terms with chapters entitled "Adequate Housing Attracts Good Migrant Labor," "Florida's Farms Tidy Work Camps," "Caldwell Labor Camp Beehive of Activity," and "California's Improved Housing Pays Off in Worker Morale and Public Relations."[168]

These Are the Braceros: Slaves or Willing Workers? written in 1958 by Elmer Kelton, agricultural editor of the *San Angelo Standard*, advanced the interests of Texas ranchers. Kelton conducted his research south of the border, interviewing so-called satisfied *braceros* represented in chapters such as "Mexicans Are Eager for Return U.S. Trip," "Even Mexico Employers Think Program is Good," "Tall Tales of Abuse 'Loco' Say Workers," and "Here's How Worker Gets Job Under Rigid Rules."[169] Kelton claimed, "A lot of adverse publicity has been given to the *bracero* program, charging all manner of exploitation and injustice. . . . What we actually found was a considerable surprise."[170] And what Kelton documents is the happy dependence of Mexican laborers on the U.S. market economy. With Mexico's labor surplus, Texas's high demand for Mexican labor, a strong agricultural lobby, and enduring government support of the *bracero* agreement, reports like these did little more than salve the public conscience.

As vociferous as their campaign remained, the American GI Forum and García did nothing to alter the growing dependence of the United States on Mexican labor. The issue was well beyond García's, the American GI Forum's, and even the state's spheres of influence. The 1954 *Stanford Law Review* article "Wetbacks: Can the State Act to Curb Illegal Entry" concludes:

The practice of employing Wetback labor has taken on a vested right aspect in the agricultural communities of the Southwest. The fact that illegal entry is a crime under federal law has meant little to employers who know that they can count on local law enforcement officers for an 'understanding' of their problems—particularly during planting and harvesting seasons. There is nothing to guarantee that the enactment of a state statute subjecting employers themselves to penalties would do anything to change this.[171]

The Stanford Law Review article acknowledges the intricacies of the issues and the overall impotence of the government's ability to reverse circular migration patterns.

García's troubled anti-*bracero*, anti-"wetback" campaign, however, was not a unidirectional discourse. It worked at multiple levels and targeted numerous audiences. It is important to tease out those strands to better understand García's role in Mexican American civil rights history and to map his influence in the post-war rhetorical situation. García's representation of the plight of the Mexican farm worker stirred the national imagination, putting a new face on racism in America. His portrayal of the country's poorest citizens contradicted America's post-war national self-image as just, egalitarian, and democratic.

César Chávez and the emergent Chicano movement of the 1960s would reweave and recast these same representations of the migrant farm worker to a more sympathetic American public ten years later. And García himself would march in solidarity with thousands of Rio Grande farm workers from the Valley to the state capitol in Austin on Labor Day 1966 to demand minimum-wage legislation for agricultural laborers. Carrying signs emblazoned with the word "J.U.S.T.I.C.E." and waving the American GI Forum flag, García and Forumeers united forces with farm workers to demonstrate against enduring exploitation of the Mexican American people.[172] Chávez's 1972 letter to García, greeting him as "Dear Brother," both thanks García for his support in "our struggle" and enlists his help in the historic Safeway stores boycott.[173] This public display of solidarity with farm laborers signaled a close to the fifteen year anti-"wetback" campaign.

However, the transformation of García's rhetoric of advocacy into a rhetoric of scapegoating had replicated racist discourses and stereotypes. The disturbing portraits provided by the Saunders and Lyle report and the American GI Forum pamphlet *What Price Wetbacks?* employed the same racist tactics García had so vociferously resisted in his earlier projects. Moreover, García and the American GI Forum's support of Operation Wetback was a grave violation of the human rights project García had so boldly conducted during medical school in the *colonias* of Galveston, during military service in overseas hospitals, and during the early years of his medical practice in South Texas migrant labor camps of the late 1940s.

Disturbingly, there is no doubt that García took an active, even if behind-the-scenes, role in the American GI Forum's program of blaming the victim. García understood the persuasive power of imagery. He had used the findings from his earliest research in the 1948 labor camps to shock the media and government officials into action. García also knew that change happened slowly if at all. Rather than resist the dominant discourse, García adopted it. He exploited the Caucasian Race Resolution of the 1940s and McCarthyism of the 1950s, twisting the words of white America to accommodate his people. Political rhetoric in racist post-war America was a dirty game, and García learned how to play it. Tragically, it also played him.

García and the Representation of the Farm Worker in Popular Culture

García's anti-*bracero* campaign made racism visible. He exposed the biases, prejudices, and myths based on race, class, and citizenship—those within the Anglo community as well as those within the Mexican American community. Unwittingly, García also exposed his own shortcomings. He was not alone. The circulation of anti-Mexican immigrant discourses by Mexican Americans, especially in the wake of Governor Coke Stevenson's 1943 Caucasian Race Resolution, was not unique to García. Other prominent Mexican American leaders well before García argued that Mexican immigrants were the obstacle to full inclusion of Mexican Americans in U.S. society.

Moreover, Mexican American activists such as the gifted orator and attorney Gus García of San Antonio exploited loopholes in segregation laws and definitions of whiteness to press for the inclusion of Mexican Americans. Gus García won a case in the U.S. District Court by arguing that Mexican-origin peoples were "whites and therefore Texas had no legal right to mix them with Negroes." The claim was sustained, declaring segregation against Mexican-origin peoples a violation of the Fourteenth Amendment of the Constitution.[174] Even Héctor García's most vocal opponent against the Saunders and Leonard report, Alonso Perales, insisted that segregation should not apply to Mexican Americans because they belonged to the "Caucasian race." In his 1948 book *Are We Good Neighbors?* Perales asserts that injustice toward Mexican Americans could be ended "by enacting both federal and state legislation forbidding discrimination against persons of Mexican and Spanish extraction and other descendents of the Caucasian race."[175] Yet by identifying with and appealing to the Anglo hegemony, Gus García, LULAC, Alonso Perales, Héctor García, and the American

GI Forum along with a growing contingent of Mexican American leaders replicated the very tenets of white supremacism that oppressed them.

In 1951, the same year that the report by Saunders and Leonard was published, *Look* magazine featured an article entitled "Texas' Forgotten People" focusing on García's work with the South Texas migrant laborers. This article illustrates how García's rhetoric operated at multiple levels, and in some cases, helped to forge new levels of racial consciousness in the American public. "Texas' Forgotten People" captured the attention and compassion of readers throughout America, eliciting letters to García and the editors of *Look*. Harriet Barker, letter editor of *Look*, writes García, "*Look*'s article has had some response that is heart-warming, and I only hope it will be effective in quarters where the most good can be accomplished by it."[176] She notes an enclosure of $3.00 in bills sent by a reader in Syracuse, New York, who "states his intention to send $3.00 each month." R. N. Jones from Corpus Christi, Texas, writes to *Look*,

> Heartfelt congratulations for your frank article on Mexican-Americans. . . . You may be surprised at the amount of indignation stirred up by your report. . . . Many of my fellow Texans still cling to the theory of racial inferiority of the Mexican. This theory explains everything but Dr. Hector Garcia, whom they dismiss as a quack, a trouble-maker and agitator.[177]

"Texas' Forgotten People" describes the "million and a half Mexican-Americans" in Texas living on "little more than hope." It includes pages of photographs of malnourished children, toiling elderly women, and desperately ill bedridden patients. The article documents the growing incidence of tuberculosis, poverty, unemployment, and death in *las colonias* where "disease obeys no color line."[178] The article tells the story of a young and devoted García tending the hopeless cases that Texas and America preferred to ignore. The article reports:

> The truth is simply this: Nowhere else in America is a group of people so downtrodden . . . and nowhere are human dignity and life held in such low regard. . . . In Corpus Christi, Dr. Hector Garcia, a 36-year-old veteran and the dedicated leader of his people in the city recently visited a 33-year-old woman T. B. sufferer. The home was a typical two-room hut occupied by the parents and nine children. The woman was gaunt, tired-looking. Her cheeks, topped by the characteristic high cheekbones of the Mexican Indian, were flushed and unhealthy. Garcia spoke scoldingly to her in Spanish. Her eyes dropped, she wheezed as she spoke, ended by slowly raising her palms upward in a stoic gesture.

"She came to me three years ago," he explained. "It had just begun. Had she kept coming and getting her shots regularly, we would have had it under control. She's too far gone now—not long for this world." Then he raised his palms in a similar gesture.[179]

Photographs show García administering injections to an elderly woman and child and examining the broken knee of a man who lived in an old chicken coop. The writer depicts García taking "a fistful of rumpled bills out of his pocket" to give to his patients for medicine. The writer carefully portrays García's tenacity and intense devotion, exposing in painfully explicit detail the end result of institutionalized racism.

García's growing national reputation especially captivated the interest of popular novelist Edna Ferber. Her long and productive career paralleled the major events in twentieth-century history, generating more than a dozen collections of short stories, a dozen novels, and six plays. Ferber was at the close of her well-respected career when she contacted García. She traveled to Corpus Christi in early 1950 to consult with him on a book about Texas, loosely based on the history of the world's largest ranching operation, the King Ranch located in South Texas. *Giant* would become her best selling novel. She spent three weeks traveling through South Texas and *las colonias* with García, studying the lives and circumstances of the Mexican people. In *The American GI Forum: In Pursuit of the Dream, 1948–1983*, Ramos concludes that "Ferber's work offered Americans one of the first popular portraits of broad-based inequality in America beyond the circumstances confronting black Americans."[180] But Ferber, through the guidance and perspective of García, offered Americans not only the first vivid portrait of racism against Mexican-origin people in the United States, she also demonstrated the inequalities generalized across groups in modern American society based on race, class, caste, and citizenship. Her fictional representation, like the national drama of the Longoria incident, helped to change the national conversation on race.

Giant focuses on a wealthy Anglo family in a cattle and oil boom town of South Texas in the first half of the twentieth-century. The fictitious town of Benedict, named after rancher Jordan Benedict's family, faintly reflects the world-renowned home of the King family for whom the town of Kingsville, Texas, was named. Jordan, or "Bick," manages his 595,000 acre "Benedict Reata Ranch" as his irrepressible Virginia socialite wife, Leslie, confronts the poverty, illness, and discrimination that plagues the impoverished Mexican migrant families. In one scene, Ferber depicts Leslie's dismay at the mass migration of Mexican laborers into Benedict:

Up and down the ranch. In and out of Benedict. . . . The workings of the little town, the pattern of its life, of the country life, of the Texas way of living and thinking, began to open up before her observant eye and keen absorbent mind.

"Jordan, what are those streams and streams of old broken down trucks and Fords that go through town with loads of Mexicans? Men and women and boys and girls and even little children. Swarms of them."

"Workers."

"Workers at what?"

"Oh, depends on the time of year. Cotton pickers. And vegetables and fruit. In the Valley."

"Where do they come from?"

"If they're Mexicans they come from Mexico. Even a bright girl like you can figure that out."

"And when everything's picked where do they go?"

"Back to Mexico, most of them. A few sometimes hide out and stay, but they're usually rooted out and tossed back."

"And where do they live while they're here, with all those children and everything? What are they paid?" . . .

"I don't know. Very little. Couple of dollars. Whatever they're paid is more than they'd get home in Mexico starving to death."

"Where do they live?"

"Camps. And don't you go near, they're a mass of dysentery and t.b. and every damn thing. You stay away. Hear me!"

"But if you know that why don't you stop it! Why don't you make them change it!"

"I'm no vegetable farmer, I'm no cotton grower. I'm a cowman. Remember?"

"What's that got to do with it! You're a Texan. You've been a great big rich powerful Texas for a hundred years. You're the one to fix it."

He shook his head. "No, thank you very much."

"Then I will."[181]

In turn, Leslie brings the benevolent Mexican American physician, Dr. Guerra (based on García), to tend the sick and dying women and children to the raging disapproval of her husband and the surrounding community. Although the themes of Mexican servitude and exploitation weave throughout the story, Dr. Guerra remains a shadow; he is lightly developed and confined to only the earliest parts of the novel. Nonetheless, García praised the book and the subsequent film.[182] He urged members of the American

GI Forum to purchase copies of the book. In his October 22, 1953, memo to the Forum, García wrote:

> It is a great honor when you have the authoress who wrote "Showboat," "So Big," "Saratoga Trunk," and "Cimarron" devote her time in writing about our work and sufferings. I understand that one of the big movie companies is trying to make a movie about "Giant." It would be best if you would become acquainted with it now before you see the movie. I recommend it very strongly.[183]

The film *Giant* was released in 1956 by Warner Brothers Pictures under the direction of George Stevens, featuring several icons of American cinema: Rock Hudson as Jordan Benedict; Elizabeth Taylor as Leslie; James Dean as the dark, brooding "wrangler-turned-rich man" Jett Rink. (It would be the last role of James Dean's "meteoric career." He died only a week after the filming for *Giant* was completed.) The character of Dr. Guerra would appear only briefly. He is momentarily shown accompanying Leslie to *las colonias* and briefly featured at the Benedict home on Christmas morning when he introduces young Jordan Benedict to his nurse, Juana, who soon becomes Jordan's young bride. Much is made of Jordan Jr.'s desire to assist Dr. Guerra and become a doctor rather than follow the ranching legacy of his father. And the marriage of Jordan Jr. to Juana, performed by a Mexican priest in solemn privacy without family consent, stirs the conflict and generates the rising convoluted action of the latter half of the film. Although the American GI Forum and García himself are generally effaced from the story, the South Texas social inequities that García struggled to make visible were projected to the American public.

In the closing line of the film, Benedict gazes at his fair-skinned blonde granddaughter and his dark-skinned *mestizo* grandson together in their playpen and muses, "My own grandson doesn't even look like us. So help us. He looks like a wetback." The closing statement, intended to signal Benedict's heightened sense of acceptance and to give closure to the family's conflicts, was both stirring and offensive. The film, all in all, made a bold statement in the midst of McCarthy-era blacklisting.

Four decades later, *Giant* provided the thematic springboard for Chicano poet Tino Villanueva's 1993 volume, *Scene from the Movie GIANT*, which won the 1994 National Book Award. Villanueva writes: "Three and a half hours had flicked by / As the sound / Trailed off into nothing/ memory would not dissolve."[184] Villanueva voices the violence of labeling, the act of exposure and erasure enacted in each frame. In "Fallingrief of Unpleasure" Villanueva depicts the visceral experience of viewing the film forty years after its release, summoning up painful recollections of his own experiences as a Texas migrant worker and life growing up in the hill country near Lyndon B. Johnson's family ranch.[185] Villanueva recalls:

> Wither on the floor, never to retrieve from darkness.
> Like fragments of thought flashing, the slow burn of
> Each frame rises into consciousness with the meaning
> Of failed belief. A fallingrief of unpleasure grows
> In you and something, call it the soul, deep is offended.
> You want to go mad or die, but turn morose instead.[186]

Villanueva's reflections depict the emotional dimensions of disfranchisement and displacement that García's earliest research attempted to quantify and empirically describe. Through García's direct guidance and indirect influence, *Giant* and Villanueva's poetic reaction to the film made racism visible to America.

The rhetorics of immigration, and more specifically the rhetorics of Mexican immigration, index the national imaginary in profound and ironic ways, exposing America's terms of identification and inclusion as well as alienation and exclusion. As Charles Paine observes in *The Resistant Writer: Rhetoric as Immunity: 1850 to Present,* "Rhetorical bodies, like bodies in the physiological sense, must become like a fortress that keeps invaders out."[187] García and the American GI Forum plumbed directly into historical ambivalences within the U.S. consciousness. Set in the context of post–World War II America, García's rhetorics of immigration (twofold assertions about the eligibility and entitlement of one Mexican-origin population over another) reflect more than Mexican Americans' struggle to improve their social standing and forge a national identity. These discourse formations index historical contradictions within America's terms of membership. Shklar maintains, "The tension between an acknowledged ideology of equal political rights and a deep and common desire to exclude and reject large groups of human beings from citizenship has marked every stage of the history of American democracy."[188]

García and the American GI Forum viewed the steady growth of Mexican immigration as a threat that undermined Mexican Americans' economic wellbeing. To wage rhetorical defense, García implicitly and explicitly manipulated negative racial and cultural stereotypes. Under Cold War political conditions, García and the American GI Forum tried to resist demographic shifts and at the same time reconcile themselves to America's historical contradiction, a contradiction that has defined the democratic imagination since the United States' beginning as an independent republic.[189]

The rhetorical scapegoating used by García and the American GI Forum is not unique to this group or even to U.S. history. In fact, rhetorical scapegoating toward one group by another has functioned as a device to mask inequitable social configurations throughout every generation of American history. "Ascriptive inequality" based on questions of race, caste, and citizenship as well as gender, creed, class, sexual orientation, and ethnolinguistic identity marks the American struggle for inclusion.[190] The residue of our first naturalization law limiting eligibility for citizenship to "free white persons" constantly seeps from national memory into contemporary political discourse.

There is no group that has stirred more overt and persistent anxiety in the American collective consciousness than the steady waves of immigrants making their way across our southernmost border from Mexico, the United States' leading source of new citizens since the institutionalization of the *bracero* immigrant labor program.[191] And, ironically, the post-war Mexican American middle class led by García and the American GI Forum served as a major force to battle that steady wave.

This blot on García's human rights record has received little if any attention in media retrospectives and is all but ignored in the few historical accounts available about García. Some of García's surviving American GI Forum contemporaries find no fault with García or the American GI Forum for the tragic course of the anti-immigrant campaign. The contradictions and silence are puzzling. The several available taped interviews with García cautiously avoid any mention of this chapter of his legacy. The elision in the record is telling. García's avoidance of the "wetback" issue suggests some measure of shame about it later in life. This was not a phase he was proud to discuss. Current political biographers ignore or minimize it. García's early labor camp investigations are touted. Operation Wetback is ignored.

However, historians' oversight of the anti-"wetback" campaign of García and the American GI Forum effaces an important dimension of the Mexican American struggle for civic inclusion. Among other consequences, ignoring the racist premises García replicated in the struggle for American civic inclusion ultimately reinforces them. Only critique can dismantle them. Intentionally and unintentionally, García made racism visible. His counterdiscourse exploited the dominant discourse, foregrounding the racist tenets of American enfranchisement. García's conflicted contributions to modern civil rights index not only the moment but the historical trajectory García both embraced and resisted.

García resonated with the American public. He struck a chord. Understanding how and why García had that kind of effect across social groups is especially efficacious from a twenty-first-century perspective as shifting demographics, growing immigration patterns, and national attitudes hauntingly echo the post–World War II moment. García inspired and instigated action in and through text, stirring controversy, sparking debate, and changing the conversation. At many levels, García's discourse on racism proved productive, especially in terms of Mexican American civil rights. The Longoria incident revealed García's vision. In contrast, García's anti-immigrant labor rhetoric proved futile and counterproductive. The "wetback" issue revealed García's blind spots. Nonetheless, as both cases dramatically illustrate, García exercised an authorial role, directly and indirectly wrapping language around the civic presence of the Mexican in American society. In the process, García exposed America to itself.

The "Imagined Fraternity" of Héctor P. García and Lyndon B. Johnson

5

*O*ver the twenty years between 1948 and 1968, Héctor P. García played an increasingly significant role in the post-war political landscape and civil rights reform.[1] The meteoric rise of the American GI Forum and García's reputation as an advocate of Mexican American civil rights paralleled Johnson's ascendancy to national prominence.[2] Through their collaborative and contentious engagement in partisan politics, García and Johnson helped to destabilize institutionalized discrimination in Texas and the nation. An examination of the García-Johnson relationship and their everyday rhetoric illustrates how García and Johnson together contributed to a social mosaic of political discourses—some of which, through complex sets of relationships and exigencies, ultimately coalesced into public policy. From disparate positions of power, García and Johnson enlarged the role of Mexican Americans in the U.S. political sphere.

From the 1949 Longoria affair to Johnson's 1965 Voting Rights Act speech, García and Johnson complicated America's terms of national belonging and recast the image of national communion.[3] Their common approaches to public rhetoric, combining formal address with accessible, colloquial speech, effectively aligned García and Johnson with America's growing middle class and the pragmatic structure of feeling of the post-war era. This chapter examines how García and Johnson's circuitous political courtship ushered in new levels of Mexican American participation in state as well as national governance. It begins by limning García's twenty-year alliance with Johnson as illustrated in their interpersonal discourse as well as illustrating García's engagement in partisan politics. Finally, this chapter analyzes the García-Johnson relationship and their role in the Longoria incident as heuristics shaping modern civil rights reform. For the first time in U.S. history, Mexican Americans took their places at the banquet table of national deliberation.

Telos *and Postwar Civil Rights Reform*

The relationship between García and Johnson offers a valuable case study of an alliance formed at "at the intersections" between legitimate social institutions and non-sanctioned political formations. The efficacy and political interdependence of the García-Johnson alliance suggest that modern civil rights reform rhetoric was informed by a number of variables and responded to many more audiences than current scholarship considers. To understand García's influence in modern civil rights history, however, demands looking at the margins of what has become the canonized discourse.

Revisionist studies that overlook the role of the Mexican American civil rights movement in Johnson's "Great Society" neglect a significant element of the rhetorical situation giving rise to social change. Generally recognized as "the strongest public discourse of Johnson's presidency," the voting rights speech marking the adoption of the Civil Rights Act of 1965 was a landmark occasion not only for Johnson and the nation, but García's reform movement as well.[4] García rallied for voting rights throughout Texas for nearly twenty years before the 1965 federal legislation was enacted. He devoted the same tenacity to voting rights issues as he directed to promoting Johnson's career across the political landscape of Texas. The 1965 Voting Rights Act was a watershed moment for both men.

The 1965 Voting Rights Act made the Fourteenth and Fifteenth Amendments enforceable for the first time in history. It provided for direct federal intervention, if and when necessary, to permit citizens to register and vote—overturning the pernicious poll tax in Texas that García and the American GI Forum had battled relentlessly. The new law also prohibited the use of literacy tests to disqualify citizens from voting, protecting the rights of citizens who do not speak English.[5] Evidence suggests that Johnson's relationship with García and the Mexican American electorate profoundly informed the imaginative construction of this historic civil rights reform policy as well as shaped the ceremonial rhetoric surrounding its introduction to the American public.

Mapping Johnson's contribution to modern civil rights reform begins with an understanding of the *telos* both revealed and masked in his relationship with García and the Mexican American constituency.[6] If we inform the historical context of Johnson's civil rights reform policies with the engaged presence of García and the Mexican American community acting as persistent agents of influence, the narrative of 1960s civil rights reform is significantly complicated. Enlarging the scope of the post-war era to include the examination of García and the Mexican American community makes it evident that Johnson's civil rights agenda began much earlier than current rhetorical studies consider. Modern civil rights rhetoric evolved out of an array of discourses, not the least of which were forged in the sustained dialectic carried on between an ambitious junior senator and a tenacious rural doctor.

The political interdependence between García and Johnson was forged in 1949 around the Longoria case. Together García and Johnson were persuasive and astute communicators who knew how to effectively navigate Anglo and Mexican American audiences. Where gaps existed in access or understanding, each relied heavily on the other to build coalitions of support. The texts circulated between García and Johnson within the context of post-war America reveal a range of rhetorical choices demonstrating the intellectual and social powers of these two important rhetoricians moving toward social change. Johnson's conflicted civil rights record finds its greatest consistency in relation to the Mexican American community.

Although Johnson's record on civil rights and his relationship with black activists such as Martin Luther King Jr. has been examined, there is scant research that considers how Johnson accommodated (and failed to accommodate) Mexican American civil rights activists and the Mexican American constituency so integral to his political career. Johnson's civil rights record, especially before the presidential period, is spotty. Contradictions in Johnson's background abound. Johnson's congressional "record on race" from 1937 to 1948 was "mixed at best." He engaged in political actions "that seemed to betray some African Americans' belief that he cared about their plight."[7] In the 1952 presidential race, Johnson endorsed Georgia senator and segregationist Richard Russell for the Democratic nomination, parting ways with the liberals or "Loyal Democrats" who had supported Truman's agenda on civil rights and social programs.[8] Johnson also opposed federal anti–poll tax and anti–lynching legislation and resisted enacting legislation to resolve racial tensions. In *The Modern Presidency: Rhetoric on Race from Roosevelt to Nixon,* Garth Pauley summarizes: "Many African Americans in Texas lashed out at Johnson for his stance on civil rights measures, yet the senator enjoyed political benefit among many whites back home for his anti–civil rights stance."[9]

Johnson's senatorial record was no less conflicted. He had "mixed feelings" about the 1954 *Brown v. Board of Education of Topeka* ruling reversing the "separate but equal" doctrine imposed by the *Plessy v. Ferguson* decision of 1896.[10] Johnson feared it would "play hell" with his leadership role in the Senate. He didn't want to argue for it, and he didn't want to argue against it. In 1956, he publicly disavowed all identification with the growing civil rights movement. As Robert Dallek argues in *Lone Star Rising:*

Lyndon Johnson and His Times, 1908–1960, Johnson believed that "his opposition to civil rights reform was not racist.[11] Johnson "had no quarrel with the aims of civil rights advocates, only their methods."[12] Johnson was frequently quoted as declaring, "I am not a civil rights advocate."[13] And yet Johnson pushed through congress the Civil Rights Act of 1957, the first civil rights bill enacted in eighty-two years. Giving new powers to the attorney general to prosecute violations at the polls, the new act was meant to protect voting rights.[14] John F. Kennedy described the bill as "an eloquent but inadequate Act."[15]

In reflection, García interpreted Johnson's inconsistent record from a different point of view:

> People say Johnson followed President Kennedy's civil rights ideals. I can't argue that way, but I say Johnson would have pushed civil rights from the very beginning if he could have. He was like this. But of course, if you were like this in '48 or '49, and you espoused it before the Texas establishment, you were a dead duck politically. . . . As it was, they started calling Johnson many bad names [as a result of his involvement in the Longoria incident]. I think they insulted the man pretty much.[16]

García understood Johnson's actions from a twenty-year vantage point. He saw Johnson's "Great Society" as the completion of a work begun in the outposts of South Texas. He pardoned Johnson's idiosyncrasies and inconsistencies as all part of the work of politics. What mattered in the end to García, the consummate pragmatist, was that Johnson got the job done. He and Johnson had set the stage for post-war America's civil rights drama early in their careers. In many respects, every other event after that was but a new act for the same script. Both García and Johnson imagined the presidency as the final, synthesizing performance.

In striking contrast to his early years, Johnson's record during his White House years represented one of the most productive civil rights periods in U.S. history. More civil rights legislation was enacted during Johnson's tenure than under any other twentieth-century president. Johnson signaled his public commitment to civil rights in 1963. When questioned why he so ardently supported the civil rights bill, he invoked the words of Martin Luther King Jr.: "Free at last, free at last. Thank God Almighty, I'm free at last."[17] Robert Dallek argues in *Flawed Giant: Lyndon Johnson and His Times, 1961–1973* that "Johnson was describing himself as liberated from his southern political bonds or as a man who could now fully put the national interest and moral concerns about political constraints imposed on a Texas Senator."[18]

For the next five years, Johnson would use the power of the rhetorical presidency for civil rights reform. Speaking from the office of the Vice President, Johnson celebrated the one-hundredth anniversary of the Gettysburg address by confronting America's racist terms of inclusion. He delivered the 1963 Memorial Day Address overlooking the graves at Gettysburg, making a bold call for racial equity and separating himself from the lackluster civil rights record of his congressional and senatorial years. His address was delivered just six months before the assassination of President John F. Kennedy. Johnson's 1963 Gettysburg message foreshadowed what would become a primary focus of his presidential administration. Marking the one-hundredth anniversary of the Gettysburg address, Johnson proclaimed:

> On this hallowed ground, heroic deeds were performed and eloquent words were spoken a century ago. . . .
>
> One hundred years ago, the slave was freed.
>
> One hundred years later, the Negro remains in bondage to the color of his skin. . . . Our nation found its soul in honor of these fields of Gettysburg one hundred years ago. We must not lose that soul in dishonor now on the fields of hate. . . .
>
> Until justice is blind to color, until education is unaware of race, until opportunity is unconcerned with the color of men's skins, emancipation will be a proclamation but not a fact. To the extent that the proclamation of emancipation is not fulfilled to fact, to that extent we shall have fallen short of assuring freedom to the free.[19]

Fourteen years after the poignant Longoria burial at Arlington, Johnson commemorated the nation's symbolic funereal occasion at Gettysburg. Moreover, Johnson employed the rhetorics of death and identification to frame his emerging civil rights agenda. "We must not lose that soul in dishonor now on the fields of hate," he reminded America.

Reflective of his early civil rights baptism by fire, Johnson's 1963 Gettysburg address poignantly echoes the 1949 telegram he sent to García in response to the Longoria case:

> I deeply regret to learn that the prejudice of some individuals extends even beyond the grave. I have no authority over civilian funeral homes, nor does the federal government. However, I have today made arrangements to have Felix Longoria reburied with full military honors in Arlington National Cemetery . . . where the honored dead of our nation's wars rest."[20]

On Memorial Day 1963, Johnson publicly extended his commitment to civil rights advocacy, first avowed to the Mexican American community of Texas in 1949, to African American citizens across the nation.

Even as a white, rich, privileged politician from Texas, Johnson remains no less a paradox than his *compadre*, Héctor P. García. Johnson's *ethos* as a leader, forged in the fires of death and identification, would attain its greatest historic value in matters of American racial equity. These seemingly contradictory facets of Johnson's political record remain as puzzling and underexamined as the inconsistencies in García's legacy of resistance. Johnson's durable, interdependent relationship with García and the Mexican American community opens up critical questions about how this constituency informed Johnson's career, as well as historic civil rights policies. Johnson's bold civil rights program makes greatest sense situated within the context of these relationships and formative experiences.

The bonds of identification formed with the Mexican American community extend across the full span of Johnson's professional life, beginning in 1928, when he was a teacher in a Texas "Mexican" school. Johnson's connection to the Mexican American constituency, more than his affiliation with any other minority group, prefigures his eventual endorsement of sweeping civil rights legislation during his White House tenure. Clearly President Johnson intended his programs and policies to impact and improve conditions for all minority groups in America. However, Johnson's association with the Mexican American community from as early as 1928, his experience with the Longoria incident as a model of social action in 1949, and his twenty-year relationship with García foreshadow important shifts within Johnson's civil rights policies that demand closer consideration.

The trajectory of the García-Johnson coalition reveals a liaison that resists strict categorization, enduring repeated rupture, shifting between the fraternal, the political, and the instrumental. A brief overview of their twenty-year relationship reveals the persistent move toward consubstantializing political energies as they grappled with national questions on race and belonging.[21] As New Deal liberal democrats, García and Johnson operated out of a common vision of government that would compensate for the limits of capitalism and historical ascriptive inequality.[22] The New Deal program and its capacity for providing pragmatic responses to immediate problems appealed to leaders like Johnson and García who wanted instant results.[23] Liberalism, never "a uniform or stable creed," provided a broad ideological umbrella for New Dealers like García and Johnson, whose politics and rhetoric were informed by alternative and even contradictory political traditions.[24] García and Johnson, however, remained true to the spirit of Franklin Roosevelt's belief in the obligation of government leaders "to work aggressively and affirmatively to deal with the nation's problems."[25]

Although their alliance was marked by periods of discord, especially over the *bracero* issue, García and Johnson realized early that in order to achieve their aims, they needed each other. In a 1969 interview, García described his relationship with Johnson:

> . . . . The question was asked of me: How is it that you can be against Texas governors and be such a great friend of Lyndon Johnson, President Johnson, Senator Johnson or Vice President Johnson? And I said, "Well, because first I served my country in wartime. I think President Johnson has always liked Mexican Americans. He has chosen me I'm sure over (perhaps I'm just imagining) the wishes of Texas governors because I have received . . . many high honors. All the recognition with the exception of my first recognition from President Kennedy, I have received from either Vice President Johnson or President Johnson.[26]

From García's first telegram to Johnson in 1949 delineating the events surrounding the Longoria case, García looked to Johnson for access to sanctioned political structures. Johnson, in turn, relied on García's influence to win over the Mexican American electorate, a margin upon which his long political career remained contingent.

Clearly, the freshman Senator Johnson quickly heeded the suggestion by Robert N. Jones of the Texas Railroad Commission to join forces with García. The vivid portrait of García's role in the South Texas Mexican American community helped to persuade Johnson to strengthen his political ties with the charismatic, indefatigable doctor. In this November 1949 "confidential report," Jones advised Johnson:

> I wish to call to your attention the results of last week's election in Nueces County, especially with regard to the part played by Dr. Hector P. Garcia of Corpus Christi. . . . The purpose of this letter is to point out why I believe it was Dr. García who brought about this landslide, and how he did it. I believe, in so doing, I am helping both you and Dr. Garcia, in guiding you to an early realization of the political potentialities of this man. . . . May I let you know what the Doctor has been doing these past few weeks. He sent out letters, inclosing a sheet in Spanish titled "El Voto de Honor," and a *marked ballot*, to two thousand voters. He went on the air for paid spot announcements during two very popular Spanish-language broadcasts. He urged all chapters of the American GI Forum, of which he is founder, busiest organizer, and state chairman. . . . Incidentally, they distributed 23,000 copies of "El Voto de Honor." He is always getting around to a great number of gatherings and dances all over South Texas, and this he did during the past campaign. Last January he held meetings in several schools for the purpose of getting

his people to pay their poll taxes, and poll taxes were sold on the spot. There the groundwork was laid for the election victory. Lots of people make speeches, yes, but Dr. Garcia has the universal admiration of these people down here. They believe in him. Everybody swears by him. He has a wonderful personality. He is an untiring worker. His idealism and integrity are beyond question. You and Rep. John Lyle were present at a recent state board meeting here in Corpus Christi of the American GI Forum. You met Dr. Garcia and you saw him at work. I think you will agree with me that the Mexican people are behind him one hundred percent. You remember the Three Rivers case—that was Dr. Garcia in action. . . . Senator, here is a man who cannot be ignored. I believe that thousands of devoted people see in Dr. Garcia, a savior, no less. He is the one man who seems capable of making Texas a decent place for Mexican-Americans to live. I say this as my cautious estimate of the situation: Dr. Hector P. Garcia is destined to carry a lot of weight in South Texas, Mr. Senator.[27]

This portrait of García was not exaggerated. García mobilized more voters than any other South Texas Mexican American leader of his day. Johnson listened to Jones's recommendations and established an open line of communication with García that would prove again and again to be productive. Strained and frayed with the tensions of partisan politics, their relationship was never severed. Even though they straddled different positions, answered to different interest groups, and claimed membership in disparate social entities, García and Johnson consistently moved together to coalesce political forces.[28]

Rhetorics of Inclusion and Partisan Politics

García's reputation as a citizen, as a healer, as a veteran, and as a social activist made him a dependable ally for Johnson. García's rhetoric of inclusion, framed as an Americanist mandate rather than an anti-American critique, made him a reliable and safe collaborator. In the face of resistance and setbacks, García never abandoned or lost faith in the liberal democratic vision. García's project was at its core a reiteration of American constitutional rhetoric. His discursive acts of identification harkened back not to *lo mexicano* and revolutionary Mexico, but to the federalist vision of American "self-subordination in the name of 'unity.'"[29]

Disparities and commonalties in García's and Johnson's backgrounds provide insight into their individual and collaborative exercise of rhetorical power. There was an immediate and lasting mutual attraction that sustained their relationship in spite of their differences. As affirmed by Liz Carpenter, who served as an executive aid, personal friend, and confidante to Lyndon and Lady Bird Johnson for over thirty years, genuine affection existed between the two men. In her experience, Johnson did not like strong "outspoken" women; however, he admired strong men like García.[30] At each phase of Johnson's White House career, García enjoyed access to Johnson's inner circles.

Tracing their parallel careers reveals the critical junctures at which García and Johnson forged enduring connections in spite of their differences. In contrast to Johnson, who founded his career on birth-ascribed status as an Anglo Texas rancher and heir of the Johnson political legacy, García operated out of a self-ascribed, self-authorizing role of advocate and political activist. Both García and Johnson returned from the war to pursue careers in public service. In 1948 while Johnson was campaigning for a seat on the Senate, García was mobilizing veterans for the formation of the American GI Forum. Johnson's senatorial campaign was not a love-fest with Texas voters. It was his second attempt at trying to win the office. García's and Johnson's political paths would intersect within less than a year of the watershed moment of the first American GI Forum meeting held in March 1948.

Johnson campaigned in Corpus Christi during the 1948 Senate race only six months before the Longoria affair. The thematic juxtaposition of Johnson's July 7, 1948, radio campaign speech in Corpus Christi with García's message to the community promoting the American GI Forum offers vivid portraits of the disparities in their individual life worlds and experiences. The sense of entitlement and inherited status depicted in Johnson's radio address as he describes a bucolic South Texas and his family ranch in Johnson City stands in dramatic contrast to the Mexican American struggle for literacy, citizenship, and political enfranchisement represented by García's American GI Forum promotional flyer.

In this radio address, Johnson reflected, "As we flew up the Rio Grande Valley today, I thought about what I should say tonight to this radio audience. Beneath our plane we saw the fertile farmlands, the neat little towns and cities, farmhouses, churches, and schools, a peaceful prosperous countryside. . ."[31] Johnson's quaint depiction of South Texas contradicts at every level the experience of García's poverty-stricken people. In striking contrast, García's 1948 promotional flyer represents a very different socioeconomic condition:

> Atencion residentes de Corpus Christi: Desea usted aprender a leer y escribir? Desea usted sacar sus papeles de ciudadania americana? Quiere usted saber poner su nombre en vez de esa 'x'? Si usted esta interasado en estas ofertas entonces no deje de venir a la gran junta que habra en la escuela

Lamar ubicada en calles 19 y Morris el lunes de febrero: a las 7:30 P.M. [32] [Attention residents of Corpus Christi. Do you want to learn to read and write? Do you want to acquire your American citizenship papers? Do you want to learn to place your name instead of this "x"? If you are interested in these offers then don't miss coming to the big meeting that will be at Lamar School located at 19 and Morris Monday on February at 7:30 P.M.]

Literacy, citizenship papers, and the ability to sign one's own name—the most rudimentary emblems of national belonging—were the primary concerns of García's constituency. García and Johnson did not meet during his campaign stop in Corpus Christi; their political lives would become intertwined only six months later when the Longoria incident erupted.

After a hotly contested campaign, Johnson's senatorial bid proved successful. On January 10, 1949, only seven days after taking the oath of office, Senator Johnson was informed by Garcia of the refusal by the funeral director in Three Rivers to provide burial services for Private Félix Longoria. Senator Lyndon B. Johnson keenly understood the critical role of Mexican Americans in the military and in the future of Texas politics. As a Texas rancher, former school teacher in the Cotulla "Mexican" school, and a Navy officer, Johnson realized the implicit and explicit conditions of inclusion (and exclusion) for citizens of Mexican origin. In spite of his precarious position as a new senator, he demonstrated strong identification with Mexican Americans in response to the news. [33]

At each stage of his political career, Johnson revealed an affinity for García and the Mexican American community. Reflecting back on their relationship during a 1969 interview, García recounted with enthusiasm his first meeting with Johnson. García and Johnson met on October 30, 1949, during an American GI Forum meeting in Corpus Christi. It was a landmark moment for the American GI Forum for several reasons. The storm over the state legislature's investigation of the Three Rivers case had settled and García and the American GI Forum survived the political turbulence relatively unscathed. The Forum was experiencing tremendous growth. Chapters were sprouting up all over the state. It was during this October meeting that the American GI Forum declared itself a "state wide society." The attendance of Senator Johnson and Representative John E. Lyle at the event validated the fledgling organization. Lyle, a mutual friend whom García had first met in Italy during the war, made the introductions. García recounted this first meeting with Johnson with affection:

> I remember I met him—at one time we were having an American GI Forum meeting in Corpus Christi at the Lamar School, I think it must have been in

the early part of '49 or '50. It must have been 1950, I remember it was election year for somebody, and he came in with Congressman John E. Lyle who was still our congressman. And he talked to us. I met this tall, good-looking young senator. Of course, we went to thank him, I said, "Senator Johnson, I want to thank you because I think you've done a great thing for our people, and our country, and our soldiers." And I remember his words quite easily today. He said, "Dr. Garcia—" of course now he calls me Hector and I appreciate that because I feel he considers me a friend of his and I prefer to be his friend. He said, "Dr. Garcia, I think greatly of your organization and there is only one [piece of] advice I want to give you. You can achieve anything if you want if you just take it easy and slowly."[34]

In many respects, García did heed Johnson's advice over the next two decades. For some, García would take it too "easy and slowly." A report by J. Luz Saénz, president of the McAllen, Texas, chapter of the American GI Forum describes the occasion of García and Johnson's first meeting in detail. Luz foreshadows many of the recurring themes circulated between García and Johnson for the next twenty years.

> On October 30, 10 A.M. at La Mar Elementary School of Corpus Christi, state officers and advisors, GI Forum presidents and a substantial number of members met for the first time after declaring our organization a state wide society.
>
> Before beginning our business session, we were honored by the presence of U. S. Senator Lindon (sic) Johnson and U. S. Representative Johnnie Lyle. Both of them addressed our assembly. . . . Their talks were short, to the point, inspiring, touchy, sincere, and solemn. They gave us the opportunity to review our past activities specially in regard to the unfortunate Three Rivers incident.
>
> We [Mexican Americans] had known Lindon Johnson since his college student days at SWSTC [Southwest Texas State Teachers College] at San Marcos, and as a teacher in the public schools where he taught children of our race. . . . It was due to much of his untiring, patriotic, altruistic, democratic, and Christian efforts that the remains of our racial brother Felix Longoria were buried at Arlington National Cemetery after such funeral service were denied by an inferior type of funeral undertaking concern of Three Rivers, because of the debased racial prejudice of its owners. . . .
>
> Congressman Lyle, a champion of people's rights as Senator Lindon Johnson had designated him, delivered a short, rhetorically adorned peroration in which he mentioned his and Dr. Garcia's comradeship on the battle fields of Italy when Dr. Garcia once gave him a lift on his

ambulance. The brotherhood created on such precarious instances of life are everlasting.[35]

Johnson's teaching experiences in South Texas, the Longoria affair, the Arlington burial, and the themes of racism, comradeship, democracy, patriotism, and brotherhood all appear in this brief vignette. It was an intimate and critical moment for both García and Johnson. On behalf of the American GI Forum, García publicly named Johnson as *nuestro verdadero amigo,* our true friend.[36] The occasion prefigured what would become the most productive era in modern American civil rights history. In the process, García and his generation would become the "most politically successful" Mexican American civic activists in the twentieth century.[37]

García and the Mexican American electorate of Texas never forgot Johnson's act of intervention on behalf of Félix Longoria. "[E]very election since that time . . . we—the Mexican Americans—have given him 98 percent of the votes, and I think that is certainly a tribute to this man," García once recounted. In the decades following the Longoria incident, García consistently credited Johnson for the international impact of the moment at Arlington cemetery:

> And this is how I got to know this great man, who came to us in a moment of sadness, need, and suffering. And this action restored a great amount of faith in the system, and certainly in the State, and in our government. I don't know what I would have done at that moment without the help of Senator Lyndon Johnson because our people were very restless and very, very upset and certainly we were very unhappy.[38]

In the controversy of the Longoria case, García and Johnson found reliable helpmates in each other.

As young leaders, García and Johnson shared "a boundless energy and drive."[39] García was only six years Johnson's junior. Having served as officers in the war, they held in common a strong military *ethos.* Neither had fought on the front lines of action but both were proud and vocal about their participation in the war effort. García spent over two years overseas; Johnson spent only seven months on active duty.[40] "We were kindred spirits," García once described. "We understood each other."[41] Even more importantly, García and Johnson shared a great interest in higher education. Johnson respected and admired García's educational accomplishments. Johnson, whose spotty academic record made him ineligible for admission to the University of Texas, was never the student García was but nonetheless valued education as much as García did. Johnson was often "ashamed of his education and [would] compare it unfavorably with that of other contemporary political leaders."[42] He recognized the exceptional discipline and determination required for García to attain what he had achieved, academic credentials that far exceeded his own.

Both García and Johnson knew intimately the historical divisions that separated their two worlds—a privileged Anglo and a poor Mexican immigrant. Johnson understood the barriers that García had to overcome to reach his level of accomplishment. Johnson's first job, as a teacher in the "Mexican" school in Cotulla, Texas, in 1928 gave, him firsthand knowledge of the realities of García's world—his home, his struggle, and the unrelenting burdens facing his community.[43] During the summer of 1928, Johnson had dropped out of South West Texas State Teachers College in San Marcos for a year to teach and pay off debts and to save money to finish college. His performance in his coursework was less than stellar, and he needed a change of venue. In September 1928, Johnson drove his newly purchased Model A Ford from the luscious Texas hill country south to the dry, treeless desolation of Cotulla just sixty miles from the Mexican border.[44] Johnson was assigned to teach at the "all Mexican" Wellhausen school. Since few accredited teachers were willing to come to this part of Texas, Johnson was appointed principal.[45] He remained there one year before returning to San Marcos to finish his degree. The impact of that experience never faded. Some would even argue it caused an existential shift in Johnson. Those early years of Johnson's career became "part of the folklore of the man."[46]

When Johnson met García twenty years later in 1949, Johnson understood the educational, economic, and health conditions García confronted as a physician, decorated Army officer, and advocate for his people in South Texas. Johnson also understood the culture and the *ethos* of honor that informed García's approach to public service. The Longoria incident had demonstrated to Johnson both the character and the vision of the man who had stirred national outrage toward Three Rivers and institutionalized discrimination in Texas. Set in the context of post-war Texas, the very act of forming an alliance transgressed social boundaries. Symbolically, politically, and rhetorically, García and Johnson together confronted a century of social conventions dividing Texas Anglos and Mexicans.

Under the barrage of political fire during and after the Longoria incident, García and Johnson had withstood attack with unwavering resolve. "I could not understand the antagonism or viciousness of their insult toward Johnson," García recalled. "No sooner had Felix been buried than the Texas legislature decided they were going to hold an investigation, and the investigation really meant at this time to try to embarrass me and to try to embarrass Senator Johnson."[47] The legislative investigations had placed García and Johnson together under international scrutiny. They were implicated for the same "crime:" exposing racism in Texas. They were convicted and celebrated at the same time. This was a battlefield kind of experience—ideological and political. Metaphorically, they had gone to war together, survived, shared battle wounds, and walked away from the scene as brothers, men in arms.

García's deep loyalty aligned with Johnson's uncompromising demand for allegiance of those admitted and retained within his circle of influence. Like García, Johnson was pragmatic, passionate, and very demanding of his followers. LBJ's former aid, James Wilson, once compared Johnson's expectations of his followers to a "lover relationship."[48] He expected to be adored. Johnson's aggressive style was in many respects like García's, who was often accused of being dogmatic and authoritarian. Both have been characterized as being inconsistent, shifting stances when it was politically expedient.

Johnson, like García, was not always straightforward or consistent. Whereas García's conflicted anti-*bracero* and anti-immigrant campaign had polarizing effects on the Mexican-origin community, Johnson's conflicted record on civil rights alienated black voters.[49] García even warned Johnson when he was a presidential hopeful in 1960, of black voters' misgivings about Johnson's sincerity on civil rights issues.[50] Nevertheless, as noted by James Wilson, Johnson's senatorial aid, "He had a very deep commitment on the civil rights issue."[51] García further confirmed this observation in 1969:

> I say overall the Mexican-American people loved this man, respected him and still love him. And in fact we are still working that somewhere down the line we will give him recognition that he deserves from us. The Mexican-American people themselves went through a little revolutionary crisis and when this turbulence is settled, we will again see the greatness of this man. . . .
>
> And speaking as a citizen, I should say he is one of the greatest presidents this country has ever had. And as history is written you'll find out that Johnson will stand out very high in the love and respect, not only of the Americans, but the world. He will come out being one of our greatest presidents. He set himself aside from the every day common point of politics in order to achieve what he thought was more important than his political future, which meant stability and world peace. I was hoping it could have been accomplished before he finished his tenure of office.[52]

From disparate positions of power, García and Johnson managed to advance common political aims, negotiate disparate points of view, and ultimately enlarge the role of Mexican Americans in the U.S. political sphere. They were loquacious but not eloquent communicators. Their use of a middling style of public oratory mixing formal and colloquial speech proved especially effective.[53] Characteristically informal, rich with slang and regional discourse features, and direct, plain speaking, this middling flavor of García's and Johnson's rhetoric was in line with America's growing middle class and the pragmatic tenor of the post-war era.

American GI Forum and Political Training Grounds

Prior to World War II, Mexican-origin people in America were a fragmented, "forgotten" minority. Reflective of other civil rights leaders of the post-war era, García articulated "core communal values" and offered a liberal, Judeo-Christian paradigm "that sought to manage the tension between individual rights and communal duty."[54] The brotherhood García imagined, mobilized, and fabricated can be seen as the "embodiment of a dynamic rhetorical process" that ultimately complicated the national conversation on race and citizenship in America.[55] Under García's leadership, Mexican Americans became a civic presence demanding recognition.

García and the American GI Forum were initiated into national-level partisan politics with the Adlai Stevenson campaign of 1952. García was appointed to the Texas steering committee for the Stevenson campaign. "After all, I was Stevenson's manager for South Texas because no one else would support him," García recalled.[56] The American GI Forum took an enthusiastic and active role in the Stevenson presidential bid while Johnson waited in the wings. García broadcast a series of radio talks in the style of "fireside chats" to stir voters. In his first address, García urged Mexican American listeners to claim their place as full citizens:

> Senor o senora si usted es nacido en este pais usted debe comprar su poll tax o personal ahorita mismo. Toda persona nacida en este pais o naturalizada es ciudadano americano y tiene el derecho de comprar su poll tax por $1.75 y votar en todas las elecciones. Usted es tan buen ciudadano y tan Americano como los que se llamen Jones, Smith, Ragland, Weinerts, Schumaker, etc. pues nuestro pais democratico no conoce distincion de ciudadania.[57] [Ladies and gentlemen if you are born in this country you should buy your poll tax immediately. Every person born in this country or naturalized is an American citizen and has the right to buy his poll tax for $1.75 and vote in all elections. You are as good a citizen and as good an American as those named Jones, Smith, Ragland, Weinerts, Schumaker in a democratic country that knows no distinction of citizenship.]

García openly confronted the stigma of Mexican-origin and demanded that members of the community take their rightful place in the national electorate.

In his second radio address, García exposed the racist, discriminatory intent of the poll tax. He educated and challenged his listeners to resist institutionalized discrimination by exercising their right to vote:

> Habla su amigo el doctor Hector Garcia de Corpus Christi en su segunda plactica donde espero que pueda convencer a los miles de gente nuestra que nunca vote que este ano lo debe de hacer. Ahoy hablo el poll tax en Texas y porque o existe el poll tax en otros estados de la nacion.
>
> Senores quiero que sepan que unicamente Texas y 4 otros estados requiren que se pague por votar. Esta taxa o contribucion se llama "el poll tax" hace varios despues de la guerra civil Americana del 1865 se pasaron leyes por muchos estados del sur de nuestro pais que tenian por proposito quitarles el derecho de votar muchos de la gente de color. Se figuraba que si el negro recientemente libre tenia que pagar por votar naturalmente no iba a votar porque no obstante que eran libres no iban a gastar su poco dinero por votar.
>
> La mayoria de los estados poco y poco quitaron estas leyes y "poll tax" injustos porque eran contra la Constitucion y anti-democraticos. Ahora no hay mas que unos cuatro estados que tienen y requieren que se pague por el derecho de votar. Los otros estados que tienen este poll tax para votar las teinen para que los Negroes no voten y no tengan fuerza politica. Yo siento mucho decir pero es mi opinion personal que Texas mantienen este "Poll Tax Law" con la intencion de que la gente de origen mejicana se desanime, no compre por su poll tax.[58] [Your friend Dr. Héctor García speaks from Corpus Christi in his second chat where I hope that I can convince thousands of our people that never vote that this year they should do so. Today I will talk about the poll tax in Texas and why it doesn't exist in other states of the nation. Gentlemen, I want you to know that only Texas and four other states require that one pays for voting. This tax or contribution is called the "poll tax." After a number of years after the Civil War of 1865 they passed laws for many states in the south of our country for the purpose of impeding the right to vote for many of the people of color. They figured that if the recently liberated "Negro" had to pay for voting naturally he was not going to vote because even though he was free he was not going to spend his little money for voting.]

García introduces himself in the third person then shifts to first person in the same utterance, engaging his audience in a middling rhetorical style,

a mix of formal and informal discourses. The shift in perspective culti-
vates identification with his audience across a continuum of social positions: venerated public figure, compassionate physician, reliable friend,
friendly neighbor, ardent activist. He makes an implicit comparison
between the political status of Mexican Americans in Texas and "people
of color" and the "Negro" in the south, educating his constituency about
their voting rights.

García felt encouraged by the eager reception of Mexican American listeners of his broadcasts. He read their interest as a sign of heightened voter
consciousness and interest. García celebrated his first political milestone
on the campaign trail; he was breaking through the fear and apathy among
the Mexican American electorate. He made a tape recording in Spanish
recounting his experience on the campaign trail entitled "Adlai Stevenson
Presidential Campaign, November 4, 1952" and had it broadcast around
Texas. He sent a letter to the National Democratic Committee in October
1952 with the tape recording of his speech and an English translation.
García reported:

> I am very much enthused about the reception that our people have given this
> report of my personal meeting with Governor Stevenson. . . . I do not wish
> to appear presumptuous, but knowing Spanish-speaking people as well as I
> have, and having contacts with them in Chicago, Texas, Colorado, Arizona,
> New Mexico, and California, I believe our party should see that this tape-
> recording is played in as many places outside of Texas as possible.[59]

Johnson took a background role throughout the campaign, making as few
appearances as possible on behalf of the doomed candidate.[60] Johnson was
in a quandary. He did not like Stevenson's politics and was not comfortable
with Stevenson's "patrician, intellectual Princeton-educated" demeanor.[61]
In the end, he worked with Senator Sam Rayburn and García to keep the
Democratic party together as many of the more conservative party members
gravitated toward General Dwight Eisenhower. "The Democratic party is
best for Texas and the South and the nation," Johnson declared. "It's a firm
conviction with me and I can't go against my convictions."[62] García later
confirmed that Johnson tried to help Stevenson and remained faithful to
the party. García recalled: "Johnson was the only one in Texas who helped
and traveled statewide. When we had Stevenson, there were no Democratic
politicians who would come out and be *seen* with him! Senator Johnson took
him in his car and stood with him and would introduce him."[63] Although
the campaign failed, García's mobilization efforts foreshadowed the highly
successful organization of the Viva Kennedy and Viva Johnson Clubs of

the 1960s. The tallies overall were highly unfavorable for Stevenson, but in Texas he lost by less than the national average.[64]

García and the American GI Forum received their political baptism by fire in 1952 in the gritty work canvassing South Texas precincts. However, they had diligently campaigned for Stevenson only to discover that they were not yet a cohesive group, not large enough or compelling enough to draw notice from the Democratic National Party. "Mexican Americans were simply too far removed from decision-makers to warrant serious consideration," observes historian Ignacio García.[65] The Democratic National Party failed to give credit to García or the Mexican American community for their efforts.

In 1953, the Democratic Party did not solicit representation from "Spanish speaking" voters and ignored Mexican American issues as they prepared for the next campaign. Even García was not invited to attend a highly publicized Democratic function in Corpus Christi. No Mexican Americans were on the guest list. García reacted with anger and disappointment. In a June 1953 letter to Lyndon Johnson, García lambasted the Democratic party:

> This county and some of the counties of South Texas went for Stevenson mostly through votes of the Americans of Mexican origin. I am sincere when I say that I did more traveling and spent more of my personal money in South Texas than any other individual. Our people worked hard; our people sent out close to 100,000 envelopes for Mr. Stevenson. Yet as usual when the Honors are passed out we are left out in the cold. . . .
>
> Of course I do feel slighted also and even at this time, an invitation would be too late. The publicity and names were already given to the paper. Our people are upset and angry. I am embarrassed and the question is "Does the Democratic Party want us, or does it want to use us?" I am not asking for favors right now; I am merely submitting a report as a small cog in the gigantic Democratic Wheel. Certainly, if a satisfactory explanation can be given our Democratic people here, I would be glad to pass it on.[66]

García threatened to resign from the party as he did on a number of occasions throughout his career. Johnson quelled García's dissatisfaction by attending the American GI Forum National Convention. He was up for re-election, and he needed García's support. Election years were anxious times for Johnson. He felt vulnerable, complaining that he was "called a Dixiecrat in Washington and a Communist in Texas."[67] The 1953 American GI Forum National Convention in August would help to restore confidence in García and Johnson's relationship and their partnership in partisan politics.

In spite of García's persistent disappointment and disillusionment with the Democratic National Committee, participation in the Democratic Party proved especially productive for Mexican American reformers by the mid-1960s. Rodolfo Rosales observes in *The Illusion of Inclusion: The Untold Story of San Antonio*:

> As it turns out, the Democratic party, even though it was dominated by conservative Jim Crow advocates, was the one institution that provided the arena from which Chicanos were able to consolidate and broaden their political base in the face of seemingly overwhelming political and economic obstacles that confronted them during that early period.[68]

García learned to play the game with increasing finesse, but his growing sophistication did not inoculate him against further disappointment or frustration.

LBJ and the American GI Forum

The American GI Forum was celebrating its fifth anniversary in 1953. In a display of hospitality, García invited Senator Johnson to address the 1953 American GI Forum National Convention. It was an honor also extended to but not accepted by Eleanor Roosevelt, someone García much admired and respected as a symbol of the ideals of FDR's New Deal vision.[69] Johnson enthusiastically accepted García's invitation and would address the American GI Forum in the same spirit of brotherhood that he had expressed during the celebrative 1949 American GI Forum meeting when he was applauded for his role in the Longoria case. Johnson's effervescent address not only came on the heels of García's disappointment with the Democratic National Committee but followed the most significant rupture in the García-Johnson alliance. Just one year before this occasion, the 1952 American GI Forum Convention in San Antonio had adopted the searing resolution censuring Johnson for his failure to support an appropriation bill for the U.S. Immigration and Naturalization Service and Texas border patrol.[70]

On August 1, 1953 in Fort Worth, Johnson gave the opening address for the annual American GI Forum banquet, embracing the Mexican American veterans in an *ethos* of friendship and national manhood. Johnson states:

> . . . . I am flattered to believe that there is a reciprocal feeling of friendship between us—between you and me. . . .
>
> My first job, after I reached young manhood, was teaching in a Latin-American school. It was an experience that has stayed with me all the years since then. I thoroughly enjoyed the work, and I think that in many respects, I learned as much as my pupils. I am proud to say I still have friends I made among my students in that school. Since I am in the business of politics, I am

aware that people have wondered sometimes why we always stick together, the Latin-American people and me. It is true I always have the comforting feeling that I can depend on you. I sincerely hope I have never given you, and will never give you, any reason to doubt that you can depend on me. We do stay with one another, but there is no mystery about it. I have always respected the accomplishments of the Spanish-speaking people of Texas. I have always liked them personally. So far, I am very happy to say, you seem to have reciprocated that feeling. I see nothing mysterious about it. That's how friendships are made—true, enduring friendships.[71]

Johnson's performance cemented the vision of an "imagined fraternity" between the American GI Forum and himself. Even more significantly, the major themes and images embedded in Johnson's 1953 American GI Forum address prefigure his historic 1965 Voting Rights Act speech. The narrative quality of his speech recalling memories of his Cotulla school experiences and the notions of manhood, friendship, reciprocal emotion, duty, and commitment infuse Johnson's 1953 speech with a personal and intimate quality. He conveys a high level of awareness of the burden of his office and mutual interdependence between him and his constituents. These features of Johnson's 1953 speech anticipate some of the most compelling qualities of Johnson's 1965 Voting Rights Act address, as will be examined later. García and Johnson's alliance was secured.

García and the American GI Forum gave Johnson their vote. Johnson won the 1954 election. By January 1955 he was elected majority leader of the Senate and, at the same time, battled illness, McCarthyism, and the upheaval in Indochina. His political positions on current issues waffled between conservative and liberal stances. And he dodged civil rights issues whenever pressed. Like García, historians believe that through the mid to late 1950s, "Johnson was not ready to move much ahead of the country."[72] They suggest, however, that to step too far ahead would have been political suicide for Johnson. Johnson worked with Eisenhower and defended his support of the Republican president by asserting:

Some people say I've been petticoatin' around with Eisenhower. Well, that's not true. . . . I want to make absolutely sure that the Communists don't play one branch of the government against the other, or one party against the other as happened in the Korean War.[73]

Johnson might not have been moving as quickly as García wanted on Mexican American issues such as immigration, voting rights, and labor issues, but the communist threat was one issue García also understood and exploited. As examined in chapter 4, García often used the same rationale to argue for increased border controls and the termination of the *bracero* agreements. On this much they agreed. Vigilance against communism, subversives, and spies needed to be the country's number one priority.

Much of the correspondence between García and Johnson during the 1950s centers on the *bracero* program, its renewal, and modifications over the decade. None of García's recommendations received Johnson's support. As previously discussed, García and Johnson never reached consensus on the Mexican labor issue. Dozens of letters were fired back and forth between them with little display of rhetorical marksmanship. García and the American GI Forum had publicly criticized Johnson in 1952, but would never repeat the performance. The relationship with Johnson was maintained in a climate of benign neglect. García continued to endorse Johnson's candidacy for the Senate even with little evidence of payback. One legislator at least partially sympathetic to Mexican Americans' issues was better than none at all.

García's importance to Johnson's political aspirations increased, however, by the close of the decade. In October 1957, Johnson asked García, "Could you visit with me in Corpus Christi on October 21? . . . I would like a few words of advice and counsel and a few relaxing moments with you and the other friends upon whom I rely so heavily."[74] Johnson knew that García kept his finger on the pulse of the South Texas electorate. García understood the issues, and he knew all the key players. Johnson had been "bitten by the presidential bug" in 1956.[75] He began marshalling his resources. And no one knew the potential of the South Texas Mexican American electorate like García.

Johnson extended several professional courtesies to García. In a gesture of support for a book project about Mexican American veterans by Raul Morin, Johnson agreed to write the foreword. At García's request, Johnson offered his assistance to the author. Johnson's April 15, 1958, letter to Morin indicates: "At the request of our mutual friend, Dr. Hector P. García, I have prepared a brief statement about the contribution of the American soldier of Mexican Origin during World War Two."[76] It took over five years before the project was finally published. Released in 1963, Vice President Lyndon B. Johnson's foreword to Morin's *Among the Valiant* lauds the sacrifices of Mexican Americans to U.S. military service. Johnson recounts:

> As a Navy officer and as a member of Congress during World War Two, I had occasion to become familiar with the contributions made during the conflict by American soldiers of Mexican origin. . . . The American soldiers of Mexican origin served with distinction. They fought courageously. They gave their lives, when need be, valiantly.[77]

Nearly fifteen years after the Longoria incident, Johnson's tribute reasserted his recognition of Mexican Americans' place in the national communion. Once again, Johnson invoked his own personal experience to represent Mexican American civic participation. Johnson not only testified as a witness, but took an active role in this portrait of Mexican American valor and sacrifice.

By 1960, García and the American GI Forum had been actively involved with partisan politics for over a decade with varying degrees of success. The Stevenson campaign had been a good training ground for grassroots mobilization. García and the post-war Mexican American leadership had matured and acquired some measure of status. As Ignacio García explains, "These reformers were non-ideological and usually quite pragmatic. While many had traces of the New Deal in their personal philosophies, more were simply individuals hypersensitive to the disparity between their community and the society at large."[78] They were distrustful of state and local government but maintained an enduring confidence in the federal government and its institutions.[79]

With the 1960 presidential election close at hand, the American GI Forum sought to forge a stronger alliance with the Democratic National Committee. They were ready to establish a presence on the national political scene. García wanted to ensure that they didn't get "left out in the cold" again. García's method, the construction and invocation of the "imagined fraternity," would be his primary rhetorical strategy. Early in the campaign process, García extended offers to assist both Kennedy and Johnson in the presidential campaign, two potential candidates who showed promise in attending to the needs of minority groups. García covered all the bases. Eventually both candidates would enlist García's support.

García made a trip to Washington, D.C., early in 1959. He informed Johnson that he would be available to meet with him. In a letter of February 4, 1959, Johnson invited García to a meeting: "Dear Doctor, I am especially delighted that you re going to be in Washington for the next couple of days. I am sending this letter to the Mayflower Hotel and when you receive it, I hope you will call my office."[80] Although the content of that meeting remains unclear, it appears that García wanted to secure a clear and active role in the presidential election. He didn't want to be left out again. García decided that it would be prudent to join forces with Johnson, if he decided to run. He was also willing to support Kennedy but didn't enjoy the same access to Kennedy that he had with Johnson. García was prepared to assist both possible candidates, even if they were initially opposing forces.

Ignacio M. García observes that neither Héctor García nor Albert Peña Jr. supported Kennedy at first.[81] Peña was still devoted to Stevenson, and García was devoted to Johnson. However, many liberals like García were unhappy with Johnson's performance in the Senate. "They disliked his cautious pace, his penchant for compromise, and his rapport with the Republican president."[82] García's biggest issue against Johnson, the Mexican labor problem, was far from being resolved. The *bracero* program had just been renewed with Johnson's tacit approval in 1958. At some level, García may not have been completely confident in Johnson's commitment to Mexican American labor concerns.

Johnson was an Anglo and a Southerner with strong ties to the Texas political machine. Kennedy, on the other hand, was an Ivy League intellectual, very refined, and a practicing Catholic—all qualities García valued. Setting aside his ten-year history with Johnson, García was willing to take a risk on Kennedy. Moreover, there was always the possibility that Johnson wouldn't come through and run for the office. In any case, Kennedy had already begun courting García and other Mexican American leaders. The political promenade over the next year played out like a traditional Texas square dance with García swinging and joining hands with different partners all around the Democratic Party dance floor.

In this April 1959 letter, Johnson thanked García for his invitation to address the 1959 National Convention of the American GI Forum, which he declined to attend with this explanation:

> You are far better to me than I deserve but I suppose that among friends such excesses are understandable and certainly I must admit I enjoy them and appreciate them. You and I and the members of the American GI Forum are indeed "amigos." I am very proud of this fact and I hope very sincerely that I always conduct myself in such a way as to justify your respect and confidence. Doctor, there is nothing that I would enjoy more than an opportunity to be in Los Angeles on August 14th to speak to the National Convention of the American GI Forum. However, there is a strong possibility that Congress will still be in session.[83]

On July 14, 1959, in the weeks just before the American GI Forum National Convention, Johnson sent another letter to García attempting to restore relations. Johnson wrote:

> People can have opposite views and still remain good friends. I am sure at times you do not approve 100% of everything I do. But on the other hand when we might be in disagreement, you are the type of man who will understand there

might be two sides to the question. I have enjoyed many enlightening talks with you. It has been a great pleasure to work with you for what we think is best for our state and nation, and we will continue to do that.[84]

The letter was little more than an obligatory bow to your partner, however. García was examining the best candidate for his endorsement to the Mexican American electorate. Johnson knew that García did not always understand nor approve of his actions, but neither could afford to sever ties over their disputes. Johnson needed the Mexican American vote as much as García desired a reliable link to the federal government. Johnson wanted to make a bid for the presidency but wasn't ready to go public with an announcement yet.

By the time the 1959 American GI Forum National Conference came around, Johnson had not yet thrown his hat into the ring and, in fact, insisted he had no designs on the presidency. Johnson vacillated, "encouraging supporters to work on his behalf but refusing to announce his candidacy."[85] Pycior explains Johnson's indecision:

> To complicate matters, Johnson viewed his 1955 heart attack as a harbinger, a reminder that the men in his family died by the age of sixty. He raged against his fate by drinking, womanizing, and throwing tantrums—what George Reedy called "some kind of colossal mid-life crisis."[86]

In the throes of indecision, Johnson didn't want to burn any bridges. He succinctly summed up his debt to the American GI Forum and the Mexican American constituency in another letter to García. Johnson's August 6, 1959, letter declared: "Hector, the only office that I am interested in is that of being Senior Senator from the state of Texas. You helped put me here and I hope you and your friends will keep me here."[87] In spite of Johnson's minimalization of his own presidential aspiration, this moment would usher in a new level of inclusion for García, who moved to the forefront of the presidential campaign propaganda wave. García and the American GI Forum established the National Viva Clubs during the 1959 American GI Forum Convention. García wasn't going to be held back by Johnson's indecision. The Forum was gearing up even faster than the potential candidates could organize themselves. García began generating letters, memos, reports, and circulars telling Mexican American voters not only of the public promises made to them by the Kennedy campaign but also of the personal assurances of the candidate and his brother.[88]

The Kennedys capitalized on García's mobilizing power. As early as 1959, well before Kennedy and Johnson joined forces on the same ticket, Kennedy sought García's guidance on rallying the support of "Spanish speaking" voters. Kennedy's December 28, 1959, letter solicited García's advice: "I would appreciate having your comments and suggestions for the best ways in which the Democratic Party can achieve victory in 1960."[89] Kennedy organized a civil rights conference in New York City that included a number of prominent Spanish-speaking leaders: Héctor García; Henry B. Gonzalez of San Antonio; Albert Peña Jr.; Carlos McCormick, a law student from Arizona; attorney Henry López of Los Angeles; and several Puerto Rican figures.[90] The meeting would lead to the official formation of the Viva Kennedy Clubs.[91]

García represented untapped political possibilities for both Johnson and Kennedy. Johnson also extended an invitation to García to serve as an unofficial advisor during the 1960 campaign. Finally getting off the fence, Johnson made explicit his intentions to run for the presidency. He enlisted García's support after the American GI Forum National Convention had already laid the groundwork for the National Viva Kennedy Clubs. Nevertheless, García was poised to rally for Kennedy, Johnson, or both. Each candidate respected García's instinct and clout. García's political dance card was finally full. The National Democratic Party had taken notice.

In the spring of 1960, Johnson asked García to conduct a survey to assess his appeal among Mexican Americans if he ran against Kennedy for the democratic ticket. García recounted:

> I was asked by Senator Johnson to take a survey among the Southwest to find out what did people think of Senator Johnson for President. It was getting close to the national convention. I ran a survey on my own, talking mostly to Mexican-Americans, Hispanos, and Spanish surnamed people. There was no question, Kennedy was the first choice. In fact my report that I still conserve, sent to Senator Johnson, was simply this: "That as far as the Mexican-Americans were concerned, he couldn't win." That my suggestion to him would be to run as vice president, and I think later he could win as president . . . I was one of the few people at that time who guessed this thing right. And I still have this report as a document. I still have the original with my signature. Because by that time the Kennedy enchantment, or vision, or charisma had spread to our Mexican people. He seemed like an idealist. It was not so much that Johnson was not an idealist, it was the fear again, to us that he was still a Texan, and we felt he could be controlled by the Texas interests which are against us. But I was one of the few ones . . . and I told him the truth and the truth came out.[92]

García's 1960 confidential report to Johnson concluded, "There is no doubt that Kenedy is the most popular democratic candidate in spite of his religious handicap."[93] García, a devout Catholic, certainly did not object to Kennedy's religious affiliation but understood that the question would be an issue in the Kennedy campaign. He also understood that Kennedy's appeal among minorities would far exceed Johnson's. García disclosed his findings to Johnson:

> Some of the report may not be to our liking but I believe that in order for you to find a solution you must know there is a problem. . . . As your devoted friend, I speak honestly for our benefit.
>
> Most people believe that you are better qualified, trained, disciplined, experienced than Kenedy and others. Why they preferred Kenedy on a popular vote was hard for me to determine except that they thought that he was the "more liberal" and they still connected you with the "Deep South or at least South Prejudices."
>
> . . . They fear that you will not be accepted by the North and Eastern voters and that you will be hard to sell to them since they consider you "too Southern." . . . All welcome a Johnson Kenedy ticket. They believe you are for Latin Americans but believe you are against Negroes (mostly anti-civil rights). You hace wonderful appeal, personality, ability, and looks but you are not selling it down to the level of the little people and neither is the little man given an opportunity to help you.[94]

García also advised Johnson to invite several Kennedy Democrats to serve under him should he get the nomination and to include African American and Mexican American delegates for the Democratic National Convention. Johnson's campaign managers did not heed García's suggestions nor did they entertain the validity of his findings. Johnson formally announced his candidacy for the presidency just days before the national convention. García's warning that Johnson lagged two to one behind Kennedy among Mexican American voters did not endear him to the Johnson campaign. His recommendation that Johnson should take the vice president slot on the ticket "put him in cold storage" until after the convention.[95]

In the final analysis, García favored Johnson for the presidential pick, but knew Johnson would never stand a chance against Kennedy. Moreover, García's carefully executed grassroots fact-finding mission did not elicit the intended response. Johnson did not offer a prompt reply. Even more, Johnson overlooked García as a delegate for the National Democratic Convention in Los Angeles. García missed out on the big moment. Assuming a rhetorical stance more reflective of one who had been stood up for prom than delivering a report, García wrote Johnson one week later on June 17, 1960:

I wish to congratulate you on our splendid victory in Austin. I was there but did not have the opportunity to talk with you. I was on the stage behind the curtain waiting to see but evidently the message never got to you. . . . I certainly am sorry that my name was struck out from the delegate list. . . . Naturally, I am very much chagrined and dumbfounded since I have always been a loyal friend of yours. I have stood up for you and spoke for you and defended you like a brother. . . . But the damage is done and I feel left out.[96]

It is not clear why García had been overlooked as a delegate in 1960. Albert Peña Jr. was selected as the only Texas Mexican American Democratic delegate. Rodolfo Rosales explains how the Democratic deal was cut:

> By 1960, civil rights was a major issue for liberal Democrats in Texas. As a consequence, Johnson was afraid that the liberal factions, which included delegations from San Antonio and Houston, were going to rump the conservative-dominated state if their concerns were not addressed. This would threaten his chances of consolidating a unanimous Texas vote for his candidacy at the national convention. His first step in consolidating support was to negotiate concessions with the liberal factions.
>
> In San Antonio's case, the liberal faction included Black leader G. J. Sutton, and was chaired by Albert Peña Jr. When Johnson solicited the support of these two leaders at the state convention, he struck a deal with the full backing of the delegation. In return for their full support, labor (Jack Martin), Black (G. J. Sutton), Chicano (Albert Peña Jr.) representatives would be included in the delegation representing Texas at the National Democratic Convention.[97]

It would seem that Johnson already knew that he had García and the moderate American GI Forum in his corner. But Peña and the liberal faction were still wild cards. He could afford to ignore García, but he couldn't afford to ignore Peña and still be assured of his support. García was his friend—Peña was not. The emotional fallout of that action played out like a lover's spat. In an act of reconciliation, Johnson's June 22, 1960, reply to García placated his dejected friend:

> Hector, I don't know anything about the reason you were not named a delegate. . . . I am very sorry that you feel left out. . . . I read the report you prepared for me and simply did not have an opportunity to thank you for it before now. Needless to say, it was a very valuable report and I am deeply grateful for the diligence and accuracy you gave to it. You remain one of my dearest friends.[98]

The record does not reflect if García's advice to Johnson to take the vice president position was ever taken to heart. The fact that García had accurately assessed the political situation and Johnson's place within it, however, certainly enhanced his *ethos* as a shrewd analyst. It showed Johnson that not only would García be honest with him but that García's political instincts were worth listening to.

Additionally, it is difficult to judge what Johnson means by "dearest friend." Examining Johnson's pattern of behavior with García beside other political alliances, García was indeed among Johnson's most favored men. According to James Wilson, Johnson's former aid, Johnson quickly cast off "friends" and associates as soon as they were no longer useful.[99] "Ceremonial chewing-outs" and relational ruptures were part of Johnson's style. He didn't routinely worry about the fallout. Wilson observes: "I was impressed with the lack of—what appeared to me to be a lack of genuineness in the relationship with constituents. Since then, I've become reconciled to the fact that this is a necessity of winning, at least, in the order of magnitudes that Lyndon Johnson won in Texas."[100] However, Johnson never cast off García from his circle. Even though he repeatedly disappointed and even rejected García, Johnson always worked to repair the ruptures in their relationship. At the very least, García remained too useful and important to Johnson to abandon. It appears, though, that Johnson had some measure of enduring respect and affection for García. Johnson had met his match.

Although he was not selected to attend the National Democratic Convention, García refused to be left out of the conversation. In his disappointment, García sent a statement to the Democratic National Committee, Nationalities Division. The "Statement of Dr. Hector P. Garcia, Founder of the American GI Forum, To Be Presented to the Democratic National Committee Nationalities Division" signaled that Mexican Americans were an assertive and potentially powerful force. This statement was eventually published in the *American GI Forum News Bulletin* and became a core document for "The American of Mexican Descent: A Statement of Principle"[101] promulgated by the Viva Kennedy Clubs. García charged:

> As an American citizen belonging to a minority group in our country I deplore the lack of representation of our groups within the two major parties. Good examples of the lack of representation of our groups are the very few delegates to the National Convention of the Democratic Party of Mexican origin . . . [102]

With this declaration on the record, García then extended his full support to Kennedy and quickly worked to build a bond between *compadres*, wholeheartedly endorsing the Kennedy/Johnson ticket. It was in this same spirit that he promoted Kennedy to Mexican American voters. Recognizing his far-reaching influence with the Mexican American electorate, the Kennedy campaign appointed García a national cochairman of the Viva Kennedy organization. García asserted in a memo to campaign coworkers:

> The main purpose [of the Viva Kennedy Clubs] is to prove to the world that we believe in the true American democracy and that even though we may be a minority that if we unite we may win the election. Senator Kennedy and Senator Johnson are counting heavily on our vote to win the election. States like Texas, New Mexico, Arizona, California, Colorado, and others may go "Democratic" with our support. If those states win and we throw our support in the other thirty states or so than we will have received the recognition that we deserve and that has never been given to us.[103]

With García in the forefront of the Viva Clubs, Johnson extended a personal invitation to help with the campaign. The gesture would help to fortify their political partnership. On August 25, 1960, Johnson invited:

> Dear Hector, The thing I would like to particularly emphasize is any suggestions . . . you have for improving the lot of our Latin American friends. From time to time I will be making speeches in general areas they are interested in and I would like for you to give me some help on these speeches and join me on the plane.[104]

The Viva Kennedy Clubs represented a watershed moment for Mexican Americans in the political arena. Their success demonstrated that the Latino vote was a significant new political force. The campaign gave Mexican American leaders like García a national level forum from which to lobby their interests. Reflective of García's mobilization style, the Viva Kennedy Club evolved in free-for-all manner appearing first in areas where American GI Forum chapters were already established. They grew more rapidly than the national offices were prepared to handle. Like the American GI Forum, the Viva Kennedy/Viva Johnson Clubs were grassroots, localized groups with an immediate goal. In *Viva Kennedy: Mexican Americans in Search of Camelot*, Ignacio M. García concludes: "The thing that kept them bound as a 'national' organization was the desire to elect John F. Kennedy president and the prospect of receiving a payback from a grateful winner."[105] The win came as desired; the payback did not.

President Kennedy's November 11, 1960 telegram of congratulations praised García: "The margin of victory in Bexar, Nueces, El Paso Counties, and the Rio Grande alley was a prominent significance in carrying

Texas."[106] The Democratic party received more than 90 percent of the Spanish-speaking vote in the 1960 presidential election.[107] There were precincts in "Spanish-speaking" communities around the country, especially in the Southwest, which produced one hundred percent returns for Kennedy.[108] At the national level, of course, the election was close. Kennedy won 49.7% of the popular vote, 303 electoral votes. Nixon won 49.5% of the popular vote, 219 electoral votes. The "Spanish-speaking" vote had made a difference.

García invested over $5,000 of his own money in the Kennedy campaign, draining his savings account and his office building fund; he was unable to pay his phone bill and office salaries when the successful campaign finally came to an end.[109] The sacrifices did not go completely unnoticed. In November 1961, García and his wife, Wanda, attended a White House dinner in honor of the governor of Puerto Rico, featuring a historic performance by the celebrated Spanish cellist Maestro Pablo Casals.[110] On February 11, 1961, García served as Kennedy's envoy to the West Indies for the signing of a treaty marking the inauguration of a worldwide mutual security program.[111] This assignment marked the beginning of García's diplomatic service period, distinguishing him as one of the first Mexican Americans to serve the United States in this capacity. Before García, few diplomatic posts had been held by minorities.[112]

Kennedy's gesture was little more than symbolic, however. In spite of a steady stream of letters to Kennedy requesting Mexican American appointments to the federal judgeship post in South Texas and other diplomatic posts, García did not exercise influence with Kennedy nor enjoy the kind of access he thought he would. Those anticipated high-level appointments never came during Kennedy's administration. In spite of numerous recommendations from García, only Kennedy's staff assistant, a Mexican American attorney from Arizona named Carlos McCormick, made the 1961 short list for Kennedy's administration. Kennedy's "Latest List" of proposed presidential appointments did not include a single member of the American GI Forum cadre.[113]

García remained hopeful and faithful to the "imagined fraternity," nevertheless. As early as August 1960, García solicited Kennedy to appoint Judge E. D. Salinas of Webb County to fill the vacancy on the U.S. District Court of the Southern District of Texas following Judge James V. Allred's death. García wrote:

> I want to take this opportunity to congratulate you and thank you for all the wonderful things that you have done for our people. I was not able to go to the Democratic National Convention in Los Angeles inspite of the fact I wanted to very badly. I would like to offer my services to help you

in every way possible since I am a personal friend of Senator Lyndon B. Johnson. . . . I would like to meet with you and talk about our situation for a few minutes.

In the meantime, there is a vacancy in the Southern District of the United States for Federal Judgeship. We believe that Honorable E. D. Salinas is the man most qualified to receive this judgeship. . . . As you know it will be a great feather in our cap and it will be a great selling point of Democracy in South and Central America and in Mexico if we could say that we have a federal judge of Mexican origin in the Southern area of the United States.[114]

He received no reply. García reiterated his request for Salinas' appointment to Robert Kennedy in this congratulatory letter of November 18, 1960 letter:

I am enclosing materials to you . . . which will prove the point that our Spanish speaking precints averaged about 95% of our votes cast and we cast about 96% of our potential voters. In south Texas we lost two counties: Zavala county had about 50% of its citizens out as migrants and could not vote. The other one Live Oak county is the seat of the Felix Longoria funeral refusal case. This county will allways be anti-Johnson in spite of the great Humanitarian work done by the Senator. I hope you will find this report as inspiring and as proof of the devotion and love that our people have for your brother and Senator Johnson. Several precints went 100%. I feel that when I met with you in Washington and I promised that our people would vote this way that you thought perhaps I was exaggerating. You will appreicate the fact that through this office, the one in Austin, and throughout the state we reached 98% of our people with individual and personal letters and sample ballots. I sincerely hope that we are given the opportunity to serve under your administration and it would be encouraging to have Judge E. D. Salinas appointed. . . . Que viva Bob Kennedy. Your amigo, Dr. Hector P. Garcia.[115]

The Kennedy administration turned a deaf ear. García persisted and sent additional recommendations. He called for the appointment of Vicente Ximenes to the diplomatic post of assistant secretary of state to Latin America in a letter to Kennedy in January 1961. He also recommended Ralph Estrada for the position of ambassador to a Latin American country in February 1961.[116] None of García's recommendations were approved. Arturo Morales Carrion, a Puerto Rican, was given the assistant secretary of state slot and another Puerto Rican, Teodoro Moscoso, received the ambassador appointment to Latin America.[117] After a stormy appointment process, Salinas was added to the list under consideration but in the end was not awarded the judgeship. President Kennedy announced his appointment of District Judge Reynaldo G. Garza to the federal bench on March 23, 1961. During a post-election meeting of Viva Kennedy Club organizers on March 26, 1961, in Phoenix, Arizona, García offered his assessment of the new Kennedy administration and its failure to recognize Mexican American leadership. García called for the formation of a national organization of *la raza*. García asserted:

> I am a doctor. I diagnose, study, treat, and operate when necessary. I speak honestly, I have to tell the truth. I am very unhappy. The Kennedy's promised several meetings with us, which were never kept. We went ahead and did the work and you know the results of our Viva Kennedy work throughout the country. The appointments of people [such as Judge Garza] from Texas were made without our consultation. I think that there is collusion that goes beyond the Congressional Representatives from Texas. . . . Johnson never consults with us. We expected it. Bob Kennedy had something to do with this. Why?. . .
>
> My feeling is that nobody in this country of ours wants us to get organized. We have a king. The King is LA RAZA. We must get organized, or else the KING will perish. We must sacrifice, We must fight and struggle until our King, LA RAZA is respected, recognized, and taken into account.
>
> Is Bob Kennedy interested in seeing the Mexican-American organized?
>
> Does our President want for us to get organized?
>
> You may not like what I say, but it is the truth and truth must be served. I SEE COLLUSION OVER, ABOVE, AND BEYOND TEXAS SENATORS AND CONGRESSMEN. Let us know and remember at all times that we are now locked in a battle with the men of great power in our country. But they too can be defeated. United strength alone will do it. A NATIONAL, POLITICAL, NON-PARTISAN ORGANIZATION will do it.
>
> A ti tambien te han usado Carlitos. Y te quiero como hermano. Necesitamos estar unidos. No hay diferencia entre los Tejanos, Californianos y Neoyorkinos de habla hispana . . . porque todos sufrimos a cajeamos del mismo pie. Nos han usado. But we must do something about it, and we start right here, right now.[118] [You also have been used Carlitos (Carlos McCormick). I love you as a brother. We need to be united. There is no difference between Spanish-speaking Texans, Californians, and New Yorkers because we all suffer and travel the same road. They used us.]

This public rebuke of the Kennedy administration represents one of García's most militant political speeches. He assumes the stance of political warrior, conveying anger, suspicion, resolve, and conviction. García reveals a loss of confidence in bipartisan politics and directly confronts institutionalized discrimination in the U.S. political system. Unlike other speeches directed to mixed audiences, García's rhetoric makes no attempt to accommodate an Anglo audience. He reaches out to unite *La Raza* in an act reflective of *el grito* [cry] for justice as signified in his use of codeswitching. His message is an embrace of all Latinos in the United States, no longer directing his focus exclusively on Mexican Americans.

This gathering of Viva Kennedy organizers formed the nucleus of new national-level organization called PASO (Political Association of Spanish Speaking Organizations).[119] García and Albert Peña Jr. were appointed cochairs of organization and program development for PASO. In an April 3, 1961, letter to Vicente Ximenes, García justified the need for the organization of PASO by summarizing, "We are getting the runaround" with the Kennedys.[120] Although relatively short-lived, PASO would provide fertile ground for the evolution of the Chicano nationalist political party, *La Raza Unida*, a party from which García ultimately divorced himself.[121]

García's *el grito* against the Kennedy administration persisted. He made numerous suggestions, but Kennedy favored none of his recommendations. García's September 21, 1961, letter to President Kennedy directly expressed his dissatisfaction:

> I feel it is my duty and responsibility to tell you that the political situation in Texas and nationally is taking a bad turn against you. This includes the Latin-American people nationally who are not too happy about their lack of recognition and your few appointments. Also we are disappointed in the lack of action taken by the civil rights section of the Attorney General's department. Secondly, a great percentage of Texas democrats are turning over to the republicans. This includes a great number of Latin American democrats.[122]

García was no more pleased with the progress of PASO as reflected in his letter to Manuel Avila Jr., a U.S. State Department employee stationed in Venezuela. García confided:

> I am still disappointed since we have not been able to get PASO off the ground. I am writing letters and letters, but I am unable to get people interested. Sometimes I feel like giving up knowing well that we need organizations so badly, but people aren't not even willing to contribute one dollar to get it moving. Of course, my time is sometimes limited and I cannot do much more than I am doing, but I will continue to try. . .
>
> The Negroes seem to be doing alright. The Italian-Americans seem to be doing alright, the Irish-Americans seem to be doing alright, the Polish-

Americans seems to be doing alright, but why in the Lord's name we cannot organize our people, Manuel. I do not know.

We constantly have to do a lot of fighting for them, just the group of us that are determined and willing to fight for them. But sometimes they don't even respect us or thank us for our work.

I hope that this letter does not sound too despondent, because I am not despondent. I am just fighting mad again and when I get fighting mad, I get down to do more work and more work every day.[123]

Ignacio M. García argues that the Viva Kennedy leaders' failure to get the appointments they had anticipated "represented a bitter repudiation" of their efforts. Garza's selection for the federal judgeship was a grave disappointment even though Garza, a South Texas Mexican American, had won the appointment over an Anglo attorney. Ignacio García explains:

> While Garza was a good judge and a respected member of the South Texas community, he was too moderate and accommodating for the likes of those pushing for more militancy. Garza came across as being more anxious to do what was "appropriate" than in helping his own people. He represented the elite families of South Texas who fought against racial stereotypes but who were content with the class distinctions so common in predominantly Mexican American communities that were governed by Anglo American politicians.[124]

García and the American GI Forum wanted to do more than secure the civil rights of the Mexican American elite. They wanted the new judge to foment change on behalf of working-class Mexican Americans as well.

The Kennedy administration did not fulfill its purported promises to the Mexican American constituency. In his role as attorney general, Robert Kennedy addressed the 1963 National Convention of the American GI Forum, praising the organization for its leadership and support.[125] Nonetheless, the policies and appointments implemented during the Kennedy years made no measurable impact on the lives of Mexican Americans. As Ignacio García concludes, "Camelot" by and large, eluded them. And Johnson knew it. García was as unhappy with Johnson's performance after the election as he was Kennedy's. Three months after the formation of PASO, García reports to Manuel Avila Jr.:

> I am very sorry to have to tell you that things are not marching according to what we expected. Evidently, we are going to have to buck the Democratic Party real hard. . . . Certainly to be honest with you, I don't think we can expect anything from the Anglo Politicians. I am sure that we will have to keep on working. . . .

In answer to your question again, Johnson and other Congressmans and all those peoples are worried now, but the problem is the same. Estos desgraciados no nos quieren dar ni agua. Quieren usarnos and we are just beginning to revolt.[126] [Those ungratefuls won't even give us water. They just want to use us.]

Although enraged by Kennedy's failure to appoint Mexican Americans to top level government positions, García's role in the Viva Kennedy/Viva Johnson Clubs had given him a toe-hold in Johnson's inner circle. Immediately following the successful 1960 election, García's January 19, 1961, letter acknowledges the newly elected Vice-President Johnson's gift of "the beautiful necktie that you sent me for Christmas." The closing line of his thank-you letter uses codeswitching and inserts the 1960 campaign slogan as a solidarity marker: "Muchas gracias y que viva Lyndon B. Johnson!"[127] [Thank you very much and long live Lyndon B. Johnson!] Johnson's July 1961 letter invited García to the LBJ Ranch: "Lady Bird and I hope that you can come out to the LBJ Ranch on Sunday, July 16 to attend the barbecue which we are giving in honor of the President of Pakistan, His Excellency Mohammad Ayub Khan."[128] García received personal invitations to the 1960 and 1964 inaugurations, and he attended a number of celebrations and social events sponsored by Johnson. The relationship would become more than social, however.

Vice President Johnson's acts of conciliation and gestures of appreciation repeatedly punctuated his correspondence to García. García's July 3, 1963, letter recognized Johnson's symbolic acts of friendship, closing with a note of unintended but nevertheless tragic foreshadowing:

> I want to thank you very much for the pictures that you sent to me. . . . It will be a great pleasure and honor to put this picture that I have with you along with the rest of the pictures that I have in my front office, one being when I met with the President in Washington, D.C. when organizing the Viva-Kennedy-Viva Johnson Clubs. . . . We hope the time is not too far when you will be the President of the United States.[129]

Three months later, García's November 22, 1963 telegram to a grieving President Johnson extended these condolences:

> Honorable Lyndon B. Johnson: At this moment of gried and sadeness let me assure you that we are suffering and shocked as much as you are.
>
> However let me assure you that we are aware of the tremendous responsibility that you carry on such a moment of crisis.
>
> The American GI Forum and the Mexican Americans of the U.S. are ready to go along with you in your moments of need. Please call on us.

Texas will now awaken to the fact that we the Mexican Americans have always known that you are a great man and will be a great president.[130]

In his November 29, 1963, reply, Johnson offers, "Dear Hector, Nothing has meant more to me during these hours of sorrow after the death of President John Fitzgerald Kennedy than the messages from friends like you. I appreciate your thoughtfulness. I shall cherish your prayers in the days ahead."[131] García was deeply shaken by Kennedy's death and confided in a letter to Vicente Ximenes:

> At this time there is nothing much that I can say concerning the assassination of our President. I will say, though, that the people from Texas are generally to blame. Personally, I even feel a great amount of guilt since I believe that we could have gotten this state to be a liberal state and that the racial discrimination, hatred, and prejudice would have never have created the favorable climate in this state for the assassination of our beloved friend and President. However, I have tried very hard as any human could, but you know the results. Right now we are not thinking of anything else, but mourn his death. Everybody is sadden and I am, too, but more than sadden, I am angry and bitter that this state contributed to his death. . . . At times like this I am praying to God to give me more faith because I have lost alot of it."[132]

For García, racism, violence, and hate remained at the root of what was wrong in America. Moreover, Kennedy's death signaled that the state of Texas had once again denied his people hope and social justice.

President Lyndon B. Johnson, García, and the Mexican American Electorate

García sent encouraging messages to Johnson throughout his first year at the helm of the nation and promoted Johnson for his 1964 presidential bid. García helped to mobilize the Viva National Clubs once again, assuring Johnson's White House victory. At his recommendation, Vicente Ximenes was appointed the national chairman of the Viva Johnson campaign. By 1964, Johnson no longer distanced himself from the image of civil rights activist and strategically cultivated his *ethos* as an advocate for Mexican American issues.

Promotional materials for the 1964 election such as "President Lyndon B. Johnson Has a Lifetime Record of Personal Concern and Public Assistance to Americans of Mexican or Spanish Origin" portray Johnson as an incomparable friend and benefactor to Mexican Americans. "Mr. Johnson has publicly credited South Texas and Rio Grande Valley voters with providing the margin in the close 1960 election of him and John F. Kennedy," this pamphlet asserts.[133] García's congratulations to Johnson on the 1964 presidential election gazed into the future:

> ... Being a student of history, I will prophesy that you will do more to bring democracy and happiness to more Americans than any president before your time.
>
> Being your friend and from a minority group I want to assure you that we minority members are grateful and proud of what you have done.
>
> There have been great presidents, Washington, Jefferson, Lincoln, Roosevelt, and Kennedy. These presidents did great things and put forth great ideas and great plans, but it will be you who will put some of these ideas and plans into *practical reality* that will actually benefit a great number of citizens who only heard about these plans and ideas but never experienced their applications.
>
> Under your administration and your Great Society things will be different. As your admirer and friend if there is anything I can do to help please feel free to call on me.[134]

No other post-war civil rights activist claimed such immediate or intimate access to a U.S. president as García did. He circulated in Johnson's inner "concentric circles" and counted himself a part of the spheres to which so many Johnson devotees were "constantly maneuvering to try to get into."[135]

In unprecedented reciprocity between a president and a civil rights organizer, Johnson's presidency faithfully honored a number of García's recommendations for Mexican American candidates to high-level government appointments. Johnson brought the plight of Mexican Americans to a national forum.[136] The alliance between García and Johnson reached its apex during these presidential years. In addition to moving in Johnson's social spheres, García accepted a number of diplomatic posts during the Johnson administration. He fondly called Johnson, "Mi Presidente," and assumed the role of Johnson's emissary, often at substantial personal financial cost. At times, he was unable to pay his staff and had to leave his patients in the care of his sister, Dr. Cleo, and his brother, Dr Xico. "I would go broke every time he called me," García once reflected.[137]

Johnson appointed García as Special Ambassador to Venezuela in March 1964, extending the U.S. Good Neighbor policies to Latin America. Johnson also appointed García a member of the National Citizens Committee for Community Relations in 1964, the first civil rights advisory board of the Johnson administration organized to prevent and resolve racial disputes through "reason, persuasion, and conciliation."[138] Significantly, Johnson framed his conceptualization of the problems of racism for all groups in terms that were closely aligned with García's personal narrative.

In January 1965, President Johnson accepted García's invitation to address the National Conference on Poverty in the Southwest held in Tucson, Arizona, sponsored by the American GI Forum. Johnson's attendance reaffirmed his commitment to Mexican American civil rights issues. The National Conference on Poverty in the Southwest also featured guest speakers Sargent Shriver (commissioner of the Office of Economic Opportunity) and Archbishop Robert Lucey of San Antonio (a vocal farm worker advocate) and held "citizen hearings" to allow community workers and activists to make suggestions to the Johnson administration.[139]

In March 1965, during the same month of his Voting Rights Act address, Johnson met briefly with a gathering of Mexican American business, professional, and organizational leaders.[140] The Mexican American representatives, men and women from the Southwest and Midwest, expressed their concerns that the Johnson administration had been slow to appoint Mexican Americans to government posts or programs. Sustained pressure from the Mexican American community paralleled the increasingly vocal and visible civil rights protests led by black activists leading up to Johnson's 1965 Voting Rights Act.

By 1966, Mexican American issues were clearly on Johnson's presidential agenda. On March 4, 1966, he named García to supervise the National Advisory Council on Economic Opportunity, a position from which García would call for additional Mexican American representation at the federal level.[141] On May 26, 1966, Johnson held a historic White House meeting with representatives from the American GI Forum, LULAC, and the Mexican American Political Association (MAPA). It was the first time a president met at the White House with Mexican Americans to focus entirely on their concerns.[142] According to Vicente Ximenes, it was a groundbreaking moment for Mexican Americans, because it set the foundation for the eventual formation of an entirely new cabinet post with the establishment of the Inter-agency of Mexican American Affairs. This meeting also set the stage for the coordination of the historic Cabinet Committee Hearings on Mexican American Affairs held in El Paso, Texas, the following year in October 1967. "If a Mexican American was ever included in anything, it was because Johnson personally demanded it," Ximenes reflected.[143]

In addition to approving funding for the Service, Employment, and Re-Development (SER) Jobs for Progress program launched by García and the American GI Forum, Johnson endorsed García's first pick for commissioner of the Equal Employment Opportunity Commission (EEOC). Honoring García's recommendation, Johnson appointed Vicente Ximenes, a founding leader of the American GI Forum.[144] García recounted:

We had another problem at that time. The SER organization, which means Service, Employment, and Re-Development in skills, had been proposed for many months but never funded. We wanted SER which is a joint operation of the American GI Forum and LULAC, to place people in jobs for job training, manpower, migrant education, and also skill bank. . . . At a White House conference . . . I complained to President Johnson. . . . I said, "Mr. President, you know, I wish you would go ahead and get us the money for SER. He said, "You mean it hasn't been funded?" I said, "No, Mr. President." He said, "Jacobsen," (he called him Jake) "I want you to go over there right away and before these people leave, get them the SER money." And before we left the White House Conference, and I remember as we were sitting at a table having coffee and cake, within the hour Jacobsen came back. He said, "Mr. President, they will be funded."[145]

García walked away from the meeting with a five million dollar package to begin the program.[146] President Johnson further confirmed his commitment to the Mexican American community by attending Vicente Ximenes's swearing-in ceremony as commissioner of EEOC on June 9, 1967. Johnson gave a brief address, invoking once again his most recurring theme. Johnson harkened back to his early teaching career experiences in the "Mexican" school in Cotulla, Texas, and reiterated his vow to use his office to benefit every American equally. Johnson also made the historic announcement, declaring his intention to "establish the highest level committee a president can create."

Johnson's new committee represented a cabinet-level group called the Inter-agency Committee on Mexican American Affairs. García recalled:

> While in Washington at the installation [of Ximenes as commissioner of EEOC] and out of the clear blue sky, he said, "I have created the Interagency Committee for Mexican-American Affairs and I appointed as the chairman of this new cabinet level committee, Mr. Vicente Ximenes and under him would be the Secretary of Commerce, Secretary of Equal Employment Opportunity, Secretary on the War on Poverty, Sargent Shriver, and down the line." And mind you, no one had ever asked him for the creation of this agency, nobody knew anything about it. Nobody had heard about it, and certainly how would we know, because we had no precedent.[147]

Johnson's staff praised his performance at the installation ceremony, claiming, "the President was at his best."[148] In a press release announcing the appointment of Ximenes, Johnson delineated the purpose of the agency as to: "assure that Federal programs are reaching the Mexican Americans and providing the assistance they need and seek out new programs that may be necessary to handle problems that are unique to the Mexican American community."[149]

Ximenes headed the new Inter-agency Committee on Mexican American Affairs, pushing for affirmative action at all levels of government. Henry A. J. Ramos observes, "Aside from Hector García, who wielded a uniquely influential relationship with LBJ, the most persuasive representative of Hispanic concerns during the Johnson administration was Vicente Ximenes."[150] From the beginning, Ximenes "noticed that Johnson was the one administration official who invariably took the lead on Mexican American issues."[151] With Johnson's enthusiastic support, Ximenes led the first Cabinet Committee Hearings on Mexican American Affairs in El Paso, Texas, on October 27, 1967, an unprecedented government sponsored event.

The American GI Forum was well represented at the El Paso hearings, including García. However, labor activist César Chávez declined attending. Chávez boycotted the event with these words in a September 27, 1967, letter to Ximenes:

> Your and the President's concern for *most* Mexican-American problems is commendable. We have not participated in any such meetings and are reluctant to do so as we do not want to embarrass the administration. It is our considered opinion that the administration is not ready to deal with specific problems affecting farm workers.[152]

George I. Sánchez also declined an invitation to attend, saying, "I cannot accept the El Paso Conference as a sort of 'consolation prize,' with all due respect to the White House."[153] Other prominent Chicano activists such as Reies López Tijerina, who was under federal indictment for leading a raid on a New Mexico courthouse, were omitted from the guest list. Many of the Mexican American community's more militant leaders such as Bert Corona, "Corky" González, and Ernesto Galarza boycotted the El Paso hearings and criticized the Johnson administration policies, including U.S. involvement in the Vietnam War.[154] Johnson insisted that the hearings be held in El Paso rather than in Washington so as to be located close to U.S.-Mexican border. The President strategically set the date for the hearings to coincide with the international signing of the Chamizal Treaty with Mexico. "He wanted the hearings to get international attention," Ximenes explained.[155] Johnson's choice of timing and location infuriated not only the Chicanos, but the organizers of the Chamizal ceremony and the city fathers of El Paso who were afraid of protests and "bad press." In spite of varying degrees of resistance, the hearings were both peaceful and productive. Ramos summarizes:

> The El Paso hearings proceeded nevertheless, with more than one thousand participants including President Johnson, Vice-President Hubert Humphrey, OEO Director Sergeant [*sic*] Shriver, and the secretaries of Agriculture, Labor, Housing and Urban Development, and Health, Education, and Welfare. In fact, this was an unprecedented event in the Mexican-American's long pursuit of justice and equal opportunity. Never before had such a group of high-ranking government officials met outside of Washington with a group of citizens to discuss their problems.[156]

Both García and Ximenes considered the El Paso hearings a major turning point for Mexican American civil rights. Ximenes further reflected:

> Many of the cabinet members came a little reluctantly perhaps, a little apprehensive about what to anticipate. . . . But as witness after witness spoke before the cabinet officials and told their individual stories, you began to see their whole demeanor change . . . I think, they began to comprehend the level of suffering *mexicano* people were having to endure in this country. I think each of those officials was deeply touched by what they saw and heard at the hearings. Each of them left with a little spark of enthusiasm about new initiatives we might forge on behalf of the people they had come to better understand in El Paso.[157]

As in the Longoria case, García and Johnson brought the plight of the Mexican American community to the nation. However, this time, with the power of the executive office, Johnson brought the nation's leaders to the Mexican American community. The following year brought a number of important and unprecedented administration initiatives on behalf of Mexican Americans, including a 41 percent increase in Hispanic federal employees over the 1965 figures. New programs emerged such as federally subsidized migrant educational benefits and the Bilingual Education Act.[158]

Johnson's February 21, 1968 statement, "A New Focus on Opportunity for the Spanish Speaking American," delineated:

> Last October in El Paso, I attended a conference of high purpose. There, with the Vice President and members of the Cabinet, I met with 1,200 Spanish speaking Americans. This was the first time that the Mexican American community had an opportunity to discuss matters of direct concern—ranging from education to economic opportunity, housing to health—with the highest officials of government.

The aim of the three-day conference was to assure that America's second largest minority was receiving its fair and just share of Federal programs in these areas. . . . Based on the recommendations of the [Cabinet-level Committee on Mexican American Affairs]—many of which stemmed from the El Paso Conference—I have taken the following actions:

I have signed into law the first Federal bilingual education program. . . .

I have asked Congress to provide funds to expand and improve adult and vocational educational programs. . . .

I have instructed the Secretary of Health, Education, and Welfare to: accelerate the training of specially-trained teachers to work with Mexican American school children and migrant workers. . . .

insure compliance with Title VI of the 1964 Civil Rights Act. . . .

I have appointed a distinguished Mexican American scholar, Dr. Julian Samora, to a Presidential Commission evaluating the Nation's welfare system. I have directed the Secretary of the Department of Housing and Urban Development to work with Laredo, Texas and its sister city in Mexico, Nuevo Laredo, in an international cooperative effort . . . that will improve the condition of life in this border area.[159]

Johnson's statement reflected the primary concerns of García's twenty-year civil rights campaign. Before the close of the year, Johnson would recognize García's key role in his civil rights reform program by appointing him to the United States Commission on Civil Rights.

Additional appointments would come for García: he served as an ambassador to the United Nations in September 1967, and as a member of the National Advisory Council on Economic Opportunity in March 1967. On March 30, 1968, García, along with Vice President Hubert Humphrey, served as Johnson's ambassador for the signing of the Treaty of Tlatelolco in Mexico, which prohibited nuclear weapons in the Latin American Zone, dazzling the Latin American leaders with his speech in "perfect" Spanish. García's diplomacy impressed Latin American countries and their ambassadors. "Hector, I'm pleased with you," Johnson praised, "Because you made headlines in the *Baltimore Sun* . . . and peeved the Russians a little bit. Because they didn't quite expect an American to be speaking Spanish."[160] García's final appointment from Johnson came in October 1968 when Johnson nominated García to the United States Commission on Civil Rights.

Johnson declared García's nomination on October 13, 1968, while on vacation at the LBJ Ranch, and pushed his staff to take immediate action on the appointment.[161] Johnson's term was coming to a close and he wanted to finish what he had started with the 1967 El Paso hearings. García's appointment to the Civil Rights Commission was one he neither sought nor expected. García recounted:

> Before I knew it, President Johnson called me. Of course, by this time, I
> had security clearance for the United Nations. I served the government
> on several missions. So he appointed me. . . . Because he knew I had been
> working on civil rights for twenty years. The American GI Forum started
> with the Felix Longoria case, we had gone into police brutality, lack of
> representation in juries, lack of representation in draft boards, lack of
> representation in schools, he knew that I knew civil rights. I knew civil rights
> as a Mexican-American, I knew the problems, I knew where they were. And
> this, I believe, is why he asked me. And of course, I think he was pleased
> with the fact that I had done my duty as his choice to be the Ambassador
> to the United Nations.[162]

Johnson was confident in García's keen ability to shuttle between cultures, his linguistic alacrity, rhetorical acumen, and strong public appeal. García was sworn in on November 7, 1968, and attended his first meeting of the Commission in Washington D.C.[163]

García became the first Mexican American to serve on the Civil Rights Commission. His term was short-lived, however. He was promptly replaced under the Nixon administration by Manuel Ruiz Jr., an attorney and businessman from Los Angeles in October 1969. In his brief period of service, nonetheless, García presided over the first hearing ever conducted by the Civil Rights Commission "devoted exclusively to the problems of Mexican Americans." García extended what Johnson and Ximenes initiated with the El Paso hearings. The commission's hearing on Texas civil rights issues was held in December 1968 in San Antonio, Texas, at Our Lady of the Lake College, attracting over three hundred participants and drawing national media attention.[164] García stated:

> The hearings are designed to identify some of the major barriers encountered
> by Mexican Americans as they attempt to gain an education, to earn a
> livelihood, and achieve economic stability, and to receive equal treatment
> and protection under the law in their communities, their state, and their
> country.[165]

The hearings lasted for a full week, examining issues of police brutality, farm worker benefits, school segregation, welfare policies, and the minimum wage. García and the Mexican American community played a visible and unprecedented role in Johnson's bold and imaginative construction of the "Great Society" and civil rights reform. It is, therefore, not surprising to find that the plight of the Mexican-origin citizens in America informed Johnson's vision of the 1965 Voting Rights Act and his public identification with America's minority groups.

The Rhetorical Imagination of Johnson's Voting Rights Reform

On January 15, 1965, at the peak of the black civil rights protest era, President Johnson offered advice to Martin Luther King Jr. during a taped phone conversation recently released by the Lyndon B. Johnson Presidential Library.[166] While their conversation reflects mutual respect and rapport, Johnson and King's alliance would be, by comparison, short-lived, never reaching the level of intimacy Johnson achieved with García. Exactly three months before his Voting Rights Act Speech, Johnson made it explicitly clear to King that the newly drafted voting rights act represented the interests of not only the "Negro" but the "Mexican" as well. Johnson conducted the phone call with King from the LBJ Ranch in the same month he addressed the National Conference on Poverty in the Southwest sponsored by the American GI Forum. What is important to consider is that there was a sustained and growing dialogue between the Johnson administration and civil rights leaders from both African American and Mexican American camps at this point in history. Moreover, Johnson's recommendation to King outlined a model of resistance to discrimination strongly reflective of García's successful representation of the Félix Longoria incident.[167] King opened the conversation:

> Well, I certainly appreciate your returning my call and I don't want to take but a minute of your time. First, I want to thank you for that great State of the Union message. It was really a powerful presentation. We are on our way now toward a Great Society.

Johnson responded:

> I'll tell you what our problem is. We have got to try with every force at our command . . . and I mean every force—to get these education bills . . . we have to get them passed before the vicious forces concentrate and get them a coalition that can block them. Then we have got to . . . get these big things through medicare, education. . . .
>
> There is not going to be anything, though, Doctor, as effective as all of them voting. That will get you a message that all the eloquence in the world won't bring because the fellow will be coming to you then instead of you calling him. . . . I think it is very important that we not say that we are doing this and we are not doing it just because it is Negroes or Whites. We take the position that every person born in this country and reaches a certain age

that he has a right to vote, just as he has a right to fight, that we just extend it whether it is a Negro, a Mexican or whoever it is. And number two, we don't want a special privilege for anybody. We want equality for all and we can stand on that principle. . . .

[I]f you can find the worst condition that you run into in Alabama, or Mississippi or Louisiana or South Carolina where—I think one of the worst I ever heard of is the President of the School at Tuskegee or Head of the Government Department there or something being denied the right to cast a vote and if you take that one illustration and get it on the radio, get it on television, get it in the pulpits, get it in the meetings—every place you can then pretty soon the fellow who didn't do anything but drive a tractor would say well that is not right—that is not fair.

Then that will help us in what we are going to shove through in the end. . . . And if we do that we will break through. It will be the greatest breakthrough of anything not even except in this '64 Act. I think the greatest achievement of my Administration—the greatest achievement in Foreign policy—I said to a group yesterday—was the passage of the 1964 Civil Rights Act, but I think this will be bigger because it will do things that even the '64 Act couldn't do.[168]

The portrait of national resistance that Johnson paints, an event that would resonate for even the "fellow who drives a tractor" harkens back to the Longoria drama. Johnson's imaginative "worst" case scenario echoes reactions he witnessed nearly twenty years before in the attitudes and feelings expressed through the numerous letters written by American citizens from every corner of the country responding to the Longoria affair.

The broad scope of the 1965 Voting Rights Act would be the landmark piece of legislation of Johnson's presidency. He took greatest pride in this reform bill. The Voting Rights Act was painstakingly developed. Moreover, Johnson's rhetoric indicates that this bill was not only the culmination of a very long process, but the fulfillment of an abiding relationship with the Mexican American community. To overlook the process and the relationships that represent the *telos* of Johnson's voting rights reform policy is to miss the heart of Johnson's rhetoric.

Not only are the motivating forces behind this policy much more complex, but the intended inclusivity of the 1965 Voting Rights Act is much broader than generally recognized. Johnson's January 15, 1965, phone conversation with Martin Luther King Jr., the narrative dimensions of Johnson's March 15, 1965, speech to the televised Joint Session of Congress, and his March 24, 1965, letter to García reflecting on the speech all underscore the fact that Johnson understood civil rights reform in terms of an "imagined fraternity" that included

Mexican Americans as well as African Americans. Johnson's assertion to King that the most effective weapon against racism would be to rally public opinion around the "worst case of discrimination" echoes García's strategic handling of the Longoria case. The success of the Longoria affair provided Johnson a rhetorical heuristic from which to re-imagine the national civil rights crisis of 1965. This was not a new drama for Johnson, but rather another act of the same script performed nearly twenty years ago.

Johnson offered this heuristic to King both as a corrective and a cautionary tale. As President, he was willing "to shove through" legislation, but knew that in order to transform the national will civil rights activists like Martin Luther King Jr. would need to evoke the American will, find the resonant chord to exhort the nation to resist ascriptive inequality as García had done in 1949 in response to the Longoria incident. Johnson was cautiously warning King against any social action that threatened to rupture the national communion, a limit García had understood and honored. In Johnson's mind the Longoria incident served as a model of national civil rights reform. García observed:

> [The Longoria case] was a turning point for many things. It was a turning point for the American GI Forum; it was a turning point for Lyndon Johnson—I think it pushed Johnson into national prominence; it was turning point for the thinking of some Anglo Texans. It was a catalyst for the cause of Mexican American civil rights.[169]

Frank Oltorf, former Texas state representative and author of the minority report for the legislative investigative hearings on the Longoria case, likewise considered the Three Rivers incident as a defining moment in Johnson's career:

> I was in the legislature; we were back in session. And this Mexican soldier had either been killed in Korea or died in service overseas. His name was Longoria. Yes, L-O-N-G-O-R-I-A. I think this is interesting, because it was Lyndon Johnson's first real endeavor in the field of civil rights, you might say. This soldier had been killed, and they brought his body back to Three Rivers where he was from, a little town in South Texas. And the undertaker refused to bury him in the cemetery where the white people were buried. There his body was, and the widow had desperately contacted the brand new junior senator from Texas, and Johnson had gotten him buried in Arlington. So it of course was a wonderful thing for him to do. But it made some of those bigots down there so mad, the publicity that he got in all the papers about this soldier having been buried in Arlington, that they decided that they would have their representative, a man named Gray, call for a

legislative investigation of the thing. . . . So we went down to Three Rivers
and held this investigation. Johnson's attitude was that he wanted neither
glory nor anything else out of it. . . . [I]t was one of the most remarkable
experiences in my life. . . .

But all during this thing . . . there was no doubt in my mind of Lyndon
Johnson's real feeling about this thing: that this man had been discriminated
against and that there wasn't any political consideration in what he had
done. He was outraged.[170]

The successful outcome of the Longoria affair reinforced Johnson's confidence in the "imagined fraternity, "an egalitarian union of men," as the
foundation of his vision of the "Great Society." As long as King subscribed
to these tenets, Johnson was willing to work with him as he had worked
with García for nearly twenty years.

Johnson's engagement on behalf of Mexican Americans in 1949 was
bold and unprecedented. His identification with Longoria, the blameless
victim, a man both dead and imagined, proved symbolically potent in the
mid-twentieth-century war-torn moment. Johnson enlarged this sense of an
all-inclusive brotherhood to encompass Mexican Americans as an invisible,
neglected American constituency. Relocating their disparate affiliations
and locally conceived identities as Mexican American and Anglo males
toward what Dana Nelson calls the ideal of "national manhood," García
and Johnson successfully constructed and connected notions of manhood
to a common civic identity.[171]

Nearly two centuries after the Constitutional era formalization of the national communion (a fraternity limited exclusively to free white men), García
and Johnson reaffirmed the national communion around the emblem of the
fallen hero and a mythos of death. Theirs was "a reformulation of manhood—
purified, unified, vigorous, brotherly, national manhood—as a corrective to
a whole range of frictions and anxieties men were experiencing as a result of
post-war political, economic, and social dislocation."[172] This *ethos* of sacrifice,
honor, and national service provided the ideological and affective foundation
of García and Johnson's relationship as well as the reconceptualization of
post-war civil rights reform. Unfortunately, rather than contest the referential
power of white manhood and the limits of liberal democracy, García and
Johnson sought to enlarge its scope and make it more inclusive.

García and Johnson did not challenge but instead reasserted the founda-
tional terms of citizenship and the qualifications for belonging. They saw
themselves individually and collectively as heirs of liberal democracy, a
modern reinvention of constitutional America. Anita Haya Patterson's *From
Emerson to King: Democracy, Race, and the Politics of Protest* argues:

Rights are markers of citizenship that allow us to exist in legally protected formal relationships to one another. . . . In the tradition of liberal nationalism rights have been defined as entailing obligations that bind individuals together as a political community, a community that is—in theory but often not in practice—infinitely permeable and expansive because any person who meets the qualifications for citizenship can join.[173]

García and Johnson's alliance was more a reaffirmation rather than a reformulation of the traditional civic fraternity. Their relationship was forged less on a Lockean archetype of citizenship as a contractual obligation, and more on an Emersonian model of friendship and American nationalism. Conceived around a paradigm of Christian civic brotherhood and continuously reaffirmed with "affection, reverence, love, and ultimately, human kindness," the García-Johnson relationship represented the performance of a national *ethos*.[174]

García and Johnson's partnership reflected both an ideal and a distortion of the Constitutional vision of the national fraternity. They saw themselves as faithful American citizens. Each perceived himself a white man. And yet the question of race and whiteness always overshadowed them, with García claiming whiteness on one hand, and decrying discrimination on the other, embracing his "Mexican" origins in one moment and attacking the "wetbacks" the next. There was a difference that they could never quite wrap words around, an inequity they could never quite articulate. They were both blinded by the myth of American exceptionalism and its implicit tenets of white supremacism.

In the final analysis, it was García's fidelity that provided the emotional glue binding them against difference. Continuously cemented by his fealty and unswerving support of Johnson, García offered a level of fidelity no other civil rights activist would dare extend to Johnson. King and others would always keep a safe distance. In the final months before his assassination, King was no longer welcome in Johnson's inner circle. Also on the periphery of Johnson's inner circle were Bayard Rustin, who planned the March on Washington, Stokely Carmichael of the Student Non-Violent Coordinating Committee, and Floyd McKissick of the Congress of Racial Equality. As soon as King and other leaders began to attack Johnson and his policies concerning U.S. involvement in the Vietnam War, they overstepped Johnson's terms of inclusion.[175] Johnson eschewed those who preferred "agitation over legislation."[176]

The "imagined fraternity" Johnson offered had a number of unspoken membership requirements. García not only abided by those terms, but maintained a devotion to Johnson that withstood the test of time. Garcia also helped to define those membership requirements by acting as a model member. Garcia's correspondence consistently reflects an enduring fealty that helped to sustain his access to Johnson as illustrated in this June 10, 1960, report to presidential hopeful Senator Johnson. García offered:

> I am ready to serve you in any way whatsoever. Please remember that this is a personal report sent to you by your true, devoted friend who is for you all the way. . . . I wish you the best of luck and I for one feel confident that you will be our next president. I am for you because not only are you my firend but you are the greatest, ablest, truest candidate for president of my country.[177]

García and Johnson's interchanges operated emblematically, circulating power between them toward an enlarged national communion. And this is the vision of national communion that Johnson extended to Martin Luther King Jr. in their March 15, 1965, phone call. It was a bargain that King did not want to make.

What made the García-Johnson relationship work was García's enduring patience and willingness to give in order to gain. Even under fire, García was willing to remain Johnson's ardent supporter. Grounded in a Judeo-Christian *ethos* of atonement, García was willing to make sacrifices. Theirs was an ideological and political exchange with very clear parameters. Because García understood and abided by the terms, Johnson risked engagement for the benefit of a larger communion. Had García adopted a more publically militant stance, he would not have been a safe risk for Johnson, the cautious and consummate politician. Even more importantly, García was faithful. He once predicted, "I have been in the United Nations and been traveling throughout the world. I know a little bit about history . . . and I say this: when the history of our times is written—of this era—Lyndon Johnson is going to come up mighty high."[178] Confident in LBJ's moderate course toward social change, García played a key role in the outcome of national civil rights reform.

Twelve years after his 1953 address to the American GI Forum asserting his devotion to the Mexican Americans of Texas, President Johnson appeared on national television to announce his new civil rights program. He wanted his proposal to be more than just a policy, but part of a comprehensive plan to confront the historical inequities that plagued the country. On March 15, 1965, President Johnson spoke before a joint session of Congress on national television in support of the Voting Rights Act. Responding to mounting pressure from García and other Mexican American leaders to repeal poll taxation in Texas, the Department of Justice had been coalescing voting rights reform proposals under Johnson's direction.[179] The necessity of voting rights reform, further accelerated by the demands of black civil rights activists from the South, had been actively promoted by García and the American GI Forum since 1949.[180] Johnson's conflicted civil rights record finds its greatest consistency in his allegiance to the Mexican American community, extending back to his experiences in the Cotulla "Mexican" school and the Longoria incident. Ramos observes in *The American GI Forum: In Pursuit of the Dream*:

> The passage of the Voting Rights Act of 1965 marked Johnson's initial investment in the Great Society. . . . LBJ's emotional, nationally televised remarks on the Voting Rights Act marked the first time an American president had placed America's race problems outside the parameters of merely black/white relations. In fact, Johnson's remarks bore special significance for their relevance to Mexican Americans across the United States.[181]

García and other civil rights leaders had long argued for repealing poll taxation in Texas. This process was hastened by demands of black civil rights activists in Alabama and other states.[182] Johnson instructed the Department of Justice to draft voting rights legislation soon after the 1964 presidential election.[183] A December 28, 1964 memo circulated between Johnson and the Justice Department outlined suggestions for dealing with the voting rights problem. The recommendations included the elimination of voting restrictions and qualifications such as literacy tests. Johnson's January 4, 1965, State of the Union Address hinted at his intention to eliminate remaining obstacles to the access and the right to vote.[184]

Three months later, on March 15, 1965, Johnson came forward with a detailed voting rights program. Appropriating Martin Luther King Jr.'s theme, "we shall overcome," Johnson's speech reflects not only his identification with African Americans but Mexican Americans. His address accommodated civil rights leaders of both groups and at the same time exercised his nation-maintaining role. Johnson's speech celebrated the black civil rights movement at its peak and reaffirmed the value of nonviolent protest as a tactic and philosophy.[185] Even more importantly, Johnson's address established the responsibility for confronting institutionalized discrimination squarely at the center of the executive office. Johnson's invocation of duty to his former students in Cotulla, Texas, not only fulfills a lifelong personal commitment but finally brings to completion the first duty of the president—to protect equally the civic participation of each member of the polis.

The narrativistic and entelechial qualities of Johnson's address work at multiple dimensions. His folksy style helps to disarm resistance, diffusing the volatility of the race issue under question. At the same time, Johnson's heart-felt disclosure to the nation about his former students humanizes both the man and the office. Johnson appears at the same time vulnerable and powerful. Through the rhetoric of story-telling, Johnson personalizes as well as universalizes the central role of enfranchisement in the imagined communion of constitutional America. He illustrates through imagery the effects of obstructed access to full democratic participation: poverty, prejudice, privation. Johnson described to the nation:

> My first job after college was as a teacher in Cotulla, Texas, in a small Mexican American school. . . . They knew in their youth the pain of prejudice. They never seemed to know why people disliked them. But they knew it was so, because I saw it in their eyes. I often walked home late in the afternoon, after classes were finished, wishing there was more I could do. But all I knew was to teach them the little I knew, hoping that it might help them against the hardships that lay ahead. . . . Somehow you never forget what poverty and hatred can do when you see its scars on the hopeful face of a young child. I never thought then, in 1928, that I would be standing here in 1965. It never occurred to me in my fondest dreams that I might have the chance to help the sons and daughters of those students and to help people like them all over this country. But now I do have that chance—and I'll let you in on a secret—I mean to use it.[186]

In the exercise of the rhetorical presidency, Johnson demonstrated not only responsiveness but leadership. He traces a trajectory, a life course, and a call to leadership. In so doing, the moment becomes a culmination of the journey of not only a man, but a nation.

Johnson historicizes racial inequity and personalizes discrimination through the faces of his Mexican American students. In this way, Johnson illustrates to the nation that racism is still with us. It is all around us. It has always been with us even in places and among people we don't even know—in the most remote and silent corners of our country. Johnson complicates the black/white binary by demonstrating the effects of racism and discrimination. He reasserts that "Negroes are not the only victims." African Americans, Mexican Americans, and Americans of all origins can be victims of discrimination. Only equal access to the ballot can ensure that each citizen has an equal voice. Johnson called for bold change with practical and immediate application. He promoted his voting rights act not only as the realization of a daring vision but the application of reasoned action.

Finally, Johnson, ever the skilled politician, wrapped an *ethos* of progressive liberalism around a national crisis without appearing to cave in to the demands of this tense and violent period in American race relations.

Marking his initial investment in Great Society legislation, Johnson made clear to the nation that his convictions on voting rights were rooted in his experience as a young teacher of Mexican American children in the South Texas town of Cotulla.[187] It was a disclosure that moved the country. The speech, on the whole, stirred reaction. But there was a different quality to this address that people struggled to identify. The day following the address, Jack Valenti, Johnson's White House aid, informed the president and his staff about public and media reactions. Valenti's March 16, 1965, memo "Report to the President" notes:

> There is considerable speculation and interest in the President's speech of Monday night: Who was the principal writer? How was it written, the method, and the timing, etc?
>
> I have responded . . . with the following:
>
> The President wrote the speech. He talked out what he wanted to say—and as drafts were prepared in response to his dictation, the President personally edited and revised. . . .
>
> The President kept revising the speech, even until the final minutes.[188]

Valenti made it clear that Johnson was responsible for the "principal creative effort." Addressing the question of authenticity was especially important to Johnson, suggesting that he did not want his address to be dismissed as merely business-as-usual politics. The personal dimensions revealed in Johnson's appeal to the nation on behalf of Mexican Americans remain one of the most distinguishing features of his speech. Historians and rhetorical analysts have since recognized Johnson's voting rights address as the most moving speech of his career.[189]

For García, the event signified Mexican Americans' inclusion in the national "imagined fraternity." Johnson had poignantly introduced the problems of Mexican Americans into the national narrative on civil rights. They were no longer a "forgotten people." But the implications went even deeper than that. García read Johnson's message as a personal tribute to their relationship. In many respects, it was an accurate interpretation.

García quickly signaled his approval of Johnson's actions with a personal letter followed by commendations from the American GI Forum. García and the American GI Forum promptly passed a resolution praising Johnson's performance. With the expiration of the *bracero* program on December 31, 1964 finally behind them, the American GI Forum's March 1965 resolution celebrated the symbolic incorporation of Mexican American citizens into the national communion. The Forum praised the president:

> Whereas, President Johnson in his message to Congress expressed himself with love, warmth, and understanding towards the problems of the Americans of Mexican origin since his days as a school teacher in Cotula [*sic*], Texas. . . . Now, therefore, be it resolved, that the American GI Forum on the 17th anniversary go on record of highly commending President Lyndon B. Johnson for his great leadership, moral encouragement, and personal assistance in achieving First Class Citizenship for Americans of Mexican origin."[190]

The resolution was a bold claim, and perhaps more wishful thinking than truth. It did, however, credit Johnson for breaking the silence on the condition of Mexican-origin citizens in American society. Interestingly, the emblems of "love," "warmth," and "understanding" echo the same terms used by and about Johnson to describe his relationship with the American GI Forum during the 1949 and 1953 conventions. Coming full circle, the American GI Forum resolution invokes the celebrative feelings formed when their alliance was first established. The discursive exchange between the American GI Forum and Johnson surrounding the Voting Rights Act address chronicles a life cycle of partnering—the honeymoon, the joy of reconciliation, and the milestone moment of a mid-life anniversary.

The Voting Rights Act speech, which aired on Monday, March 15, was still making headlines when Johnson wrote his reply to García. Johnson was moved by García's tribute. His March 24, 1965 thank-you letter to García reveals uncharacteristic humility and joy. In very carefully chosen words, Johnson acknowledged García's presence in the long process leading up to the formation of the Voting Rights Act. He directly connects the Voting Rights Act address to his relationship with García and the Longoria affair. Johnson's allusion to the Three Rivers case describes a moment upon which not only their friendship but Johnson's understanding of civil rights issues was founded. His letter conveys a sense of enduring comradeship and intimacy in the use of the metaphor of "the long road." An archetype of passage, the image of the road comes to represent the sixteen-year journey leading them to this moment. Johnson wrote:

> As I thought of Cotulla, I also had in my mind the memories of our own associations in times past—particularly at Three Rivers—as we walked together the long road that led to last Monday night. . . . [191]

There is roundedness to Johnson's message, a feeling of completion. His message suggests the fulfillment of something begun long before this occasion, a moment finally coming full circle. Affection and generosity of spirit circulate between author and reader. The extension of the "imagined fraternity" had been performed on national prime-time television. Johnson's debt to the Mexican American constituency was finally paid. Even more significantly, Johnson suggests that his efforts were not entirely political. This was something more. He both recognizes García's leadership as well as García's faithful friendship. "For all you have meant in the past . . . I thank you," Johnson closes.

Although the level of inclusion that the 1965 Voting Rights Act was designed to protect was not immediately realized by Mexican Americans or African Americans, and though the "first class citizenship" which García and the American GI Forum claimed in 1965 was partial at best, the moment marked the emergence of a small socially incorporated Mexican American middle class. García and his generation of reformers along with an emerging Chicano rights movement would continue to challenge the limits of the Great Society. There was much left undone. The occasion of the 1965 Voting Rights Act Address, however, unequivocally illustrated that belonging is rhetorical.

Conclusion: Revising the History of American Civil Rights Reform

arcía's story can be read as a romance with America, a love affair with a vision—the multiplicity of the polis and the possibilities of democracy. García was an immigrant revisioning, reasserting, and reclaiming the core tenets of the U.S. Constitution. García's performance of civic identity both resonates and resists the romantic self-image proffered by the "imagined fraternity" of white America—the seamless union of the Federalists, the cohesive brotherhood of Emerson, the embodied patriotism of Whitman. In each phase of his political history from the Longoria affair through the *bracero* battle and into the Democratic Party alliance with LBJ, García exploited the passion and imagination contained in the nation's democratizing discourses.

García's story is more than a love story, however. It is also a tragedy. García's receipt of the Presidential Medal of Freedom in 1984 was in truth a tortuous moment of ironic contradiction as he stood on an exalted stage beside President Ronald Reagan, the figurehead of an administration García considered "pure Hollywood."[1] The contributions of Héctor P. García to modern civil rights reform, like the construction of Mexican American civil rights history, do not resolve into a decisive narrative of progress. García's legacy of resistance does not fit neatly into a coherent and close-ended story of hard-won justice.

At the turn of the twenty-first century, Mexican-origin peoples continue to have the lowest rates of educational achievement and economic mobility and the highest incidence of poverty, unemployment, infant mortality, and birth defects in the nation. The exigencies that spurred García to action fifty years ago still exist. And the permeable border García tried to seal remains a wound separating an international superpower from the so-called third world realities of Latin America—a wound that continues to resist suturing.[2]

In late October 2005, Governor Bill Richardson of New Mexico authorized the U.S. Army to dispatch fourteen armored vehicles in a surveillance mission tagged "Operation Rolling Thunder." This military exercise combined efforts with the U.S. border patrol, state police, and civilian volunteers called the Minutemen Civil Defense Corps to patrol the southern borders of New Mexico. Instead of "spies, subversives, and wetbacks," these patrols stand on alert for terrorists and undocumented workers displaced by global market and political trends impacting Mexico and Central America who are crossing the U.S. border in waves searching for work, food, and asylum. Hauntingly, the week of October 24, 2005, also marked the loss of the two thousandth U.S. soldier in Iraq, as well as the death of civil rights activist Rosa Parks. The threads of history reweave themselves.

García's civil rights movement offers a representative anecdote of the history of Mexican American civic inclusion. The Longoria incident can be read as the symbolic enactment of Mexican people's ritual sacrifice for citizenship in the United States. The national drama of the Longoria case provides illustration of an enduring cycle of rejection, the continuing struggle from displacement to honor that has historically characterized the Mexican American journey toward enfranchisement. As a narrative of the Mexican presence in America, the Longoria case continues to reinvent itself into an ongoing drama transforming death and erasure into viability and presence.

Five decades later, the town of Three Rivers erupted once again over the controversy of the burial rites for Private Félix Longoria. A recent proposal to rename the city post office in honor of Longoria has reignited old animosities. In May 2004, the city hall in Three Rivers was packed beyond capacity as the city council listened to the public debate rehashing the events of fifty years ago. Following heated deliberation, the city council ruled that it would not oppose the proposal drafted by Representative Lloyd Dogget, D-Texas, to rename the post office. Local newspapers reported that Longoria's sister left the city hall in tears and vowed to protect the family name. "I'm hoping and praying that it will all end now."[3]

Meanwhile, the ritual sacrifice for inclusion continues on the border between the United States and Mexico as a routine performance for the thousands of undocumented workers who risk their lives to gain entry. Rick Ufford-Chase of BorderLinks, a Tucson-based public awareness group, observes, "We've made the act of looking for a better job in the United States a crime that carries the death penalty."[4] The question of *bracero* labor and the place of undocumented migrant workers in the U.S. social, political, and economic landscape is as volatile today as it was fifty years ago. Echoes of Cold War rhetorical scapegoating reverberate in current political rhetorics. Politicians and social commentators portray the porosity of the U.S. border and historical dependence on Mexican labor as an unsolicited, unilateral arrangement in which the U.S. has fallen victim to Mexico's economic agenda. Political columnist Robert Samuelson writes in "The Limits of Immigration: The United States Cannot Be a Sponge for Mexico's Poor":

> But we surely don't need more poor and unskilled immigrants, and Mexicans fall largely in this category. The stakes here transcend economics. . . . The most obvious consequence of allowing more Mexican immigrants into the country would be to hurt those already here. . . . A possible perverse side effect is a rise in prejudice against Hispanic-Americans, who are confused for immigrants, even though they've often lived here for generations. There is a difference between having open borders for goods and for people."[5]

The anti-immigrant battle and rhetoric are still with us, demanding that we extricate the implicit and explicit racism in our national discourses toward Mexico and its people.

Civic identity is symbolic performance, rhetorically constituted and socially performed. Inclusion requires symbolic identification. In the national imaginary, whiteness still operates as a master trope, an index of citizenship, a marker of privilege, and a reduction of the whole person. The metonymic function of whiteness as a trope forges a distinction between categorical whiteness and nonwhiteness and reduces one perceived racial phenomenon in relation to the other. The metonymy of race, as such, performs its rhetorical work as a symbolic turn that simultaneously twists and subordinates categories.

American civil rights history has not adequately contextualized the rhetorical work of leaders like García and the post-war generation against the racial backdrop of white privilege. In the forty years since sweeping civil rights reform, the hereditary privilege of whiteness continues to permeate multiple dimensions of U.S. culture and social structure. Whiteness is intuitively recognized and ritually masked in the laws we construct, the images we generate, the lexicon we construct, the values we celebrate, and the privileges we afford. The failure to recognize that the desire for inclusion is inflected by a complex mythos of race involves an act of complicity—subliminal consent—to agree to resist naming the symbolic reduction.[6] The process by which whiteness as a class is sustained as the national standard still eludes notice. Race is understood in everyday terms only in relation to color, anything that is not white.

Examined against the grain of a post-9/11 moment, García's legacy demonstrates that stirring resistance to injustice is a quintessentially patriotic act. War and the fear of the invader are occasions for the assertion and celebration, not the retraction, of civil rights. The infidel in our midst is the intractable presence of hate, prejudice, intolerance, and racism within our borders. As García's story attests, these may be a far greater threat to our national integrity than the invisible "other" beyond our borders. Neither the national euphoria over victory in World War II nor the politically repressive Cold War period silenced García. Deprived of access to public services in restaurants, hotels, and swimming pools as well as to equal employment, school, and housing, García sought to make social inequities visible. The epistemic nature of García's everyday rhetoric illustrates, among other things, how social justice is both constructed and dismantled at the level of discourse—the discourse of disputation, dialogue, and ultimately policymaking.

Héctor P. García sparked mobilization of the most politically successful group of reformers in twentieth-century Mexican American history. García's rhetorical career shows that mobilization is less about eloquence and more about resonance—making a connection across groups. He showed time and again that effective rhetorical action strikes a chord of discontent yet embeds itself with hope. Inclusion was a shifting target that he was always trying to pin down through discourse. He illustrated that civic inclusion requires the effective use of the everyday rhetorics, common language and literacy practices that build identification within and across communities. Never a stranger to conflict or controversy, García demonstrated that communicative competence depends upon complex strategies of shuttling between rupture and repair across social groups. He also revealed that effective reform rhetoric begins by negotiating power differentials and resolves by healing division, even as it reveals and names the racism that would defeat it.

For García, democracy was not only a way of governing but a way of knowing. Local knowledge and the rhetorics of the everyday shaped social action. Furthermore, he demonstrated that the impetus for social action begins in the subjective and gains momentum through identification with others. Sociolinguistic alacrity and his ability to identify with diverse constituencies ultimately enhanced his discursive agency. Civic identity was symbolic performance, socially enacted and rhetorically constituted. Finally, for García civic *ethos* was synergistic, more than the sum of his social roles.

While historians Patrick Carroll and Ignacio García and documentarian Jeff Felts limn the emergence of the American GI Forum and the role of Dr. Héctor P. García as its national-level figure head, they overlook the complex discourse formations of the American GI Forum's fifty year civil rights campaign. What is gained from each narrativization of García is the textualization of a social actor, an unsung Mexican American hero previously effaced and recovered. What is lost is the ideological and discursive dimensionality of García's rhetoric, the historical moment and the dissonant discourses he resisted, regenerated, replicated, and recirculated. Without examination of the dissonance and contradiction, the narrativization of post-war reform history resolves into a reaffirmation of the civil rights narrative of progress, a once-done-always-done fiction of racial equality. Among the dangers of heroizing, erasing, or demonizing Héctor P. García in U.S. post-war civil rights reform history is the inadvertent affirmation and replication of whiteness as a trope of inclusion.

The recent reemergence and momentum of white supremacist movements and ideology in the United States (and throughout the world) underscore the need for, among other things, a critique that disrupts the discourse formations and premises upon which white hegemony maintains power. García's everyday rhetoric reflects a lifetime of grappling with the phenomenon of hereditary privilege from diverse class positions: impoverished Mexican immigrant to esteemed professional to political insider. García understood the human condition from the inside out—the human body, the human spirit, the human community. As a community leader, he struggled with the endemic force of racism, an affliction from which no one—not even he—was immune.

García rejected the subordinate subject position constructed and assigned to him by first attempting to expand—but failing to deconstruct—the vaulted category of whiteness. García and his followers understood intuitively that to disavow and dismantle the myth of white superiority was to relinquish simultaneously the access and mobility that comes with first-class citizenship, paths to the opportunity they fought so ardently to acquire. It would require the revocation of whiteness and the construction of a *mestizo* mythos by the Chicano movement to bring this contradiction to the foreground of the Mexican American civil rights movement.

García's journey is a counterstory, an unfinished journey. The once-done-always-done myth of racial justice in the United States becomes increasingly evidenced in the reversal of affirmative action policies, the persistent dismantling of bilingual education programs, anti-immigrant legislation in southwestern states such as California, Colorado, and Arizona, and the growing marginalization of liberal democratic discourses across the nation. These divisions are further exacerbated by the assertion of white dominance in public culture, political arenas, government institutions, and educational settings, which are increasingly returning to racially segregated patterns. To resist the resurgence of totalizing discourses demands dismantling black-white binaries.

The equalization of historical racial power differentials necessitates the rhetorical reconstruction of U.S. civil rights history complicated by the dissonance as well as the resonance of visible and passionate leaders like García positioned at the nexus of the black-white binary. His struggle at the fulcrum of U.S. civil rights discourse powerfully illustrates the teeter-totter of racism. Leaders like García go forward into the minefields of contradiction. The recovery and representation of the multifaceted journeys of complex civil rights reform leaders—their victories, failures, and foibles—provide historical touchstones critical to current reflective exegesis.

U.S. Representative Solomon Ortiz and Texas state senator Carlos Truan credit García's leadership and tenacity for Mexican Americans' social progress. García's interrogation of institutionalized discrimination, his role in the deliberative process of national policymaking, and his forty-year legacy as a social activist unquestionably distinguish him as a prodigious leader in modern civil rights history. Building on García's achievements and those of the post–World War II generation, an established middle class and an upper middle class of college-educated, fully enfranchised Mexican Americans exist today.

However, as a political force, this now economically secure sector of the Hispanic populace has shifted over time to the political right. Even Ed Idar Jr., one of the few remaining American GI Forum founders, a self-ascribed "yellow dog Democrat" through the early post-war years, became disillusioned by the Democratic party through the 1990s and resolutely voted for George W. Bush in the 2000 presidential election. Palatial Shoreline Drive in Corpus Christi is marked by the sparse but symbolic testaments of late-twentieth- and early-twenty-first-century Hispanic prosperity in the Spanish surnames designating the homes and offices of the city's prominent attorneys, physicians, accountants, and entrepreneurs. Meanwhile, the rapidly growing majority of the newly arrived Mexican-origin population in Texas lives on the borders of belonging, subsisting desperately below the national poverty level.[7]

The American GI Forum, García's national organization, is in decline. In yet another ironic twist, the charter of the Dr. Héctor P. García chapter of the American G.I. Forum was revoked by the national committee in July 2006 after charges of financial mismanagement. Moreover, García's accolades have been emptied of much of their symbolic value beside the enduring impoverishment of his people. How could an influential figure like Dr. Héctor P. García, a leader at the forefront, and behind-the-scenes of some of the major civil rights events of twentieth-century American history, elude scholarly consideration until recently? The paradox of position and the enigma of border identity constitute part of the answer. García belonged to everyone and to no one.

After Lyndon B. Johnson's administration, García became less significant to key political figures. The Chicano intelligentsia dismissed him as "too bourgeois and conservative a subject to warrant serious study or meaningful acknowledgment."[8] The Political Association of Spanish Speaking Organizations (PASO), defunct by 1964, gave way to more radical voices in the Mexican American movement. César Chávez and the United Farm Workers captured the attention of liberal democrats like Robert F. Kennedy, signaling the fact that García's liberal agenda was no longer liberal enough. Even World War II generation leader Albert Peña Jr. was calling for more militant action, claiming that Mexican Americans "are about four years behind our black brothers."[9] By the summer of 1967, a new emerging political force, under the direction of José Ángel Gutiérrez, a graduate student at St. Mary's University in San Antonio, was beginning to mobilize young Chicanos. García not only was out of step with the times but was losing his foothold in the sanctioned political structures. As Johnson receded from power, so did García.

The war and violence that was ripping the nation apart in 1968 cast a long shadow over García and the American GI Forum. The failure in Vietnam, the massacre of three hundred student protesters in Tlatelolco Plaza before the 1968 Olympics in Mexico, and military action against students at Kent State and across the United States called into question the integrity of elected officials and the efficacy of the male military *ethos*. The leadership qualities reflective of post-war figures like García and Johnson came under severe public scrutiny. Military action was no longer a productive solution against the threats to American democracy. The Great Society was closing down.

Johnson announced his decision not to run for reelection on March 26, 1968, with these words: "For thirty-seven years in the service of our Nation . . . I have put the unity of the people first . . . and ahead of any divisive partisanship."[10] Johnson's renunciation of his candidacy foreshadowed the final hour of New Deal liberalism and the erosion of the civil rights advances of the 1960s. As Vicente Ximenes recalls, "We knew the party was over the day Johnson renounced his candidacy for reelection." The tragic assassination of the visionary Martin Luther King Jr., on April 4, 1968, and of presidential hopeful Robert Kennedy on June 5, 1968, overwhelmed the nation and seared the collective memory. Fear, grief, and self-preservation reshaped the national tenor. The nation retreated to the right.

The vision of national Latino unity would become an unattainable goal by the end of the 1960s, the last hopes of which remain inscribed in García's militant rhetorical exhortations during the era following the Viva Kennedy National Political Leadership Conference.[11] The fracturing that occurred between generations of World War II and Vietnam War Mexican American civil rights activists would be a point of great distress and disappointment for García. The national solidarity Mexican Americans forged as a political presence through the late 1950s to the middle 1960s would be unrecoverable by the late 1960s, a condition García lamented. García regretted the militant rhetoric of the Chicanos and consistently condemned their strategies, which he believed led to violence.[12] He correctly predicted that the movement would have negligible long-term impact on American political and social structures. In its comparatively short life, the Chicano movement would not have the suasory influence over state and national policymaking that García's coalition achieved over its twenty-year journey. And at the same time, by the close of the Vietnam War, the American GI Forum would no longer generate the global appeal it enjoyed in the early post–World War II years.

Mexican Americans of the 1960s became more politically, linguistically, and culturally heterogeneous. The politically centrist Mexican American middle class eschewed the label and ideology of the Chicano movement, but they no longer responded to the 1950s "rhetoric of atonement" proffered by the American GI Forum. Middle-class Mexican Americans shifted to the right in the post-Johnson years as the new generation of Chicano civil rights activists marched to the left. They were united only in their skepticism toward Anglo politicians and the White House. A growing lack of confidence in the government, across all generations, did not engender Mexican American participation in the political process or encourage broad mobilization.

Moreover, in the 1960s, there was no collective emblem as potent and global as the Longoria incident around which to catalyze Mexican American activism across generations and classes. The rhetorical situation of the post–World War II era and the Longoria incident as exigence could not be recovered or repeated. García had provided the object and the leadership that moved the South Texas community interdependently toward broad, historically conditioned goals. He understood the value of *kairos*, time and place, and he knew how to rally people around an issue and a moment. Yet, by the end of the 1960s, the moments, the leaders, and the ideologies were far too many and diffuse to be united around a common emblem.

The symbol of the dead soldier in the 1960s became a rallying cry of a different kind for Chicanos. Death in war was a dubious sacrifice, an unholy price to pay for the promise of inclusion. Chicanos and many other American youth raised their voices against the Vietnam War and refused to serve. Entire families split over this ideological and social schism. "Hell no, we won't go" rang out across the nation, no less in Texas than in California. Chicano activists resisted the disproportionate representation of Mexican Americans on the front lines of action. This was not a point of honor as it had been for the World War II generation. This was a travesty. The post-war Mexican American generation, who had gained access to the "American Dream" through the military, found themselves once again alienated from their government, but even more tragically, alienated from their children, whose language, politics, and culture no longer reflected their own.

Popular rhetorics tend to portray the 1960s as a moment when the disinherited finally stood up and claimed their rightful place in the polis, a narrative construction that too comfortably resolves into a "once-done-always-done" notion of American civil rights reform.[13] The construction of modern civil rights history in popular as well as scholarly text too narrowly circumscribes the struggle for racial social justice to one period and one people.[14] In so doing, the myth-making of American civil rights reform replicates the binaries of race. The rhetorical construction of twentieth century civil rights as a black and white issue rests on an either-or fallacy rather than a hologram of possibilities. García's legacy complicates this narrative of progress.

Mobilization of the Mexican American civil rights movement suggests that the discursive action of post–World War II American civil rights was not linear, direct, or decisive. There was not one civil rights movement, but many. Civil rights reform was and continues to be an imaginative construction, the linguistically mediated exercise of will and vision performed in and on the world. The polyvocal texts left in the wake of García's mobilization efforts provide testimony to the contradictory, inconsistent, and conflicted process of social justice. They also attest to the ability to exercise a "moral voice" and to "plumb our moral sensibilities and convictions."

Movements are processes—five steps forward and three steps backward. They are linguistically and textually constructed with lives, deaths, and reincarnations. Social movements are sustained and extended conversations, diffuse, complex, and dynamic as the nature of language itself. In the case of García's civil rights movement, the premises he advanced aligned closely with Americanist Constitutional rhetoric. And yet García's rhetoric introduced a dissonance, exposing the disparity between America's ideals and America's practices. There is no end of the story—a clean, clear culmination. Justice is never achieved once and for all. Because we are grappling with language, its loops, its connections and dis-connections, the narratives tangle into new discourses that reinvent themselves into still other discourses, other texts, other genres. How we read these emanations of the rhetorical struggle of marginalized groups in America remains contingent on what stories we canonize and codify.

Reading García from an Americanist meta-narrative of progress would call for a story of a man in control of his text, achieving his aims, wielding power, and changing the world. Instead García's legacy illustrates a rhetor turning language loose in the world with intended and unintended consequences, conflicted results, and tenuous impact. If the Longoria case is mentioned at all, history attributes Lyndon B. Johnson with the bold outcome. The "wetback" issue remains a tragic and shameful blot on García's human rights record. And the historic mobilization of the Mexican American electorate in the Viva Kennedy and Viva Johnson campaigns does not warrant even a single file in the John F. Kennedy Library. The tragic turns of his life and work did not transform García into a martyr or saint but a frail and despondent old man.

In December 1972, Harry Middleton, director of the newly established Lyndon B. Johnson Presidential Library, organized an unprecedented national-level symposium on civil rights. As Middleton describes it: "The major thrust of the symposium will be to probe the future—to question and discuss what steps the nation should take in the decade ahead to pursue our commitment to the cause of equal opportunity and equal justice for all Americans."[15] Featured speakers included Chief Justice Earl Warren; Reynaldo Garza, federal judge of the Southern District of Texas; U.S. Representative Henry B. Gonzales; state senator Barbara Jordan; Vernon Jordan, executive director of the National Urban League; Roy Wilkins, executive director of the NAACP; Senator Hubert Humphrey; Vicente Ximenes; and Lyndon B. Johnson.

García received a personal invitation to attend this exclusive gathering. He was, however, not included on the program. Current archival evidence does not indicate if García attended or not. According to Vicente Ximenes, García regretted his omission from the list of civil rights dignitaries. Nonetheless, the first symposium on civil rights included three Mexican Americans of the post-war era alongside prominent African American leaders. In a critical moment of American self-reflection and vision-making, Mexican Americans joined in the conversation.

García's connection to LBJ ended in the early 1970s, when Johnson died at the LBJ Ranch on January 22, 1973.[16] The stalwart García would survive his political *compadre* by more than twenty years, continuing in his battle against discrimination. García's condolences to Lady Bird were rushed by telegram the same day of Johnson's death. His words reiterate the devotion and affection of a well-tempered twenty-five year relationship. García openly grieved:

> Johnson's loss will forever be remembered by Mexican Americans as their own loss. After all he was also our "Presidente." I personally feel that his death is like a loss in my own family. May the Lord give you strength. We loved him. We love you. Your Friend. Dr. Hector P. Garcia, Founder American GI Forum of U.S.[17]

García's words bring closure to his emotional ties to Johnson and their enduring relationship. In no uncertain terms, García asserts, "We loved him." The textualization of their relationships and legacy would prove particularly problematic. A year after Johnson's death, on April 2, 1974, Lady Bird wrote to García requesting his permission to include his oral history in the archives of Lyndon B. Johnson Presidential Library. Archivist David McComb conducted the oral history for the National Archives and Records Service on July 9, 1969. However, García withheld permission to release the transcript for five years. Lady Bird wrote:

> You and Lyndon worked in the same vineyards, each from your own "vantage point" and it would be a most regrettable omission not to have what you have to say on those turbulent times here for scholars and researchers after we are gone.[18]

Pushing the issue, Lady Bird conveys a strong sense of urgency for constructing a textual history of García and LBJ's relationship and roles in the twentieth century. In a show of mutual respect and affection, she signs her letter, "Fondly, Lady Bird." Without further delay, García signed the release form on April 5, 1974, and promptly donated the transcript recording his memories of Johnson to the Lyndon B. Johnson Presidential Library. However, his own papers would not be given to the LBJ Library, or to the University of Texas (his alma mater), or to the Benson Latin American Collection in Austin, which houses many of the papers of twentieth-century Mexican American civil rights activists, including those of his mentor, George I. Sánchez. Although these institutions and others solicited his records, García resisted. García waited twenty years before depositing his papers at Texas A&M University–Corpus Christi. He had a different vision.

García had plans to write a book on Mexican American civil rights history. There are no manuscripts or working papers available. Tracing García's intentions for this project leads to only one letter, written by the

Reverend Theodore M. Hesburgh, president of Notre Dame University, who served with García on the U.S. Civil Rights Commission in 1968. Hesburgh's February 4, 1975, letter encouraged García in his plans:

> Dear Hector, Your plan to write a history of the civil-rights movement of the Mexican Americans sounds exciting to me. I asked Howard Glickstein [former staff director of the United States Commission on Civil Rights] to come up with some suggestions as to where it might be possible for you to obtain funding for a research assistant. I am enclosing a list of suggestions. . . .
>
> Finally, I am enclosing a letter of endorsement which you might wish to submit with your funding request. My best regards. Regards also from Howard Glickstein who is a great admirer of yours.[19]

Hesburgh's endorsement of García's proposed book project indicated:

> I have known Dr. Garcia for many years. We served together on the United States Commission on Civil Rights. He was a creative and vigorous member of the body. Dr. García's interests are broad and universal. . . .
>
> There is a great need for further research in the history, development, and current problems of our Mexican American population. In many respects, Mexican Americans have been forgotten Americans. Dr. Garcia is in a unique position to enlighten the country about the history and problems of this group. He has been a stalwart in the fight for Mexican American civil rights and is an internationally recognized leader. Any book written by Dr. Garcia would be a major contribution.[20]

García, however, was not a writing professional. When his patients weren't demanding his attention, other community issues did. The book project never happened. His legacy was turned over to the public in fragments with the establishment of the Dr. Héctor P. García Papers at Texas A&M University–Corpus Christi. He envisioned that Corpus Christi would remain the site from which to protect, preserve, and promote his legacy.

García and his generation of reformers became the most politically influential group of Mexican American activists in the twentieth century. They would capture two congressional seats, one governorship, and a number of elected offices. Although they failed to attain their own political "Camelot," they did hold power and open the doors for generations of Mexican Americans to participate in American politics.[21] García remained politically active for more than twenty years after Johnson's death and the closing of the "Great Society," battling school segregation, promoting Mexican American candidates, and fighting for services for the poor of South

Texas. García built the first national-level Mexican American coalition of resistance to discrimination in post–World War II America.

García once reflected on his experience of coalition building. García thoughtfully described his approach to civic activism:

> In the matter of organization for civic action one runs into many problems and complexities which one has not faced in any other field either professional or elective. Consequently, one must take into consideration all of the possible phases of community life and even, the approach and organizational work will by necessity be on a trial and error method.
>
> There is no question in anyone's mind that civic action must be on an organized basis in order to bring the desired results which should be "the assumption of all obligations and the enjoyment of all benefits of first class citizenship.
>
> Naturally, in the organizational field, my efforts, failures, and successes have been limited to the Spanish-speaking population of the Southwest and mostly to the state of Texas. . . .
>
> There was never any question in my mind that in order to attain first class citizenship for our Spanish-speaking population, we must become organized. Naturally, the question arose not only as to how to organize, but also as to what level should we organize.
>
> The only experience that most of our people have had as far as organization, has been in the army. We find that officers and non-commissioned officers make the best organizers and usually the best leaders when they return to their people in their own communities. Of course there are a few union people or labor people in our group who are also good organizers. We also find that young women or young men who had Catholic social action in the Catholic youth groups develop into good organizers.
>
> The main problem was still the fact that organizational work amongst the Spanish-speaking people of the state was practically unknown. I would venture the guess that were it not for the organizational work in the Army during the last world war, our efforts in organizing our civic groups throughout the state would have been failures.
>
> The whole process of organization of civic groups had to be done on a trial and error method. There were no texts. There were no instructions as how to develop organizing leaders or even as to how to study or meet the problems of organization.
>
> We definitely decided that we must organize our people and the only possibility for a successful organizational work should be to organize them on the basis of their Army experience.

Thus, in order to insure the success, our people had to organize themselves into veterans' organizations complete with Ladies Auxiliaries, Junior Groups, and all, the object still being the same and that was to develop our people into becoming first class American citizens.

Civic action in the long run may show its overall success on state or national level. However, the permanency of organizational work should have its basis, the development of "local grass-roots leadership." Development of local leadership, therefore, become our primary objective and we set forth plans and ideas as to how to develop local leaders.[22]

García maintained an enduring faith in the power of the local community to stir national change. García's role as a civil rights leader evolved not in an isolated corner on the U.S.-Mexico border, but in relation to global shifts in the twentieth-century social order. His legacy of public service paralleled an era of universal disintegration and regeneration, performing the role of physician and advocate in a localized South Texas context as well on a world stage riddled with rupture and unrest. García's rhetorical engagement in partisan politics, as such, evolved into a collective performance of Mexican American civic identity. Through instrumental rhetoric, a discourse of guidance and governance, García moved the Mexican American community to act in force, to perform as one body, to form a unified voting bloc.[23]

Desire moves leaders like Héctor P. García to speak, to act, and to compel communities and the nation into being. The failure in rhetorical studies to consider the broad range of "emotional ties," the complex connective tissue of the nation's civil rights history, even its fissures, ultimately truncates reflective and projective vision. The absence of actors like García in our narratives of civil rights reform effaces the messy process of national ontogenesis and replicates the myth of American exceptionalism. Tracing the history of modern civil rights rhetoric and social action demands that rhetorical and cultural studies work in concert to tease out the complex strands and to seek not only the idiosyncratic but the syncretic meanings. The poignancy of García's legacy rests in the margins of his achievements and his failures. García's story is a reaffirmation of American democracy and a testimony to our unfinished work.

Notes
Selected Bibliography
Index

Notes

1. Introduction: "The Rhetorics of the Everyday" and Civic Belonging

1. Héctor P. García, "Need for Organized Civic Action" (address to the Catholic Conference on the Spanish Speaking People of Texas, April 24, 1952). Box 57, Folder 1, Dr. Héctor P. García Papers. Special Collections and Archives, Mary and Jeff Bell Library, Texas A&M University—Corpus Christi (henceforth abbreviated as HPG Papers).

2. Ralph Cintron, *Angels' Town: Chero Ways, Gang Life, and Rhetorics of the Everyday* (Boston: Beacon Press, 1997), xv.

3. For Michel de Certeau, the "ordinary man" is the universal "anonymous hero," "an ubiquitous character," "the murmuring voice of societies." Because the discourse of the anonymous hero generally does not command representation, he (or she) remains invisible to history. As Certeau observes, "In all ages, he comes before texts." See Michel de Certeau, *The Practice of Everyday Life*, trans. Steven F. Rendall. (Berkeley: University of California Press, 1984).

4. Reflective of the discourse conventions of García's era, the terms "United States" and "America" are used interchangeably in this book. The term "American" as used by García and the post-war generation generally referred to a U.S. citizen.

5. *Paideia* represents a process of teaching, apprenticeship, and mentorship in the arts of rhetoric.

6. *Phronesis* as rhetorical practice relies on the practical wisdom of lived experience for social action.

7. *Koinonia* is the formation of partnership and identification through the act of rhetoric.

8. *Kairos* invokes consideration of time, place, and circumstance in the generation and engagement of argument.

9. To honor the authenticity of García's texts, I have not edited nonstandard orthographic features or annotated them with the conventional marker "sic." Moreover, orthographic conventions for the representation of Spanish words in written English remain inconsistent and in continuous flux. John C. Hammerback, Richard J. Jensen, and José Ángel Gutiérrez explain the problem in their introduction to *A War on Words: Chicano Protest in the 1960s and 1970s*. They contend:

> Authors and publishers, including many of those cited in our footnotes, have been notoriously inconsistent and occasionally incorrect in their use of accents for Spanish words. This inconsistency creates confusion for some readers. Moreover, whether Spanish words are accented or not, those readers familiar with Spanish will be likely to know correct pronunciation while those unfamiliar will not. Therefore, we have decided not to accent Spanish words in this book (8).

My approach to orthographic inconsistencies differs. Consistent with my understanding of Spanish linguistics and my desire to clearly represent the cultural, social, and political features of bicultural/bilingual/binational realities of the historical context about which I am writing, I have applied Spanish accents where convention dictates. I have used accents to reflect those primary and secondary sources that use them and have omitted them only when they have been omitted. The end result while seemingly inconsistent most accurately reflects the changing nature of language and text in the ever-shifting sphere of cultures in contact.

10. I conducted research at the Dr. Héctor P. García Papers at Texas A&M University-Corpus Christi, the Lyndon B. Johnson Presidential Library, the John F. Kennedy Presidential Library, and the W.E. B. Du Bois Collection at the University of Massachusetts, Amherst during the summer of 2001. In addition to over twelve interviews with family, colleagues, American GI Forum members, and scholars, I visited the offices of Dr. Xico P. García (Héctor García's brother) and the home of Mrs. Wanda García (Héctor García's widow) in Corpus Christi.

11. Thomas Rosteck, introduction, *At the Intersections: Cultural Studies and Rhetorical Studies* (New York: Guilford Press, 1999), 7.

12. Rosteck, preface, *At the Intersections: Cultural Studies and Rhetorical Studies,* viii.

13. Walter Beale synthesizes notions of the aims of discourse as advanced by Aristotle, Kenneth Burke, James Kinneavy, and pragmatists Charles Pierce, William James, and John Dewey into what he calls a "system of placement" or a model of "theoretical alignments of the aims of discourse." See Walter H. Beale, *A Pragmatic Theory of Rhetoric* (Carbondale: Southern Illinois University Press, 1987), 162.

14. Beale, *A Pragmatic Theory of Rhetoric,* 94.

15. In addition to Beale, this argument is informed by the ethnopoetic examination of the "rhetorics of the everyday" offered by Ralph Cintron in *Angels' Town: Chero Ways, Gang Life, and the Rhetorics of the Everyday* (Boston: Beacon Press, 1997).

16. Beale's model of instrumental rhetoric and Dewey's notion of "pragmatic attitude" helped me to situate the discourses practices of Héctor P. García within the scope of rhetorical studies. Because of a narrow understanding of rhetoric as public oratory, scholars have overlooked García's repository of instrumental discourse for its rhetorical as well as historical significance.

17. See Lloyd F. Bitzer, "The Rhetorical Situation" in *Rhetoric: Concepts, Definitions, Boundaries,* William A. Covino and David A. Jolliffe, eds. (Boston: Allyn & Bacon, 1995), 300–310; and in the same volume, Richard E. Vatz, "The Myth of the Rhetorical Situation," 461–67.

18. Victor Villanueva examines the "bootstraps" myth of social mobility in *Bootstraps: From an American Academic of Color* (Urbana, IL: NCTE Press, 1993).

19. Alan Brinkley, *Liberalism and Its Discontents* (Cambridge: Harvard University Press, 1998), 107.

20. Héctor P. García, telegram to Allan Shivers, November 22, 1949. Box 147, Folder 1, HPG Papers.

21. Héctor P. García, letter to Allan Shivers, December 4, 1949. Box 147, Folder 1, HPG Papers.

22. For an examination of Truman's use of reform rhetorics see: Garth E. Pauley, *The Modern Presidency and Civil Rights: Rhetoric on Race from Roosevelt to Nixon*, (College Station: Texas A&M University Press, 2001), 46.

23. Dean Hinnen. "Discrimination Roots Examined." *Hutchinson News* (Kansas) February 13, 1971.

24. Dean Hinnen. "Discrimination Roots Examined." *Hutchinson News* (Kansas) February 13, 1971.

25. Seymoure Martin Lipset, *American: A Double-Edged Sword* (New York: W.W. Norton, 1996), 3.

26. Chaim Perelman, *The Realm of Rhetoric,* trans. William Kluback. (Notre Dame: University of Notre Dame Press, 1982), 11.

27. Perelman, *The Realm of Rhetoric*, 13.

28. Héctor P. García, interview with Thomas Kreneck, July 16, 1991. Oral History Papers, HPG Papers.

29. Perelman, *The Realm of Rhetoric*, xii.

30. Rolando Hinojosa-Smith, e-mail interview by author, August 24, 2001.

31. Will Potter, "War Showed Soldiers America's Opportunities," *Narratives: Stories of U.S. Latinos and Latinas and World War II*, 2 (2000), 1, 3.

32. Rodolfo Rosales, *The Illusion of Inclusion: The Untold Political Story of San Antonio* (Austin: University of Texas Press, 2000), 4.

33. The political evolution of *chicanismo* and Chicano resistance to first generation post-war reformers such as Héctor P. García is chronicled by Ignacio M. García in *Hector P. García: In Relentless Pursuit of Justice* (Houston: Arte Público Press, 2002); *Viva Kennedy: Mexican Americans in Search of Camelot* (College Station: Texas A&M University Press, 2000); *Chicanismo: The Forging of a Militant Ethos Among Mexican Americans* (Tucson: University of Arizona Press, 1997); and *United We Stand: The Rise and Fall of La Raza Unida Party* (Tucson: MASRC, University of Arizona, 1989).

34. Thomas H. Kreneck, "The Dr. Hector P. García Papers: A Research Resource for Texas, and More," *Texas Library Journal* 72 (1996), 80–83.

35. Archive research for this book began in 1999. During the following three years, I circulated my work widely among the Texas scholarly community.

36. Maggie Rivas-Rodriguez, *Mexican Americans and World War II* (Austin: University of Texas Press, 2005).

37. Michelle Hall Kells, "Legacy of Resistance: Héctor P. García, the Félix Longoria Incident, and the Construction a Mexican American Civil Rights Rhetoric" (Ph.D. diss., Texas A&M University, 2002).

38. Ignacio M. García, *Hector P. García: In Relentless Pursuit of Justice* (Houston: Arte Público Press, 2002).

39. *Justice for My People: The Dr. Héctor P. García Story*. Prod. Jeff Felts. (Corpus Christi, KEDT-TV, 2002). For further information about this documentary see http://www.justiceformypeople.org

40. Patrick J. Carroll, *Felix Longoria's Wake: Bereavement, Racism, and the Rise of Mexican American Activism* (Austin: University of Texas Press, 2003).

41. Julie Pycior qtd. in *Justice for My People: The Dr. Héctor P. García Story*. Prod. Jeff Felts. (Corpus Christi, KEDT-TV, 2002).

42. Ignacio M. García, *Hector P. García: In Relentless Pursuit of Justice*, xvii.

43. Dr. Héctor P. García was awarded the Presidential Medal of Freedom, the highest civilian award given in the United States, by President Reagan on March 26, 1984. For a list of García's lifetime achievements, see "Dr. Hector P. Garcia," *Corpus Christi Caller Times*, July 3, 1993, F8, F9.

44. Hayden White, *Metahistory: The Historical Imagination in Nineteenth-Century Europe* (Baltimore: Johns Hopkins University Press, 1973), x.

45. Lipset, *American Exceptionalism: A Double-Edged Sword*, 14.

46. Henry B. Gonzalez to Oscar Phillips, January 10, 1958. Semi-Processed, HPG Papers.

47. Philippe-Joseph Salazar, *An African Athens: Rhetoric and the Shaping of Democracy in South Africa* (Mahwah, NJ: Lawrence Erlbaum, 2002), xiv

48. Perelman, *The Realm of Rhetoric*, 93.

49. For further discussion of the role of Héctor P. García in the post–World War II era, see Ignacio M. García, *Viva Kennedy: Mexican Americans in Search of Camelot* (College Station: Texas A&M University Press, 2000).

50. "State Senate Passes Resolution Honoring Dr. Hector Garcia." See Semi-Processed, HPG Papers.

51. Ron George "More of a Compromiser Than an Antagonist," *Corpus Christi Caller Times*, July 27, 1996: A1, A11.

52. Guadalupe San Miguel Jr. *"Let Them All Take Heed:" Mexican Americans and the Campaign for Educational Equality in Texas, 1910–1981* (Austin: University of Texas Press, 1987).

53. Juan Gómez-Quiñones, *Chicano Politics: Reality and Promise, 1940–1990* (Albuquerque: University of New Mexico Press, 1990), 61.

54. Rodolfo Acuña, *Occupied America: A History of Chicanos*. 3rd ed. (New York: Harper & Row, 1988), 334

55. Ignacio M. García, *Chicanismo: The Forging of a Militant Ethos among Mexican Americans* (Tucson: University of Arizona Press, 1997), 18.

56. Winthrop Yinger, *Cesar Chavez: The Rhetoric of Nonviolence* (Hicksville, NY: Exposition Press, 1975); John C. Hammerback and Richard J. Jensen, *The Rhetorical Career of César Chávez* (College Station: Texas A&M University Press, 1998).

57. Richard J. Jensen and John C. Hammerback, eds. *The Words of César Chávez* (College Station: Texas A&M University Press, 2002).

58. John C. Hammerback, Richard J. Jensen, and José Ángel Gutiérrez, *A War of Words: Chicano Protest in the 1960s and 1970s* (Westport, CT: Greenwood Press, 1985).

59. Jorge C. Rangel and Carlos M. Alcala, "Project Report: De Jure Segregation of Chicanos in Texas Schools," *Harvard Civil Rights–Civil Liberties Law Review* 7 (1972), 308–91.

60. Matt S. Meier and Margo Gutiérrez, introduction, *Encyclopedia of the Mexican American Civil Rights Movement* (Westport, CT: Greenwood Press, 2000), xviii.

61. Meier and Gutiérrez, introduction, *Encyclopedia of the Mexican American Civil Rights Movement,* xv; appendix D includes a copy of the Treaty of Hidalgo, the binational agreement of 1848 guaranteeing the civil rights of Mexican citizens after the annexation of Texas to the United States, 277–278.

62. Edna Ferber, *Giant* (New York: Doubleday, 1952); *Giant,* prod. George Stevens and Henry Ginsberg. Warner Brothers Communications Co., 1956. For the portrayal of Héctor P. García's role in popular culture, see Carl Allsup, *The American GI Forum: Origins and Evolution* (Austin: Center for Mexican American Studies, 1982), 63–64; Tino Villanueva, *Scene from the Movie Giant* (Willimantic, CT: Curbstone Press, 1993). Further examination of these texts and the representation of Héctor P. García in the film *Giant* is provided in chapter 3.

63. For examination of the history of Chicano thought and politics, see Rodolfo Acuña, *Occupied America: A History of Chicanos.* 3rd ed. (New York: Harper & Row, 1988); Ignacio M. García, *United We Stand: The Rise and Fall of La Raza Unida Party* (Tucson: MASRC, University of Arizona, 1989); Ignacio M. García *Chicanismo: The Forging of a Militant Ethos Among Mexican Americans* (Tucson: University of Arizona Press, 1997); Ignacio M. García, *Viva Kennedy: Mexican Americans in Search of Camelot* (College Station: Texas A&M University Press, 2000); Mario T. García, *Mexican Americans: Leadership, Ideology, and Identity;* Devon G. Peña, ed. *Chicano Culture, Ecology, Politics: Subversive Kin* (Tucson: University of Arizona Press, 1998); Juan Gómez-Quiñones, *Chicano Politics: Reality and Promise, 1940–1990* (Albuquerque: University of New Mexico Press, 1990); Juan Gómez-Quiñones, *Roots of Chicano Politics, 1600–1940* (Albuquerque: University of New Mexico Press, 1994); David Montejano, ed. *Chicano Politics and Society in the Late Twentieth Century* (Austin: University of Texas Press, 1999); Francisco A. Rosales, *¡Chicano!: The History of the Mexican American Civil Rights Movement* (Houston: Arte Público, 1996); Carlos G. Vélez-Ibáñez, *Border Visions: Mexican Cultures of the Southwest United States* (Tucson: University of Arizona Press, 1996); and Emilio Zamora, Cynthia Orozco, and Rodolfo Rocha, eds., *Mexican Americans in Texas History* (College Station: Texas A&M University Press, 2000).

64. The notion of rhetorical context offered by Martin Medhurst in the introduction to *Beyond the Rhetorical Presidency* (College Station: Texas A&M University Press, 1996) also informs this examination of the discursive action of Héctor P. García and the rhetorical situation in which he operated. Accord-

ing to Medhurst: "A rhetorical context is the unique array of forces—rhetorical, historical, sociological, psychological, strategic, economic, and personal—that exists at any given moment in time and that impacts the speaker's selection and presentation of topics, the ways in which the message is composed and treated, and the manner in which the audience is invited to experience and understand the discourse" (xix).

65. Eduardo Bonilla-Silva, *White Supremacy and Racism in the Post-Civil Rights Era* (Boulder, CO: Lynne Rienner, 2001); Garth E. Pauley, *The Modern Presidency and Civil Rights: Rhetoric on Race from Roosevelt to Nixon* (College Station: Texas A&M University Press, 2001).

66. Oscar Phillips, unpublished manuscript, "Personal Papers" Box, Semi-Processed, HPG Papers.

67. The term "New American Pragmatism" is offered by Nancy Muller Milligan in "W. E. B. Du Bois: American Philosopher," *Journal of American Culture* 8 (1985), 31–37.

68. Héctor P. García, interview by David G. McComb, July 9, 1969. AC74–277, University of Texas Oral History Project, National Archives and Records Service, Lyndon B. Presidential Library (hereafter cited as LBJ Library).

69. Héctor P. García, interview by David G. McComb, July 9, 1969. AC74–277, University of Texas Oral History Project, National Archives and Records Service, LBJ Library.

70. Kenneth Burke's *A Grammar of Motives* (Berkeley: University of California Press, 1969) and *A Rhetoric of Motives* (Berkeley: University of California Press, 1969) set the framework for this pragmatic approach to analysis of Héctor P. García's civil rights discourse.

71. Cornel West, *The American Evasion of Philosophy: A Genealogy of Pragmatism* (Madison: University of Wisconsin Press, 1989), 229.

72. Ernest Morgan, "A Profile of Dr. Hector Garcia: A Man of Controversy," *Corpus Christi Caller Times*, December 12, 1966, B4, B5, B12. Available in Semi-Processed, HPG Papers; Office of John Macy Files. Box 203, "Garcia, Hector P." Folder, LBJ Library.

73. Theodore M. Hesburgh to Héctor P. García, February 4, 1975. Box 122, Folder 50, HPG Papers.

74. Beale, *A Pragmatic Theory of Rhetoric*, 65–66.

75. Héctor P. García to the League of United Latin American Citizens, January 27, 1979. *LULAC: Fifty Years of Serving Hispanics: Golden Anniversary, 1929–1979* (Corpus Christi: N. p., 1979).

76. Thomas S. Sutherland, "Texas Tackles the Race Problem," *Saturday Evening Post*, January 12, 1952, 66.

2. *The American GI Forum and the Rhetoric of Civic Presence*

1. Héctor P. García, interview by Thomas Kreneck, Corpus Christi, July 16, 1991, Oral History Papers, HPG Papers.

2. For further explication of the term "structure of feelings," see Raymond Williams, *The Long Revolution: An Analysis of the Democratic, Industrial, and Cultural Changes Transforming Our Society* (New York: Columbia University Press, 1961) and *Culture and Society, 1780–1950* (New York: Columbia University Press), 1983.

3. The term heuristic is used here to refer to a social constructionist method of teaching and discovery; a systematic approach to problem-solving and mapping experience. García applied heuritics or models and templates as thinking devices to cultivate creative approaches to problem solving among his followers.

4. Héctor P. García to Concha Noyola, January 23, 1952. Box 147, Folder 9, HPG Papers.

5. Pauline Kibbe Povall to Ruth Morton, April 20, 1953. Box 141, Folder 6, HPG Papers.

6. Although García resisted the subject position of victim, he exploited the role of "charism" or vicar of sacrifice. As exemplified in the mythos of the Judeo-Christian martyr, the role of charism attains honor, and ultimately beatification, through the act of volition or assent of the self-sacrificing agent. Without consent, there is victimization not redemption. García's civil rights agenda sought secular redemption for Mexican-origin people by resisting victimization through personal and collective sacrifice.

7. García identified deeply with the displacement and class segmentation described by David Gutíerrez, *Walls and Mirrors: Mexican Americans, Mexican Immigrants, and the Politics of Ethnicity* (Berkeley: University of California Press, 1995).

8. Héctor P. García, interview by Thomas Kreneck, Corpus Christi, July 16, 1991. Oral History Papers, HPG Papers.

9. Héctor P. García, interview by David G. McComb, July 9, 1969. AC74–27, University of Texas Oral History Project, National Archives and Records Service, Austin, Texas. LBJ Library.

10. Héctor P. García, taped interview by Julie Leininger Pycior, June 20, 1989, "History of Lyndon B. Johnson: Relationship to Mexican Americans" tapes. Unprocessed File. Box 1, Tape 1, Benson Latin American Collection, University of Texas.

11. Maury Maverick, foreword, *A Cotton Picker Finds Justice: The Saga of the Hernandez Case.* Compiled by Ruben Munguia. n.p., n.d. Box 82, Folder 7, HPG Papers.

12. Ernest Morgan, "Profile of Dr. Hector Garcia: A Man of Controversy," *Corpus Christi Caller Times,* December 12, 1966, B4, B5, B12. Semi-Processed, Personal Papers of Héctor P. García, HPG Papers; also available in Office of John Macy Files. Box 203, "Garcia, Hector P." Folder, LBJ Library.

13. Tyrone Meighan, "Dr. Hector P. Garcia." *Corpus Christi Caller Times,* July 3, 1993, F2.

14. Thomas Kreneck, interview by author, October 15, 2001, Corpus Christi.

15. Jim Wood, "Discrimination Here Charged: Unit on Civil Rights Ends Stormy Session," *Corpus Christi Caller Times,* April 17, 1966, 12.

16. Héctor P. García to Gerald Saldana, March 13, 1954. Box 141, Folder 13, HPG Papers.

17. "American GI Forum of Texas Financial Statement," May 31, 1951. Box 141, Folder 12, HPG Papers.

18. Thomas H. Kreneck, "The Dr. Hector P. García Papers," *Texas Library Journal* 72 (1996), 80–83.

19. Tyrone Meighan, "Dr. Hector P. Garcia," *Corpus Christi Caller Times,* July 3, 1993, F1–F5.

20. H. S. Thayer, introduction. *Pragmatism.* William James (Cambridge: Harvard University Press, 1975), xiv.

21. Gunnar Myrdal, *An American Dilemma: The Negro Problem and Modern Democracy.* Vol. 1(New York: Harper, 1944), 4.

22. The "American Dilemma," in Myrdal's analysis, was "the ever-raging conflict between, on the one hand, the valuations preserved on the general plane which we shall call the 'American Creed,' where the American thinks, talks, and acts under the influence of high national and Christian precepts, and on the other hand, the valuations on specific planes of individual and group living, where personal and local interests; economic, social and sexual jealousies; considerations for community prestige and conformity; group prejudice against particular persons or types of people; and all sorts of miscellaneous wants, impulses, and habits dominate his outlook" *(*4*)*.

23. Héctor P. García, "South Texas War Dead Have Returned!" October 30, 1947. Box 131, Folder 3, HPG Papers.

24. State Senator Carlos Truan, mentored by Dr. Héctor P. García, called Dr. García "a prophet with honor" and sponsored a 1989 state senate resolution to honor García's contributions to civil rights in Texas. See Tyrone Meighan, "Dr. Hector P. Garcia," *Corpus Christi Caller Times,* July 3, 1993, F7.

25. Héctor P. García to Civil Rights Commission, Washington, D.C., May 5, 1948. Box 107, Folder 25, HPG Papers.

26. Vicente Ximenes to Héctor P. García, December 13, 1957; Vicente Ximenes to Héctor P. García, January 28, 1958, Semi-Processed, HPG Papers; Vicente Ximenes, e-mail interview with author, October 29, 2004.

27. Héctor P. García to Harry S. Truman, April 14, 1951. Box 142, Folder 2, HPG Papers.

28. Meighan, "Dr. Hector P. Garcia," *Corpus Christi Caller Times,* July 3, 1993. F5.

29. Clotilde P. García, interviewed by Thomas Kreneck, February 17, 1994. Oral History 14.1, HPG Papers.

30. Meighan, "Dr. Hector P. Garcia," F9.

31. Héctor P. García, interview by Thomas Kreneck, May 21, 1991. Oral History Papers, HPG Papers.

32. Héctor P. García, interview by Thomas Kreneck, May 21, 1991. Oral History Papers, HPG Papers.

33. Clotilde P. García, interview by Thomas Kreneck, February 17, 1994. Oral History 14.1, HPG Papers.

34. Clotilde P. García, interview by Thomas Kreneck, February 17, 1994. Oral History 14.1, HPG Papers.

35. For an examination of the statutes of blood purity in colonial Mexico, see Richard Greenleaf, *Mexican Inquisition of the Sixteenth Century* (Albuquerque: University of New Mexico Press, 1969).

36. According to the reflections of Wanda Fusillo García, the extended family of Héctor P. García exhibited similar racial attitudes, a strong preference for those members of the family who possessed "Spanish" features (light skin, light eyes, and European physical qualities) over those whose dark features were more reflective of "los indios." Héctor was one of the most favored who could "pass" for a European or white American when he was overseas during World War II. She expressed her shock and dismay to discover when she arrived in the U.S. that her husband, even as an educated physician and veteran, was not recognized as white and did not have access to equal privileges. She recalled that the one thing that Héctor was even more proud of than her light hair was her Ph.D. Wanda Fusillo García, interview by author, October 15, 2001, Corpus Christi.

37. Clotilde P. García, interview by Thomas Kreneck, February 17, 1994. Oral History 14.1, HPG Papers.

38. Clotilde P. García, interview by Thomas Kreneck, February 17, 1994. Oral History 14.2, HPG Papers.

39. Clotilde P. García, interview by Thomas Kreneck, February 17, 1994. Oral History 14.2, HPG Papers.

40. The Many Faces of Dr. Cleo García." *Memorial Medical Center Mirror* (Corpus Christi), Mar–April 1974, 6.

41. Héctor P. García, interview by Thomas Kreneck, July 17, 1991, Corpus Christi. Oral History Papers, HPG Papers.

42. Richard A. García, *Rise of the Mexican American Middle Class, San Antonio, 1929–1941* (College Station: Texas A&M University Press, 1991), 279.

43. Richard A. García, *Rise of the Mexican American Middle Class, San Antonio, 1929–1941,* 279.

44. Richard A. García, *Rise of the Mexican American Middle Class, San Antonio, 1929–1941,* 278–79.

45. Héctor P. García, interview by Thomas Kreneck, July 16, 1991. Dr. Héctor P. García Papers, Oral History Papers, HPG Papers.

46. R. N. Jones to editor of *Look m*agazine, March 14, 1951. Box 141, Folder 2, HPG Papers.

47. Héctor P. García, interview by Thomas Kreneck, July 23, 1991. Oral History Papers, HPG Papers.

48. Héctor P. García to José G. García, April 9, 1943. Semi-Processed, HPG Papers.

49. Wanda Fusillo García, interview by author, October 15, 2001, Corpus Christi.

50. Wanda Fusillo García, interview by author, October 15, 2001, Corpus Christi.

51. Héctor P. García, interview by Thomas Kreneck, July 23, 1991. Oral History Papers, HPG Papers.

52. Héctor P. García, interview by Thomas Kreneck, Corpus Christi, July 16, 1991. Oral History Papers, HPG Papers.

53. Héctor P. García, interview by Thomas Kreneck, July 23, 1991. Oral History Papers, HPG Papers.

54. Wanda Fusillo García, interview by author, October 15, 2001, Corpus Christi.

55. Wanda Fusillo García, interview by author, October 15, 2001, Corpus Christi.

56. Héctor P. García to Mathis School Board of Education, May 5, 1948; Héctor P. García to LULAC Council No. 1, November 22, 1948. Box 107, Folder 25, HPG Papers; Also see Carl Allsup, *The American GI Forum: Origins and Evolution* (Austin: Center for Mexican American Studies, 1982), 29–38.

57. Héctor P. García to LULAC Council No. 1, November 22, 1948. Box 107, Folder 25, HPG Papers.

58. For further elaboration on the term "organic intellectual" see Antonio Gramsci, *Selections from the Prison Notebooks,* ed. and trans. Quintin Hoare and Geoffrey Nowell Smith (New York: International Publishers, 1971); Cornel West, *Prophetic Fragments* (Grand Rapids: Eerdmans, 1988); and Cornel West, *The American Evasion of Philosophy: A Genealogy of Pragmatism* (Madison: University of Wisconsin Press, 1989).

59. Héctor P. García to George R. Herrman, February 12, 1948. Semi-Processed, HPG Papers.

60. Convention Memorandum, Hector P. García, September 24, 1949. Box 147, Folder 1, HPG Papers.

61. Héctor P. García, "Need for Organized Civic Action" (address to the Catholic Conference on the Spanish Speaking People of Texas, April 24, 1952). Box 57, Folder 1, HPG Papers.

62. Héctor P. García to J. A. García, February 3, 1948. Box 107, Folder 25, HPG Papers.

63. Tyrone Meighan, "Helping Veterans, Many More: Born of Discrimination, Group Fights for Equality for All," *Corpus Christi Caller Times,* July 3, 1993, F10.

64. Cornel West, *The American Evasion of Philosophy: A Genealogy of Pragmatism,* 211–39.

65. Raul Morin, *Among the Valiant: Mexican Americans in World War II and Korea* (Alhambra, CA: Borden Publishing, 1963), 278.

66. Morin, *Among the Valiant: Mexican Americans in World War II and Korea*, 27.

67. The historical and statistical value of Latinos' and Latinas' contributions to World War II has been assessed by Maggie Rivas-Rodriguez, "What 'Narratives' Is About," *Narratives: Stories of U.S. Latinos and Latinas and World War II*, 1 (1999), 2. For further information about the U.S. Latinos and Latinas World War II Oral History Project see www.utexas.edu/projects/latinoarchives.

68. Morin, *Among the Valiant: Mexican Americans in World War II and Korea*, 277. American Population

69. Star Castillo, "Editorial," *LULAC News* 12 (July 1945); Reprint: *LULAC: Fifty Years of Serving Hispanics: Golden Anniversary, 1929–1979* (Corpus Christi: N.p., 1979).

70. For an overview of the discourses in circulation among South Texas Mexican American middle class leaders and intelligentsia, see Alonso S. Perales, *Are We Good Neighbors?* (San Antonio: Artes Gráficas, 1948); and *LULAC: Fifty Years of Serving Hispanics, 1929–1979* (Corpus Christi: N.p., 1979).

71. Mobilizing trends in Mexican American political activism is examined in detail by Julie Leininger Pycior's "La Raza Organizes: Mexican American Life in San Antonio, 1915–1930 as Reflected in Mutualista Activities" (Ph.D. diss., University of Notre Dame, 1979).

72. Cynthia Orozco's "The Origins of the United League of Latin American Citizens (LULAC) and the Mexican American Civil Rights Movement in Texas with an Analysis of Women's Political Participation in a Gendered Context, 1910–1929" (Ph.D. diss., University of California, Los Angeles, 1992) credits LULAC for initiating the Mexican American civil rights movement in Texas.

73. Orozco, "The Origins of the United League of Latin American Citizens (LULAC) and the Mexican American Civil Rights Movement in Texas," xi.

74. For further examination of the development of LULAC, see Benjamin Márquez, "The Politics of Race and Class: The League of United Latin American Citizens in the Post World War II Period," *Social Science Quarterly* 68 (March 1987), 84–101; Benjamin Márquez, *LULAC: The Evolution of a Mexican American Political Organization* (Austin: University of Texas Press, 1993); Richard A. García, *Rise of the Mexican American Middle Class, San Antonio, 1929–1941*; Cynthia E. Orozco, "The Origins of the League of United Latin American Citizens (LULAC) and the Mexican American Civil Rights Movement in Texas with an Analysis of Women's Political Participation in a Gendered Context, 1910–1929;" and O. Douglas Weeks, "The League of United Latin American Citizens: A Texas-Mexican Organization," *Political and Social Science Quarterly* 10 (1929), 257–78.

75. Héctor P. García to the League of United Latin American Citizens, January 27, 1979, in *LULAC: Fifty Years of Serving Hispanics, 1929–1979* (Corpus Christi: N.p., 1979).

76. George I. Sánchez to Héctor P. García, October 7, 1949. Box 147, Folder 1, HPG Papers.

77. Mario T. García underscores that LULAC's approach to political activism, like the American GI Forum's strategy, stressed citizenship and "Americanism"

and members carefully avoided being labeled political agitators. See Mario T. García, *Mexican Americans: Leadership, Ideology, and Identity, 1930–1960* (New Haven: Yale University Press, 1989).

78. García, *Mexican Americans: Leadership, Ideology, and Identity, 1930–1960*, 40.

79. "Minutes of March 26, 1948." Box 76, Folder 57, HPG Papers.

80. Héctor P. García, interview by David G. McComb, July 9, 1969. AC74-277, University of Texas Oral History Project, National Archives and Records Service, LBJ Library.

81. Pauline Kibbe Povall to Ruth Morton, April 20, 1953. Box 141, Folder 6, HPG Papers; Pauline R. Kibbe, *Latin Americans in Texas* (Albuquerque: University of New Mexico Press, 1946; rpt. New York: Arno Press, 1974).

82. Vicente Ximenes, interview by author, November 5, 2004, Albuquerque, New Mexico.

83. Grace Charles, interview by author, October 15, 2001, Corpus Christi.

84. "Gran Junta de Veteranos," poster, December 30, 1948. Box 14, Folder 40, HPG Papers.

85. Héctor P. García, "A Brief History of the American GI Forum," November 19, 1958. Album 1.1, HPG Papers.

86. Rogers Kelley to Héctor P. García, June 14, 1949. Box 111, Folder 40, HPG Papers; Rogers Kelley, "Constitutional Amendment," n.d. Box 147, Folder 1, HPG Papers.

87. Héctor P. García to Edna Ferber, June 15, 1949. "Personal Papers of Dr. Héctor P. García," Semi-Processed, HPG Papers.

88. Héctor P. García to W. F. Kelly, October 4, 1949. Box 147, Folder 6, HPG Papers.

89. Thomas Sutherland to M. B. Morgan, September 21, 1949. Box 147, Folder 1, HPG Papers.

90. García's leadership role in the American GI Forum was enduring and multifaceted, a legacy well documented by Carl Allsup, *The American GI Forum: Origins and Evolution* (Austin: CMAS, University of Texas, 1982) and Henry A. J. Ramos, *The American GI Forum: In Pursuit of the Dream, 1948–1983* (Houston: Arte Público Press, 1998).

91. "Minutes of March 26, 1948." Box 76, Folder 57, HPG Papers.

92. Ramos, *The American GI Forum: In Pursuit of the Dream, 1948–1983*, 5.

93. Ramos, *The American GI Forum: In Pursuit of the Dream, 1948–1983*, 5.

94. "Prayer of St. Francis," adopted September 25, 1949. Box 147, Folder 1, HPG Papers.

95. Héctor P. García, letter to Allan Shivers, January 19, 1951. Box 141, Folder 2, HPG Papers.

96. "Constitution and By Laws of American GI Forum." Unprocessed, HPG Papers.

97. Héctor P. García to Eluterio L. Perez, October 12, 1953. Box 141, Folder 16, HPG Papers.

98. Héctor P. García, "A Brief History of the American GI Forum." Album 1.1, HPG Papers.

99. Héctor P. García, memo, October 22, 1953. Box 141, Folder 16, HPG Papers.

100. Ed Idar to Héctor P. García. Box 142, Folder 14, HPG Papers.

101. Guadalupe San Miguel Jr., "Mexican American Organizations and the Changing Politics of School Desegregation," *Latino Language and Education: Communication and the Dream Deferred,* ed. Antoinette Sedillo López (New York: Garland Publishing, 1995), 191.

102. John F. Kennedy to Héctor P. García, August 1, 1961. Box 104, Folder 27, HPG Papers.

103. Hector P. García to Eleanor Roosevelt, n.d. Box 141, Folder 6, HPG Papers.

104. Henri J. M. Nouwen, *The Wounded Healer* (Garden City, NY: Image, 1979).

105. Garry Wills, *Certain Trumpets: The Call of Leaders* (New York: Simon & Schuster, 1994), 32.

106. Héctor P. García to the League of United Latin American Citizens, January 27, 1979. *LULAC: Fifty Years of Serving Hispanics: Golden Anniversary, 1929–1979.*

107. Wills, *Certain Trumpets: The Call of Leaders,* 33.

108. Garth E. Pauley, *The Modern Presidency and Civil Rights: Rhetoric on Race from Roosevelt to Nixon,* 24.

109. Pauley, *The Modern Presidency and Civil Rights: Rhetoric on Race from Roosevelt to Nixon,* 30; Wills, *Certain Trumpets: The Call of Leaders,* 34.

110. Jim Wood, "Discrimination Here Charged: Unit on Civil Rights Ends Stormy Session," *Corpus Christi Caller Times,* April 17, 1966, 1, 12.

111. Héctor P. García, interview by David G. McComb, July 9, 1969. AC74–277, University of Texas Oral History Project, National Archives and Records Service, LBJ Library.

112. See Dana D. Nelson, *National Manhood: Capitalist Citizenship and the Imagined Fraternity of White Men* (Durham, NC: Duke University Press, 1998).

113. Grace Charles, interview by author, October 15, 2001, Corpus Christi.

114. Ernest Morgan, "Profile of Dr. Hector Garcia: A Man of Controversy," *Corpus Christi Caller Times,* December 12, 1966, B12.

115. Rolando Hinojosa-Smith, e-mail to author, August 24, 2001.

116. Juan C. Guerra, letter to author, June 30, 2005.

117. "The American GI Forum," *Border Trends* 1 (September 1948), 1–2. Available Box 55, Folder 64, HPG Papers.

118. "Civil Rights: Strength or Weakness?" *Quick* (September 24, 1941), 10–12. Available Box 94, Folder 97, HPG Papers.

119. Lewis W. Gillenson, "'Texas' Forgotten People," *Look* (March 26, 1951), 29–36.

120. Daniel A. McAteer Jr. to Héctor P. García, March 18, 1951. Semi-Processed, "Personal Papers of Héctor P. García," HPG Papers.

121. Manuel Reyes to Raymond Venezia, March 31, 1951. Box 141, Folder 2, HPG Papers.

122. Sutherland, "Texas Tackles the Race Problem," *Saturday Evening Post,* 64, 66.

123. Sutherland, "Texas Tackles the Race Problem," 22–23.

124. Sutherland, "Texas Tackles the Race Problem," 22.

125. Carl Allsup, *The American GI Forum: Origins and Evolution* (Austin: Center for Mexican American Studies, 1982).

126. Jorge C. Rangel and Carlos M. Alcala, "Project Report: De Jure Segregation of Chicanos in Texas Schools," *Harvard Civil Rights-Civil Liberties Law Review* 7 (1972), 308–91; "Wetbacks: Can the States Act to Curb Illegal Entry?" *Stanford Law Review* 6 (March 1954), 287–322.

127. Richard H. Kraemer, Ernest Crain, and Earl Maxwell, *Understanding Texas Politics* (New York: West Publishing Company, 1975), 76.

128. Ed Idar Jr., interview by author, tape recording, August 10, 2000, San Antonio; Virgilio Roel, interview by author, tape recording, August 10, 2000, Austin; Xico P. García, interview by author, June 13, 2001, Corpus Christi.

129. For further examination of the evolution of La Raza Unida Party, see Ignacio M. García, *United We Stand: The Rise and Fall of La Raza Unida Party*; Ignacio M. García, *Chicanismo: The Forging of a Militant Ethos among Mexican Americans.*

130. Héctor P. García to Richard H. Kraemer, September 16, 1977. Box 45, Folder 43, HPG Papers.

131. Richard H. Kraemer to Héctor P. García, October 6, 1977. Box 69, Folder 79, HPG Papers.

132. Ernest Crain and Earl Maxwell to Héctor P. García, October 5, 1977. Box 69, Folder 79, HPG Papers.

133. Si Dunn, "The Legacy of Pvt. Longoria," *Dallas Morning News,* "Scene," April 6, 1975, n.p.

134. James De Anda to editor, *Corpus Christi Caller Times,* August 15, 1963. Box 138, Folder 37, HPG Papers.

135. For examination of the concept of the national "imagined fraternity" see Benedict Anderson, *Imagined Communities: Reflections on the Origin and Spread of Nationalism* (London: Verso, 1983); Dana D. Nelson, *National Manhood: Capitalist Citizenship and the Imagined Fraternity of White Men* (Durham: Duke University Press, 1998); Rogers M. Smith, *Civic Ideals: Conflicting Visions of Citizenship in U.S. History* (New Haven: Yale University Press, 1997); Judith N. Shklar, *American Citizenship: The Quest for Inclusion* (Cambridge: Harvard University Press, 1991).

136. Ed Idar Jr., interview by author, tape recording, August 10, 2000, San Antonio; Virgilio Roel, interview by author, tape recording, August 10, 2000, Austin.

137. Héctor P. García, interview by Thomas Kreneck, May 21, 1991. Oral History Papers, HPG Papers.

138. Héctor P. García, interview by David G. McComb, July 9, 1969. AC74–277, University of Texas Oral History Project, National Archives and Records Service, LBJ Library.

139. Héctor P. García, interview by David G. McComb, July 9, 1969. AC74–277, University of Texas Oral History Project, National Archives and Records Service, LBJ Library.

140. Héctor P. García, "Statement to the Democratic National Committee," July 12, 1960. Box 75, Folder 34, HPG Papers.

141. Daniel A. McAteer Jr. to Héctor P. García, May 18, 1951. Semi-Processed, Personal Papers of Héctor P. García, HPG Papers.

142. Memorial Medical Center of Corpus Christi named its indigent health care clinic after Dr. Héctor P. García at a tribute to his forty-seven years of service on June 12, 1993.

143. Tyrone Meighan, "Dr. as Doctor: Amid Other Duties Garcia Always Made Time for Patients," *Corpus Christi Caller Times,* July 3, 1993, F9.

144. Tyrone Meighan, "A Community in His Debt," *Corpus Christi Caller Times,* July 3, 1993, F6.

145. Tyrone Meighan, "Dr. Hector P. Garcia," *Corpus Christi Caller Times,* July 3, 1993, F5.

146. Héctor P. García to Xico P. García, July 21, 1981. Papers of Dr. Xico P. García.

147. Héctor P. García, interview by David G. McComb, July 9, 1969. AC74–277, University of Texas Oral History Project, National Archives and Records Service, LBJ Library.

148. Héctor P. García, interview by David G. McComb, July 9, 1969. AC74–277, University of Texas Oral History Project, National Archives and Records Service, LBJ Library.

149. Wills, *Certain Trumpets: The Call of Leaders,* 34.

150. Henry David Thoreau, "Civil Disobedience" in *Walden and Civil Disobedience,* ed. Sherman Paul (Cambridge: Riverside Press, 1960), 245.

151. Belia Chabot, interview by author, June 13, 2001, Corpus Christi.

152. Wills, *Certain Trumpets: The Call of Leaders,* 40.

153. Wanda Fusillo García, interview by author, October 15, 2001, Corpus Christi.

154. "House of Representatives: Ortiz Salutes Dr. Hector Garcia," *Congressional Record* 174.75 (June 26, 1996), 1. Available in Dr. Héctor P. García Papers, Special Collections and Archives, Texas A&M University-Corpus Christi Bell Library, Exhibit Case.

155. Tyrone Meighan, "Dr. Hector P. Garcia," *Corpus Christi Caller Times,* July 3, 1993, F3.

156. Wanda Fusillo García, interview by author, October 15, 2001, Corpus Christi.

3. The Félix Longoria Incident:
Drama, Irony, and "The American Dilemma"

1. A segment of this chapter was presented at the Conference of the Texas State Historical Association, El Paso, March 2003.

2. William James, "Lecture II: What Pragmatism Means." *Pragmatism.* (Cambridge: Harvard University Press, 1975), 38.

3. Gary A. Greenfield and Don B. Kates Jr., "Mexican American Racial Discrimination and the Civil Rights Act of 1866." 63.3 (1975), 727.

4. George Gold, "The Racial Prerequisite in the Naturalization Law," Boston University Law Review 15 (1935), 425.

5. Gold, "The Racial Prerequisite in the Naturalization Law," 495.

6. Gunnar Myrdal, *An American Dilemma: The Negro Problem and Modern Democracy.* Vol. 1 (New York: Harper, 1944), 4.

7. Garth Pauley notes that Truman was "the first president to define civil rights as a crisis." See Pauley, *The Modern Presidency and Civil Rights: Rhetoric on Race from Roosevelt to Nixon* (College Station: Texas A&M University Press, 2001), 33.

8. *The Good War and Those Who Refused to Fight It,* prod. and dir. Judith Erlich and Rick Tejada-Flores, Berkeley, CA: Paradigm Productions, 2002. For further information on the role of World War II's conscientious objectors in modern civil rights history, see www.pbs.org/itvs/thegoodwar/film.html

9. Pauley, *The Modern Presidency and Civil Rights: Rhetoric on Race from Roosevelt to Nixon,* 38.

10. George J. Garza, "Founding and History of LULAC," *LULAC: Fifty Years of Serving Hispanics: Golden Anniversary, 1929–1979,* (Corpus Christi, 1979), n.p.

11. For discussion of the role of the Good Neighbor Commission in Texas immigration issues, see Allsup, *The American GI Forum: Origins and Evolution,* 64–65; George Norris Green, "The Felix Longoria Affair," *Journal of Ethnic Studies* 19 (1991): 24–25; Gutiérrez, *Walls and Mirrors: Mexican Americans, Mexican Immigrants, and the Politics of Ethnicity,* 140–41.

12. "Caucasian Race—Equal Privileges," H.C.R. No. 105, April 15, 1943, passed by the Regular Session in General and Special Laws of the State of Texas, of the Forty-Eighth Regular Session of the Forty-Eighth Legislature, Austin. Convened January 12, 1943 and Adjourned May 11, 1943 (Austin: State of Texas, 1943).

13. Héctor P. García to J. A. García, February 3, 1948. Box 107, Folder 25, HPG Papers.

14. Wills, *Certain Trumpets: The Call of Leaders,* 32.

15. *W. E. B. Du Bois, Color and Democracy: Colonies and Peace* (New York: Harcourt, Brace, 1945), 72.

16. Du Bois, *Color and Democracy,* 18, 85.

17. W. E. B. Du Bois, "The Color Line Belts the World," *Collier's Weekly* (October 20, 1906), 30. Available, MS 312. Box 361, Folder 61, Special Collections and Archives, W. E. B. Du Bois Library, University of Massachusetts Amherst (hereafter cited as WEB Du Bois Library).

18. Lawrence J. Oliver, *Brander Matthews, Theodore Roosevelt, and the Politics of American Literature, 1880–1920* (Knoxville: University of Tennessee Press, 1992), 36.

19. Oliver, *Brander Matthews, Theodore Roosevelt, and the Politics of American Literature, 1880–1920,* 199.

20. Franklin H. Giddings, *Democracy and Empire* (New York: Macmillan, 1900); Franklin H. Giddings, "The American People," *International Quarterly* 7 (June 1903), 281–299.

21. W. E. B. Du Bois, "The First Universal Races Congress," *Independent* 71 (August 23, 1911), 402. Available, MS 312. Box 362, Folder 17, WEB Du Bois Library. For further examination of Du Bois's application of pragmatism to issues of race, see Homer L. Meade, "A Pragmatist: William Edward Burghart Du Bois" (M.A. thesis, University of Massachusetts, 1989) and "Homer L. Meade, W. E. B. Du Bois and His Place in the Discussion on Racism" (Ph.D. diss., University of Massachusetts, 1987).

22. David Montejano, *Anglos and Mexicans in the Making of Texas, 1836–1986* (Austin: University of Texas Press, 1987), 263.

23. Armando C. Alonzo, *Tejano Legacy: Rancheros and Settlers in South Texas, 1734–1900* (Albuquerque: University of New Mexico Press, 1998), 133–34.

24. Douglas E. Foley, *From Peones to Politicos: Ethnic Relations in a South Texas Town, 1900–1987* (Austin: University of Texas Press, 1988), 45.

25. Foley, *From Peones to Politicos: Ethnic Relations in a South Texas Town, 1900–1987,* 47.

26. Montejano, *Anglos and Mexicans in the Making of Texas, 1836–1986,* 262.

27. Reproduction of complex racial myths through Texas and U.S. history resulted in a naturalized system of racism that impacted every dimension of the lives of Mexican peoples, culturally, linguistically, and socioeconomically on both sides of the border. The legacy of white supremacy in the Americas, however, predates Anglo occupation of Greater Mexico and begins with Spanish colonization and the migration of Sephardic Jews who fled from Spain under the threat of the Spanish Inquisition.

28. For examination of racial attitudes in the Americas, see Rogers Smith, *Civic Ideals: Conflicting Visions of Citizenship in U.S. History* (New Haven: Yale University Press, 1997).

29. For further discussion on the mythos of mestizaje, see Suzanne Oboler, *Ethnic Labels, Latino Lives: Identity and the Politics of (Re)Presentation in the United States* (Minneapolis: University of Minnesota Press, 1995); Frederick B. Pike, *The United States and Latin America: Myths and Stereotypes of Civilization and Nature* (Austin: University of Texas Press, 1992); James W. Russell, *After the Fifth Sun: Class and Race in North America* (Englewood Cliffs, NJ: Prentice Hall, 1994); Henry C. Schmidt, *The Roots of Lo Mexicano: Self and Society in Mexican Thought, 1900–1934* (College Station: Texas A&M University Press, 1978).

30. For examination of the impact of the Spanish Inquisition on Sephardic Jews and the colonization of the Americas, see Richard E. Greenleaf, *The Mexican*

Inquisition of the Sixteenth Century (Albuquerque: University of New Mexico Press, 1969); Stanley M. Hordes, "The Crypto-Jewish Community of New Spain, 1620–1649" (Ph.D. diss. Tulane University, 1980).

31. Anglo colonists' project of maintaining separation and ultimately establishing economic domination over Mexico involved the elaborate construction of narratives of Anglo-European supremacism and American exceptionalism in conjunction with the reification of negative social images of Mexican peoples.

32. Neil Foley examines in *The White Scourge: Mexicans, Blacks and Poor Whites in Texas Cotton Culture* (Berkeley: University of California Press, 1997) how the color line of the southern states was extended into Texas and excluded Mexican Americans as well as African Americans from social power structure.

33. For examination of the racialized stereotypes and the politics of labeling of Latin Americans, see Suzanne Oboler, *Ethnic Labels and Latino Lives;* Frederick B. Pike, *The United States and Latin America: Myths and Stereotypes of Civilization and Nature.*

34. Du Bois, "The Color Line Belts the World," 30.

35. Du Bois's mission—to construct a scientific response to the issues of racism—led to his formation of an epistemological framework from which to counter the discourse of white supremacism. Du Boisian pragmatism, integral to twentieth-century theory on race and social stratification, is reflected in García's handling of the Longoria case and subsequent civil rights project.

36. Du Bois outlines his vision in the preface of *Color and Democracy: Colonies and Peace:* "Henceforth, the majority of the inhabitants of earth, who happen for the most part to be colored, must be regarded as having the right and the capacity to share in human progress and to become co-partners in that democracy which alone can ensure peace among men, by the abolition of poverty, the education of the masses, protection from disease, and the scientific treatment of crime."

37. Gunnar Myrdal, *An American Dilemma: The Negro Problem and Modern Democracy.* Vol. 1(New York: Harper, 1944), 21.

38. Du Bois, *Color and Democracy: Colonies and Peace,* 85.

39. Héctor P. García to Allan Shivers, December 4, 1949. Box 147, Folder 1, HPG Papers.

40. W. E. B. Du Bois, "Caste in America: That is the Root of the Trouble," *Des Moines Register and Leader,* October 19, 1904, 5. Available, MS 312. Box 360, Folder 71, W. E. B. Du Bois Library

41. Beatrice Longoria, "Statement," February 9, 1949, PPC File. Box 3, "Longoria" Folder, LBJ Library.

42. William E. Smith to Department of the Army, Fort Worth Quartermaster Depot, December 1, 1948, Lyndon B. Johnson Presidential Library, Pre-Presidential Confidential File. Box 2, "Longoria," LBJ Library.

43. According Beatrice Longoria's "Statement" of February 9, 1949, she met with Thomas Kennedy on January 7, 1949. Kennedy's letter of apology and published statement indicates they met on January 8, 1949. See "Mr. Kennedy's

Statement," *Live Oak County Herald,* January 20, 1949, 1; Si Dunn, "The Legacy of Pvt. Longoria," *Dallas Morning News,* "Scene," April 6, 1975.

44. Lyndon B. Johnson to Shag Floore, February 3, 1949, PPC File. Box 2, "Longoria," LBJ Library.

45. For accounts of the refusal by Rice Funeral Home to provide service for the Longoria family, see "Minority Report on the Longoria Investigation," April 7, 1949, *House Journal,* Fifty-First Legislature:1424; Héctor P. García, "Statement," February 9, 1949, PPC File. Box 3, "Longoria" Folder, LBJ Library.

46. Beatrice Longoria, "Statement," February 9, 1949, PPC File. Box 3, "Longoria" Folder, LBJ Library.

47. "Nation Honors Latin-American: Three Rivers Soldier Buried in Arlington," *Austin American Statesman,* February 17, 1949, n.p. Available, PPC File. Box 3, "Longoria," LBJ Library.

48. Dunn, "The Legacy of Pvt. Longoria," *Dallas Morning News,* "Scene," April 6, 1975, n.p.

49. Richard Zelade, "Last Rites, First Rights," *Texas Monthly* (January 1986), 192–94.

50. Guadalupe Longoria, Sr., "Statement," February 20, 1949, PPC File. Box 3, "Longoria" Folder, LBJ Library; Sara Moreno, "Statement," February 18, 1949, PPC File. Box 3, "Longoria" Folder, LBJ Library.

51. William F. Chestnutt to Lyndon B. Johnson, January 14, 1949, PPC File. Box 2, "Longoria" Folder, LBJ Library.

52. Gladys Blucher, "Statement," February 9, 1949, PPC File. Box 3, "Longoria" Folder, LBJ Library.

53. George Groh, "Statement," February 18, 1949, PPC File. Box 3, "Longoria" Folder, LBJ Library.

54. Héctor P. García, telegram to Lyndon B. Johnson, January 10, 1949, PPC File. Box 2, "Longoria" Folder, LBJ Library.

55. Héctor P. García, "Statement," February 9, 1949, PPC File. Box 3, "Longoria" Folder, LBJ Library.

56. John B. Connally, "Memo for the Files," January 11, 1949, John B. Connally, "Memorandum: Re: Felix Longoria File, January 14, 1949; John B. Connally, "Memo for the Files: Summary of Conversations with Mr. Paul J. Reveley," February 24, 1949; Paul J. Reveley to Lyndon B. Johnson, March 8, 1949; Lyndon B. Johnson to Frank Oltorf, March 12, 1949; all available, PPC File. Box 2, "Longoria" Folder, LBJ Library.

57. Shag Floore to Lt. Col. Stanley H. Partridge, January 21, 1949, PPC File. Box 2, "Longoria" Folder, LBJ Library.

58. "Gran Junta de Protesta," poster, January 11, 1949, Exhibit Case, HPG Papers.

59. George Groh, "Arlington Burial for Three Rivers Veteran Planned," *Corpus Christi Caller Times,* January 12, 1949, n. p.; Lyndon B. Johnson, telegram to Héctor P. García, January 11, 1949, PPC File. Box 3, "Longoria" Folder, LBJ Library.

60. John B. Connally, "Memorandum Re: Felix Longoria File," January 14, 1949, PPC File. Box 2, "Longoria" Folder, LBJ Library; Lyndon B. Johnson to Shag Floore, February 3, 1949, PPC File. Box 2, "Longoria" Folder, LBJ Library.

61. Lyndon B. Johnson to Shag Floore, February 3, 1949, PPC File. Box 2, "Longoria" Folder, LBJ Library.

62. George Groh "Arlington Burial for Three Rivers Veteran Planned," *Corpus Christi Caller Times,* January 12, 1949, n.p. Available, PPC File. Box 3, "Longoria" Folder, LBJ Library.

63. Harry H. Vaughn, telegram to Héctor P. García, January 12, 1949. Box 130, Folder 4, HPG Papers.

64. T. W. Kennedy to Beatrice Longoria, January 12, 1949, PPC File. Box 2, "Longoria" Folder, LBJ Library.

65. "Texas Town Offers Apology to Widow," *New York Times,* January 14, 1949, 1.

66. Paul J. Reveley to Lyndon B. Johnson, March 8, 1949, PPC File. Box 2, "Longoria" Folder, LBJ Library.

67. "A Hero's Return: Bigotry in Texas," Detroit Free Press, January 14, 1949, n.p. Available PPC File. Box 3, "Longoria" Folder, LBJ Library.

68. Garry Wills, *Lincoln at Gettysburg: The Words That Remade America* (New York: Simon & Schuster, 1992), 74.

69. Wills, *Lincoln at Gettysburg: The Words That Remade America,* 89.

70. William S. White, "GI of Mexican Origin, Denied Rites in Texas, to Be Buried in Arlington," *New York Times,* January 13, 1949, 1, 11.

71. "A Hero's Return: Bigotry in Texas," January 14, 1949, *Detroit Free Press* n.p. Available, PPC File. Box 3, "Longoria" Folder, LBJ Library.

72. Clifford A. Bishop to Lyndon B. Johnson, January 17, 1949, PPC File. Box 3, "Longoria" Folder; Rose Mae Goldstad to Lyndon B. Johnson, January 19, 1949, PPC File. Box 3, "Longoria" Folder, LBJ Library.

73. Mason L. Cashion to Lyndon B. Johnson, January 26, 1949, PPC File. Box 3, "Longoria," LBJ Library.

74. Nelson A. Rockefeller to Lyndon B. Johnson, January 13, 1949, PPC File. Box 2, "Longoria," LBJ Library.

75. V. G. Roel to Lyndon B. Johnson, January 14, 1949, PPC File. Box 2, "Longoria," LBJ Library.

76. Edwin A. Elliott to Lyndon B. Johnson, January 19, 1949, PPC File. Box 2, "Longoria," LBJ Library.

77. Wick Fowler, "Case of Pvt. Longoria: Three Rivers Digs Out of Blizzard of Abuse," *Dallas Morning News,* January 30, 1949, n.p. Available, PPC File. Box 3, "Longoria" Folder, LBJ Library.

78. George N. Green, "The Felix Longoria Affair," *Journal of Ethnic Studies* 19 (1991), 26.

79. Shag Floore to Lt. Col. Stanley H. Partridge, January 21, 1949, PPC File. Box 2, "Longoria" Folder, LBJ Library.

80. R. E. Smith to Héctor P. García, January 17, 1949, PPC File. Box 2, "Longoria" Folder, LBJ Library.

81. "Texas Town Offers Apology to Widow," *New York Times*, January 14, 1949, 1.

82. Beatrice Longoria to T. W. Kennedy, January 14, 1949, PPC File. Box 2, "Longoria" Folder; "Letter from Mrs. Longoria," *Three Rivers News*, January 20, 1949, 1. Available, PPC File. Box 2, "Longoria" Folder, LBJ Library.

83. "Doctor Accuses Funeral Home Head in Longoria Burial Controversy," *San Antonio Express News*, March 12, 1949: 1, 2. Available, PPC File. Box 3, "Longoria," LBJ Library.

84. Shag Floore to Lt. Col. Stanley H. Partridge, January 21, 1949, PPC File. Box 2, "Longoria" Folder, LBJ Library.

85. Shag Floore to Lt. Col. Stanley H. Partridge, January 21, 1949, PPC File. Box 2, "Longoria" Folder, LBJ Library.

86. Héctor P. García to American GI Forum, March 5, 1949, Exhibit Case, HPG Papers; Héctor P. García to Mathis School Board of Education, May 5, 1948. Box 107, Folder 25, HPG Papers.

87. John B. Connally to Lyndon B. Johnson, February 25, 1949, PPC File. Box 2, "Longoria" Folder, LBJ Library.

88. Beatrice Longoria et al. to Lyndon B. Johnson, January 31, 1949, PPC File. Box 2, "Longoria" Folder, LBJ Library.

89. John B. Connally to Lyndon B. Johnson, February 25, 1949, PPC File. Box 2, "Longoria" Folder, LBJ Library.

90. David Botter, "Services Brief and Moving: Arlington Cemetery Rites Held for Private Longoria," *Dallas Morning News*, February 17, 1949, 1, 19.

91. Lyndon B. Johnson to Héctor P. García, February 16, 1949, PPC File. Box 3, "Longoria" Folder, LBJ Library.

92. "Three Rivers C of C Brands Reburial Story 'Bad Publicity,'" *Corpus Christi Caller Times*, January 14, 1949, n.p. Available, PPC File. Box 3, "Longoria" Folder, LBJ Library.

93. "Bigotry Is Unpopular." *Santa Fe New Mexican*, January 14, 1949, n.p. Available, PPC File. Box 3, "Longoria" Folder, LBJ Library.

94. Roy Grimes, "Threat to Safety: Lugs of Solon's Car Loosened," *San Antonio Express Evening News*, February 20, 1949, 1, 4; Fred Williams, "Good Neighbor Panel Seeks 'Full' Probe," *Austin American*, February 20, 1949, n.p. Available, PPC File. Box 3, "Longoria" Folder, LBJ Library.

95. Letter to Lyndon B. Johnson, January 20, 1949, PPC File. Box 3, "Longoria" Folder, LBJ Library.

96. "An Open Letter to Senator Johnson," *Three Rivers News*, February 20, 1949, n.p. Available, PPC File. Box 3, "Longoria" Folder, LBJ Library.

97. The term "ascriptive inequality" offered by Smith, *Civic Ideals: Conflicting Visions of Citizenship in U.S. History*.

98. Sara Moreno Posas qtd. in Karen Lister, "Longoria Family Never Forgot García's Help in Burying World War II Veteran," *Corpus Christi Caller Times,* July 1996, A18.

99. Proceedings, *House Journal,* Fifty-First Legislature, Regular Session, February 17, 1949, Austin, 319.

100. Pycior, *LBJ and Mexican Americans: The Paradox of Power,* 72.

101. Dunn, "The Legacy of Private Longoria," n.p.

102. Johnnie Brown, "'Obscene' Mail on Longoria Case Sent Three Rivers Mayor: Dr. Garcia Repeats Forum Charge of Discrimination," *Corpus Christi Caller Times,* March 11, 1949, 1, 18.

103. Gus García to Lyndon B. Johnson, March 16, 1949, PPC File. Box 3, "Longoria" Folder, LBJ Library.

104. Gus García to Lyndon B. Johnson, March 25, 1949, PPC File. Box 3, "Longoria" Folder, LBJ Library.

105. Gus García to John B. Connally, April 7, 1949, PPC File. Box, "Longoria," LBJ Library.

106. Proceedings, *House Journal,* Fifty-First Legislature, Regular Session, April 17, 1949, Austin, 1514.

107. Proceedings, House Journal, Fifty-First Legislature, Regular Session, April 17, 1949, Austin, 1515.

108. Dunn, "The Legacy of Private Longoria," n.p.

109. "Tragic Blot: Kelly Raps Three Rivers Case Report," *Corpus Christi Caller Times,* April 8, 1949, n.p.

110. Héctor P. García to José Cueva, April 21, 1949. Box 147, Folder 1, HPG Papers.

111. Enrique R. Lamadrid. "El Corrido de Tomóchic:" Honor, Grace, Gender, and Power in the First Ballad of the Mexican Revolution." *Journal of the Southwest* 41.4 (Winter 1999), 449.

112. Manuel H. Peña. "Folksong and Social Change: Two Corridos as Interpretive Sources." *Aztlán* 13 (1982), 16.

113. The need for a "broader, ideologically 'uncommitted framework' for understanding the ways in which discourse and works of discourse 'mean' and construct understanding" is examined in Walter Beale, *A Pragmatic Theory of Rhetoric* (Carbondale: Southern Illinois University Press, 1987). Beale argues, "Burke's pentadic framework of concepts—Act, Scene, Agent, Agency, Purpose—is based upon the insight that discourse 'means' not merely by referring (as positivists would have it) but also by participating in human action" (56).

114. Beale, *A Pragmatic Theory of Rhetoric,* 56.

115. Burke, *A Grammar of Motives,* 59–61; 323–25.

116. Kenneth Burke, *A Grammar of Motives* (Berkeley: University of California Press), 1969: 59–61; 323–25.

117. Russell Riley, *The Presidency and the Politics of Racial Inequality* (New York: Columbia University Press, 1999), ix.

118. Riley, *The Presidency and the Politics of Racial Inequality,* x.

119. Manuel H. Peña. "Folksong and Social Change: Two Corridos as Interpretive Sources." *Aztlán* 13 (1982), 15.

120. Israel Bustamente, "A Soldier Named Felix Longoria." Box 130, Folder 1, HPG Papers.

121. For examination of the cultural values of the Mexican folk ballad, see Enrique R. Lamadrid. "El Corrido de Tomóchic:" Honor, Grace, Gender, and Power in the First Ballad of the Mexican Revolution." *Journal of the Southwest* 41.4 (Winter 1999), 450.

122. Botter, "Services Brief and Moving: Arlington Cemetery Rites Held for Private Longoria," *Dallas Morning News,* February 17, 1949: 1, 19.

123. "Nation Honors Latin-American: Three Rivers Soldier Buried in Arlington," *Austin American Statesman,* February 17, 1949, n.p. Available, PPC File. Box 3, "Longoria," LBJ Library.

124. For further examination of the Longoria incident, see Patrick J. Carroll *Felix Longoria's Wake: Bereavement, Racism, and the Rise of Mexican American Activism* (Austin: University of Texas Press, 2003).

125. Leland M. Griffin "A Dramatistic Theory of the Rhetoric of Movements," in *Critical Responses to Kenneth Burke, 1924–1966,* ed. William H. Rueckert (Minneapolis: University of Minnesota Press, 1969), 456–78.

126. Griffin, "A Dramatistic Theory of the Rhetoric of Movements," 462.

127. Griffin, "A Dramatistic Theory of the Rhetoric of Movements," 456.

128. Kenneth Burke, *The Rhetoric of Religion: Studies in Logology* (Berkeley: University of California Press, 1970), 4–5.

129. Manuel H. Peña. "Folksong and Social Change: Two Corridos as Interpretive Sources." *Aztlán* 13 (1982), 22–23.

130. Auxesis includes a range of rhetorical strategies used for amplification or heightening effect (e.g. to situate in a climactic series). For further definitions and etymological roots of the term, auxesis, see Richard A. Lanham, *A Handlist of Rhetorical Terms.* 2nd ed. (Berkeley: University of California Press, 1991), 26–28.

131. Beale, *A Pragmatic Theory of Rhetoric,* 162.

132. Wills, Garry. *Lincoln at Gettysburg: The Words That Remade America* (New York: Simon & Schuster, 1992), 41.

133. Plato, *Phaedrus,* in *The Rhetorical Tradition: Readings from Classical Times to the Present,* ed. Patricia Bizzell and Bruce Herzberg, (Boston: Bedford/St. Martin's Press, 1990), 137.

134. Kenneth Burke, *A Rhetoric of Motives* (Berkeley: University of California Press, 1969), 177.

135. Héctor P. García to Pauline Kibbe, April 16, 1949. Box 147, Folder 1, HPG Papers.

136. The location and the content of the Longoria radio broadcast is unknown as per Grace Charles, e-mail to author, November 15, 2001.

137. Ramos, *The American GI Forum,* 71.

138. Rodolfo Rosales, interview by author, August 24, 2001, San Antonio.

4. Immigration and the Rhetorics of Race, Caste, and Citizenship

1. Segments of this chapter were presented at the 2001 George Bush School of Government and Public Service Conference on Presidential Rhetoric, "The White House and Immigration Policy." College Station, March 2001, and at the 2004 Rhetoric Society of America Conference, Austin, May 29, 2004 for the session panel, "Latino/a Discourses and Rhetorics of Self-Representation." An earlier version of this chapter appears as "Héctor P. García, Lyndon B. Johnson, and the Polemics of the Bracero Immigrant Labor Program: Questions of Race, Caste, and Citizenship" in *Who Belongs in America? Presidents, Rhetoric, and Immigration,* ed. Vanessa Beasley (College Station: Texas A&M University Press, 2006).

2. This notion of the "open texture" in U.S. civil rights law and the necessity of "counterstories" to reflect "the Mexican American experience" is proposed by George Martinez, "Legal Indeterminacy, Judicial Discretion, and the Mexican American Litigation Experience: 1930–1980," *University of California, Davis Law Review* 27 (1994), 555–618.

3. For a copy of bracero legislation, "Agreement of August 4, 1942, for the Temporary Migration of Mexican Agricultural Workers to the United States," see Juan Ramon García, *Operation Wetback: The Mass Deportation of Mexican Undocumented Workers in 1954,* appendix 1, 242–45.

4. Juan Ramon García, *Operation Wetback: The Mass Deportation of Mexican Undocumented Workers in 1954,* 25.

5. For further discussion of the bracero program see Richard Craig, *The Bracero Program: Interest Groups and Foreign Policy* (Austin: University of Texas Press, 1971); Barbara A. Driscoll, *The Tracks North: The Railroad Bracero Program of World War II* (Austin: CMAS Publications, 1998); Erasmo Gamboa, *Mexican Labor and World War II: Braceros in the Pacific Northwest, 1942–1947* (Austin: University of Texas Press, 1990); Julian Samora, *Los Mojados: The Wetback Story* (Notre Dame: University of Notre Dame Press, 1971).

6. "Agreement between the United States of America and Mexico Respecting the Temporary Migration of Mexican Agricultural Workers," *United States Statutes at Large: Laws and Concurrent Resolutions Enacted during the Second Session of the Seventy-Seventh Congress of the United States.* Vol. 56, pt. 2. (Washington, DC: United States Government, 1942), 1759–69.

7. For historical patterns of violence and discrimination against Mexican-origin peoples in the U.S., see George Martinez, "Legal Indeterminacy, Judicial Discretion, and the Mexican American Litigation Experience: 1930–1980," *University of California, Davis Law Review* 27 (1994), 555–618. For analysis of "the confluence of stereotype and law" see: Steven W. Bender, *Greasers and Gringos: Latinos, Law, and the American Imagination* (New York: New York University Press, 2003).

8. Chandler Davidson, *Race and Class in Texas Politics* (Princeton: Princeton University Press, 1990), 5.

9. "Agreement between the United States of America and Mexico" (1942), 1766.

10. "Caucasian Race-Equal Privileges, H.C.R. No. 105. General and Special Laws of the State of Texas. Passed by the Regular Session of the Forty-Eighth Legislature, Convened at the City of Austin Jan. 12, 1943 and Adjourned May 11, 1943: 1119.

11. George Martinez, "Legal Indeterminacy, Judicial Discretion, and the Mexican American Litigation Experience: 1930–1980." *University of California, Davis Law Review* 27 (1994).

12. "Caucasian Race-Equal Privileges, H.C.R. No. 105. General and Special Laws of the State of Texas. Passed by the Regular Session of the Forty-Eighth Legislature, Convened at the City of Austin Jan. 12, 1943 and Adjourned May 11, 1943: 1119.

13. "Caucasian-Race Equal Privileges," 1119.

14. For precedents related to the racial classification of Mexican-origin peoples in litigation and naturalization cases, see: Richard Delgado and Vicky Palacios, "Mexican Americans as a Legally Cognizable Class under Rule 23 and Equal Protection Clause." *Notre Dame Law Review* 50 (1975), 393–418; George Gold, "The Racial Prerequisite in the Naturalization Law," *Boston University Law Review* 15 (1935), 462–506; Cheryl Harris, "Whiteness as Property," *Harvard Law Review* 106 (1993), 1707–1791; Gary A. Greenfield and Don B. Kates Jr., "Mexican American Racial Discrimination and the Civil Rights Act of 1866." 63.3 (1975), 662–731.

15. Fernando Peñalosa, "Toward an Operational Definition of the Mexican American." *Aztlan* 1.1 (1970), 3.

16. Peñalosa, "Toward an Operational Definition of the Mexican American," 3.

17. Neil Foley, "Becoming Hispanic: Mexican Americans and the Faustian Pact with Whiteness." *Reflexiones: New Directions in Mexican American Studies* (Austin: Center for Mexican American Studies, 1997), 53–70.

18. Ian F. Haney López, *White By Law: The Legal Construction of Race* (New York: New York University Press, 1996), 169.

19. Cheryl Harris, "Whiteness as Property," 1713.

20. Foley, "Reflexiones," 58.

21. Foley, "Reflexiones," 65.

22. A copy of the LULAC constitution is available in Richard A. García, *Rise of the Mexican American Middle Class, San Antonio, 1929–1941* (College Station: Texas A&M University Press, 1991), 268–69.

23. Green, "The Felix Longoria Affair," 24.

24. Foley, *The White Scourge: Mexicans, Blacks, and Poor Whites in Texas Cotton Culture*, 206.

25. Carlos K. Blanton, May 4, 2004, e-mail to author.

26. Haney López, *White By Law*, 46.

27. Haney López, *White By Law*, 43.

28. Hanry López, *White By Law*, 10.

29. Rogers Smith, *Civic Ideals: Conflicting Visions of Citizenship in U.S. History* (New Haven: Yale University Press, 1997). Smith's notion of "inegalitarian

ascriptive Americanist tradition" is a cover term for a system of beliefs which maintain that: "'true' Americans are 'chosen by God, history, or nature to possess superior moral and intellectual traits associated with their race, ethnicity, religion, gender, and sexual orientation. Hence many ascriptive Americanists believed that nonwhites, women, and various others should be governed as subjects and second-class citizens, not as equals, denied full individual rights, including many property rights, and sometimes excluded from the nation altogether" (508).

30. George Gold, "The Racial Prerequisite in the Naturalization Law," *Boston University Law Review* 15 (1935), 463.

31. Lyle Saunders and Olen E. Leonard, "The Wetback of the Lower Rio Grande Valley of Texas" (Austin: University of Texas, Inter-American Education Occasional Papers 7, July 1951); *What Price Wetbacks? American GI Forum of Texas and Texas State Federation of Labor* (Austin), 1953; "Wetbacks: Can the States Act to Curb Illegal Entry?" *Stanford Law Review* 6 (1954), 287–322; Lewis W. Gillenson, "Texas' Forgotten People," *Look* (March 26, 1951), 29–36; Edna Ferber, *Giant* (Garden City, NY: Double Day, 1952); *Giant,* prod. George Stevens and Henry Ginsberg, Warner Brothers Communications Company, 1956, videocassette.

32. Craig, *The Bracero Program: Interest Groups and Foreign Policy*, ix.

33. Juan Ramon García, *Operation Wetback: The Mass Deportation of Mexican Undocumented Workers in 1954,* 236.

34. Alexander Monto, *The Roots of Mexican Labor Migration* (Westport, CT: Praeger, 1994), xiii.

35. Richard A. Garcia, *Rise of the Mexican American Middle Class: San Antonio, 1929–1941,* 4.

36. Gutiérrez, *Walls and Mirrors: Mexican Americans, Mexican Immigrants, and the Politics of Ethnicity,* 4–5.

37. Monto, *The Roots of Mexican Labor Migration,* 204.

38. For additional historical background on the development and implementation of the 1942 bracero program, see Foley, *The White Scourge: Mexicans, Blacks, and Poor Whites in Texas Cotton Culture;* Otey M. Scruggs, "Evolution of the Mexican Farm Labor Agreement of 1942," *Agricultural History* 34 (1960), 140–49.

39. Doc Neuhaus to Lyndon B. Johnson, April 14, 1958, Senate Papers, 1958 Subject Files. Box 604, Labor "Mexican" Folder, LBJ Library.

40. Dallas Stites to Lyndon B. Johnson, April 15, 1958, Senate Papers, 1958 Subject Files. Box 605, Labor "Mexican," Folder, LBJ Library.

41. Héctor P. García, American GI Forum Resolution, September 26, 1949, Semi-Processed, HPG Papers.

42. Ralph C. Guzmán, *The Political Socialization of the Mexican American People* (New York: Arno Press, 1976).

43. Carl Allsup, *The American GI Forum: Origins and Evolution,* 33.

44. Héctor P. García to U.S. Civil Rights Commission, Washington D.C., May 5, 1948. Box 107, Folder 25, HPG Papers.

45. Héctor P. García to Maurice Tobin, June 20, 1949, Semi-Processed, American GI Forum Correspondence, HPG Papers.

46. Héctor P. García to Emanuel Celler, April 11, 1951. Box 142, Folder 2, HPG Papers.

47. Héctor P. García to Philip Murray, October 6 1949. Box 147, Folder 6, HPG Papers.

48. Héctor P. García qtd. in Julie Leininger Pycior, *LBJ and Mexican Americans: The Paradox of Power* (Austin: University of Texas, 1997), 60.

49. Héctor P. García to Ed Idar, June 29, 1953. Box 141, Folder 6, HPG Papers.

50. Héctor P. García to George I. Sánchez, April 18, 1961. Box 146, Folder 13, HPG Papers.

51. Héctor P. García to Manuel Avila, August 28, 1961. Box 46, Folder 27, HPG Papers.

52. Héctor P. García to Manuel Avila, August 28, 1961. Box 46, Folder 27, HPG Papers.

53. Letter to Vicente Ximenes, November 15, 1956. Box 146, Folder 17, HPG Papers.

54. In his discussion of the nineteenth-century origins of the terms "greaser" and "spic," Bender offers a number of explanations including the speculation that "the 'greasers' label may derive from long-standing conceptions of Mexicans as unkempt and unclean, with unwashed, greasy black hair (xiii)." This stereotype of uncleanliness links to the codes of *limpieza de sangre* and attitudes toward the *braceros* by some Anglo and Mexican American groups; see Steven W. Bender, *Greasers and Gringos: Latinos, Laws, and the American Imagination* (New York: New York University Press, 2003). For further examination of ethnolinguistic labels and language attitudes of Mexican Americans, see: Anthony G. Dworkin, "Stereotypes and Self-Images Held by Native Born and Foreign Born Mexican Americans" *Sociology and Social Research* 49.2 (1965), 214–224; Juan Guerra, "Emerging Representations, Situated Literacies, and the Practice of Transcultural Repositioning" in Michelle Hall Kells, Valerie Balester, and Victor Villanueva, eds. *Latino/a Discourses: On Language Identity, and Literacy Education* (Portsmouth, NH: Heinemann-Boynton/Cook, 2004), 7–23; "Linguistic Contact Zones in the College Writing Classroom: An Examination of Ethnolinguistic Identity and Language Attitudes" *Written Communication* 19.1 (2002), 5–43; Marilyn Montenegro, *Chicanos and Mexican-Americans: Ethnic Self-Identification and Attitudinal Differences* (San Francisco: R&E Research Associates, 1976); Fernando Peñalosa, "Toward an Operational Definition of the Mexican American" *Aztlan* 1.1 (1970), 1–12; Emma Pérez, *The Decolonial Imaginary: Writing Chicanos into History* (Bloomington: Indiana University Press, 1999).

55. Marilyn Montenegro, *Chicanos and Mexican-Americans: Ethnic Self-Identification and Attitudinal Differences* (San Francisco: R&E Research Associates, 1976).

56. Montenegro, *Chicanos and Mexican-Americans: Ethnic Self-Identification and Attitudinal Differences*, 5.

57. The phrase "limits of legal imagination" is offered by Richard Delgado and Jean Stefancic, *Failed Revolutions: Social Reform and the Limits of Legal Imagination* (Boulder: Westview Press, 1994).

58. Wanda Fusillo García, interview with author, Corpus Christi, Texas, October 15, 2001.

59. For perspectives of Dr. Clotilde García about racial attitudes in the García family, see Cleotilde P. García, interview by Thomas Kreneck, February 17, 1994, Dr. Héctor P. García Papers, Oral History 14.1, HPC Papers.

60. The term "ultimate identification" drawn from Burke's *A Rhetoric of Motives* (328); Neil Foley offers the term, "Faustian Pact" in *Reflexiones*.

61. "Biography of Héctor P. García," The American GI Forum of Texas 45th Annual Convention: Tribute to an American Hero: Dr. Héctor P. García," July 1993, American GI Forum Extended Collection, Small Collection, HPG Papers.

62. American GI Forum, *Forum News Bulletin*, January 15, 1952. Box 141, Folder 12, HPG Papers.

63. Héctor P. García to A. Maceo, September 15, 1953. Box 142, Folder 9, HPG Papers.

64. American GI Forum of the U.S. National Convention, Resolutions, August 1960. Box 76, Folder 52, HPG Papers.

65. Carlos Blanton, "Review: *Félix Longoria's Wake: Bereavement, Racism, and the Rise of Mexican American Activism.*" *Journal of South Texas* 17.1 (Spring 2004), 92–95.

66. Carroll, *Felix Longoria's Wake: Bereavement, Racism, and the Rise of Mexican American Activism*, 114; Carlos Blanton, "Review: *Félix Longoria's Wake: Bereavement, Racism, and the Rise of Mexican American Activism.*" *Journal of South Texas* 17.1 (Spring 2004), 92–95.

67. Héctor P. García, memo, January 23, 1962; "Hotel Incident: Garcia Sends Protest Wire to Gov. Daniel," *Corpus Christi Caller Times*, January 22, 1962: 5B. Available, White House Central Files, White House Central Name File. Box 946, "Garcia, Hector P." Folder, John F. Kennedy Library (hereafter cited as JFK Library).

68. For a discussion of the origin of the concept of Mexican Americans as a "linguistically constructed" people, see Ignacio M. García, *Viva Kennedy: Mexican Americans in Search of Camelot*, 15.

69. Barkan, Elazar, *The Retreat of Scientific Racism: Changing Concepts of Race in Britain and the United States between the World Wars* (New York: Cambridge University Press, 1992), xi.

70. Barkan, *The Retreat of Scientific Racism*, 280.

71. Héctor P. García, "Labor Camp Investigation and Report," April 22, 1948. Box 12, Folder 39, HPG Papers.

72. Héctor P. García, "Labor Camp Investigation and Report," April 22, 1948. Box 12, Folder 39, HPG Papers.

73. Héctor P. García to Thomas Sutherland, May 5, 1948. Box 107, Folder 25, HPG Papers.

74. Héctor P. García to Beauford Jester, May 6, 1948. Box 107, Folder 25, HPG Papers.

75. Héctor P. García to Thomas Sutherland, May 5, 1948. Box 107, Folder 25, HPG Papers.

76. Héctor P. García to Lyndon B. Johnson, October 20, 1950, State Departmental Files. Box 927, "Labor-Garcia, Hector P." Folder, LBJ Library.

77. Thomas Sutherland to M. B. Morgan, September 21, 1949. Box 147, Folder 1, HPG Papers.

78. Héctor P. García to Ignacio Garza, October 7, 1949. Box 147, Folder 1, HPG Papers.

79. Héctor P. García, "Notes on Wetback Pickers," July 24, 1950. Box 141, Folder 2, HPG Papers.

80. Ethel Esken to Héctor P. García, n.d. Box 147, Folder 1, HPG Papers.

81. Héctor P. García, letter to editor, *Edinburg Valley Review,* January 7, 1949. Box 147, Folder 1, HPG Papers.

82. Héctor P. García to *Life* magazine, May 6, 1948. Box 107, Folder 25, HPG Papers.

83. Héctor P. García to Ignacio Garza, May 7, 1949. Box 147, Folder 1, HPG Papers.

84. Héctor P. García to Ignacio Garza, May 7, 1949. Box 147, Folder 1, HPG Papers.

85. Héctor P. García to Harry S. Truman, October 5, 1949. Box 147, Folder 6, HPG Papers.

86. Héctor P. García to Dwight D. Eisenhower, October 17, 1953. Box 141, Folder 16, HPG Papers.

87. Héctor P. García to John F. Kennedy, September 30, 1961, White House Central Files. Box 946, Folder "Garcia, Hector P.," JFK Library.

88. Héctor P. García to Leslie A. Wheeler, October 5, 1949. Box 147, Folder 6, HPG Papers.

89. Gutiérrez, *Walls and Mirrors: Mexican Americans, Mexican Immigrants, and the Politics of Ethnicity,* 141.

90. Judith N. Shklar, *American Citizenship: The Quest for Inclusion* (Cambridge: Harvard University Press, 1991), 3.

91. Shklar, *American Citizenship: The Quest for Inclusion,* 8.

92. Shklar, *American Citizenship: The Quest for Inclusion,* 6.

93. U.S. Congress, "Naturalization Act" (March 26, 1790) 103 Public Statutes at Large of the United States of America.

94. Gutiérrez, *Walls and Mirrors: Mexican Americans, Mexican Immigrants, and the Politics of Ethnicity,* 154–55.

95. Gutiérrez, *Walls and Mirrors: Mexican Americans, Mexican Immigrants, and the Politics of Ethnicity,* 138.

96. Gutiérrez, *Walls and Mirrors: Mexican Americans, Mexican Immigrants, and the Politics of Ethnicity,* 6.

97. Gutiérrez, *Walls and Mirrors: Mexican Americans, Mexican Immigrants, and the Politics of Ethnicity,* 151.

98. "A Cotton Picker Finds Justice: The Saga of the Hernandez Case," compiled by Ruben Munguia (1954). Box 82, Folder 7, HPG Papers.

99. Héctor P. García to Don Larin, October 4, 1949. Box 147, Folder 6, HPG Papers.

100. Héctor P. García, "Resolution of the American GI Forum of Texas, September 26, 1949, Unprocessed, "AGIF 1949," HPG Papers.

101. Otey M. Scruggs, "Texas, Good Neighbor?" *Southwestern Social Science Quarterly* 43 (1962), 118.

102. Gutiérrez, *Walls and Mirrors: Mexican Americans, Mexican Immigrants, and the Politics of Ethnicity,* 141.

103. Susan Ferriss and Ricardo Sandoval, *The Fight in the Fields: Cesar Chavez and the Farmworkers Movement* (New York: Harcourt Brace, 1997), 4.

104. Héctor P. García to Thomas Sutherland, April 8, 1949. Box 147, Folder 10, HPG Papers.

105. Héctor P. García to Miguel Calderon, January 19, 1951. Box 141, Folder 2, HPG Papers.

106. Héctor P. García, letter to Jerry Holleman, February 10, 1962, White House Central Files, White House Central Name File. Box 946, Folder "Garcia, Hector P.," JFK Library.

107. Juan Ramon García, *Operation Wetback: The Mass Deportation of Mexican Undocumented Workers in 1954,* 125.

108. Ed Idar Jr., interview by author, tape recording, August 10, 2000 San Antonio; Virgilio Roel, interview by author, tape recording, August 10, 2000 Austin.

109. American GI Forum and Texas State Federation of Labor, *What Price Wetbacks?* (Austin, Texas), 2.

110. American GI Forum and Texas State Federation of Labor, *What Price Wetbacks?* (Austin, Texas), 1.

111. For discussion of the construct of "structure of feeling" see Raymond Williams, *Culture and Society, 1780–1950* (New York: Columbia University Press, 1983); Raymond Williams, *The Long Revolution: An Analysis of the Democratic, Industrial, and Cultural Changes Transforming Our Society* (New York: Columbia University Press, 1961).

112. For examination of the emergence of the Mexican American middle class, see Richard A. García, *Rise of the Mexican American Middle Class, San Antonio, 1929–1941* (College Station: Texas A&M University Press, 1991).

113. "What Price Wetbacks?" 59.

114. Richard A. García, *Rise of the Mexican American Middle Class, San Antonio, 1929–1941,* 310.

115. "Report on Wetback Problem Published by Forum, AFL." *American GI Forum News Bulletin* 2 (December 1953), 1.

116. Ed Idar Jr., interview by author, tape recording, August 10, 2000, San Antonio; Virgilio Roel, interview by author, tape recording, August 10, 2000, Austin.

117. Ed Idar Jr., interview by author, tape recording, August 10, 2000, San Antonio.

118. Ed Idar Jr., interview by author, tape recording, August 10, 2000, San Antonio; Virgilio Roel, interview by author, tape recording, August 10, 2000, Austin.

119. Juan Ramon García, *Operation Wetback: The Mass Deportation of Mexican Undocumented Workers in 1954,* 172.

120. Ed Idar Jr., interview by author, tape recording, August 10, 2000 San Antonio; Virgilio Roel, interview by author, tape recording, August 10, 2000 Austin; Juan Ramon García, *Operation Wetback: The Mass Deportation of Mexican Undocumented Workers in 1954,* 210.

121. Juan Ramon García, *Operation Wetback: The Mass Deportation of Mexican Undocumented Workers in 1954,* 212.

122. Acuña, *Occupied America: A History of Chicanos,* 267.

123. Ed Idar to Joseph M. Swing, August 14, 1954, Semi-Processed, HPG Papers.

124. Emma Pérez, "Gulf Dreams." In Carla Trujillo, ed. *Chicana Lesbians: The Girls Our Mothers Warned Us About,* (Berkeley: Third Woman Press, 1991), 102.

125. Acuña, *Occupied America: A History of Chicanos,* 268.

126. Juan Ramon García, *Operation Wetback: The Mass Deportation of Mexican Undocumented Workers in 1954,* 221.

127. Shklar, *American Citizenship: The Quest for Inclusion,* 64.

128. Héctor P. García to Lyndon B. Johnson, October 6, 1949. Box 147 Folder 6, HPG Papers.

129. Lyndon B. Johnson to Héctor P. García, October 13, 1949. Box 147, Folder 1, HPG Papers.

130. Wright G. Boyd to Lyndon B. Johnson, January 11, 1958, Senate Papers, 1958 Subject Files. Box 604, "Mexican Labor" Folder, LBJ Library.

131. Pycior, *LBJ and Mexican Americans: The Paradox of Power,* 107.

132. Peary Wilemon to Lyndon B. Johnson, May 10, 1958, Senate Papers, 1958 Subject Files. Box 604, "Mexican Labor" Folder, LBJ Library.

133. E. L. Wetzig, Sr. to Lyndon B. Johnson, August 4, 1958, Senate Papers, 1958 Subject Files. Box 604, "Mexican Labor" Folder, LBJ Library.

134. "Resolution of the American GI Forum of Texas," LBJA Selected Names File. Box 20, Folder "I," LBJ Library.

135. "Resolution of the American GI Forum of Texas," LBJA Selected Names File. Box 20, Folder "I," LBJ Library.

136. Ed Idar Jr., interview by author, tape recording, August 10, 2000. San Antonio.

137. Lyndon B. Johnson to Ed Idar Jr., November 14, 1952, LBJA Selected Names File. Box 20, Folder "I," LBJ Library.

138. Lyndon B. Johnson, "Address by Lyndon B. Johnson Before the Annual Banquet of the American GI Forum" (August 1, 1953). "Statements of Lyndon B. Johnson." Box 13, LBJ Library.

139. Lyndon B. Johnson to Héctor P. García, August 11, 1953, Unprocessed, "LBJ 1953." Box 1, Folder 2, HPG Papers.

140. A review of the García archives does not yield evidence of a formal 1960 investigation conducted by García on the bracero program. It appears that García is referencing his ongoing observations of the impact of the bracero program on South Texas since 1949, not a specific report.

141. Héctor P. García to Lyndon B. Johnson, April 15, 1960, Senate Papers, 1960 Subject File. Box 778, "Labor" Folder, LBJ Library.

142. Lyndon B. Johnson to Héctor P. García, April 28, 1960, Senate Papers, 1960 Subject File. Box 778, "Labor" Folder, LBJ Library.

143. Lyndon B. Johnson to Héctor P. García, May 31, 1960, Senate Papers, 1960 Subject File. Box 778, Folder 1, LBJ Library.

144. Saunders and Leonard, "The Wetback in the Lower Rio Grande Valley of Texas" (Austin: University of Texas, Inter-American Educational Occasional Papers VII, 1951).

145. Ed Idar Jr., interview by author, tape recording, August 10, 2000, San Antonio; Virgilio Roel, interview by author, tape recording, August 10, 2000 Austin.

146. Héctor P. García to Leslie A. Wheeler, October 5, 1949. Box 147, Folder 6, HPG Papers.

147. J. T. Canales to Héctor P. García, April 29, 1952. Box 141, Folder 12, HPG Papers.

148. George I. Sánchez, foreword, "The Wetback in the Lower Rio Grande Valley of Texas," 3.

149. Saunders and Leonard, preface, "The Wetback in the Lower Rio Grande Valley of Texas," 6.

150. Saunders and Leonard, "The Wetback in the Lower Rio Grande Valley of Texas," 65.

151. Saunders and Leonard, "The Wetback in the Lower Rio Grande Valley of Texas," 66.

152. Saunders and Leonard, "The Wetback in the Lower Rio Grande Valley of Texas," 66.

153. Saunders and Leonard, "The Wetback in the Lower Rio Grande Valley of Texas," 67.

154. Saunders and Leonard, "The Wetback in the Lower Rio Grande Valley of Texas," 67.

155. Saunders and Leonard, "The Wetback in the Lower Rio Grande Valley of Texas," 70.

156. Saunders and Leonard, "The Wetback in the Lower Rio Grande Valley of Texas," 70.

157. For correspondence concerning the statements in "The Wetback in the Lower Rio Grande Valley of Texas," see letters of Alonso Perales, George I. Sánchez, J. T. Canales, Ed Idar, Gus García, and Héctor P. García. Available, Box 141, Folder 12, HPG Papers.

158. Alonso S. Perales to George I. Sánchez, December 3, 1951. Box 141, Folder 12, HPG Papers.

159. "Importante Junta en Mission," flyer, n.d. Box 141, Folder 12, HPG Papers.

160. J. T. Canales, letter to Héctor P. García, April 29, 1952. Box 141, Folder 12, HPG Papers.

161. Héctor P. García, to La Prensa, December 13, 1951. Box 141, Folder 12, HPG Papers.

162. George I. Sánchez to Héctor P. García, December 20, 1951. Box 141, Folder 12, HPG Papers.

163. Héctor P. García to George I. Sánchez, December 31, 1951. Box 141, Folder 12, HPG Papers.

164. "Resolution," January 20, 1951. Box 141, Folder 12, HPG Papers.

165. "What Price Wetbacks?" 6.

166. Ed Idar to Héctor P. García, May 19, 1954. Box 142, Folder 14, HPG Papers.

167. Irwin Unger and Debi Unger, *LBJ: A Life* (New York: John Wiley & Sons, 1999), 166.

168. *Progress in Housing for Migratory Farm Workers* (U.S. Department of Labor, Bureau of Employment Security, March 1958), No. 11.

169. Elmer Kelton, "These Are the Braceros: Slaves or Willing Workers?" *San Angelo Standard*, 1958.

170. Kelton, "These Are the Braceros: Slaves or Willing Workers?" n.p.

171. "Wetbacks: Can the State Act to Curb Illegal Entry?" *Stanford Law Review* 6 (1954), 321.

172. "Texans March for Better Wage: Rio Grande Valley to Austin, Texas," *The Forumeer* 13 (October 1966), 1.

173. César E. Chávez to Héctor P. García, December 23, 1972. Unprocessed, HPG Papers.

174. Lewis W. Gillenson, "Texas' Forgotten People," *Look*, 15 (March 27, 1951), 35.

175. Alonso S. Perales, *Are We Good Neighbors?* (San Antonio: Artes Gráficas, 1948), 9.

176. Harriet Barker to Héctor P. García, March 27, 1951. Box 141, Folder 2, HPG Papers.

177. R. N. Jones to editor of *Look*, March 14, 1951. Box 141, Folder 2, HPG Papers.

178. Gillenson, "Texas' Forgotten People," 32.

179. Gillenson, "Texas' Forgotten People," 32.

180. Ramos, *The American GI Forum: In Pursuit of the Dream, 1948–1983*, 25.

181. Ferber, *Giant*, 268–69.

182. For García's attitudes toward the film *Giant* see Julie Leininger Pycior, *LBJ and Mexican Americans: The Paradox of Power*, 102.

183. Héctor P. García to American GI Forum, October 22, 1953. Box 141, Folder 16, HPG Papers.

184. Tino Villanueva, "The 8 O'clock Movie," from *Scene from the Movie Giant* (Willimantic, CT: Curbstone Press, 1993), 16.

185. Pycior, *LBJ and Mexican Americans: The Paradox of Power*, 101.

186. Villanueva, "Fallingrief of Unpleasure," from *Scene from the Movie Giant*, 29.

187. Charles Paine, *The Resistant Writer: Rhetoric as Immunity: 1850 to Present.* (Albany: State University of New York Press, 1999), 5.

188. Shklar, *American Citizenship: The Quest for Inclusion*, 80.

189. For further examination of the development of U.S. naturalization policies see James H. Kettner, *The Development of American Citizenship, 1608–1870* (Chapel Hill: University of North Carolina Press, 1978); Dana D. Nelson, *National Manhood: Capitalist Citizenship and the Imagined Fraternity of White Men;* Constance Perin, *Belonging in America: Reading Between the Lines* (Madison: University of Wisconsin, 1988); Riley, *The Presidency and the Politics of Racial Inequality;* Benjamin B. Ringer and Elinor Lawless, *Race—Ethnicity and Society* (New York: Routledge, 1989); Shklar, *American Citizenship: The Quest for Inclusion;* Smith, *Civic Ideals: Conflicting Visions of Citizenship in U.S. History* (New Haven: Yale University Press, 1997).

190. For historical examination of patterns of "ascriptive inequality" in the formation of U.S. citizenship laws, see Smith, *Civic Ideals: Conflicting Visions of Citizenship in U.S. History.*

191. For examination of U.S. immigration trends and attitudinal patterns see Roger Daniels, *Coming to America: A History of Immigration and Ethnicity in American Life* (New York: HarperCollins, 1999); Jorge Durand and Douglas S. Massey, *Miracles on the Border: Retablos of Mexican Migrants to the United States* (Tucson: University of Arizona Press, 1995); María Herrera-Sobek, *Northward Bound: The Mexican Immigrant Experience in Ballad and Song* (Indianapolis: Indiana University Press, 1993); Nelson, *National Manhood: Capitalist Citizenship and the Imagined Fraternity of White Men;* Alejandro Portes and Rubén G. Rumbaut, *Immigrant America: A Portrait* (Berkeley: University of California Press, 1996); Lawrence A. Cardosa, *Mexican Emigration to the United States, 1897–1931: Socioeconomic Patters* (Tucson: University of Arizona Press, 1980); Marcelo M. Suárez-Orozco, ed., *Crossings: Mexican Immigration in Interdisciplinary Perspectives* (Cambridge: Harvard University David Rockefeller Center for Latin American Studies, 1998).

5. The "Imagined Fraternity" of Héctor P. García and Lyndon B. Johnson

1. The concept of "imagined fraternity" coalesces in the works of Benedict Anderson, *Imagined Communities: Reflections of the Origin and Spread of Nationalism* (London: Verso, 1983); George M. Fredrickson, *The Comparative Imagination: On the History of Racism, Nationalism, and Social Movements* (Berkeley: University of California Press, 1997); Dana D. Nelson, *National Manhood: Capitalist Citizenship and the Imagined Fraternity of White Men* (Durham, NC: Duke University Press, 1998); Anita Haya Patterson, *From Emerson to King: Democracy, Race, and the Politics of Protest* (New York: Oxford University Press, 1997); Judith

N. Shklar, *American Citizenship: The Quest for Inclusion* (Cambridge: Harvard University Press, 1991); Rogers M. Smith, *Civic Ideals: Conflicting Visions of Citizenship in U.S. History* (New Haven: Yale University Press, 1997).

2. A segment of this chapter was presented at the Conference of the Rhetoric of Society of America, Las Vegas, May 2002.

3. Anderson, *Imagined Communities: Reflections of the Origin and Spread of Nationalism,* 15.

4. Garth E. Pauley, "Rhetoric and Timeliness: An Analysis of Lyndon B. Johnson's Voting Rights Address," *Western Journal of Communication* 62 (1998), 26.

5. These protections were further extended in 1975 to protect linguistically diverse citizens by requiring bilingual ballots in various regions. See Meier and Gutiérrez, *Encyclopedia of the Mexican American Civil Rights Movement,* 248–49.

6. In *A Grammar of Motives,* Burke extends Aristotle's notion of telos with this explanation:

> Everything that comes into existence moves toward an end. This end is the principle of its existence; and it comes into existence for the sake of this end. This state of completion is its full actuality, and "it is for the sake of this that the potency is acquired. . . . Since an action contains some ingredient of purpose, or end, Aristotle uses the term "entelechy" ("having its end within itself") as synonym for "actuality" (262–62).

7. Garth E. Pauley, *The Modern Presidency: Rhetoric on Race from Roosevelt to Nixon* (College Station: Texas A&M University Press, 2001), 163.

8. Julie Leininger Pycior, *LBJ and Mexican Americans: The Paradox of Power* (Austin: University of Texas Press, 1997), 87.

9. Pauley, *The Modern Presidency: Rhetoric on Race from Roosevelt to Nixon,* 165.

10. Irwin Unger and Debi Unger, *LBJ: A Life* (New York: John Wiley & Sons, 1999), 167.

11. Robert Dallek, *Lone Star Rising: Lyndon Johnson and His Times, 1908–1960* (New York: Oxford University Press, 1991), 367.

12. Dallek, *Lone Star Rising,* 367–68.

13. Pauley, *The Modern Presidency: Rhetoric on Race from Roosevelt to Nixon,* 166.

14. Harris Wofford, "Notes for Briefing on Civil Rights for TV Debate," September 23, 1960, Robert F. Kennedy Papers, Pre-Administration, General Subject File, 1959–1960. Box 34, JFK Library.

15. John F. Kennedy, "Protecting the Right to Vote," March 21, 1960, Pre-Presidential Papers, Speeches, Statements, and Sections, 1958–1960. Box 1028, JFK Library.

16. Héctor P. García qtd. in Dunn, "The Legacy of Private Longoria," n.p.

17. Robert Dallek, *Flawed Giant: Lyndon Johnson and His Times, 1961–1973* (New York: Oxford University Press, 1998), 113.

18. Dalleck, *Flawed Giant,* 113.

19. "Remarks of Vice President Lyndon B. Johnson," Unprocessed, "LBJ" Box, HPG Papers.

20. Lyndon B. Johnson, telegram to Héctor P. García, January 11, 1949, PPC File. Box 3, "Longoria" Folder, LBJ Library.

21. Historian Julie Leininger Pycior observes in *LBJ and Mexican Americans: The Paradox of Power:*

> When it came to political leadership, men largely forged bonds with men, particularly during the Cold War with its male military *ethos,* as in the Three Rivers case that linked Lyndon Johnson and Héctor García. Women conducted much of the grass-roots organizational activity, as when Longoria's sister brought up the issue to Dr. García, but they operated mostly behind the scenes (95).

22. In *Civic Ideals: Conflicting Visions of Citizenship in U.S. History,* Smith defines "inegalitarian ascriptive Americanist" ideology as a belief system founded on the following tenets: "'true' Americans are 'chosen' by God, history, or nature to possess superior moral and intellectual traits associated with their race, ethnicity, religion, gender, and sexual orientation" (508). For further examination of the notion of "American exceptionalism" see Seymour Martin Lipset, *American Exceptionalism: A Double-Edged Sword* (New York: Norton, 1996).

23. See Alan Brinkley, *Liberalism and Its Discontents* (Cambridge: Harvard University Press, 1998), 18.

Brinkley describes New Deal liberalism as "a confusing amalgam of visions and instincts—a program that seemed to have something in it to please everyone." The New Deal liberalism to which García and Johnson subscribed was ideologically diffuse and action-oriented.

24. Brinkley, *Liberalism and Its Discontents,* xi.

25. Brinkley, *Liberalism and Its Discontents,* 18.

26. Héctor P. García, interview by David G. McComb, July 9, 1969. AC74–277, University of Texas Oral History Project, National Archives and Records Service, LBJ Library.

27. Robert N. Jones to Lyndon B. Johnson, November 13, 1949. Box 147, Folder 1, HPG Papers.

28. Burke observes in *A Rhetoric of Motives:* "Identification is affirmed with earnestness precisely because there is division. Identification is compensatory to division" (22).

29. Nelson, *National Manhood: Capitalist Citizenship and the Imagined Fraternity of White Men,* xi.

30. Liz Carpenter, Rhetoric Society of America Pre-Conference Address, May 27, 2004, Lyndon B. Johnson Presidential Library, Austin. Liz Carpenter was born Elizabeth Sutherland in Salado, in 1920. She attended the University of Texas from 1938–1942 and received a degree in journalism. She joined the Tufty News Service

in Washington, D.C., after graduation in 1942, where she first met Congressman Lyndon B. Johnson and Lady Bird Johnson. As the sister of Thomas Sutherland, executive secretary of the Good Neighbor Commission during the Longoria incident, she had first-hand knowledge of case. Liz Carpenter became the press secretary for LBJ during the 1960 presidential campaign, the executive assistant to LBJ during his vice presidency and chief of staff for Lady Bird during the presidential years.

31. Lyndon B. Johnson, Speech, July 7, 1948, "Statements of Lyndon B. Johnson." Box 7, LBJ Library.

32. "Atencion Residentes." Flyer. Box 141, Folder 7, HPG Papers.

33. Lyndon B. Johnson telegram to Héctor P. García, January 11, 1949, Pre-Presidential Confidential File. Box 2, "Longoria," LBJ Library.

34. Héctor P. García, interview by David G. McComb, July 9, 1969. AC74-277, University of Texas Oral History Project, National Archives and Records Service, LBJ Library.

35. "American GI Forum Officers and Advisory Board Meeting," October 30, 1949. Box 147, Folder 1, HPG Papers.

36. Héctor P. García, interview by David G. McComb, July 9, 1969. AC74-277, University of Texas Oral History Project, National Archives and Records Service, LBJ Library.

37. Ignacio M. García, *Viva Kennedy: Mexican Americans in Search of Camelot* (College Station: Texas A&M University Press, 2000), 8.

38. Héctor P. García, interview by David G. McComb, July 9, 1969. AC74-277, University of Texas Oral History Project, National Archives and Records Service, LBJ Library.

39. Pycior, *LBJ and Mexican Americans: The Paradox of Power,* 70.

40. Unger and Unger, *LBJ: A Life,* 113.

41. Héctor P. García, taped interview by Julie Leininger Pycior, June 20, 1989, "History of Lyndon B. Johnson: Relationship to Mexican Americans" tapes, Unprocessed File. Box 1, Tape 1, Benson Latin American Collection, University of Texas.

42. Unger and Unger, *LBJ: A Life,* 21

43. For further examination of Lyndon B. Johnson's early career as a teacher in Cotulla, Texas, see Pycior, *LBJ and Mexican Americans: The Paradox of Power,* 3–22.

44. Unger and Unger, *LBJ: A Life,* 26.

45. Unger and Unger, *LBJ: A Life,* 26.

46. Pycior, *LBJ and Mexican Americans: The Paradox of Power,* 4.

47. Héctor P. García, interview by David G. McComb, July 9, 1969. AC74-277, University of Tex Oral History Project, National Archives and Records Service, LBJ Library.

48. James W. Wilson, interview by Joe B. Frantz, February 26, 1971, AC78-22, University of Texas Oral History Project, National Archives and Records Service, LBJ Library.

49. Pauley, *The Modern Presidency and Civil Rights: Rhetoric on Race from Roosevelt to Nixon,* 163–67.

50. Héctor P. García to Lyndon B. Johnson, June 10, 1960, Unprocessed, "LBJ 1960," HPG Papers.

51. James W. Wilson, interview by Joe B. Frantz, February 26, 1971, AC78–22, University of Texas Oral History Project, National Archives and Records Service, LBJ Library.

52. Héctor P. García, Héctor P. García, interview by David G. McComb, July 9, 1969. AC74–277, University of Texas Oral History Project, National Archives and Records Service, LBJ Library.

53. Kenneth Cmiel, *Democratic Eloquence: The Fight over Popular Speech in Nineteenth Century America* (New York: William Morrow, 1990), 66.

54. Miller et al., *Martin Luther King Jr. and the Sermonic Power of Public Discourse,* 9.

55. Miller et al., *Martin Luther King Jr. and the Sermonic Power of Public Discourse,* 10.

56. Héctor P. García, Héctor P. García, interview by David G. McComb, July 9, 1969. AC74–277, University of Texas Oral History Project, National Archives and Records Service, LBJ Library.

57. Héctor P. García, 1952 radio transcript, no. 1, Unprocessed, HPG Papers.

58. Héctor P. García, 1952 radio transcript, no. 2, Unprocessed, HPG Papers.

59. Héctor P. García to the National Democratic Committee, October 21, 1952; Héctor P. García, report, "Adlai Stevenson Presidential Campaign," November 4, 1952. Box 53, Folder 19, HPG Papers.

60. Pycior, *LBJ and Mexican Americans: The Paradox of Power,* 89.

61. Unger and Unger, *LBJ: A Life,* 159.

62. Unger and Unger, *LBJ: A Life,* 160.

63. Héctor P. García, interview by David G. McComb, July 9, 1969. AC74–277, University of Texas Oral History Project, National Archives and Records Service, LBJ Library.

64. Unger and Unger, *LBJ: A Life,* 160.

65. Ignacio M. García, *Viva Kennedy: Mexican Americans in Search of Camelot,* 14.

66. Héctor P. García to Lyndon B. Johnson, June 23, 1953. Box 141, Folder 6, HPG Papers.

67. Unger and Unger, *LBJ: A Life,* 176.

68. Rodolfo Rosales, *The Illusion of Inclusion: The Untold Political Story of San Antonio* (Austin: University of Texas Press, 2000), 28.

69. The invitation to Eleanor Roosevelt was largely symbolic, reflecting García's enduring commitment to New Deal values and programs. See Hector P. García to Eleanor Roosevelt, n.d. Box 141, Folder 6, HPG Papers.

70. The 1952 American GI Forum Convention resolved that Johnson's inaction was "in utter disregard of the friendship and high regard in which he has been held by thousands of citizens of Mexican-descent." The American GI Forum's punitive

resolution had captured Johnson's attention. Fearing the loss of support from the Mexican American constituency, Johnson worked to restore his relationship with García and the American GI Forum. See "Resolution of the American GI Forum of Texas," July 6, 1952, "LBJA Selected Names." Box 20, Folder "I," LBJ Library.

71. Lyndon B. Johnson, "Address by Lyndon B. Johnson before the Annual Banquet of the American GI Forum," August 1, 1953, "Statements of Lyndon B. Johnson." Box 13, LBJ Library.

72. Unger and Unger, *LBJ: A Life*, 181.

73. Lyndon B. Johnson qtd. in Unger and Unger, *LBJ: A Life*, 176.

74. Lyndon B. Johnson to Héctor P. García, August 6, 1959, Unprocessed, "LBJ 1958–1959." Box 1, Folder 4, LBJ Library.

75. Unger and Unger, *LBJ: A Life*, 177.

76. Lyndon B. Johnson to Raul Morin, April 15, 1958, Unprocessed, "LBJ 1958–1959." Box 1, Folder 5, HPG Papers.

77. Morin, *Among the Valiant: Mexican Americans in World War II and Korea*, 7.

78. Ignacio M. García, *Viva Kennedy: Mexican Americans in Search of Camelot*, 35.

79. Ignacio M. García, *Viva Kennedy: Mexican Americans in Search of Camelot*, 37.

80. Lyndon B. Johnson, letter to Héctor P. García, February 4, 1959, Unprocessed, "LBJ 1958–1959." Box 1, Folder 5, HPG Papers.

81. Ignacio M. García, *Viva Kennedy: Mexican Americans in Search of Camelot*, 43.

82. Unger and Unger, *LBJ: A Life*, 182.

83. Lyndon B. Johnson to Héctor P. García, April 22, 1959, Unprocessed, "LBJ 1958–1959." Box 1, Folder 5, HPG Papers.

84. Lyndon B. Johnson to Héctor P. García, July 14, 1959, Unprocessed, "LBJ 1958–1959." Box 1, Folder 5, HPG Papers.

85. Pycior, *LBJ and Mexican Americans: The Paradox of Power*, 111.

86. Pycior, *LBJ and Mexican Americans: The Paradox of Power*, 111.

87. Lyndon B. Johnson to Héctor P. García, August 6, 1959, Unprocessed, "LBJ 1958–1959." Box 1, Folder 5, HPG Papers.

88. Ignacio M. García, *Viva Kennedy: Mexican Americans in Search of Camelot*, 102.

89. John F. Kennedy to Héctor P. García, December 28, 1959, "Viva Kennedy" Box, HPG Papers.

90. There are conflicting dates in the literature as to when this meeting occurred. According to Héctor García in his interview with David G. McComb, the meeting occurred "in late '59, if not early '60." Pycior's *LBJ and Mexican Americans* records the meeting on October 31, 1960;

91. Héctor P. García, interview by David G. McComb, July 9, 1969. AC74-277, University of Texas Oral History Project, National Archives and Records Service, LBJ Library.

92. Héctor P. García, interview by David G. McComb, July 9, 1969. AC74–277, University of Texas Oral History Project, National Archives and Records Service, LBJ Library.

93. Héctor P. García, "Confidential Report for Senator Lyndon Johnson," June 10, 1960, Unprocessed, "LBJ 1969." Box 1, Folder 6, HPG Papers.

94. Héctor P. García, "Confidential Report to Lyndon B. Johnson," June 10, 1960, Unprocessed, "LBJ 1960." Box 1, Folder 6, HPG Papers.

95. Pycior, *LBJ and Mexican Americans: The Paradox of Power,* 114.

96. Héctor P. García to Lyndon B. Johnson, June 17, 1960, Unprocessed, "LBJ 1960." Box 1, Folder 6, HPG Papers.

97. Rosales, *The Illusion of Inclusion: The Untold Political Story of San Antonio,* 59.

98. Lyndon B. Johnson to Héctor P. García, June 22, 1960, Senate Papers. Box 67, Folder "Gar 1960," LBJ Library.

99. James W. Wilson, interview by Joe B. Frantz, February 26, 1971, AC78–22, University of Texas Oral History Project, National Archives and Records Service, LBJ Library.

100. James W. Wilson, interview by Joe B. Frantz, February 26, 1971, AC78–22, University of Texas Oral History Project, National Archives and Records Service, LBJ Library.

101. Viva Kennedy Texas Organization, "The American of Mexican Descent: A Principle of Statement," n.d. Box 107, Folder 66, HPG Papers.

102. Héctor P. García, "Statement of Dr. Hector P. Garcia, Founder of the American GI Forum to Be Presented to the Democratic National Committee Nationalities Division," June 12, 1960. Box 75, Folder 34, HPG Papers.

103. Héctor P. García, memo, "Viva Kennedy Clubs of the U.S.," n.d., Personal Papers of Dr. Héctor P. García," Semi-Processed, HPG Papers.

104. Lyndon B. Johnson, letter to Héctor P. García, August 25, 1960, Lyndon B. Johnson Presidential Library, LBJ Senate Papers. Box 68, File "Gar" 1960, LBJ Library.

105. Ignacio M. García, *Viva Kennedy: Mexican Americans in Search of Camelot,* 59.

106. John F. Kennedy, telegram to Héctor P. García, November 11, 1960, Unprocessed, Personal Papers of Héctor P. García, HPG Papers.

107. "Spanish American Leaders Assail Administration Patronage Policy," Colorado Federation of Latin American Groups, 10 (February 1962), 1. Available in Semi-Processed, "PASO" Box, HPG Papers.

108. "Narrative Report of the National Political Leadership Conference," March 26, 1961, Unprocessed, Personal Papers of Héctor P. García, HPG Papers.

109. Héctor P. García, letter to Carlos McCormick, November 22, 1960, Unprocessed, Personal Papers of Héctor P. García, HPG Papers.

110. Maestro Pablo Casals' last performance at the White House had been in 1904 during the Theodore Roosevelt administration. John F. Kennedy describes

the event in his November 14, 1961, thank you letter to Casals: "There are very few unforgettable evenings, but everyone who was present last night will regard this one as such." John F. Kennedy Library and Museum, Exhibit Case; also see thank you letter to John F. Kennedy by Héctor P. García, letter to John F. Kennedy, November 22, 1961, Unprocessed, Personal Papers of Héctor P. García, HPG Papers.

111. "Statement by Hector P. Garcia, Public Member of the U.S. Delegation of the Occasion of the Signing of the Two Project Agreements," February 11, 1961, Album. Box 2, Folder 2, HPG Papers.

112. James Weldon Johnson, an accomplished black writer of the Harlem Renaissance and fluent in Spanish, served as United States consul to Venezuela and Nicaragua for seven years from 1906 to 1913 during Theodore Roosevelt's administration. Lauded as a "pioneer of the American diplomatic service," James Weldon Johnson, like García, had won presidential favor by his pragmatic strategies and celebration of Americanist principles. See Lawrence J. Oliver, "'Jim Crowed' in Their Own Country: James Weldon Johnson's New York Age Essays on Colonialism during the Wilson Years," in *Critical Essays on James Weldon Johnson*, Kenneth M. Price and Lawrence J. Oliver, eds. (New York: G. K. Hall, 1997), 209–22.

113. "Latest List," Presidential Appointments Proposed 11/17/60–1/3/61, John F. Kennedy Presidential Library, Robert F. Kennedy Papers, Pre-Administration, Political Papers, General Subject Files, 1959–1960. Box 46, JFK Library.

114. Héctor P. García, letter to John F. Kennedy, August 2, 1960, Unprocessed, Personal Papers of Héctor P. García, HPG Papers.

115. Héctor P. García to Robert Kennedy, November 18, 1960, Unprocessed, Personal Papers of Héctor P. García," HPG Papers.

116. Héctor P. García to John F. Kennedy, January 11, 1961, Robert F. Kennedy Papers, Pre-Administration Political Files. Box 11, "Garcia" Folder, JFK Library; Héctor P. García to John F. Kennedy, February 22, 1961, Unprocessed, Personal Papers of Héctor P. García, HPG Papers.

117. Ignacio M. García, *Viva Kennedy: Mexican Americans in Search of Camelot*, 109–111.

118. "Narrative Report of National Political Leadership Conference, March 26, 1961, Semi-Processed, HPG Papers.

119. The Political Association of Spanish Speaking Organizations was established March 26, 1961 in Phoenix, Arizona, during the National Political Leadership Conference of the Viva Kennedy Club. The name of the new organization was passed by vote. The acronyms of PASSO and PASO are used interchangeably in the literature. See "Narrative Report of National Political Leadership Conference, March 26, 1961, Semi-Processed, HPG Papers.

120. Héctor P. García to Vicente Ximenes, April 3, 1961. Box 146, Folder 13, HPG Papers.

121. This sample of García's public rhetoric is one of the few examples representing his more militant discourse. Over the next few years, García's rhetoric increasingly moderated as his access to the federal government increased. For

further discussion on PASO and La Raza Unida, see Ignacio M. García, *United We Stand: The Rise and Fall of La Raza Unida Party;* Ignacio M. García, *Chicanismo: The Forging of a Militant Ethos among Mexican Americans.*

122. Héctor P. García to John F. Kennedy, September 22, 1961, Unprocessed, Personal Papers of Héctor P. García, HPG Papers.

123. Héctor P. García to Manual Avila Jr., September 18, 1961. Box 46, Folder 27, HPG Papers.

124. Ignacio M. García, *Viva Kennedy: Mexican Americans in Search of Camelot,* 120.

125. "Speech by Attorney General Robert F. Kennedy," *American GI Forum News Bulletin* 10 (December 1963), 2.

126. Héctor P. García to Manuel Avila Jr., July 22, 1961. Box 46, Folder 27, HPG Papers.

127. Héctor P. García, letter to Lyndon B. Johnson, January 19, 1961, Unprocessed, "LBJ 1961." Box 1, Folder 7, HPG Papers.

128. Lyndon B. Johnson to Héctor P. García, July 7, 1961, Unprocessed, "LBJ 1961." Box 1, Folder 7, HPG Papers.

129. Héctor P. García to Lyndon B. Johnson, July 3, 1963, Unprocessed, "LBJ 1963." Box 1, Folder 9, HPG Papers.

130. Héctor P. García telegram to Lyndon B. Johnson, November 22, 1963, Unprocessed, "LBJ 1963." Box 1, Folder 9, HPG Papers.

131. Lyndon B. Johnson to Héctor P. García, November 29, 1963, Unprocessed, "LBJ 1963." Box 1, Folder 9, HPG Papers.

132. Héctor P. García to Vicente Ximenes, November 29, 1963, Semi-Processed, HPG Papers.

133. "President Lyndon B. Johnson Has a Lifetime Record of Personal Concern and Public Assistance to Americans of Mexican or Spanish Origin," n.d., Unprocessed, "LBJ" Box, HPG Papers.

134. Héctor P. García to Lyndon B. Johnson, January 13, 1965, Semi-Processed, "LBJ 1965." Box 1, Folder 12, HPG Papers.

135. James W. Wilson, interview by Joe B. Frantz, February 26, 1971, AC78–22, University of Texas Oral History Project, National Archives and Records Service, LBJ Library.

136. See *Corpus Christi Caller Times,* July 3, 1993, sec. F.

137. Xico P. García, interview with author, June 13, 2001, Corpus Christi; Héctor P. García, taped interview with Julie Leininger Pycior, June 20, 1989, Corpus Christi. "History of Lyndon B. Johnson: Relationship to Mexican Americans" tapes, Unprocessed. Box 1, Tape 1, Benson Latin American Collection, University of Texas.

138. Lyndon B. Johnson telegram to Héctor P. García, July 10, 1964, Unprocessed, "LBJ 1964." Box 1, Folder 10.

139. Pycior, *LBJ and Mexican Americans: The Paradox of Power,* 153.

140. Pycior, *LBJ and Mexican Americans: The Paradox of Power,* 154.

141. Pycior, *LBJ and Mexican Americans: The Paradox of Power,* 195.

142. Pycior, *LBJ and Mexican Americans: The Paradox of Power*, 169.

143. Vicente Ximenes, interview with author, November 5, 2004, Albuquerque, NM.

144. Pycior, *LBJ and Mexican Americans: The Paradox of Power*, 169, 196–197.

145. Héctor P. García, interview by David G. McComb, July 9, 1969. AC74–277, University of Texas Oral History Project, National Archives and Records Service, LBJ Library.

146. Ramos, *The American GI Forum: In Pursuit of the Dream, 1948–1983*, 102.

147. Héctor P. García, interview by David G. McComb, July 9, 1969. AC74–277, University of Texas Oral History Project, National Archives and Records Service, LBJ Library.

148. Pycior, *LBJ and Mexican Americans: The Paradox of Power*, 201.

149. Lyndon B. Johnson, Memorandum of the Office of the White House Press Secretary, June 9, 1967, Semi-Processed, HPG Papers.

150. Ramos, *The American GI Forum: In Pursuit of the Dream, 1948–1983*, 94.

151. Pycior, *LBJ and Mexican Americans: The Paradox of Power*, 201.

152. César Chávez qtd. in Pycior, *LBJ and Mexican Americans: The Paradox of Power*, 204.

153. George I. Sánchez qtd. in Pycior, *LBJ and Mexican Americans: The Paradox of Power*, 203.

154. Ramos, *The American GI Forum: In Pursuit of the Dream, 1948–1983*, 104.

155. Vicente Ximenes, interview with author, November 5, 2004, Albuquerque.

156. Ramos, *The American GI Forum: In Pursuit of the Dream, 1948–1983*, 105.

157. Vicente Ximenes qtd. in Ramos, *The American GI Forum: In Pursuit of the Dream, 1948–1983*, 105.

158. Ramos, *The American GI Forum: In Pursuit of the Dream, 1948–1983*, 106.

159. "Statement by the President: A New Focus on Opportunity for the Spanish Speaking American," February 21, 1968, Unprocessed LBJ File, HPG Papers.

160. Héctor P. García, interview by David G. McComb, July 9, 1969. AC74–277, University of Texas Oral History Project, National Archives and Records Service, LBJ Library.

161. Matthew B. Coffey memo to Bill Hopkins, October 14, 1968, White House Central Files, Name File "Hector Garcia." Box 29, LBJ Library.

162. Héctor P. García, interview by David G. McComb, July 9, 1969. AC74–277, University of Texas Oral History Project, National Archives and Records Service, LBJ Library.

163. John W. Macy to Lyndon B. Johnson, November 5, 1968, White House Central Files, Name File "Hector Garcia." Box 29, LBJ Library.

164. "Civil Rights Commission: Dr. Garcia, Many Forumeers at Texas Rights Hearing," *Forumeer*, January 1969, 1, 3; "Hearing in San Antonio Outline," agenda, November 5, 1968, Semi-Processed, HPG Papers.

165. Héctor P. García qtd. in "Civil Rights Commission: Dr. Garcia, Many Forumeers at Texas Rights Hearing," *Forumeer*, January 1969, 1, 3.

166. Harry Middleton, former aid to Lyndon B. Johnson and director of the Lyndon B. Johnson Presidential Library, recently released hundreds of audio tapes which include the January 15, 1965, taped telephone conversation between Lyndon B. Johnson and Martin Luther King Jr. about the Voting Rights Act. Recent news releases provide clips from these audio tapes: Michael Beschloss, "Lyndon Johnson on the Record," *Texas Monthly,* December 2001, 107–115; Kelley Shannon, "Tapes Showed LBJ's Anguish: Release of Recordings Saw a President's Image Changed," *Bryan–College Station (Texas) Eagle,* September 16, 2001, B4; Chris Williams, "Johnson Tapes Reveal Power of Persuasion: Conversations with Wallace, King Released," *Bryan–College Station (Texas) Eagle,* May 27, 2000, A1, 14.

167. Taped phone conversation, Lyndon B. Johnson and Martin Luther King Jr., January 15, 1965, WH6501.04 Phone Conversation, Service Set II, Recordings and Transcripts of Telephone Conversations and Meetings, WH Series, Program 2, LBJ Library.

168. "President Johnson's Notes on Conversation with Martin Luther King Jr., January 15, 1965, transcript of taped phone conversation, January 1965 Chrono File, Citation 6736–6737. Box 6, LBJ Library.

169. Dunn, "The Legacy of Pvt. Longoria," *Dallas Morning News,* "Scene," Apr. 6, 1975 n.p.

170. Frank "Posh" Oltorf, interview by David G. McComb, August 3, 1971, AC78–53, University of Texas Oral History Project, National Archives and Records Service, LBJ Library.

171. Nelson, *National Manhood: Capitalist Citizenship and the Imagined Fraternity of White Men,* ix.

172. Nelson, *National Manhood: Capitalist Citizenship and the Imagined Fraternity of White Men,* x.

173. Anita Haya Patterson, *From Emerson to King: Democracy, Race, and the Politics of Protest* (New York: Oxford University Press, 1997), 3.

174. Patterson, *From Emerson to King: Democracy, Race, and the Politics of Protest,* 101.

175. For an expanded discussion of Martin Luther King Jr.'s rhetorical strategies see Richard Lischer, *The Preacher King: Martin Luther King Jr. and the Word that Moved America* (New York: Oxford University Press, 1995).

176. Rowland Evans and Robert Novak. "New LBJ Strategy on Civil Rights." The World Journal Tribune, February 24, 1967 n.p. Semi-Processed, HPG Papers.

177. Héctor P. García to Lyndon B. Johnson, June 10, 1960, Semi-Processed Papers, "LBJ 1960." Box 1 Folder 6, HPG Papers.

178. Héctor P. García, interview by David G. McComb, July 9, 1969. AC74–277, University of Texas Oral History Project, National Archives and Records Service, LBJ Library.

179. Ramos, *The American GI Forum: In Pursuit of the Dream, 1948–1983,* 92.

180. Rogers Kelly to Héctor P. García, April 21, 1949. Box 147, Folder 1, HPG Papers.

181. Ramos, *The American GI Forum: In Pursuit of the Dream, 1948–1983,* 92.

182. Rogers Kelly to Héctor P. García, April 21, 1949. Box 147, Folder 1, HPG Papers.

183. Pauley, "Rhetoric and Timeliness: An Analysis of Lyndon B. Johnson's Voting Rights Address," 31; Ramos, *The American GI Forum: In Pursuit of the Dream, 1948–1983,* 92.

184. Pauley, "Rhetoric and Timeliness: An Analysis of Lyndon B. Johnson's Voting Rights Address," 31.

185. Pauley, "Rhetoric and Timeliness: An Analysis of Lyndon B. Johnson's Voting Rights Address," 45.

186. Lyndon B. Johnson, "Civil Rights Address to the Joint Session of the Congress," March 15, 1965, Statements of Lyndon B. Johnson. Box 141, LBJ Library; Excerpts of speech also available in Julie Leininger Pycior, *LBJ and Mexican Americans,* 3–4; Pycior, "Lyndon, La Raza, and the Paradox of Texas History" in *Lyndon Baines Johnson and the Uses of Power,* ed. Bernard J. Firestone and Robert C. Vogt (New York: Greenwood Press, 1988), 129; Ramos, *The American GI Forum: In Pursuit of the Dream, 1948–1983,* 93.

187. Ramos, *The American GI Forum: In Pursuit of the Dream, 1948–1983,* 93.

188. Jack Valenti to Lyndon B. Johnson, "Report to the President," March 16, 1965, Statements of Lyndon B. Johnson. Box 141, LBJ Library.

189. Pauley, "Rhetoric and Timeliness: An Analysis of Lyndon B. Johnson's Voting Rights Address," 26.

190. American GI Forum to Lyndon B. Johnson, resolution, March 27, 1965, "LBJ 1965." Box 1, Folder 12, HPG Papers.

191. Lyndon B. Johnson to Héctor P. García, March 24, 1965, White House Central Files, Name File, "Hector Garcia." Box 29, LBJ Library.

6. Conclusion: Revising the History of American Civil Rights Reform

1. Wanda Fusillo García, interview by author, October 15, 2001, Corpus Christi.

2. Alfredo Corchado and Ricardo Sandoval, "Braceros Want Old Promise Met," *Dallas Morning News,* January 27, 2002, A1.

3. Lianne Hart, "WWII Dispute again Divides Texas Town." *Bryan–College Station Eagle,* June 13, 2004. A9, A15.

4. Pauline Arrillaga and Giovanna Dell-Orto, "Border Deaths All Too Common," *Bryan-College Station Eagle,* May 27, 2001, A4; Giovanna Dell-Orto, "Economics, Enforcement Led to Deaths," *Bryan-College Station Eagle,* May 16, 2001 C1, C6.

5. Robert J. Samuelson, "The Limits of Immigration: The United States Cannot be a Sponge for Mexico's Poor," *Newsweek,* July 24, 2000, 42.

6. For discussion on the "transparency" of white racial consciousness, see: Barbara Flagg, "The Transparency Phenomenon, Race-Neutral Decisionmaking, and Discriminatory Intent." In Richard Delgado and Jean Stefancic, eds. *Critical*

White Studies: Looking Behind the Mirror (Philadelphia: Temple University Press, 1997), 220–26.

7. Robert Lee Maril, *The Poorest of Americans: The Mexican Americans of the Lower Rio Grande Valley of Texas* (Notre Dame: University of Notre Dame Press, 1989); Murdock, et al., *The Texas Challenge: Population Change and the Future of Texas* (College Station: Texas A&M University Press, 1997).

8. Ramos, *Hector P. García: In Relentless Pursuit of Justice,* xiv.

9. Albert Peña Jr. qtd. in "Del Rio Demonstration Shows Militant Spirit," n.d., n.p. Box 74, Folder 22, HPG Papers.

10. Lyndon B. Johnson qtd. in Irwin Unger and Debi Unger, *LBJ: A Life* (New York: John Wiley & Sons, 1999), 460.

11. "Narrative Report of National Political Leadership Conference," March 26, 1961, Semi-Processed, HPG Papers.

12. Ed Idar Jr., interview by author, tape recording, San Antonio, Texas, August 10, 2000; Virgilio Roel, interview by author, tape recording, Austin, Texas, August 10, 2000.

13. The construction of civil rights reform history as represented at the Civil Rights Museum in Memphis and the Birmingham Civil Rights Institute in Birmingham, like most popular media exposés on civil rights history commemorating Martin Luther King Jr., relies on a meta-narrative of progress. This observation is shared by Neil Foley in his paper "From Veteran Rights to Civil Rights: American GI Forum in the Post-War Years" for the Conference U.S. Latinos and Latinas and World War II: Changes Seen, Changes Wrought, May 27, 2000, Austin,

14. James M. Jasper, *The Art of Moral Protest: Culture, Biography, and Creativity in Social Movements* (Chicago: University of Chicago Press, 1997), 5.

15. Harry Middleton to Héctor P. García, October 27, 1972, Unprocessed, "LBJ" Box, HPG Papers.

16. According to Unger and Unger, haunted by the fear of an early death, Johnson had commissioned an actuarial study of his life expectancy in 1967 based on his own health record and the medical histories of all the men in the Johnson family. The results predicted that he would die at the age of sixty-four. Johnson died at sixty-four and half. See *LBJ: A Life,* 440.

17. Héctor P. García telegram to Mrs. Lyndon Johnson, January 22, 1973, Unprocessed, "LBJ" Box, HPG Papers.

18. Lady Bird Johnson to Héctor P. García, April 2, 1974, Unprocessed, "LBJ" Box, HPG Papers.

19. Theodore M. Hesburgh to Héctor P. García, February 4, 1975. Box 122, Folder 50, HPG Papers.

20. Theodore M. Hesburgh, letter of endorsement, February 4, 1975. Box 122, Folder 50, HPG Papers.

21. Ignacio M. García, *Viva Kennedy: Mexican Americans in Search of Camelot,* (College Station: Texas A&M University Press, 2000), 8.

22. Héctor P. García, "Need for Organized Civic Action." Address to the Catholic Conference on the Spanish Speaking People of Texas (April, 24, 1952). Box 57, Folder 1, HPG Papers.

23. Walter Beale employs the Aristotelian concept of "telos" in his definition of rhetoric as performative. According to Beale in *A Pragmatic Theory of Rhetoric*, "Rhetoric is performative in a teleological rather than a formal sense: it aims at participation in the actions of a community." Rhetoric as performative finds completion in the action of the community. The end is contained in the beginning (65–66).

Selected Bibliography

Archival Collections

Benson Latin American Collection. General Libraries, University of Texas, Austin.

W. E. B. Du Bois Papers. Special Collections and Archives, W. E. B. Du Bois Library, University of Massachusetts, Amherst.

Dr. Héctor P. García Papers. Special Collections and Archives, Mary and Jeff Bell Library, Texas A&M University—Corpus Christi.

Dr. Xico García Personal Papers, Corpus Christi, Texas.

Ed Idar Jr. Personal Papers, San Antonio, TX.

Lyndon B. Johnson Papers. Lyndon B. Johnson Presidential Library, University of Texas, Austin.

John F. Kennedy Papers. John F. Kennedy Presidential Library, University of Massachusetts, Boston.

Robert F. Kennedy Papers. John F. Kennedy Presidential Library, University of Massachusetts, Boston.

Carolyn F. Swearingen Papers. Corpus Christi Public Library, Local History Archives, Corpus Christi, Texas.

Dr. Vicente Ximenes Personal Papers, Albuquerque, New Mexico.

Books

Acuña, Rudolfo. *Occupied America: A History of Chicanos*. 3rd ed. New York: Harper & Row, 1988.

Allsup, Carl. *The American GI Forum: Origins and Evolution*. Austin: Center for Mexican American Studies, 1982.

Alonzo, Armando C. *Tejano Legacy: Rancheros and Settlers in South Texas, 1734–1900*. Albuquerque: University of New Mexico Press, 1998.

Anderson, Benedict. *Imagined Communities: Reflections on the Origin and Spread of Nationalism*. London: Verso, 1983.

Beale, Walter H. *A Pragmatic Theory of Rhetoric*. Carbondale: Southern Illinois University Press, 1987.

Brinkley, Alan. *Liberalism and Its Discontents*. Cambridge: Harvard University Press, 1998.

Burke, Kenneth. *A Rhetoric of Motives*. Berkeley: University of California Press, 1969.

Burstein, Andrew. *Sentimental Democracy: The Evolution of America's Romantic Self-Image*. New York: Hill & Wang, 1999.

Cintron, Ralph. *Angels' Town: Chero Ways, Gang Life, and Rhetorics of the Everyday*. Boston: Beacon Press, 1997.

Cmiel, Kenneth. *Democratic Eloquence: The Fight over Popular Speech in Nineteenth Century America*. New York: William Morrow, 1990.

Darsey, James. *The Prophetic Tradition and Radical Rhetoric in America.* New York: New York University Press, 1997.

Du Bois, W. E. B. *Color and Democracy: Colonies and Peace.* New York: Harcourt, Brace, 1945.

Ferber, Edna. *Giant.* New York: Doubleday, 1952.

Foley, Douglas E. *From Peones to Politicos: Ethnic Relations in a South Texas Town, 1900–1987.* Austin: University of Texas Press, 1988.

Foley, Neil. *White Scourge: Mexicans, Blacks, and Poor Whites in Texas Cotton Culture.* Berkeley: University of California Press, 1997.

Fredrickson, George M. *The Comparative Imagination: On the History of Racism, Nationalism, and Social Movements.* Berkeley: University of California Press, 1997.

García, Ignacio M. *Chicanismo: The Forging of a Militant Ethos among Mexican Americans.* Tucson: University of Arizona Press, 1997.

———. *Hector P. García: In Relentless Pursuit of Justice* (Houston: Arte Público Press, 2002)

———.*United We Stand: The Rise and Fall of La Raza Unida Party.* Tucson: MASRC, University of Arizona, 1989.

———. *Viva Kennedy: Mexican Americans in Search of Camelot.* College Station: Texas A&M University Press, 2000.

García, Juan Ramon. *Operation Wetback: The Mass Deportation of Mexican Undocumented Workers in 1954.* Westport, CT: Greenwood Press, 1980.

García, Mario T. *The Mexican American Generation: Leadership, Ideology, and Identity, 1930–1960.* New Haven: Yale University Press, 1989.

García, Richard A. *Rise of the Mexican American Middle Class, San Antonio, 1929–1941.* College Station: Texas A&M University Press, 1991.

Gómez-Quiñones, Juan. *Chicano Politics: Reality and Promise, 1940–1990.* Albuquerque: University of New Mexico Press, 1990.

Gutiérrez, David G. *Walls and Mirrors: Mexican Americans, Mexican Immigrants, and the Politics of Ethnicity.* Berkeley: University of California Press, 1995.

Guzmán, Ralph C. *The Political Socialization of the Mexican American People.* New York: Arno Press, 1976.

Hammerback, John C., Richard J. Jensen, and José Ángel Gutiérrez. *A War of Words: Chicano Protest in the 1960s and 1970s.* Westport, CT: Greenwood Press, 1985.

Haney López, Ian F. *White By Law: The Legal Construction of Race.* New York: New York University Press, 1996.

Jasper, James M. *The Art of Moral Protest: Culture, Biography, and Creativity in Social Movements.* Chicago: University of Chicago Press, 1997.

Lipset, Seymoure Martin. *American Exceptionalism: A Double-Edged Sword.* New York: Norton, 1996.

Medhurst, Martin J., ed. Introduction to *Beyond the Rhetorical Presidency.* College Station: Texas A&M University Press, 1996.

Meier, Matt S., and Feliciano Rivera. *The Chicanos: A History of Mexican Americans*. New York: Hill &Wang, 1972.

Meier, Matt S., and Margo Gutiérrez. *Encyclopedia of the Mexican American Civil Rights Movement*. Westport, CT: Greenwood Press, 2000.

Miller, Carolyn K., Calloway Thomas, and John Louis Lucaites, eds. *Martin Luther King, Jr. and the Sermonic Power of Public Discourse*. Tuscaloosa: University of Alabama Press, 1993.

Montejano, David. *Anglos and Mexicans in the Making of Texas, 1836–1986*. Austin: University of Texas Press, 1987.

Monto, Alexander. *The Roots of Mexican Labor Migration*. Westport, CT: Praeger, 1994.

Morin, Raul. *Among the Valiant: Mexican Americans in World War II and Korea*. Alhambra, CA: Borden Publishing, 1963.

Myrdal, Gunnar. *An American Dilemma: The Negro Problem and Modern Democracy*, vol.1. New York: Harper, 1944.

Nelson, Dana D. *National Manhood: Capitalist Citizenship and the Imagined Fraternity of White Men*. Durham, NC: Duke University Press, 1998.

Pauley, Garth E. *The Modern Presidency and Civil Rights: Rhetoric on Race from Roosevelt to Nixon*. College Station: Texas A&M University Press, 2001.

Patterson, Anita Haya. *From Emerson to King: Democracy, Race, and the Politics of Protest*. New York: Oxford University Press, 1997.

Perales, Alonso S. *Are We Good Neighbors?* San Antonio: Artes Gráficas, 1948.

Pycior, Julie Leininger. *LBJ and Mexican Americans: The Paradox of Power*. Austin: University of Texas Press, 1997.

Quezada, J. Giberto. *Border Boss: Manuel B. Bravo and Zapata County*. College Station: Texas A&M University Press, 1999.

Ramos, Henry A. J. *The American GI Forum: In Pursuit of the Dream, 1948–1983*. Houston: Arte Público, 1998.

Riley, Russell. *The Presidency and the Politics of Racial Inequality*. New York: Columbia University Press, 1999.

Rorty, Richard. *Achieving Our Country: Leftist Thought in Twentieth-Century America*. Cambridge: Harvard University Press, 1998.

Rosales, Rodolfo. *The Illusion of Inclusion: The Untold Political Story of San Antonio*. Austin: University of Texas Press, 2000.

Rosteck, Thomas, ed. *At the Intersections: Cultural Studies and Rhetorical Studies*. New York: Guilford Press, 1999.

Salazar, Philippe-Joseph. *An African Athens: Rhetoric and the Shaping of Democracy in South Africa*. Mahwah: Lawrence Erlbaum, 2002.

San Miguel Jr., Guadalupe. *"Let Them All Take Heed:" Mexican Americans and the Campaign for Educational Equality in Texas, 1910–1981*. Austin: University of Texas Press, 1987.

Shklar, Judith N. *American Citizenship: The Quest for Inclusion*. Cambridge: Harvard University Press, 1991.

Smith, Rogers M. *Civic Ideals: Conflicting Visions of Citizenship in U.S. History.* New Haven: Yale University Press, 1997.

Unger, Irwin, and Debi Unger. *LBJ: A Life.* New York: John Wiley & Sons, 1999.

Villanueva, Tino. *Scene from the Movie "Giant."* Willimantic, CT: Curbstone Press, 1993.

West, Cornel. *The American Evasion of Philosophy: A Genealogy of Pragmatism.* Madison: University of Wisconsin Press, 1989.

White, Hayden. *Metahistory: The Historical Imagination in Nineteenth-Century Europe.* Baltimore: Johns Hopkins University Press, 1973.

Wills, Garry. *Certain Trumpets: The Call of Leaders.* New York: Simon & Schuster, 1994.

———. *Lincoln at Gettysburg: The Words That Remade America.* New York: Simon & Schuster, 1992.

Articles, Dissertations, and Theses

"The American GI Forum." *Border Trends* 1 (September 1948): 1–2.

Bitzer, Lloyd F. "The Rhetorical Situation." In *Rhetoric: Concepts, Definitions, Boundaries,* ed. William A. Covino and David A. Jolliffe, 300–310. Boston: Allyn & Bacon, 1995.

Botter, David. "Services Brief and Moving: Arlington Cemetery Rites Held for Private Longoria." *Dallas Morning News,* February 17, 1949.

Castillo, Star. "Editorial." *LULAC News* no. 12 (July 1945): n.p.

"Civil Rights Commission: Dr. Garcia, Many Forumeers at Texas Rights Hearing." *Forumeer,* January 1969. Available at Dr. Héctor P. García Papers, Special Collections and Archives, Bell Library, Texas A&M University–Corpus Christi.

"Civil Rights: Strength or Weakness?" *Quick,* September 24, 1941, 10–12.

Cuellar, Robert A. "A Social and Political History of the Mexican American Population of Texas, 1929–1963." Master's thesis, State University, 1969. Reprint: San Francisco: R&E Research Associates, 1974.

Du Bois, W. E. B. "Caste in America: That Is the Root of the Trouble." *Des Moines Register and Leader,* October 19, 1904.

———. "The Color Line Belts the World." *Collier's Weekly,* October 20, 1906, 30.

———. "The First Universal Races Congress." *Independent,* no. 71 (August 23, 1911): 402.

Dunn, Si. "The Legacy of Pvt. Longoria." *Dallas Morning News* "Scene," April 6, 1975.

Dyer, Stanford P. and Merrell A. Knighten. "Discrimination after Death: Lyndon Johnson and Felix Longoria." *Southern Studies: An Interdisciplinary Journal of the South* 18 (Winter 1974): 411–26.

George, Ron. "More of a Compromiser Than an Antagonist." *Corpus Christi Caller Times,* July 27 1996. A1, A11.

Gillenson, Lewis W. "Texas' Forgotten People." *Look,* March 26, 1951, 29–36.

Goldzwig, Steven R. "Civil Rights in the Postmodern Era: An Introduction." *Rhetoric and Public Affairs* 2 (1999): 171–76.

Green, George Norris. "The Felix Longoria Affair." *Journal of Ethnic Studies* 19 (1991): 22–34.

Griffin, Leland M. "A Dramatistic Theory of the Rhetoric of Movements." In *Critical Responses to Kenneth Burke, 1924–1966,* ed. William H. Rueckert, 456–78. Minneapolis: University of Minnesota Press, 1969.

"A Hero's Return: Bigotry in Texas." *Detroit Free Press,* January 14, 1949. n.p.

Houston, Romona Allaniz. "African Americans, Mexican Americans, and Anglo Americans and the Desegregation of Texas, 1946–1957." Ph.D. dissertation, University of Texas, Austin, 2000.

Hutson, James H. "Written Knowledge: Illuminating Manuscripts." *Civilization: The Magazine of the Library of Congress* April/May 2000, 58–64.

Inda, Xavier. "Matter Out of Place: Mexican Immigrants, National Terrains." Ph.D. dissertation, University of California, Berkeley, 1997.

Kelton, Elmer. "These Are the Braceros: Slaves or Willing Workers?" Issued by *San Angelo Standard,* 1958. Pamphlet.

Kreneck, Thomas H. "The Dr. Hector P. García Papers: A Research Resource for Texas, and More." *Texas Library Journal* 72 (1996): 80–83.

"LULAC: Fifty Years of Serving Hispanics: Golden Anniversary, 1929–1979." Issued by the United League of Latin American Citizens, 1979. Pamphlet.

Mechling, Elizabeth Walker, and Jay Mechling. "American Cultural Criticism in the Pragmatic Attitude." In *At the Intersection: Cultural Studies and Rhetorical Studies,* ed. Thomas Rosteck, 137–67. New York: Guilford Press, 1999.

Meighan, Tyrone. "Dr. Hector P. Garcia." *Corpus Christi Caller Times,* July 3, 1993. F1–5

Miller, Carolyn R. "Genre as Social Action." *Quarterly Journal of Speech* 70 (1984): 151–67.

Milligan, Nancy Muller. "W. E. B. Du Bois: American Philosopher." *Journal of American Culture* 8 (1985): 31–37.

Morgan, Ernest. "A Profile of Dr. Hector Garcia: A Man of Controversy." *Corpus Christi Caller Times,* December 12, 1966. B4+.

Murdock, Steve H., et al. Preface to *The Texas Challenge: Population Change and the Future of Texas,* xxiii–xxvi. College Station: Texas A&M University Press, 1997.

"Nation Honors Latin-American: Three Rivers Soldier Buried in Arlington." *Austin American-Statesman,* February 17, 1949.

Orozco, Cynthia E. "The Origins of the United League of Latin American Citizens (LULAC) and the Mexican American Civil Rights Movement in Texas with an Analysis of Women's Political Participation in a Gendered Context, 1910–1929." Ph.D. dissertation, University of California, Los Angeles, 1992.

Pauley, Garth E. "Rhetoric and Timeliness: An Analysis of Lyndon B. Johnson's Voting Rights Address." *Western Journal of Communication* 62 (1998): 26–53.

Plato. "Phaedrus." In *The Rhetorical Tradition: Readings from Classical Times to the Present*, Patricia Bizzell and Bruce Herzberg, eds. 113–143. Boston: Bedford/St. Martin's Press, 1990.

"President Lyndon B. Johnson Has a Lifetime Record of Personal Concern and Public Assistance to Americans of Mexican or Spanish Origin." Issued by Viva Johnson Organization of the Democratic National Committee, 1964. Pamphlet.

Proceedings, *House Journal,* Fifty-First Legislature, Regular Session, February 17, 1949, Austin, TX.

Proceedings, *House Journal,* Fifty-First Legislature, Regular Session, April 17, 1949, Austin, TX.

Rangel, Jorge C., and Carlos M. Alcala. "Project Report: De Jure Segregation of Chicanos in Texas Schools." *Harvard Civil Rights–Civil Liberties Law Review* 7 (1972): 308–91.

"Report on Wetback Problem Published by Forum, AFL." *American GI Forum News Bulletin,* December 1953, 1.

San Miguel Jr., Guadalupe. "Mexican American Organizations and the Changing Politics of School Desegregation." In *Latino Language and Education: Communication and the Dream Deferred,* ed. Antoinette Sedillo López, 179–93. New York: Garland Publishing, 1995.

Saunders, Lyle, and Olen E. Leonard. "The Wetback of the Lower Rio Grande Valley of Texas." Austin: University of Texas, Inter-American Education Occasional Papers 7, July 1951.

Schwartz, Jerry. "Our Vanishing Veterans." *Austin American-Statesman,* May 27, 2000.

Scruggs, Otey M. "Texas, Good Neighbor?" *Southwestern Social Science Quarterly* 43 (1962): 118–25.

"Speech by Attorney General Robert F. Kennedy." *American GI Forum News Bulletin,* December 1963, 2

Sutherland, Thomas S. "Texas Tackles the Race Problem." *The Saturday Evening Post* January 12, 1952, 22–23, 64–66.

"Texas Town Offers Apology to Widow." *New York Times* January 14, 1949.

"Tragic Blot: Kelly Raps Three Rivers Case Report." *Corpus Christi Caller Times,* April 8, 1949.

Vatz, Richard E. "The Myth of the Rhetorical Situation." In *Rhetoric: Concepts, Definitions, Boundaries,* William A. Covino and David A. Jolliffe, eds. 461–67. Boston: Allyn & Bacon, 1995.

Weaver, Richard. "All Language Is Sermonic." In *The Rhetorical Tradition: Readings from Classical Times to the Present,* Bizzell and Herzberg, eds. 1044–54.

"Wetbacks: Can the States Act to Curb Illegal Entry?" *Stanford Law Review* 6 (March 1954): 287–322.

"What Price Wetbacks?" Issued by American GI Forum of Texas and Texas State Federation of Labor, 1953. Pamphlet.

White, William S. "GI of Mexican Origin, Denied Rites in Texas, to Be Buried in Arlington." *New York Times,* January 13, 1949.

Wood, Jim. "Discrimination Here Charged: Unit on Civil Rights Ends Stormy Session." *Corpus Christi Caller Times,* April 17, 1966, 12

Zelade, Richard. "Last Rites, First Rights," *Texas Monthly,* January 1986, 192–94.

Index

Michelle Hall Kells is an assistant professor of rhetoric and writing at the University of New Mexico. Her areas of research—civil rights rhetorics, sociolinguistics, and composition/literacy studies—coalesce around problems related to ethnolinguistic stratification and intercultural communication. She is coeditor of *Attending to the Margins: Writing, Researching, and Teaching on the Front Lines* (1999) and *Latino/a Discourses: On Language, Identity, and Literacy Education* (2004), which focus on teaching writing to diverse student populations. Her present research focuses on Mexican American civic discourse, and she is currently working on a new book, *Vicente Ximenes and LBJ's "Great Society": The Rhetoric of Mexican American Civil Rights Reform*.